The Tibetan Book
of Living and Dying

Also by Sogyal Rinpoche

Meditation
Glimpse After Glimpse

The Tibetan Book of Living and Dying

SOGYAL RINPOCHE

Edited by
PATRICK GAFFNEY AND ANDREW HARVEY

RIDER

LONDON · SYDNEY · AUCKLAND · JOHANNESBURG

First published in the United States in 1992
by Harper San Francisco, a division of Harper Collins Publishers, Inc.

First published in the UK in 1992 by Rider,
An imprint of The Random House Group Limited,
20 Vauxhall Bridge Road, London SW1V 2SA
Reprinted 1992 (five times), 1993 (five times), 1994 (twice)
Published in paperback by Rider in 1995
Reprinted 1995, 1996, 1997
This edition first published in 1998

10 9 8 7 6 5 4

Random House Australia (Pty) Limited
20 Alfred Street, Milsons Point, Sydney, New South Wales 2061, Australia

Random House New Zealand Limited
18 Poland Road, Glenfield, Auckland 10, New Zealand

Random House South Africa (Pty) Limited
Endulini, 5a Jubilee Road, Parktown 2193, South Africa

The Random House Group Limited Reg. No. 954009
www.randomhouse.co.uk

Printed and bound in Great Britain by
Cox & Wyman Ltd, Reading, Berkshire

Papers used by Rider are natural, recyclable products made from wood
grown in sustainable forests. The manufacturing processes conform to
the environmental regulations of the country of origin.

A catalogue record for this book is available from the British Library.

ISBN 0 7126 7139 0

I WOULD LIKE TO DEDICATE THIS BOOK *to Jamyang Khyentse Chökyi Lodrö, Dudjom Rinpoche, Dilgo Khyentse Rinpoche, Khyentse Sangyum Khandro Tsering Chödrön, and all my beloved masters, who have been the inspiration of my life.*

May this book be a guide to liberation, read by the living, and to the dying, and for the dead.

May it help all who read it and spur them on their journey to enlightenment!

Contents

Foreword
by His Holiness the Dalai Lama

IN THIS TIMELY BOOK, Sogyal Rinpoche focuses on how to understand the true meaning of life, how to accept death, and how to help the dying, and the dead.

Death is a natural part of life, which we will all surely have to face sooner or later. To my mind, there are two ways we can deal with it while we are alive. We can either choose to ignore it or we can confront the prospect of our own death and, by thinking clearly about it, try to minimise the suffering that it can bring. However, in neither of these ways can we actually overcome it.

As a Buddhist, I view death as a normal process, a reality that I accept will occur as long as I remain in this earthly existence. Knowing that I cannot escape it, I see no point in worrying about it. I tend to think of death as being like changing your clothes when they are old and worn out, rather than as some final end. Yet death is unpredictable: We do not know when or how it will take place. So it is only sensible to take certain precautions before it actually happens.

Naturally, most of us would like to die a peaceful death, but it is also clear that we cannot hope to die peacefully if our lives have been full of violence, or if our minds have mostly been agitated by emotions like anger, attachment, or fear. So if we wish to die well, we must learn how to live well: Hoping for a peaceful death, we must cultivate peace in our mind, and in our way of life.

As you will read here, from the Buddhist point of view, the actual experience of death is very important. Although how or where we will be reborn is generally dependent on karmic forces, our state of mind at the time of death can influence the quality of our next rebirth. So at the moment of death, in spite of the great variety of karmas we have accumulated, if we make a special effort to generate a virtuous state of mind, we may strengthen and activate a virtuous karma, and so bring about a happy rebirth.

The actual point of death is also when the most profound and beneficial inner experiences can come about. Through repeated acquaintance with the processes of death in meditation, an accomplished meditator can use his or her actual death to gain great spiritual realization. This is why experienced practitioners engage in meditative practices as they pass away. An indication of their attainment is that often their bodies do not begin to decay until long after they are clinically dead.

No less significant than preparing for our own death is helping others to die well. As newborn babies each of us was helpless and, without the care and kindness we received then, we would not have survived. Because the dying also are unable to help themselves, we should relieve them of discomfort and anxiety, and assist them, as far as we can, to die with composure.

Here the most important point is to avoid anything which will cause the dying person's mind to become more disturbed than it may already be. Our prime aim in helping a dying person is to put them at ease, and there are many ways of doing this. A dying person who is familiar with spiritual practice may be encouraged and inspired if they are reminded of it, but even kindly reassurance on our part can engender a peaceful, relaxed attitude in the dying person's mind.

Death and Dying provide a meeting point between the Tibetan Buddhist and modern scientific traditions. I believe both have a great deal to contribute to each other on the level of understanding and of practical benefit. Sogyal Rinpoche is especially well placed to facilitate this meeting; having been born and brought up in the Tibetan tradition, he has received instructions from some of our greatest Lamas. Having also benefitted from a modern education and lived and worked as a teacher for many years in the West, he has become well acquainted with Western ways of thought.

This book offers readers not just a theoretical account of death and dying, but also practical measures for understanding, and for preparing themselves and others in a calm and fulfilling way.

June 2, 1992

Preface

I WAS BORN IN TIBET, and I was six months old when I entered the monastery of my master Jamyang Khyentse Chökyi Lodrö, in the province of Kham. In Tibet we have a unique tradition of finding the reincarnations of great masters who have passed away. They are chosen young and given a special education to train them to become the teachers of the future. I was given the name Sogyal, even though it was only later that my master recognized me as the incarnation of Tertön Sogyal, a renowned mystic who was one of his own teachers and a master of the Thirteenth Dalai Lama.

My master, Jamyang Khyentse, was tall for a Tibetan, and he always seemed to stand a good head above others in a crowd. He had silver hair, cut very short, and kind eyes that glowed with humor. His ears were long, like those of the Buddha. But what you noticed most about him was his presence. His glance and bearing told you that he was a wise and holy man. He had a rich, deep, enchanting voice, and when he taught his head would tilt slightly backward and the teaching would flow from him in a stream of eloquence and poetry. And for all the respect and even awe he commanded, there was humility in everything he did.

Jamyang Khyentse is the ground of my life, and the inspiration of this book. He was the incarnation of a master who had transformed the practice of Buddhism in our country. In Tibet it was never enough simply to have the name of an incarnation, you always had to earn respect, through your learning and through your spiritual practice. My master spent years in retreat, and many miraculous stories are told about him. He had profound knowledge and spiritual realization, and I came to discover that he was like an encyclopedia of wisdom, and knew the answer to any question you might ask him. There were many spiritual traditions in Tibet, but Jamyang Khyentse was acclaimed as the authority on them all. He was, for everyone who knew or heard about him, the embodiment of Tibetan Buddhism, a living proof of how someone who had realized the teachings and completed their practice would be.

I have heard that my master said that I would help continue his work, and certainly he always treated me like his own son. I feel that what I have been able to achieve now in my work, and the audience I have been able to reach, is a ripening of the blessing he gave me.

All my earliest memories are of him. He was the environment in which I grew up, and his influence dominated my childhood. He was like a father to me. He would grant me anything I asked. His spiritual consort, Khandro Tsering Chödrön, who is also my aunt, used to say: "Don't disturb Rinpoche, he might be busy,"[1] but I would always want to be there next to him, and he was happy to have me with him. I would pester him with questions all the time, and he always answered me patiently. I was a naughty child; none of my tutors were able to discipline me. Whenever they tried to beat me, I would run to my master and climb up behind him, where no one would dare to go. Crouching there, I felt proud and pleased with myself; he would just laugh. Then one day, without my knowledge, my tutor pleaded with him, explaining that for my own benefit this could not go on. The next time I fled to hide, my tutor came into the room, did three prostrations to my master, and dragged me out. I remember thinking, as I was hauled out of the room, how strange it was that he did not seem to be afraid of my master.

Jamyang Khyentse used to live in the room where his previous incarnation had seen his visions and launched the renaissance of culture and spirituality that swept through eastern Tibet in the last century. It was a wonderful room, not particularly large but with a magical atmosphere, full of sacred objects, paintings, and books. They called it "the heaven of the buddhas," "the room of empowerment," and if there is one place that I remember in Tibet, it is that room. My master sat on a low seat made of wood and strips of leather, and I sat next to him. I would refuse to eat if it was not from his bowl. In the small bedroom close by, there was a veranda, but it was always quite dark, and there was always a kettle with tea bubbling away on a little stove in the corner.

Usually I slept next to my master, on a small bed at the foot of his own. One sound I shall never forget is the clicking of the beads of his *mala,* his Buddhist rosary, as he whispered his prayers. When I went to sleep he would be there, sitting and practicing; and when I awoke in the morning he would already be awake and sitting and practicing again, overflowing with blessing and power. As I opened my eyes and saw him, I would be filled with a warm and cozy happiness. He had such an air of peace about him.

As I grew older, Jamyang Khyentse, would make me preside over ceremonies, while he took the part of chant leader. I was witness to all the teachings and initiations that he gave to others; but rather than the details, what I remember now is the atmosphere. For me he was the Buddha, of that there was no question in my mind. And everyone else recognized it as well. When he gave initiations, his disciples were so overawed they hardly dared look into his face. Some would see him actually in the form of his predecessor, or as different buddhas and *bodhisattvas.*[2] Everyone called him *Rinpoche,* "the Precious One," which is the title given to a master, and when he was present no other teacher would be addressed in that way. His presence was so impressive that many affectionately called him "the Primordial Buddha."[3]

Had I not met my master Jamyang Khyentse, I know I would have been an entirely different person. With his warmth and wisdom and compassion, he personified the sacred truth of the teachings and so made them practical and vibrant with life. Whenever I share that atmosphere of my master with others, they can sense the same profound feeling it aroused in me. What then did Jamyang Khyentse inspire in me? An unshakeable confidence in the teachings, and a conviction in the central and dramatic importance of the master. Whatever understanding I have, I know I owe it to him. This is something I can never repay, but I can pass on to others.

Throughout my youth in Tibet I saw the kind of love Jamyang Khyentse used to radiate in the community, especially in guiding the dying and the dead. A lama in Tibet was not only a spiritual teacher but also wise man, therapist, parish priest, doctor, and spiritual healer, helping the sick and the dying. Later I was to learn the specific techniques for guiding the dying and the dead from the teachings connected with the *Tibetan Book of the Dead.* But the greatest lessons I ever learned about death—and life—came from watching my master as he guided dying people with infinite compassion, wisdom, and understanding.

I pray this book will transmit something of his great wisdom and compassion to the world, and, through it, you too, wherever you are, can come into the presence of his wisdom mind and find a living connection with him.

PART ONE

Living

ONE

In the Mirror of Death

MY OWN FIRST EXPERIENCE of death came when I was about seven. We were preparing to leave the eastern highlands to travel to central Tibet. Samten, one of the personal attendants of my master, was a wonderful monk who was kind to me during my childhood. He had a bright, round, chubby face, always ready to break into a smile. He was everyone's favorite in the monastery because he was so good-natured. Every day my master would give teachings and initiations and lead practices and rituals. Toward the end of the day, I would gather together my friends and act out a little theatrical performance, reenacting the morning's events. It was Samten who would always lend me the costumes my master had worn in the morning. He never refused me.

Then suddenly Samten fell ill, and it was clear he was not going to live. We had to postpone our departure. I will never forget the two weeks that followed. The rank smell of death hung like a cloud over everything, and whenever I think of that time, that smell comes back to me. The monastery was saturated with an intense awareness of death. This was not at all morbid or frightening, however; in the presence of my master, Samten's death took on a special significance. It became a teaching for us all.

Samten lay on a bed by the window in a small temple in my master's residence. I knew he was dying. From time to time I would go in and sit by him. He could not talk, and I was shocked by the change in his face, which was now so haggard and drawn. I realized that he was going to leave us and we would never see him again. I felt intensely sad and lonely.

Samten's death was not an easy one. The sound of his labored breathing followed us everywhere, and we could smell his body decaying. The monastery was overwhelmingly silent except for this breathing. Everything focused on Samten.

Yet although there was so much suffering in Samten's prolonged dying, we could all see that deep down he had a peace
and inner confidence about him. At first I could not explain
this, but then I realized what it came from: his faith and his
training, and the presence of our master. And though I felt
sad, I knew then that if our master was there, everything
would turn out all right, because he would be able to help
Samten toward liberation. Later I came to know that it is the
dream of any practitioner to die before his master and have
the good fortune to be guided by him through death.

As Jamyang Khyentse guided Samten calmly through his
dying, he introduced him to all the stages of the process he
was going through, one by one. I was astonished by the precision of my master's knowledge, and by his confidence and
peace. When my master was there, his peaceful confidence
would reassure even the most anxious person. Now Jamyang
Khyentse was revealing to us his fearlessness of death. Not
that he ever treated death lightly: He often told us that he
was afraid of it, and warned us against taking it naively or
complacently. Yet what was it that allowed my master to face
death in a way that was at once so sober and so lighthearted,
so practical yet so mysteriously carefree? That question fascinated and absorbed me.

Samten's death shook me. At the age of seven, I had my
first glimpse of the vast power of the tradition I was being
made part of, and I began to understand the purpose of spiritual practice. Practice had given Samten an acceptance of
death, as well as a clear understanding that suffering and
pain can be part of a deep, natural process of purification.
Practice had given my master a complete knowledge of what
death is, and a precise technology for guiding individuals
through it.

After Samten died we set off for Lhasa, the capital of Tibet,
a tortuous three-month journey on horseback. From there we
continued our pilgrimage to the sacred sites of central and
southern Tibet. These are the holy places of the saints, kings,
and scholars who brought Buddhism to Tibet from the seventh century onward. My master was the emanation of
many masters of all traditions, and because of his reputation
he was given a tumultuous reception everywhere we went.

For me that journey was extremely exciting, and has
remained full of beautiful memories. Tibetans rise early, in

order to make use of all the natural light. We would go to bed at dusk and rise before daybreak, and by first light the yaks carrying the baggage would be moving out. The tents would be struck, and the last ones to come down were the kitchen and my master's tent. A scout would go ahead to choose a good camping place, and we would stop and camp around noon for the rest of the day. I used to love to camp by a river and listen to the sound of the water, or to sit in the tent and hear the rain pattering on the roof.

We were a small party with about thirty tents in all. During the day I rode on a golden-colored horse next to my master. While we rode he gave teachings, told stories, practiced, and composed a number of practices specially for me. One day, as we drew near the sacred lake of Yamdrok Tso, and caught sight of the turquoise radiance of its waters, another Lama in our party, Lama Tseten, began to die.

The death of Lama Tseten proved another strong teaching for me. He was the tutor to my master's spiritual wife, Khandro Tsering Chödrön, who is still alive today. She is regarded by many as Tibet's foremost woman practitioner, a hidden master who for me is an embodiment of devotion, teaching through the simplicity of her loving presence. Lama Tseten was an immensely human and grandfatherly character. He was over sixty, quite tall and with gray hair, and exuded an effortless gentleness. He was also a highly accomplished practitioner of meditation, and just to be near him used to give me a sense of peace and serenity. Sometimes he would scold me, and I would be afraid of him; but for all his occasional sternness, he never lost his warmth.

Lama Tseten died in an extraordinary way. Although there was a monastery close by, he refused to go there, saying he did not want to leave a corpse for them to clear up. So we camped and pitched our tents in a circle as usual. Khandro was nursing and caring for Lama Tseten, as he was her tutor. She and I were the only two people in his tent when he suddenly called her over. He had an endearing way of calling her "A-mi," meaning "my child" in his local dialect. "A-mi," he said tenderly, "come here. It's happening now. I've no further advice for you. You are fine as you are: I am happy with you. Serve your master just as you have been doing."

Immediately she turned to run out of the tent, but he caught her by the sleeve. "Where are you going?" he asked. "I'm going to call Rinpoche," she replied.

"Don't bother him, there's no need," he smiled. "With the master, there's no such thing as distance." With that, he just gazed up into the sky and passed away. Khandro released herself from his grip and rushed out to call my master. I sat there, unable to move.

I was amazed that anyone who was staring into the face of death could have that kind of confidence. Lama Tseten could have had his Lama there in person to help him—something anyone else would have longed for—but he had no need. I understand why now: He had already realized the presence of the master within himself. Jamyang Khyentse was there with him always, in his mind and heart; never for one moment did he feel any separation.

Khandro did go to fetch Jamyang Khyentse. I shall never forget how he stooped to enter the tent. He gave one look at Lama Tseten's face, and then, peering into his eyes, began to chuckle. He always used to call him "La Gen," "old Lama"; it was a sign of his affection. "La Gen," he said, "don't stay in that state!" He could see, I now understand, that Lama Tseten was doing one particular practice of meditation in which the practitioner merges the nature of his mind with the space of truth. "You know, La Gen, when you do this practice, sometimes subtle obstacles can arise. Come on. I'll guide you."

Transfixed, I watched what happened next, and if I hadn't seen it myself I would never have believed it. *Lama Tseten came back to life.* Then my master sat by his side and took him through the *phowa,* the practice for guiding the consciousness at the moment before death. There are many ways of doing this practice, and the one he used then culminated with the master uttering the syllable "A" three times. As my master declared the first "A," we could hear Lama Tseten accompanying him quite audibly. The second time his voice was less distinct, and the third time it was silent; he had gone.

The death of Samten taught me the purpose of spiritual practice; Lama Tseten's death taught me that it is not unusual for practitioners of his caliber to conceal their remarkable qualities during their lifetime. Sometimes, in fact, they show them only once, at the moment of death. I understood, even as a child, that there was a striking difference between the death of Samten and that of Lama Tseten, and I realized that it was the difference between the death of a good monk who had practiced in his life and that of a much more realized practitioner. Samten died in an ordinary way and in pain,

yet with the confidence of faith; Lama Tseten's death was a
display of spiritual mastery.

Soon after Lama Tseten's funeral, we moved up into the
monastery of Yamdrok. As usual, I slept next to my master in
his room, and I remember that night watching the shadows
of the butter lamps flickering on the wall. While everyone
else slept soundly, I lay awake and cried the whole night long.
I understood that night that death is real, and that I too
would have to die. As I lay there, thinking about death and
about my own death, through all my sadness a profound
sense of acceptance began slowly to emerge, and with it a
resolve to dedicate my life to spiritual practice.

So I began to face death and its implications very young.
I could never have imagined then how many kinds of death
there were to follow, one heaped upon another. The death
that was the tragic loss of my country Tibet, after the Chinese occupation. The death that is exile. The death of losing
everything my family and I possessed. My family, Lakar
Tsang, had been among the wealthiest in Tibet. Since the
fourteenth century it had been famous as one of the most
important benefactors of Buddhism, supporting the teaching
of Buddha and helping the great masters with their work.[1]

The most shattering death of all was yet to come—that of
my master Jamyang Khyentse. Losing him I felt I had lost the
ground of my existence. It was in 1959, the year of the fall of
Tibet. For the Tibetans, my master's death was a second
devastating blow. And for Tibet, it marked the end of an era.

DEATH IN THE MODERN WORLD

When I first came to the West, I was shocked by the contrast between the attitudes to death I had been brought up
with, and those I now found. For all its technological achievements, modern Western society has no real understanding of
death or what happens in death or after death.

I learned that people today are taught to deny death, and
taught that it means nothing but annihilation and loss. That
means that most of the world lives either in denial of death
or in terror of it. Even talking about death is considered
morbid, and many people believe that simply mentioning
death is to risk wishing it upon ourselves.

Others look on death with a naive, thoughtless cheerfulness, thinking that for some unknown reason death will work
out all right for them, and that it is nothing to worry about.

When I think of them, I am reminded of what one Tibetan master says: "People often make the mistake of being frivolous about death and think, 'Oh well, death happens to everybody. It's not a big deal, it's natural. I'll be fine.' That's a nice theory until one is dying."[2]

Of these two attitudes toward death, one views death as something to scurry away from and the other as something that will just take care of itself. How far they both are from understanding death's true significance!

All the greatest spiritual traditions of the world, including of course Christianity, have told us clearly that death is not the end. They have all handed down a vision of some sort of life to come, which infuses this life that we are leading now with sacred meaning. But despite their teachings, modern society is largely a spiritual desert where the majority imagine that *this life* is all that there is. Without any real or authentic faith in an afterlife, most people live lives deprived of any ultimate meaning.

I have come to realize that the disastrous effects of the denial of death go far beyond the individual: They affect the whole planet. Believing fundamentally that this life is the only one, modern people have developed no long-term vision. So there is nothing to restrain them from plundering the planet for their own immediate ends and from living in a selfish way that could prove fatal for the future. How many more warnings do we need, like this one from the former Brazilian Minister for the Environment, responsible for the Amazon rain forest?

> *Modern industrial society is a fanatical religion. We are demolishing, poisoning, destroying all life-systems on the planet. We are signing IOUs our children will not be able to pay . . . We are acting as if we were the last generation on the planet. Without a radical change in heart, in mind, in vision, the earth will end up like Venus, charred and dead.*[3]

Fear of death and ignorance of the afterlife are fueling that destruction of our environment that is threatening all of our lives. So isn't it all the more disturbing that people are not taught what death is, or how to die? Or given any hope in what lies after death, and so what really lies behind life? Could it be more ironic that young people are so highly educated in every subject except the one that holds the key to the entire meaning of life, and perhaps to our very survival?

It has often intrigued me how some Buddhist masters I know ask one simple question of people who approach them for teaching: Do you believe in a life after this one? They are not being asked whether they believe in it as a philosophical proposition, but whether they feel it deeply in their heart. The master knows that if people believe in a life after this one, their whole outlook on life will be different, and they will have a distinct sense of personal responsibility and morality. What the masters must suspect is that there is a danger that people who have no strong belief in a life after this one will create a society fixated on short-term results, without much thought for the consequences of their actions. Could this be the major reason why we have created a brutal world like the one in which we are now living, a world with little real compassion?

Sometimes I think that the most affluent and powerful countries of the developed world are like the realm of the gods described in the Buddhist teachings. The gods are said to live lives of fabulous luxury, reveling in every conceivable pleasure, without a thought for the spiritual dimension of life. All seems to go well until death draws near, and unexpected signs of decay appear. Then the gods' wives and lovers no longer dare approach them, but throw flowers to them from a distance, with casual prayers that they be reborn again as gods. None of their memories of happiness or comfort can shelter them now from the suffering they face; they only make it more savage. So the dying gods are left to die alone in misery.

The fate of the gods reminds me of the way the elderly, the sick, and the dying are treated today. Our society is obsessed with youth, sex, and power, and we shun old age and decay. Isn't it terrifying that we discard old people when their working life is finished and they are no longer useful? Isn't it disturbing that we cast them into old people's homes, where they die lonely and abandoned?

Isn't it time also that we took another look at how we sometimes treat those suffering with terminal illnesses like cancer and AIDS? I know a number of people who have died from AIDS, and I have seen how often they were treated as outcasts, even by their friends, and how the stigma attached to the disease reduced them to despair, and made them feel their life was disgusting and had in the eyes of the world already ended.

Even when a person we know or love is dying, so often people find they are given almost no idea of how to help them; and when they are dead, we are not encouraged to give any thought to the future of the dead person, how he or she will continue, or how we could go on helping him or her. In fact, any attempt to think along these lines risks being dismissed as nonsensical and ridiculous.

What all of this is showing us, with painful clarity, is that now more than ever before we need a fundamental change in our attitude to death and dying.

Happily, attitudes are beginning to change. The hospice movement, for example, is doing marvelous work in giving practical and emotional care. Yet practical and emotional care are not enough; people who are dying need love and care, but they also need something even more profound. They need to discover a real meaning to death, and to life. Without that, how can we give them ultimate comfort? Helping the dying, then, must include the possibility of spiritual care, because it is only with spiritual knowledge that we can truly face, and understand, death.

I have been heartened by the way in which in recent years the whole subject of death and dying has been opened up in the West by pioneers such as Elisabeth Kübler-Ross and Raymond Moody. Looking deeply into the way that we care for the dying, Elisabeth Kübler-Ross has shown that with unconditional love, and a more enlightened attitude, dying can be a peaceful, even transformative experience. The scientific studies of the many different aspects of the near-death experience that followed the brave work of Raymond Moody have held out to humanity a vivid and strong hope that life does not end with death, and there is indeed a "life after life."

Some, unfortunately, did not really understand the full meaning of these revelations about death and dying. They went to the extreme of glamorizing death, and I have heard of tragic cases of young people who committed suicide because they believed death was beautiful and an escape from the depression of their lives. But whether we fear death and refuse to face it, or whether we romanticize it, death is trivialized. Both despair and euphoria about death are an evasion. Death is neither depressing nor exciting; it is simply a fact of life.

How sad it is that most of us only begin to appreciate our life when we are on the point of dying. I often think of the words of the great Buddhist master Padmasambhava: "Those who believe they have plenty of time get ready only at the time of death. Then they are ravaged by regret. But isn't it far too late?" What more chilling commentary on the modern world could there be than that most people die unprepared for death, as they have lived, unprepared for life?

THE JOURNEY THROUGH LIFE AND DEATH

According to the wisdom of Buddha, we *can* actually use our lives to prepare for death. We do not have to wait for the painful death of someone close to us or the shock of terminal illness to force us into looking at our lives. Nor are we condemned to go out empty-handed at death to meet the unknown. We can begin, here and now, to find meaning in our lives. We can make of every moment an opportunity to change and to prepare—wholeheartedly, precisely, and with peace of mind—for death and eternity.

In the Buddhist approach, life and death are seen as one whole, where death is the beginning of another chapter of life. Death is a mirror in which the entire meaning of life is reflected.

This view is central to the teachings of the most ancient school of Tibetan Buddhism. Many of you will have heard of the *Tibetan Book of the Dead.* What I am seeking to do in this book is to explain and expand the *Tibetan Book of the Dead,* to cover not only death but life as well, and to fill out in detail the whole teaching of which the *Tibetan Book of the Dead* is only a part. In this wonderful teaching, we find the whole of life and death presented together as a series of constantly changing transitional realities known as *bardos.* The word "bardo" is commonly used to denote the intermediate state between death and rebirth, but in reality bardos *are occurring continuously throughout both life and death,* and are junctures when the possibility of liberation, or enlightenment, is heightened.

The bardos are particularly powerful opportunities for liberation because there are, the teachings show us, certain moments that are much more powerful than others and much more charged with potential, when whatever you do has a crucial and far-reaching effect. I think of a bardo as being like a moment when you step toward the edge of a precipice; such a moment, for example, is when a master introduces a disciple to the essential, original, and innermost nature of his or her mind. The greatest and most charged of these moments, however, is the moment of death.

So from the Tibetan Buddhist point of view, we can divide our entire existence into four continuously interlinked realities: (1) life, (2) dying and death, (3) after death, and (4) rebirth. These are known as the four bardos: (1) the natural bardo of this life, (2) the painful bardo of dying, (3) the luminous bardo of *dharmata*, and (4) the karmic bardo of becoming.

Because of the vastness and all-comprehensiveness of the bardo teachings, this book has been carefully structured. You will be guided, stage by stage, through the unfolding vision of the journey through life and death. Our exploration necessarily begins with a direct reflection on what death means and the many facets of the truth of impermanence—the kind of reflection that can enable us to make rich use of this life while we still have time, and ensure that when we die it will be without remorse or self-recrimination at having wasted our lives. As Tibet's famous poet saint, Milarepa, said: "My religion is to live—and die—without regret."

Contemplating deeply on the secret message of impermanence—what lies in fact beyond impermanence and death—leads directly to the heart of the ancient and powerful Tibetan teachings: the introduction to the essential "nature of mind." Realization of the nature of mind, which you could call our innermost essence, that truth which we all search for, is the key to understanding life and death. For what happens at the moment of death is that the ordinary mind and its delusions die, and in that gap the boundless sky-like nature of our mind is uncovered. This essential nature of mind is the background to the whole of life and death, like the sky, which folds the whole universe in its embrace.

The teachings make it clear that if all we know of mind is the aspect of mind that dissolves when we die, we will be left with no idea of what continues, no knowledge of the new dimension of the deeper reality of the nature of mind. So it is vital for us all to familiarize ourselves with the nature of mind while we are still alive. Only then will we be prepared when it reveals itself spontaneously and powerfully at the moment of death; be able to recognize it "as naturally," the teachings say, "as a child running into its mother's lap"; and by remaining in that state, finally be liberated.

A description of the nature of mind leads naturally into a complete instruction on meditation, for meditation is the only way we can repeatedly uncover and gradually realize and stabilize that nature of mind. An explanation will then be given of the nature of human evolution, rebirth, and *karma*, so as to provide you with the fullest possible meaning and context of our path through life and death.

By this point you will have enough knowledge to be able to enter confidently the heart of the book: a comprehensive account, drawn from many different sources, of all of the four bardos and of all of the different stages of death and dying. Instruction, practical advice, and spiritual practices are set out in detail for helping both ourselves and others through life, through dying, through death, and after death. The book then concludes with a vision of how the bardo teachings can help us understand the deepest nature of the human mind, and of the universe.

My students often ask me: How do we know what these bardos are, and from where does the astonishing precision of the bardo teachings and their uncannily clear knowledge of each stage of dying, of death, and of rebirth come from? The answer may seem initially difficult to understand for many readers, because the notion of mind the West now has is an extremely narrow one. Despite the major breakthroughs of recent years, especially in mind/body science and transpersonal psychology, the great majority of scientists continue to reduce the mind to no more than physical processes in the brain, which goes against the testimony of thousands of years of experience of mystics and meditators of all religions.

From what source or authority, then, can a book like this be written? The "inner science" of Buddhism is based, as one American scholar puts it, "on a thorough and comprehensive knowledge of reality, on an already assessed, depth understanding of self and environment; that is to say, on the complete enlightenment of the Buddha."[4] The source of the bardo teachings is the enlightened mind, the completely awake buddha mind, as experienced, explained, and transmitted by a long line of masters that stretches back to the Primordial Buddha. Their careful, meticulous—you could almost say scientific—explorations and formulations of their discoveries of mind over many centuries have given us the most complete picture possible of both life and death. It is this complete picture that, inspired by Jamyang Khyentse and all my other great masters, I am humbly attempting to transmit for the very first time to the West.

Over many years of contemplation and teaching and practice, and clarifying questions with my masters, I have written

The Tibetan Book of Living and Dying as the quintessence of the heart-advice of all my masters, to be a new *Tibetan Book of the Dead* and a *Tibetan Book of Life*. I want it to be a manual, a guide, a work of reference, and a source of sacred inspiration. Only by going over this book and reading it again and again, I suggest, can its many layers of meaning be revealed. The more you use it, you will find, the more profoundly you will feel its implications, and the more you will come to realize the depth of the wisdom that is being transmitted to you through the teachings.

The bardo teachings show us precisely what will happen if we prepare for death and what will happen if we do not. The choice could not be clearer. If we refuse to accept death now, while we are still alive, we will pay dearly throughout our lives, at the moment of death, and thereafter. The effects of this refusal will ravage this life and all the lives to come. We will not be able to live our lives fully; we will remain imprisoned in the very aspect of ourselves that has to die. This ignorance will rob us of the basis of the journey to enlightenment, and trap us endlessly in the realm of illusion, the uncontrolled cycle of birth and death, that ocean of suffering that we Buddhists call *samsara*.[5]

Yet the fundamental message of the Buddhist teachings is that if we are prepared, there is tremendous hope, both in life and in death. The teachings reveal to us the possibility of an astounding and finally boundless freedom, which is ours to work for now, in life—the freedom that will also enable us to choose our death and so to choose our birth. For someone who has prepared and practiced, death comes not as a defeat but as a triumph, the crowning and most glorious moment of life.

TWO

Impermanence

There is no place on earth where death cannot find us—even if we constantly twist our heads about in all directions as in a dubious and suspect land . . . If there were any way of sheltering from death's blows—I am not the man to recoil from it . . . But it is madness to think that you can succeed . . .

Men come and they go and they trot and they dance, and never a word about death. All well and good. Yet when death does come—to them, their wives, their children, their friends—catching them unawares and unprepared, then what storms of passion overwhelm them, what cries, what fury, what despair! . . .

To begin depriving death of its greatest advantage over us, let us adopt a way clean contrary to that common one; let us deprive death of its strangeness, let us frequent it, let us get used to it; let us have nothing more often in mind than death . . . We do not know where death awaits us: so let us wait for it everywhere. To practice death is to practice freedom. A man who has learned how to die has unlearned how to be a slave.

MONTAIGNE[1]

WHY IS IT SO VERY HARD to practice death and to practice freedom? And why exactly are we so frightened of death that we avoid looking at it altogether? Somewhere, deep down, we know we cannot avoid facing death forever. We know, in Milarepa's words, "This thing called 'corpse' we dread so much is living with us here and now." The longer we postpone facing death, the more we ignore it, the greater the fear and insecurity that build up to haunt us. The more we try to run away from that fear, the more monstrous it becomes.

Death *is* a vast mystery, but there are two things we can say about it: *It is absolutely certain that we will die,* and *it is uncertain when or how we will die.* The only surety we have, then, is this uncertainty about the hour of our death, which we seize on as the excuse to postpone facing death directly. We are like children who cover their eyes in a game of hide-and-seek and think that no one can see them.

Why do we live in such terror of death? Because our instinctive desire is to live and to go on living, and death is a savage end to everything we hold familiar. We feel that when it comes we will be plunged into something quite unknown, or become someone totally different. We imagine we will find ourselves lost and bewildered, in surroundings that are terrifyingly unfamiliar. We imagine it will be like waking up alone, in a torment of anxiety, in a foreign country, with no knowledge of the land or language, no money, no contacts, no passport, no friends . . .

Perhaps the deepest reason why we are afraid of death is because we do not know who we are. We believe in a personal, unique, and separate identity; but if we dare to examine it, we find that this identity depends entirely on an endless collection of things to prop it up: our name, our "biography," our partners, family, home, job, friends, credit cards . . . It is on their fragile and transient support that we rely for our security. So when they are all taken away, will we have any idea of who we really are?

Without our familiar props, we are faced with just ourselves, a person we do not know, an unnerving stranger with whom we have been living all the time but we never really wanted to meet. Isn't that why we have tried to fill every moment of time with noise and activity, however boring or trivial, to ensure that we are never left in silence with this stranger on our own?

And doesn't this point to something fundamentally tragic about our way of life? We live under an assumed identity, in a neurotic fairy tale world with no more reality than the Mock Turtle in *Alice in Wonderland*. Hypnotized by the thrill of building, we have raised the houses of our lives on sand. This world can seem marvelously convincing until death collapses the illusion and evicts us from our hiding place. What will happen to us then if we have no clue of any deeper reality?

When we die we leave everything behind, especially this body we have cherished so much and relied upon so blindly and tried so hard to keep alive. But our minds are no more dependable than our bodies. Just look at your mind for a few minutes. You will see that it is like a flea, constantly hopping to and fro. You will see that thoughts arise without any reason, without any connection. Swept along by the chaos of every moment, we are the victims of the fickleness of our mind. If this is the only state of consciousness we are familiar with, then to rely on our minds at the moment of death is an absurd gamble.

THE GREAT DECEPTION

The birth of a man is the birth of his sorrow. The longer he lives, the more stupid he becomes, because his anxiety to avoid unavoidable death becomes more and more acute. What bitterness! He lives for what is always out of reach! His thirst for survival in the future makes him incapable of living in the present.

CHUANG TZU

After my master died, I enjoyed a close connection with Dudjom Rinpoche, one of the greatest meditation masters, mystics, and yogins of recent times. One day he was driving through France with his wife, admiring the countryside as they went along. They passed a long cemetery, which had been freshly painted and decorated with flowers. Dudjom Rinpoche's wife said, "Rinpoche, look how everything in the West is so neat and clean. Even the places where they keep corpses are spotless. In the East not even the houses that people live in are anything like as clean as this."

"Ah, yes," he replied, "that's true; this is such a civilized country. They have such marvelous houses for dead corpses. But haven't you noticed? They have such wonderful houses for the living corpses too."

Whenever I think of this story, it makes me think how hollow and futile life can be, when it's founded on a false belief in continuity and permanence. When we live like that, we become, as Dudjom Rinpoche said, unconscious, living corpses.

Most of us do live like that; we live according to a preordained plan. We spend our youth being educated. Then we find a job, and meet someone, marry, and have children. We buy a house, try to make a success of our business, aim for dreams like a country house or a second car. We go away on holiday with our friends. We plan for retirement. The biggest dilemmas some of us ever have to face are where to take our next holiday or whom to invite at Christmas. Our lives are monotonous, petty, and repetitive, wasted in the pursuit of the trivial, because we seem to know of nothing better.

The pace of our lives is so hectic that the last thing we have time to think of is death. We smother our secret fears of impermanence by surrounding ourselves with more and more goods, more and more things, more and more comforts, only to find ourselves their slaves. All our time and energy is exhausted simply maintaining them. Our only aim in life soon becomes to keep everything as safe and secure as possible. When changes do happen, we find the quickest remedy, some slick and temporary solution. And so our lives drift on, unless a serious illness or disaster shakes us out of our stupor.

It is not as if we even spare much time or thought for this life either. Think of those people who work for years and then have to retire, only to find that they don't know what to do with themselves, as they age and approach death. Despite all our chatter about being practical, to be practical in the West means to be ignorantly and often selfishly short-sighted. Our myopic focus on this life, and this life only, is the great deception, the source of the modern world's bleak and destructive materialism. No one talks about death and no one talks about the afterlife, because people are made to believe that such talk will only thwart our so-called "progress" in the world.

Yet if our deepest desire is truly to live and go on living, why do we blindly insist that death is the end? Why not at least try and explore the possibility that there may be a life after? Why, if we are as pragmatic as we claim, don't we begin to ask ourselves seriously: Where does our *real* future lie? After all, no one lives longer than a hundred years. And after that there stretches the whole of eternity, unaccounted for . . .

ACTIVE LAZINESS

There is an old Tibetan story that I love, called "The Father of 'As Famous as the Moon.'" A very poor man, after a great deal of hard work, had managed to accumulate a whole sack of grain. He was proud of himself, and when he got home he strung the bag up with a rope from one of the rafters of his house to keep it safe from rats and thieves. He left it hanging there, and settled down underneath it for the night as an added precaution. Lying there, his mind began to wander: "If I can sell this grain off in small quantities, that will make the biggest profit. With that I can buy some more grain, and do the same again, and before too long I'll become rich, and I'll be someone to reckon with in the community.

Plenty of girls will be after me. I'll marry a beautiful woman, and before too long we'll have a child . . . it will have to be a son . . . what on earth are we going to call him?" Looking round the room, his gaze fell upon the little window, through which he could see the moon rising.

"What a sign!" he thought. "How auspicious! That's a really good name. I'll call him 'As Famous as the Moon' . . ." Now while he had been carried away in his speculation, a rat had found its way up to the sack of grain·and chewed through the rope. At the very moment the words "As Famous as the Moon" issued from his lips, the bag of grain dropped from the ceiling and killed him, instantly. "As Famous as the Moon," of course, was never born.

How many of us, like the man in the story, are swept away by what I have come to call an "active laziness"? Naturally there are different species of laziness: Eastern and Western. The Eastern style is like the one practiced to perfection in India. It consists of hanging out all day in the sun, doing nothing, avoiding any kind of work or useful activity, drinking cups of tea, listening to Hindi film music blaring on the radio, and gossiping with friends. Western laziness is quite different. It consists of cramming our lives with compulsive activity, so that there is no time at all to confront the real issues.

If we look into our lives, we will see clearly how many unimportant tasks, so-called "responsibilities" accumulate to fill them up. One master compares them to "housekeeping in a dream." We tell ourselves we want to spend time on the important things of life, but there never *is* any time. Even simply to get up in the morning, there is so much to do: open the window, make the bed, take a shower, brush your teeth, feed the dog or cat, do last night's washing up, discover you are out of sugar or coffee, go and buy them, make breakfast —the list is endless. Then there are clothes to sort out, choose, iron, and fold up again. And what about your hair, or your makeup? Helpless, we watch our days fill up with telephone calls and petty projects, with so many responsibilities—or shouldn't we call them "irresponsibilities"?

Our lives seem to live us, to possess their own bizarre momentum, to carry us away; in the end we feel we have no choice or control over them. Of course we feel bad about this sometimes, we have nightmares and wake up in a sweat, wondering: "What am I doing with my life?" But our fears only last until breakfast time; out comes the briefcase, and back we go to where we started.

I think of the Indian saint, Ramakrishna, who said to one of his disciples: "If you spent one-tenth of the time you devoted to distractions like chasing women or making money to spiritual practice, you would be enlightened in a few years!" There was a Tibetan master who lived around the turn of the century, a kind of Himalayan Leonardo da Vinci, called Mipham. He is said to have invented a clock, a cannon, and an airplane. But once each of them was complete, he destroyed them, saying that they would only be the cause of further distraction.

In Tibetan the word for body is *lü,* which means "something you leave behind," like baggage. Each time we say "lü," it reminds us that we are only travelers, taking temporary refuge in this life and this body. So in Tibet people did not distract themselves by spending all their time trying to make their external circumstances more comfortable. They were satisfied if they had enough to eat, clothes on their backs, and a roof over their heads. Going on as we do, obsessively trying to improve our conditions, can become an end in itself and a pointless distraction. Would anyone in their right mind think of fastidiously redecorating their hotel room every time they booked into one? I love this piece of advice from Patrul Rinpoche:

> *Remember the example of an old cow,*
> *She's content to sleep in a barn.*
> *You have to eat, sleep, and shit—*
> *That's unavoidable—*
> *Beyond that is none of your business.*

Sometimes I think that the greatest achievement of modern culture is its brilliant selling of samsara and its barren distractions. Modern society seems to me a celebration of all the things that lead away from the truth, make truth hard to live for, and discourage people from even believing that it exists. And to think that all this springs from a civilization that claims to adore life, but actually starves it of any real meaning; that endlessly speaks of making people "happy," but in fact blocks their way to the source of real joy.

This modern samsara feeds off an anxiety and depression that it fosters and trains us all in, and carefully nurtures with a consumer machine that needs to keep us greedy to keep going. Samsara is highly organized, versatile, and sophisticated; it assaults us from every angle with its propaganda, and creates an almost impregnable environment of addiction around us. The more we try to escape, the more we seem to fall into the traps it is so ingenious at setting for us. As the eighteenth-century Tibetan master Jikmé Lingpa said: "Mesmerized by the sheer variety of perceptions, beings wander endlessly astray in samsara's vicious cycle."

Obsessed, then, with false hopes, dreams, and ambitions, which promise happiness but lead only to misery, we are like people crawling through an endless desert, dying of thirst. And all that this samsara holds out to us to drink is a cup of salt water, designed to make us even thirstier.

FACING DEATH

Knowing and realizing this, shouldn't we listen to Gyalsé Rinpoche when he says:

> *Planning for the future is like going fishing in a dry gulch;*
> *Nothing ever works out as you wanted, so give up all your schemes and ambitions.*
> *If you have got to think about something—*
> *Make it the uncertainty of the hour of your death . . .*

For Tibetans, the main festival of the year is the New Year, which is like Christmas, Easter, Thanksgiving, and your birthday all rolled into one. Patrul Rinpoche was a great master whose life was full of eccentric episodes that would bring the teaching to life. Instead of celebrating New Year's Day and wishing people a "Happy New Year" like everyone else, Patrul Rinpoche used to weep. When asked why, he said that another year had gone by, and so many people had come one year closer to death, still unprepared.

Think of what must have happened to nearly all of us one day or the other. We are strolling down the street, thinking inspiring thoughts, speculating on important matters, or just listening to our Walkman. A car suddenly races by and almost runs us over.

Switch on the television or glance at a newspaper: You will see death everywhere. Yet did the victims of those plane crashes and car accidents expect to die? They took life for granted, as we do. How often do we hear stories of people whom we know, or even friends, who died unexpectedly? We don't even have to be ill to die: our bodies can suddenly break down and go out of order, just like our cars. We can be quite well one day, then fall sick and die the next. Milarepa sang:

When you are strong and healthy,
You never think of sickness coming,
But it descends with sudden force
Like a stroke of lightning.

When involved in worldly things,
You never think of death's approach;
Quick it comes like thunder
Crashing round your head.[2]

We need to shake ourselves sometimes and really ask: "What if I were to die tonight? What then?" We do not know whether we will wake up tomorrow, or where. If you breathe out and you cannot breathe in again, you are dead. It's as simple as that. As a Tibetan saying goes: "Tomorrow or the next life—which comes first, we never know."

Some of the renowned contemplative masters of Tibet, when they went to bed at night, would empty their cups and leave them, upside down, by their bedside. They were never sure if they would wake up and need them in the morning. They even put their fires out at night, without bothering to keep the embers alight for the next day. Moment to moment, they lived with the possibility of imminent death.

Near Jikmé Lingpa's hermitage was a pond, which he had great difficulty crossing. Some of his disciples offered to build him a bridge, but he replied: "What's the use? Who knows if I'll even be alive to sleep here tomorrow night?"

Some masters try to wake us up to the fragility of life with even harsher images: They tell each of us to reflect on ourselves as a condemned prisoner taking our last walk from our cell, a fish struggling in the net, an animal lining up for its end in the slaughterhouse.

Others encourage their students to imagine vivid scenarios of their own death, as part of a calm and structured contemplation: the sensations, the pain, the panic, the helplessness, the grief of their loved ones, the realization of what they have or have not done with their lives.

Body lying flat on a last bed,
Voices whispering a few last words,
Mind watching a final memory glide past:
When will that drama come for you?[3]

It is important to reflect calmly, again and again, that *death is real, and comes without warning.* Don't be like the pigeon in the

Tibetan proverb. He spends all night fussing about, making his bed, and dawn comes up before he has even had time to go to sleep. As an important twelfth-century master, Drakpa Gyaltsen, said: "Human beings spend all their lives preparing, preparing, preparing . . . Only to meet the next life unprepared."

TAKING LIFE SERIOUSLY

Perhaps it is only those who understand just how fragile life is who know how precious it is. Once when I was taking part in a conference in Britain, the participants were interviewed by the BBC. At the same time they talked to a woman who was actually dying. She was distraught with fear, because she had not really thought that death was real. Now she knew. She had just one message to those who would survive her: to take life, and death, seriously.

Taking life seriously does not mean spending our whole lives meditating as if we were living in the mountains in the Himalayas or in the old days in Tibet. In the modern world, we have to work and earn our living, but we should not get entangled in a nine-to-five existence, where we live without any view of the deeper meaning of life. Our task is to strike a balance, to find a middle way, to learn not to overstretch ourselves with extraneous activities and preoccupations, but to simplify our lives more and more. *The key to finding a happy balance in modern lives is simplicity.*

In Buddhism this is what is really meant by discipline. In Tibetan, the term for discipline is *tsul trim*. *Tsul* means "appropriate or just," and *trim* means "rule" or "way." So discipline is to do what is appropriate or just; that is, in an excessively complicated age, to simplify our lives.

Peace of mind will come from this. You will have more time to pursue the things of the spirit and the knowledge that only spiritual truth can bring, which can help you face death.

Sadly, this is something that few of us do. Maybe we should ask ourselves the question now: "What have I really achieved in my life?" By that I mean, how much have we really understood about life and death? I have been inspired by the reports that have appeared in the studies on the near-death experience, like the books by my friend Kenneth Ring and others. A striking number of those who survive near-fatal accidents or a near-death experience describe a "panoramic life review." With uncanny vividness and accuracy, they relive the events of their lives. Sometimes they even live through the effects their actions have had on others, and experience the emotions their actions have caused. One man told Kenneth Ring:

> I realized that there are things that every person is sent to earth to real-
> ize and to learn. For instance, to share more love, to be more loving
> toward one another. To discover that the most important thing is
> human relationships and love and not materialistic things. And to
> realize that every single thing that you do in your life is recorded and
> that even though you pass it by not thinking at the time, it always
> comes up later.[4]

Sometimes the life review takes place in the company of a glorious presence, a "being of light." What stands out from the various testimonies is that this meeting with the "being" reveals that the only truly serious goals in life are "learning to love other people and acquiring knowledge."

One person recounted to Raymond Moody: "When the light appeared, the first thing he said to me was, 'What have you done to show me that you've done with your life?' or something to that effect . . . All through this, he kept stress-ing the importance of love . . . He seemed very interested in things concerning knowledge too . . . "[5] Another man told Kenneth Ring: "I was asked—but there were no words: it was a straight mental instantaneous communication—'What had I done to benefit or advance the human race?'"[6]

Whatever we have done with our lives makes us what we are when we die. And everything, absolutely everything, counts.

AUTUMN CLOUDS

At his monastery in Nepal, my master's oldest living disci-ple, the great Dilgo Khyentse Rinpoche, had come to the end of a teaching. He was one of the foremost teachers of our time, the teacher of the Dalai Lama himself, and of many other masters who looked to him as an inexhaustible treasure-house of wisdom and compassion. We all looked up at this gentle, glowing mountain of a man, a scholar, poet, and mys-tic who had spent twenty-two years of his life in retreat. He paused and gazed into the distance:

"I am now seventy-eight years old, and have seen so many things during my lifetime. So many young people have died, so many people of my own age have died, so many old peo-ple have died. So many people that were high up have become low. So many people that were low have risen to be high up. So many countries have changed. There has been so much turmoil and tragedy, so many wars, and plagues, so much terrible destruction all over the world. And yet all these changes are no more real than a dream. When you look deeply, you realize there is nothing that is permanent and constant, nothing, not even the tiniest hair on your body. And this is not a theory, but something you can actually come to know and realize and see, even, with your very own eyes."

I ask myself often: "Why is it that everything changes?" And only one answer comes back to me: *That is how life is.* Nothing, nothing at all, has any lasting character. The Buddha said:

> *This existence of ours is as transient as autumn clouds.*
> *To watch the birth and death of beings is like looking at the movements of a dance.*
> *A lifetime is like a flash of lightning in the sky,*
> *Rushing by, like a torrent down a steep mountain.*

One of the chief reasons we have so much anguish and difficulty facing death is that we ignore the truth of impermanence. We so desperately want everything to continue as it is that we have to believe that things will always stay the same. But this is only make-believe. And as we so often discover, belief has little or nothing to do with reality. This make-believe, with its misinformation, ideas, and assumptions, is the rickety foundation on which we construct our lives. No matter how much the truth keeps interrupting, we prefer to go on trying, with hopeless bravado, to keep up our pretense.

In our minds changes always equal loss and suffering. And if they come, we try to anesthetize ourselves as far as possible. We assume, stubbornly and unquestioningly, that permanence provides security and impermanence does not. But, in fact, impermanence is like some of the people we meet in life—difficult and disturbing at first, but on deeper acquaintance far friendlier and less unnerving than we could have imagined.

Reflect on this: The realization of impermanence is paradoxically the only thing we can hold onto, perhaps our only lasting possession. It is like the sky, or the earth. No matter how much everything around us may change or collapse, they endure. Say we go through a shattering emotional crisis . . . our whole life seems to be disintegrating . . . our husband or wife suddenly leaves us without warning. The earth is still there; the sky is still there. Of course, even the earth trembles now and again, just to remind us we cannot take anything for granted . . .

Even Buddha died. His death was a teaching, to shock the naive, the indolent, and complacent, to wake us up to the truth that everything is impermanent and death an inescapable fact of life. As he was approaching death, the Buddha said:

Of all footprints
That of the elephant is supreme;
Of all mindfulness meditations
That on death is supreme.[7]

Whenever we lose our perspective, or fall prey to laziness, reflecting on death and impermanence shakes us back into the truth:

What is born will die,
What has been gathered will be dispersed,
What has been accumulated will be exhausted,
What has been built up will collapse,
And what has been high will be brought low.

The whole universe, scientists now tell us, is nothing but change, activity, and process—a totality of flux that is the ground of all things:

Every subatomic interaction consists of the annihilation of the original
particles and the creation of new subatomic particles. The subatomic
world is a continual dance of creation and annihilation, of mass
changing into energy and energy changing to mass. Transient forms
sparkle in and out of existence, creating a never-ending, forever newly
created reality.[8]

What is our life but this dance of transient forms? Isn't everything always changing: the leaves on the trees in the park, the light in your room as you read this, the seasons, the weather, the time of day, the people passing you in the street? And what about us? Doesn't everything we have done in the past seem like a dream now? The friends we grew up with, the childhood haunts, those views and opinions we once held with such single-minded passion: We have left them all behind. Now, at this moment, reading this book seems vividly real to you. Even this page will soon be only a memory.

The cells of our body are dying, the neurons in our brain are decaying, even the expression on our face is always changing, depending on our mood. What we call our basic character is only a "mindstream," nothing more. Today we feel good because things are going well; tomorrow we feel the opposite. Where did that good feeling go? New influences took us over as circumstances changed: We are impermanent, the influences are impermanent, and there is nothing solid or lasting anywhere that we can point to.

What could be more unpredictable than our thoughts and emotions: do you have any idea what you are going to think or feel next? Our mind, in fact, is as empty, as impermanent, and as transient as a dream. Look at a thought: It comes, it stays, and it goes. The past is past, the future not yet risen, and even the present thought, as we experience it, becomes the past.

The only thing we really have is nowness, is now.

Sometimes when I teach these things, a person will come up to me afterward and say: "All this seems obvious! I've always known it. Tell me something new." I say to him or her: "Have you actually understood, and realized, the truth of impermanence? Have you so integrated it with your every thought, breath, and movement that your life has been transformed? Ask yourself these two questions: Do I remember at every moment that I am dying, and everyone and everything else is, and so treat all beings at all times with compassion? Has my understanding of death and impermanence become so keen and so urgent that I am devoting every second to the pursuit of enlightenment? If you can answer 'yes' to both of these, *then* you have *really* understood impermanence."

THREE

Reflection and Change

WHEN I WAS A CHILD IN TIBET, I heard the story of Krisha Gotami, a young woman who had the good fortune to live at the time of the Buddha. When her firstborn child was about a year old, it fell ill and died. Grief-stricken and clutching its little body, Krisha Gotami roamed the streets, begging anyone she met for a medicine that could restore her child to life. Some ignored her, some laughed at her, some thought she was mad, but finally she met a wise man who told her that the only person in the world who could perform the miracle she was looking for was the Buddha.

So she went to the Buddha, laid the body of her child at his feet, and told him her story. The Buddha listened with infinite compassion. Then he said gently, "There is only one way to heal your affliction. Go down to the city and bring me back a mustard seed from any house in which there has never been a death."

Krisha Gotami felt elated and set off at once for the city. She stopped at the first house she saw and said: "I have been told by the Buddha to fetch a mustard seed from a house that has never known death."

"Many people have died in this house," she was told. She went on to the next house. "There have been countless deaths in our family," they said. And so to a third and a fourth house, until she had been all round the city and realized the Buddha's condition could not be fulfilled.

She took the body of her child to the charnel ground and said goodbye to him for the last time, then returned to the Buddha. "Did you bring the mustard seed?" he asked.

"No," she said. "I am beginning to understand the lesson you are trying to teach me. Grief made me blind and I thought that only I had suffered at the hands of death."

"Why have you come back?" asked the Buddha.

"To ask you to teach me the truth," she replied, "of what death is, what might lie behind and beyond death, and what in me, if anything, will not die."

The Buddha began to teach her: "If you want to know the truth of life and death, you must reflect continually on this: There is only one law in the universe that never changes—that all things change, and that all things are impermanent. The death of your child has helped you to see now that the realm we are in—samsara—is an ocean of unbearable suffering. There is one way, and one way only, out of samsara's ceaseless round of birth and death, which is the path to liberation. Because pain has now made you ready to learn and your heart is opening to the truth, I will show it to you."

Krisha Gotami knelt at his feet, and followed the Buddha for the rest of her life. Near the end of it, it is said, she attained enlightenment.

ACCEPTING DEATH

Krisha Gotami's story shows us something we can observe again and again: A close encounter with death can bring a real awakening, a transformation in our whole approach to life.

Take, for example the near-death experience. Perhaps one of its most important revelations is how it transforms the lives of those who have been through it. Researchers have noted a startling range of aftereffects and changes: a reduced fear and deeper acceptance of death; an increased concern for helping others; an enhanced vision of the importance of love; less interest in materialistic pursuits; a growing belief in a spiritual dimension and the spiritual meaning of life; and, of course, a greater openness to belief in the afterlife. One man said to Kenneth Ring:

> I was transformed from a man who was lost and wandering aimlessly, with no goal in life other than a desire for material wealth, to someone who had a deep motivation, a purpose in life, a definite direction, and an overpowering conviction that there would be a reward at the end of life. My interest in material wealth and greed for possessions were replaced by a thirst for spiritual understanding and a passionate desire to see world conditions improve.[1]

A woman told Margot Grey, a British researcher into the near-death experience:

> The things that I felt slowly were a very heightened sense of love, the ability to communicate love, the ability to find joy and pleasures in

*the smallest and most insignificant things about me . . . I developed
a great compassion for people that were ill and facing death and I
wanted so much to let them know, to somehow make them aware that
the dying process was nothing more than an extension of one's life.*[2]

We all know how life-menacing crises such as serious illness can produce transformations of a similar depth. Freda
Naylor, a doctor who courageously kept a diary as she died of
cancer, wrote:

*I have had experiences which I never would have had, for which I
have to thank the cancer. Humility, coming to terms with my own
mortality, knowledge of my inner strength, which continually surprises
me, and more things about myself which I have discovered because I
have had to stop in my tracks, reassess and proceed.*[3]

If we can indeed "reassess and proceed" with this new-
found humility and openness, and a real acceptance of our
death, we will find ourselves much more receptive to spiritual
instructions and spiritual practice. This receptivity could well
open to us yet another marvelous possibility: that of true
healing.

I remember a middle-aged American woman who came to
see Dudjom Rinpoche in New York in 1976. She had no particular interest in Buddhism, but had heard that there was a
great master in town. She was extremely sick, and in her
desperation she was willing to try anything, even to see a
Tibetan master! At that time I was his translator.

She came into the room and sat in front of Dudjom Rinpoche. She was so moved by her own condition and his presence that she broke down into tears. She blurted out, "My
doctor has given me only a few months to live. Can you help
me? I am dying."

To her surprise, in a gentle yet compassionate way, Dudjom Rinpoche began to chuckle. Then he said quietly: "You
see, we are all dying. It's only a matter of time. Some of us
just die sooner than others." With these few words, he helped
her to see the universality of death, and that her impending
death was not unique. This eased her anxiety. Then he talked
about dying, and the acceptance of death. And he spoke about
the hope there is in death. At the end he gave her a healing
practice, which she followed enthusiastically.

Not only did she come to accept death; but by following
the practice with complete dedication, she was healed. I have

heard of many other cases of people who were diagnosed as terminally ill and given only a few months to live. When they went into solitude, followed a spiritual practice, and truly faced themselves and the fact of death, they were healed. What is this telling us? That when we accept death, transform our attitude toward life, and discover the fundamental connection between life and death, a dramatic possibility for healing can occur.

Tibetan Buddhists believe that illnesses like cancer can be a warning, to remind us that we have been neglecting deep aspects of our being, such as our spiritual needs.[4] If we take this warning seriously and change fundamentally the direction of our lives, there is a very real hope for healing not only our bodies, but our whole being.

A CHANGE IN THE DEPTHS OF THE HEART

To reflect deeply on impermanence, just as Krisha Gotami did, is to be led to understand in the core of your heart the truth that is expressed so strongly in this verse of a poem by a contemporary master, Nyoshul Khenpo:

The nature of everything is illusory and ephemeral,
Those with dualistic perception regard suffering as happiness,
Like they who lick the honey from a razor's edge.
How pitiful they who cling strongly to concrete reality:
Turn your attention within, my heart friends.[5]

Yet how hard it can be to turn our attention within! How easily we allow our old habits and set patterns to dominate us! Even though, as Nyoshul Khenpo's poem tells us, they bring us suffering, we accept them with almost fatalistic resignation, for we are so used to giving in to them. *We may idealize freedom, but when it comes to our habits, we are completely enslaved.*

Still, reflection can slowly bring us wisdom. We can come to see we are falling again and again into fixed repetitive patterns, and begin to long to get out of them. We may, of course, fall back into them, again and again, but slowly we can emerge from them and change. The following poem speaks to us all. It's called "Autobiography in Five Chapters."[6]

1) I walk down the street.
There is a deep hole in the sidewalk
I fall in.

I am lost . . . I am hopeless.
It isn't my fault.
It takes forever to find a way out.

2) I walk down the same street.
There is a deep hole in the sidewalk.
I pretend I don't see it.
I fall in again.
I can't believe I'm in the same place.
But it isn't my fault.
It still takes a long time to get out.

3) I walk down the same street.
There is a deep hole in the sidewalk
I see it is there.
I still fall in . . . it's a habit
My eyes are open
I know where I am
It is my fault.
I get out immediately.

4) I walk down the same street.
There is a deep hole in the sidewalk
I walk around it.

5) I walk down another street.

The purpose of reflecting on death is to make a real change in the depths of your heart, and to come to learn how to avoid the "hole in the sidewalk," and how to "walk down another street." Often this will require a period of retreat and deep contemplation, because only that can truly open our eyes to what we are doing with our lives.

Looking into death needn't be frightening or morbid. Why not reflect on death when you are really inspired, relaxed, and comfortable, lying in bed, or on holiday, or listening to music that particularly delights you? Why not reflect on it when you are happy, in good health, confident, and full of well-being? Don't you notice that there are particular moments when you are naturally moved to introspection? Work with them gently, for *these are the moments when you can go through a powerful experience, and your whole worldview can change quickly.* These are the moments when former beliefs crumble on their own, and you can find yourself being transformed.

Contemplation on death will bring you a deepening sense of what we call "renunciation," in Tibetan *ngé jung. Ngé* means "actually" or "definitely," and *jung* means to "come out," "emerge," or "be born." The fruit of frequent and deep reflection on death will be that you will find yourself "emerging," often with a sense of disgust, from your habitual patterns. You will find yourself increasingly ready to let go of them, and in the end you will be able to free yourself from them as smoothly, the masters say, "as drawing a hair from a slab of butter."

This renunciation that you will come to has both sadness and joy in it: sadness because you realize the futility of your old ways, and joy because of the greater vision that begins to unfold when you are able to let go of them. This is no ordinary joy. It is a joy that gives birth to a new and profound strength, a confidence, an abiding inspiration that comes from the realization that you are not condemned to your habits, that you *can* indeed emerge from them, that you *can* change, and grow more and more free.

THE HEARTBEAT OF DEATH

There would be no chance at all of getting to know death if it happened only once. But fortunately, life is nothing but a continuing dance of birth and death, a dance of change. Every time I hear the rush of a mountain stream, or the waves crashing on the shore, or my own heartbeat, I hear the sound of impermanence. These changes, these small deaths, are our living links with death. They are death's pulse, death's heartbeat, prompting us to let go of all the things we cling to.

So let us then work with these changes now, in life: that is the real way to prepare for death. Life may be full of pain, suffering, and difficulty, but all of these are opportunities handed to us to help us move toward an emotional acceptance of death. It is only when we believe things to be permanent that we shut off the possibility of learning from change.

If we shut off this possibility, we become closed, and we become grasping. Grasping is the source of all our problems. Since impermanence to us spells anguish, we grasp on to things desperately, even though all things change. We are terrified of letting go, terrified, in fact, of living at all, *since learning to live is learning to let go.* And this is the tragedy and the irony of our struggle to hold on: not only is it impossible, but it brings us the very pain we are seeking to avoid.

The intention behind grasping may not in itself be bad; there's nothing wrong with the desire to be happy, but what we grasp on to is by nature ungraspable. The Tibetans say you cannot wash the same dirty hand twice in the same running river, and, "No matter how much you squeeze a handful of sand, you will never get oil out of it."

Taking impermanence truly to heart is to be slowly freed from the idea of grasping, from our flawed and destructive view of permanence, from the false passion for security on which we built everything. Slowly it dawns on us that all the heartache we have been through from grasping at the ungraspable was, in the deepest sense, unnecessary. At the beginning this too may be painful to accept, because it seems so unfamiliar. But as we reflect, and go on reflecting, our hearts and minds go through a gradual transformation. Letting go begins to feel more natural, and becomes easier and easier. It may take a long time for the extent of our foolishness to sink in, but the more we reflect, the more we develop the view of letting go; it is then that a shift takes place in our way of looking at everything.

Contemplating impermanence on its own is not enough: You have to work with it in your life. Just as medical studies require both theory and practice, so does life; and in life the practical training is here, is now, in the laboratory of change. As changes occur we learn to look at them with a new understanding; and though they will still go on arising just as they did before, something in us will be different. The whole situation will now be more relaxed, less intense and painful; even the impact of the changes we go through we will find less shocking. With each successive change, we realize a little bit more, and our view of living becomes deeper and more spacious.

WORKING WITH CHANGES

Let's try an experiment. Pick up a coin. Imagine that it represents the object at which you are grasping. Hold it tightly clutched in your fist and extend your arm, with the palm of your hand facing the ground. Now if you let go or relax your grip, you will lose what you are clinging onto. That's why you hold on.

But there's another possibility: You can let go and yet keep hold of it. With your arm still outstretched, turn your hand over so that it faces the sky. Release your hand and the coin still rests on your open palm. You let go. And the coin is still yours, even with all this space around it.

So there is a way in which we can accept impermanence and still relish life, at one and the same time, without grasping.

Let us now think of what frequently happens in relationships. So often it is only when people suddenly feel they are losing their partner that they realize that they love them. Then they cling on even tighter. But the more they grasp, the more the other person escapes them, and the more fragile their relationship becomes.

So often we want happiness, but the very way we pursue it is so clumsy and unskillful that it brings only more sorrow. Usually we assume we must grasp in order to have that something that will ensure our happiness. We ask ourselves: How can we possibly enjoy anything if we cannot own it? How often attachment is mistaken for love! Even when the relationship is a good one, love is spoiled by attachment, with its insecurity, possessiveness, and pride; and then when love is gone, all you are left to show for it are the "souvenirs" of love, the scars of attachment.

How, then, can we work to overcome attachment? Only by realizing its impermanent nature; this realization slowly releases us from its grip. We come to glimpse what the masters say the true attitude to change can be: as if we were the sky looking at the clouds passing by, or as free as mercury. When mercury is dropped on the ground, its very nature is to remain intact; it never mixes with the dust. As we try to follow the masters' advice and are slowly released from attachment, a great compassion is released in us. The clouds of grasping part and disperse, and the sun of our true compassionate heart shines out. It is then that we begin, in our deepest self, to taste the elating truth of these words by William Blake:

> He who binds to himself a Joy,
> Does the winged life destroy;
> He who kisses the Joy as it flies,
> Lives in Eternity's sunrise.[7]

THE SPIRIT OF THE WARRIOR

Although we have been made to believe that if we let go we will end up with nothing, life itself reveals again and again the opposite: that letting go is the path to real freedom.

Just as when the waves lash at the shore, the rocks suffer no damage but are sculpted and eroded into beautiful shapes, so our characters can be molded and our rough edges worn smooth by changes. Through weathering changes we can learn how to develop a gentle but unshakeable composure. Our confidence in ourselves grows, and becomes so much greater that goodness and compassion begin naturally to radiate out from us and bring joy to others. That goodness is what survives death, a fundamental goodness that is in every one of us. The whole of our life is a teaching of how to uncover that strong goodness, and a training toward realizing it.

So each time the losses and deceptions of life teach us about impermanence, they bring us closer to the truth. When you fall from a great height, there is only one possible place to land: on the ground; the ground of truth. And if you have the understanding that comes from spiritual practice, then falling is in no way a disaster but the discovery of an inner refuge.

Difficulties and obstacles, if properly understood and used, can often turn out to be an unexpected source of strength. In the biographies of the masters, you will often find that had they not faced difficulties and obstacles, they would not have discovered the strength they needed to rise above them. This was true, for example, of Gesar, the great warrior king of Tibet, whose escapades form the greatest epic of Tibetan literature. *Gesar* means "indomitable," someone who can never be put down. From the moment Gesar was born, his evil uncle Trotung tried all kinds of means to kill him. But with each attempt Gesar only grew stronger and stronger. It was thanks to Trotung's efforts, in fact, that Gesar was to become so great. This gave rise to a Tibetan proverb: *Trotung tro ma tung na, Gesar ge mi sar,* which means that if Trotung had not been so malicious and scheming, Gesar could never have risen so high.

For the Tibetans Gesar is not only a martial warrior but also a spiritual one. To be a spiritual warrior means to develop a special kind of courage, one that is innately intelligent, gentle, and fearless. Spiritual warriors can still be frightened, but even so they are courageous enough to taste suffering, to relate clearly to their fundamental fear, and to draw out without evasion the lessons from difficulties. As Chögyam Trungpa Rinpoche tells us, becoming a warrior means that "we can trade our small-minded struggle for security for a much vaster vision, one of fearlessness, openness, and genuine heroism . . ."[8] To enter the transforming field of that much vaster vision is to learn how to be at home in change, and how to make impermanence our friend.

THE MESSAGE OF IMPERMANENCE: WHAT HOPE THERE IS IN DEATH

Look still deeper into impermanence, and you will find it has another message, another face, one of great hope, one that opens your eyes to the fundamental nature of the universe, and our extraordinary relationship to it.

If everything is impermanent, then everything is what we call "empty," which means lacking in any lasting, stable, and inherent existence; and all things, when seen and understood in their true relation, are not independent but interdependent with all other things. The Buddha compared the universe to a vast net woven of a countless variety of brilliant jewels, each with a countless number of facets. Each jewel reflects in itself every other jewel in the net and is, in fact, one with every other jewel.

Think of a wave in the sea. Seen in one way, it seems to have a distinct identity, an end and a beginning, a birth and a death. Seen in another way, the wave itself doesn't really exist but is just the behavior of water, "empty" of any separate identity but "full" of water. So when you really think about the wave, you come to realize that it is something made temporarily possible by wind and water, and is dependent on a set of constantly changing circumstances. You also realize that every wave is related to every other wave.

Nothing has any *inherent* existence of its own when you really look at it, and this absence of independent existence is what we call "emptiness." Think of a tree. When you think of a tree, you tend to think of a distinctly defined object; and on a certain level, like the wave, it is. But when you look more closely at the tree, you will see that ultimately it has no independent existence. When you contemplate it, you will find that it dissolves into an extremely subtle net of relationships that stretches across the universe. The rain that falls on its leaves, the wind that sways it, the soil that nourishes and sustains it, all the seasons and the weather, moonlight and starlight and sunlight—all form part of this tree. As you begin to think about the tree more and more, you will discover that everything in the universe helps to make the tree what it is; that it cannot at any moment be isolated from anything else; and that at every moment its nature is subtly changing. This is what we mean when we say things are empty, that they have no independent existence.

Modern science speaks to us of an extraordinary range of interrelations. Ecologists know that a tree burning in the Amazon rainforest alters in some way the air breathed by a citizen of Paris, and that the trembling of a butterfly's wing in Yucatan affects the life of a fern in the Hebrides. Biologists are beginning to uncover the fantastic and complex dance of genes that creates personality and identity, a dance that stretches far into the past and shows that each so-called "identity" is composed of a swirl of different influences. Physicists have introduced us to the world of the quantum particle, a world astonishingly like that described by Buddha in his image of the glittering net that unfolds across the universe. Just like the jewels in the net, all particles exist potentially as different combinations of other particles.

So when we really look at ourselves, then, and the things around us that we took to be so solid, so stable, and so lasting, we find that they have no more reality than a dream. Buddha said:

> Know all things to be like this:
> A mirage, a cloud castle,
> A dream, an apparition,
> Without essence, but with qualities that can be seen.

> Know all things to be like this:
> As the moon in a bright sky
> In some clear lake reflected,
> Though to that lake the moon has never moved.

> Know all things to be like this:
> As an echo that derives
> From music, sounds, and weeping,
> Yet in that echo is no melody.

> Know all things to be like this:
> As a magician makes illusions
> Of horses, oxen, carts and other things,
> Nothing is as it appears.[9]

Contemplation of this dreamlike quality of reality need not in any way make us cold, hopeless, or embittered. On the contrary, it can open up in us a warm humor, a soft, strong compassion we hardly knew we possessed, and so more and more generosity toward all things and beings. The great

Tibetan saint Milarepa said: "Seeing emptiness, have compassion." When through contemplation we really have seen the emptiness and interdependence of all things and ourselves, the world is revealed in a brighter, fresher, more sparkling light as the infinitely reflecting net of jewels that Buddha spoke of. We no longer have to protect ourselves or pretend, and it becomes increasingly easy to do what one Tibetan master has advised:

> *Always recognize the dreamlike qualities of life and reduce attachment and aversion. Practice good-heartedness toward all beings. Be loving and compassionate, no matter what others do to you. What they will do will not matter so much when you see it as a dream. The trick is to have positive intention during the dream. This is the essential point. This is true spirituality.*[10]

True spirituality also is to be aware that if we are interdependent with everything and everyone else, even our smallest, least significant thought, word, and action have real consequences throughout the universe. Throw a pebble into a pond. It sends a shiver across the surface of the water. Ripples merge into one another and create new ones. Everything is inextricably interrelated: We come to realize we are responsible for everything we do, say, or think, responsible in fact for ourselves, everyone and everything else, and the entire universe. The Dalai Lama has said:

> *In today's highly interdependent world, individuals and nations can no longer resolve many of their problems by themselves. We need one another. We must therefore develop a sense of universal responsibility . . . It is our collective and individual responsibility to protect and nurture the global family, to support its weaker members, and to preserve and tend to the environment in which we all live.*[11]

THE CHANGELESS

Impermanence has already revealed to us many truths, but it has a final treasure still in its keeping, one that lies largely hidden from us, unsuspected and unrecognized, yet most intimately our own.

The Western poet Rainer Maria Rilke has said that our deepest fears are like dragons guarding our deepest treasure.[12] The fear that impermanence awakens in us, that nothing is real and nothing lasts, is, we come to discover, our greatest friend because it drives us to ask: If everything dies and changes, then what is really true? Is there something behind the appearances, something boundless and infinitely spacious, something in which the dance of change and impermanence takes place? Is there something in fact we can depend on, that does survive what we call death?

Allowing these questions to occupy us urgently, and reflecting on them, we slowly find ourselves making a profound shift in the way we view everything. With continued contemplation and practice in letting go, we come to uncover in ourselves "something" we cannot name or describe or conceptualize, "something" that we begin to realize lies behind all the changes and deaths of the world. The narrow desires and distractions to which our obsessive grasping onto permanence has condemned us begin to dissolve and fall away.

As this happens we catch repeated and glowing glimpses of the vast implications behind the truth of impermanence. It is as if all our lives we have been flying in an airplane through dark clouds and turbulence, when suddenly the plane soars above these into the clear, boundless sky. Inspired and exhilarated by this emergence into a new dimension of freedom, we come to uncover a depth of peace, joy, and confidence in ourselves that fills us with wonder, and breeds in us gradually a certainty that there is in us "something" that nothing destroys, that nothing alters, and that cannot die. Milarepa wrote:

> In horror of death, I took to the mountains—
> Again and again I meditated on the uncertainty of the hour of death,
> Capturing the fortress of the deathless unending nature of mind.
> Now all fear of death is over and done.[13]

Gradually, then, we become aware in ourselves of the calm and sky-like presence of what Milarepa calls the deathless and unending nature of mind. And as this new awareness begins to become vivid and almost unbroken, there occurs what the Upanishads call "a turning about in the seat of consciousness," a personal, utterly non-conceptual revelation of what we are, why we are here, and how we should act, which amounts in the end to nothing less than a new life, a new birth, almost, you could say, a resurrection.

What a beautiful and what a healing mystery it is that from contemplating, continually and fearlessly, the truth of change and impermanence, we come slowly to find ourselves face to face, in gratitude and joy, with the truth of the changeless, with the truth of the deathless, unending nature of mind!

FOUR

The Nature of Mind

CONFINED IN THE DARK, narrow cage of our own making which we take for the whole universe, very few of us can even begin to imagine another dimension of reality. Patrul Rinpoche tells the story of an old frog who had lived all his life in a dank well. One day a frog from the sea paid him a visit.

"Where do you come from?" asked the frog in the well.

"From the great ocean," he replied.

"How big is your ocean?"

"It's gigantic."

"You mean about a quarter of the size of my well here?"

"Bigger."

"Bigger? You mean half as big?"

"No, even bigger."

"Is it . . . as big as this well?"

"There's no comparison."

"That's impossible! I've got to see this for myself."

They set off together. When the frog from the well saw the ocean, it was such a shock that his head just exploded into pieces.

Most of my childhood memories of Tibet have faded, but two moments will always stay with me. They were when my master Jamyang Khyentse introduced me to the essential, original, and innermost nature of my mind.

At first I felt reticent about revealing these personal experiences, as in Tibet this is never done; but my students and friends were convinced that a description of these experiences would help others, and they pleaded with me and kept on insisting that I write about them.

The first of these moments occurred when I was six or seven years old. It took place in that special room in which

Jamyang Khyentse lived, in front of a large portrait statue of his previous incarnation, Jamyang Khyentse Wangpo. This was a solemn, awe-inspiring figure, made more so when the flame of the butter-lamp in front of it would flicker and light up its face. Before I knew what was happening, my master did something most unusual. He suddenly hugged me and lifted me up off my feet. Then he gave me a huge kiss on the side of my face. For a long moment my mind fell away completely and I was enveloped by a tremendous tenderness, warmth, confidence, and power.

The next occasion was more formal, and it happened at Lhodrak Kharchu, in a cave in which the great saint and father of Tibetan Buddhism, Padmasambhava, had meditated. We had stopped there on our pilgrimage through southern Tibet. I was about nine at the time. My master sent for me and told me to sit in front of him. We were alone. He said, "Now I'm going to introduce you to the essential 'nature of mind.'" Picking up his bell and small hand-drum, he chanted the invocation of all the masters of the lineage, from the Primordial Buddha down to his own master. Then he did the introduction. Suddenly he sprung on me a question with no answer: "What is mind?" and gazed intently deep into my eyes. I was taken totally by surprise. My mind shattered. No words, no names, no thought remained—no mind, in fact, at all.

What happened in that astounding moment? Past thoughts had died away, the future had not yet arisen; the stream of my thoughts was cut right through. In that pure shock a gap opened, and in that gap was laid bare a sheer, immediate awareness of the present, one that was free of any clinging. It was simple, naked, and fundamental. And yet that naked simplicity was also radiant with the warmth of an immense compassion.

How many things I could say about that moment! My master, apparently, was asking a question; yet I knew he did not expect an answer. And before I could hunt for an answer, I knew there was none to find. I sat thunderstruck in wonder, and yet a deep and glowing certainty I had never known before was welling up within me.

My master had asked: "What is mind?" and at that instant I felt that it was almost as if everyone knew there was no such thing as mind, and I was the last to find out. How ridiculous it seemed then even to look for mind.

The introduction by my master had sown a seed deep inside me. Later, I came to realize that this was the method of introduction employed in our lineage. Not knowing this then, however, made what happened completely unexpected, and so more astonishing and powerful.

In our tradition we say that "three authentics" must be present for the nature of mind to be introduced: the blessing of an authentic master, the devotion of an authentic student, and the authentic lineage of the method of introduction.

The President of the United States cannot introduce you to the nature of your mind, nor can your father or your mother. It doesn't matter how powerful someone may be, or how much they love you. It can only be introduced by someone who has fully realized it, and who carries the blessing and experience of the lineage.

And you, the student, must find and constantly nourish that openness, breadth of vision, willingness, enthusiasm, and reverence that will change the whole atmosphere of your mind, and make you receptive to the introduction. That is what we mean by devotion. Without it, the master may introduce but the student will not recognize. The introduction to the nature of mind is only possible when both the master and student enter into that experience together; only in that meeting of minds and hearts will the student realize.

The method is also of crucial importance. It is the very same method that has been tried and tested for thousands of years and enabled the masters of the past themselves to attain realization.

When my master gave me the introduction so spontaneously, and at such an early age, he was doing something quite out of the ordinary. Normally it is done much later, when a disciple has gone through the preliminary training of meditation practice and purification. That is what ripens and opens the student's heart and mind to the direct understanding of the truth. Then, in that powerful moment of introduction, the master can direct his or her realization of the nature of mind—what we call the master's "wisdom mind"—into the mind of the now authentically receptive student. The master is doing nothing less than introducing the student to what the Buddha actually *is*, awakening the student, in other words, to the living presence of enlightenment within. In that experience, the Buddha, the nature of mind, and the master's wisdom mind are all fused into, and revealed as, one. The student then recognizes, in a blaze of gratitude, beyond any shadow of doubt, that there is not, has never been, and could not ever be, any separation: between student and master, between the master's wisdom mind and the nature of the student's mind.

Dudjom Rinpoche, in his famous declaration of realization, wrote:

> Since pure awareness of nowness is the real buddha,
> In openness and contentment I found the Lama in my heart.
> When we realize this unending natural mind is the very nature of the Lama,
> Then there is no need for attached, grasping, or weeping prayers or artificial complaints,
> By simply relaxing in this uncontrived, open, and natural state,
> We obtain the blessing of aimless self-liberation of whatever arises.[1]

When you have fully recognized that the nature of your mind is the same as that of the master, from then on you and the master can never be separate because the master is *one* with the nature of your mind, always present, as it is. Remember Lama Tseten, whom I had watched dying as a child? When given the chance to have his master physically present at his deathbed, he said: "With the master, there's no such thing as distance."

When, like Lama Tseten, you have recognized that the master and you are inseparable, an enormous gratitude and sense of awe and homage is born in you. Dudjom Rinpoche calls this "the homage of the View." It is a devotion that springs spontaneously from seeing the View of the nature of mind.

For me there were many other moments of introduction: in the teachings and initiations, and later I received the introduction from my other masters. After Jamyang Khyentse passed away, Dudjom Rinpoche held me in his love and took care of me, and I served as his translator for a number of years. This opened another phase of my life.

Dudjom Rinpoche was one of Tibet's most famous masters and mystics, and a renowned scholar and author. My master Jamyang Khyentse always used to talk about how wonderful a master Dudjom Rinpoche was, and how he was the living representative of Padmasambhava in this age. Therefore I had a profound respect for him, although I had no personal connection with him or experience of his teaching. One day, after my master had died, when I was in my early twenties, I paid a courtesy call on Dudjom Rinpoche at his home in Kalimpong, a hill-station in the Himalayas.

When I arrived I found that one of his first American students was there, receiving some instruction. She was having a very frustrating time, as there was no translator with English good enough to translate teachings on the nature of mind. When he saw me come in, Dudjom Rinpoche said: "Oh! You are here. Good! Can you translate for her?" So I sat down and began to translate. In one sitting, in the course of about an hour, he gave an amazing teaching, one that embraced everything. I was so moved and inspired there were tears in my eyes. I realized that this was what Jamyang Khyentse had meant.

Immediately afterward, I requested Dudjom Rinpoche to give me teachings. I would go to his house every afternoon and spend several hours with him. He was small, with a beautiful and gentle face, exquisite hands, and a delicate, almost feminine presence. He wore his hair long and tied up like a yogin in a knot; his eyes always glittered with secret amusement. His voice seemed the voice of compassion itself, soft and a little hoarse. Dudjom Rinpoche would sit on a low seat covered with a Tibetan carpet, and I sat just below him. I will always remember him sitting there, the late sun streaming in through the window behind him.

Then one day, when I was receiving the teaching and practicing with him, I had the most astounding experience. Everything I had ever heard about in the teachings seemed to be happening to me—all the material phenomena around us were dissolving—I became so excited and stammered:

"Rinpoche . . . Rinpoche . . . it's happening!" I will never forget the look of compassion on his face as he leaned down toward me and comforted me: "It's all right . . . it's all right. Don't get too excited. In the end, it's neither good nor bad . . ." Wonder and bliss were beginning to carry me away, but Dudjom Rinpoche knew that although good experiences can be useful landmarks on the path of meditation, they can be traps if attachment enters in. You have to go beyond them into a deeper and more stable grounding: It was to that grounding that his wise words brought me.

Dudjom Rinpoche would inspire again and again the realization of the nature of mind through the words of the teaching he gave; the words themselves kindled glimpses of the real experience. For many years, every day, he would give me the instructions on the nature of mind known as the "pointing out" instructions. Although I had received all the essential training from my master Jamyang Khyentse like a seed, it was Dudjom Rinpoche who had watered it and made it blossom. And when I began to teach, it was his example that inspired me.

THE MIND AND THE NATURE OF MIND

The still revolutionary insight of Buddhism is that *life and death are in the mind, and nowhere else.* Mind is revealed as the universal basis of experience—the creator of happiness and the creator of suffering, the creator of what we call life and what we call death.

There are many aspects to the mind, but two stand out. The first is the ordinary mind, called by the Tibetans *sem.* One master defines it: "That which possesses discriminating awareness, that which possesses a sense of duality—which grasps or rejects something external—that is mind. Fundamentally it is that which can associate with an 'other'—with any 'something', that is perceived as different from the perceiver."[2] Sem is the discursive, dualistic, thinking mind, which can only function in relation to a projected and falsely perceived external reference point.

So sem is the mind that thinks, plots, desires, manipulates, that flares up in anger, that creates and indulges in waves of negative emotions and thoughts, that has to go on and on asserting, validating, and confirming its 'existence' by fragmenting, conceptualizing, and solidifying experience. The ordinary mind is the ceaselessly shifting and shiftless prey of external influences, habitual tendencies, and conditioning: The masters liken sem to a candle flame in an open doorway, vulnerable to all the winds of circumstance.

Seen from one angle, sem is flickering, unstable, grasping, and endlessly minding others' business; its energy consumed by projecting outwards. I think of it sometimes as a Mexican jumping bean, or as a monkey hopping restlessly from branch to branch on a tree. Yet seen in another way, the ordinary mind has a false, dull stability, a smug and self-protective inertia, a stone-like calm of ingrained habits. Sem is as cunning as a crooked politician, sceptical, distrustful, expert at trickery and guile, "ingenious," Jamyang Khyentse wrote, "in the games of deception." It is within the experience of this chaotic, confused, undisciplined, and repetitive sem, this ordinary mind, that, again and again, we undergo change and death.

Then there is the very nature of mind, its innermost essence, which is absolutely and always untouched by change or death. At present it is hidden within our own mind, our sem, enveloped and obscured by the mental scurry of our thoughts and emotions. Just as clouds can be shifted by a strong gust of wind to reveal the shining sun and wide-open sky, so, under certain special circumstances, some inspiration may uncover for us glimpses of this nature of mind. These glimpses have many depths and degrees, but each of them will bring some light of understanding, meaning, and freedom. This is because the nature of mind is the very root itself of understanding. In Tibetan we call it *Rigpa*, a primordial, pure, pristine awareness that is at once intelligent, cognizant, radiant, and always awake. It could be said to be the knowledge of knowledge itself.[3]

Do not make the mistake of imagining that the nature of mind is exclusive to our mind only. It is in fact the nature of everything. It can never be said too often that to realize the nature of mind is to realize the nature of all things.

Saints and mystics throughout history have adorned their realizations with different names and given them different faces and interpretations, but what they are all fundamentally experiencing is the essential nature of the mind. Christians and Jews call it "God"; Hindus call it "the Self," "Shiva," "Brahman," and "Vishnu"; Sufi mystics name it "the Hidden Essence"; and Buddhists call it "buddha nature." At the heart of all religions is the certainty that there is a fundamental truth, and that this life is a sacred opportunity to evolve and realize it.

When we say Buddha, we naturally think of the Indian prince Gautama Siddhartha who reached enlightenment in the sixth century B.C., and who taught the spiritual path followed by millions all over Asia, known today as Buddhism. *Buddha,* however, has a much deeper meaning. It means a person, any person, who has completely awakened from ignorance and opened to his or her vast potential of wisdom. A buddha is one who has brought a final end to suffering and frustration, and discovered a lasting and deathless happiness and peace.

But for many of us in this skeptical age, this state may seem like a fantasy or a dream, or an achievement far beyond our reach. It is important to remember always that Buddha was a human being, like you or me. He never claimed divinity, he merely knew he had the buddha nature, the seed of enlightenment, and that everyone else did too. The buddha nature is simply the birthright of every sentient being, and I always say, "Our buddha nature is as good as any buddha's buddha nature." This is the good news that the Buddha brought us from his enlightenment in Bodhgaya, and which many people find so inspiring. His message—*that enlightenment is within the reach of all*—holds out tremendous hope. Through practice, we too can all become awakened. If this were not true, countless individuals down to the present day would not have become enlightened.

It is said that when Buddha attained enlightenment, all he wanted to do was to show the rest of us the nature of mind and share completely what he had realized. But he also saw, with the sorrow of infinite compassion, how difficult it would be for us to understand.

For even though we have the same inner nature as Buddha, we have not recognized it because it is so enclosed and wrapped up in our individual ordinary minds. Imagine an empty vase. The space inside is exactly the same as the space outside. Only the fragile walls of the vase separate one from the other. Our buddha mind is enclosed within the walls of our ordinary mind. But when we become enlightened, it is as if that vase shatters into pieces. The space "inside" merges instantly into the space "outside." They become one: There and then we realize they were never separate or different; they were always the same.

THE SKY AND THE CLOUDS

So whatever our lives are like, our buddha nature is always there. And it is always perfect. We say that not even the Buddhas can improve it in their infinite wisdom, nor can sentient beings spoil it in their seemingly infinite confusion. Our true nature could be compared to the sky, and the confusion of the ordinary mind to clouds. Some days the sky is completely obscured by clouds. When we are down on the ground, looking up, it is very difficult to believe there is anything else there but clouds. Yet we only have to fly in a plane to discover up above a limitless expanse of clear blue sky. From up there the clouds we assumed were everything seem so small and so far away down below.

We should always try and remember: the clouds are not the sky, and do not "belong" to it. They only hang there and pass by in their slightly ridiculous and non-dependent fashion. And they can never stain or mark the sky in any way.

So where exactly is this buddha nature? It is in the sky-like nature of our mind. Utterly open, free, and limitless, it is fundamentally so simple and so natural that it can never be complicated, corrupted, or stained, so pure that it is beyond even the concept of purity and impurity. To talk of this nature of mind as sky-like, of course, is only a metaphor that helps us to begin to imagine its all-embracing boundlessness; for the buddha nature has a quality the sky cannot have, that of the radiant clarity of awareness. As it is said:

> It is simply your flawless, present awareness, cognizant and empty, naked and awake.

Dudjom Rinpoche wrote:

> No words can describe it
> No example can point to it
> Samsara does not make it worse
> Nirvana does not make it better
> It has never been born
> It has never ceased
> It has never been liberated
> It has never been deluded
> It has never existed
> It has never been nonexistent
> It has no limits at all
> It does not fall into any kind of category.

Nyoshul Khen Rinpoche[4] said:

> Profound and tranquil, free from complexity,
> Uncompounded luminous clarity,
> Beyond the mind of conceptual ideas;
> This is the depth of the mind of the Victorious Ones.
> In this there is not a thing to be removed,
> Nor anything that needs to be added.
> It is merely the immaculate
> Looking naturally at itself.

THE FOUR FAULTS

Why is it that people should find it so difficult even to conceive of the depth and glory of the nature of mind? Why does it seem to many such an outlandish and improbable idea?

The teachings speak of four faults, which prevent us from realizing the nature of mind right now:

1. The nature of mind is just too *close* to be recognized. Just as we are unable to see our own face, mind finds it difficult to look into its own nature.

2. It is too *profound* for us to fathom. We have no idea how deep it could be; if we did, we would have already, to a certain extent, realized it.

3. It is too *easy* for us to believe. In reality, all we need do is simply to rest in the naked, pure awareness of the nature of mind, which is always present.

4. It is too *wonderful* for us to accommodate. The sheer immensity of it is too vast to fit into our narrow way of thinking. We just can't believe it. Nor can we possibly imagine that enlightenment is the real nature of *our* minds.

If this analysis of the four faults was true in a civilization like Tibet, devoted almost entirely to the pursuit of enlightenment, how much more strikingly and poignantly true must it be of modern civilization, which is largely devoted to the pursuit of the cult of delusion. There is no general information about the nature of mind. It is hardly ever written about by writers or intellectuals; modern philosophers do not speak of it directly; the majority of scientists deny it could possibly be there at all. It plays no part in popular culture: No one sings about it; no one talks about it in plays; and it's not on TV. We are actually educated into believing that nothing is real beyond what we can perceive with our ordinary senses.

Despite this massive and nearly all-pervasive denial of its existence, we still sometimes have fleeting glimpses of the nature of mind. These could be inspired by a certain exalting piece of music, by the serene happiness we sometimes feel in nature, or by the most ordinary everyday situation. They could arise simply while watching snow slowly drifting down, or seeing the sun rising behind a mountain, or watching a shaft of light falling into a room in a mysteriously moving way. Such moments of illumination, peace, and bliss happen to us all and stay strangely with us.

I think we do, sometimes, half understand these glimpses, but modern culture gives us no context or framework in which to comprehend them. Worse still, rather than encouraging us to explore these glimpses more deeply and discover where they spring from, we are told in both obvious and subtle ways to shut them out. We know that no one will take us seriously if we try to share them. So we ignore what could be really the most revealing experiences of our lives, if only we understood them. This is perhaps the darkest and most disturbing aspect of modern civilization—its ignorance and repression of who we really are.

LOOKING IN

Let's say we make a complete shift. Let's say we turn away from looking in only one direction. We have been taught to spend our lives chasing our thoughts and projections. Even when "mind" is talked about, what is referred to is thoughts and emotions alone; and when our researchers study what they imagine to be the mind, they look only at its projections. No one ever really looks into the mind itself, the ground from which all these expressions arise; and this has tragic consequences. As Padmasambhava said:

> Even though that which is usually called "mind" is widely esteemed and much discussed,
> Still it is not understood or it is wrongly understood or it is understood in a one-sided manner only.
> Since it is not understood correctly, just as it is in itself,
> There come into existence inconceivable numbers of philosophical ideas and assertions.
> Furthermore, since ordinary individuals do not understand it,
> They do not recognize their own nature,
> And so they continue to wander among the six destinies of rebirth within the three worlds, and thus experience suffering.
> Therefore, not understanding your own mind is a very grievous fault.[5]

How can we now turn this situation around? It is very simple. Our minds have two positions: looking out and looking in.

Let us now look in.

The difference that this slight change in orientation could make is enormous, and might even reverse those disasters that threaten the world. When a much larger number of people know the nature of their minds, they'll know also the glorious nature of the world they are in, and struggle urgently and bravely to preserve it. It's interesting that the word for "Buddhist" in Tibetan is *nangpa*. It means "inside-er": someone who seeks the truth not outside, but within the nature of mind. All the teachings and training in Buddhism are aimed at that one single point: to look into the nature of the mind, and so free us from the fear of death and help us realize the truth of life.

Looking in will require of us great subtlety and great courage—nothing less than a complete shift in our attitude to life and to the mind. We are so addicted to looking outside ourselves that we have lost access to our inner being almost completely. We are terrified to look inward, because our culture has given us no idea of what we will find. We may even think that if we do we will be in danger of madness. This is one of the last and most resourceful ploys of ego to prevent us discovering our real nature.

So we make our lives so hectic that we eliminate the slightest risk of looking into ourselves. Even the idea of meditation can scare people. When they hear the words "egoless" or "emptiness," they think experiencing those states will be like being thrown out of the door of a spaceship to float forever in a dark, chilling void. Nothing could be further from the truth. But in a world dedicated to distraction, silence and stillness terrify us; we protect ourselves from them with noise and frantic busyness. Looking into the nature of our mind is the last thing we would dare to do.

Sometimes I think we don't want to ask any real questions about who we are, for fear of discovering there is some other reality than this one. What would this discovery make of how we have lived? How would our friends and colleagues react to what we now know? What would we do with the new knowledge? With knowledge comes responsibility. Sometimes even when the cell door is flung open, the prisoner chooses not to escape.

THE PROMISE OF ENLIGHTENMENT

In the modern world, there are few examples of human beings who embody the qualities that come from realizing the nature of mind. So it is hard for us even to imagine enlightenment or the perception of an enlightened being, and even harder to begin to think we ourselves could become enlightened.

For all its vaunted celebration of the value of human life and individual liberty, our society in fact treats us as obsessed only with power, sex, and money, and needing to be distracted at any moment from any contact with death, or with real life. If we are told of or begin to suspect our deep potential, we cannot believe it; and if we can conceive of spiritual transformation at all, we see it as only possible for the great saints and spiritual masters of the past. The Dalai Lama talks often of the lack of real self-love and self-respect that he sees in many people in the modern world. Underlying our whole outlook is a neurotic conviction of our own limitations. This denies us all hope of awakening, and tragically contradicts the central truth of Buddha's teaching: that we are all already essentially perfect.

Even if we were to think of the possibility of enlighten-ment, one look at what composes our ordinary mind—anger, greed, jealousy, spite, cruelty, lust, fear, anxiety, and turmoil— would undermine forever any hope of achieving it, if we had not been told about the nature of mind, and the possibility of coming to realize that nature beyond all doubt.

But enlightenment is real, and there are enlightened mas-ters still on the earth. When you actually meet one, you will be shaken and moved in the depths of your heart and you will realize that all the words, such as "illumination" and "wisdom," which you thought were only ideas, are in fact true. For all its dangers, the world today is also a very exciting one. The modern mind is slowly opening to different visions of reality. Great teachers like the Dalai Lama and Mother Teresa can be seen on television; many masters from the East now visit and teach in the West; and books from all the mys-tical traditions are winning an increasingly large audience. The desperate situation of the planet is slowly waking people up to the necessity for transformation on a global scale.

Enlightenment, as I have said, is real; and each of us, who-ever we are, can in the right circumstances and with the right training realize the nature of mind and so know in us what is deathless and eternally pure. This is the promise of all the mystical traditions of the world, and it has been fulfilled and is being fulfilled in countless thousands of human lives.

The wonder of this promise is that it is something not exotic, not fantastic, not for an elite, but for all of humanity; and when we realize it, the masters tell us, it is unexpectedly ordinary. Spiritual truth is not something elaborate and eso-teric, it is in fact profound common sense. When you realize the nature of mind, layers of confusion peel away. You don't actually "become" a buddha, you simply cease, slowly, to be deluded. And being a buddha is not being some omnipotent spiritual superman, but becoming at last a true human being.

One of the greatest Buddhist traditions calls the nature of mind "the wisdom of ordinariness." I cannot say it enough:

Our true nature and the nature of all beings is not something extraordinary. The irony is that it is our so-called ordinary world that is extraordinary, a fantastic, elaborate hallucination of the deluded vision of samsara. It is this "extraordinary" vision that blinds us to the "ordinary," natural, inherent nature of mind. Imagine if the buddhas were looking down at us now: How they would marvel sadly at the lethal ingenuity and intricacy of our confusion!

Sometimes, because we are so unnecessarily complicated, when the nature of mind is introduced by a master, it is just too simple for us to believe. Our ordinary mind tells us this cannot be, there must be something more to it than this. It must surely be more "glorious," with lights blazing in space around us, angels with flowing golden hair swooping down to meet us, and a deep Wizard of Oz voice announcing, "Now you have been introduced to the nature of your mind." There is no such drama.

Because in our culture we overvalue the intellect, we would imagine that to become enlightened demands extraordinary intelligence. In fact many kinds of cleverness are just further obscurations. There is a Tibetan saying that goes, "If you are too clever, you could miss the point entirely." Patrul Rinpoche said: "The logical mind seems interesting, but it is the seed of delusion." People can become obsessed with their own theories and miss the point of everything. In Tibet we say: "Theories are like patches on a coat, one day they just wear off." Let me tell you an encouraging story:

One great master in the last century had a disciple who was very thick-headed. The master had taught him again and again, trying to introduce him to the nature of his mind. Still he did not get it. Finally, the master became furious and told him, "Look, I want you to carry this bag full of barley up to the top of that mountain over there. But you mustn't stop and rest. Just keep on going until you reach the top." The disciple was a simple man, but he had unshakeable devotion and trust in his master, and he did exactly what he had been told. The bag was heavy. He picked it up, and started up the slope of the mountain, not daring to stop. He just walked and walked. And the bag got heavier and heavier. It took him a long time. At last, when he reached the top, he dropped the bag. He slumped to the ground, overcome with exhaustion but deeply relaxed. He felt the fresh mountain air on his face. All his resistance had dissolved, and with it, his ordinary mind. Everything just seemed to stop. At that instant, he suddenly realized the nature of his mind. "Ah! This is what my master has been showing me all along," he thought. He ran back down the mountain, and, against all convention, burst into his master's room.

"I think I've got it now . . . I've really got it!"

His master smiled at him knowingly: "So you had an interesting climb up the mountain, did you?"

Whoever you are, you too can have the experience the disciple had on that mountain, and it is that experience that will give you the fearlessness to negotiate life and death. But what is the best, quickest, and most efficient way to set about it? The first step is the practice of meditation. It is meditation that slowly purifies the ordinary mind, unmasking and exhausting its habits and illusions, so that we can, at the right moment, recognize who we really are.

FIVE

Bringing the Mind Home

OVER 2,500 YEARS AGO, a man who had been
searching for the truth for many, many lifetimes came to a
quiet place in northern India and sat down under a tree. He
continued to sit under the tree, with immense resolve, and
vowed not to get up until he had found the truth. At dusk, it
is said, he conquered all the dark forces of delusion; and early
the next morning, as the star Venus broke in the dawn sky,
the man was rewarded for his age-long patience, discipline,
and flawless concentration by achieving the final goal of
human existence, enlightenment. At that sacred moment,
the earth itself shuddered, as if "drunk with bliss," and as
the scriptures tell us, "No one anywhere was angry, ill, or sad;
no one did evil, none was proud; the world became quite
quiet, as though it had reached full perfection." This man
became known as the Buddha. Here is the Vietnamese master
Thich Nhat Hanh's beautiful description of the Buddha's
enlightenment:

> Gautama felt as though a prison which had confined him for thou-
> sands of lifetimes had broken open. Ignorance had been the jailkeeper.
> Because of ignorance, his mind had been obscured, just like the moon
> and stars hidden by the storm clouds. Clouded by endless waves of
> deluded thoughts, the mind had falsely divided reality into subject and
> object, self and others, existence and non-existence, birth and death,
> and from these discriminations arose wrong views—the prisons of feel-
> ings, craving, grasping, and becoming. The suffering of birth, old age,
> sickness, and death only made the prison walls thicker. The only
> thing to do was to seize the jailkeeper and see his true face. The
> jailkeeper was ignorance. . . . Once the jailkeeper was gone, the jail
> would disappear and never be rebuilt again.[1]

What the Buddha saw was that ignorance of our true nature is the root of all the torment of samsara, and the root of ignorance itself is our mind's habitual tendency to distraction. To end the mind's distraction would be to end samsara itself; the key to this, he realized, is to bring the mind home to its true nature, through the practice of meditation.

The Buddha sat in serene and humble dignity on the ground, with the sky above him and around him, as if to show us that in meditation you sit with an open, sky-like attitude of mind, yet remain present, earthed, and grounded. The sky is our absolute nature, which has no barriers and is boundless, and the ground is our reality, our relative, ordinary condition. The posture we take when we meditate signifies that we are linking absolute and relative, sky and ground, heaven and earth, like two wings of a bird, integrating the sky-like deathless nature of mind and the ground of our transient, mortal nature.

The gift of learning to meditate is the greatest gift you can give yourself in this life. For it is only through meditation that you can undertake the journey to discover your true nature, and so find the stability and confidence you will need to live, and die, well. Meditation is the road to enlightenment.

TRAINING THE MIND

There are so many ways to present meditation, and I must have taught on it a thousand times, but each time it is different, and each time it is direct and fresh.

Fortunately we live in a time when all over the world many people are becoming familiar with meditation. It is being increasingly accepted as a practice that cuts through and soars above cultural and religious barriers, and enables those who pursue it to establish a direct contact with the truth of their being. It is a practice that at once transcends the dogma of religions and is the essence of religions.

Generally we waste our lives, distracted from our true selves, in endless activity; meditation, on the other hand, is the way to bring us back to ourselves, where we can really experience and taste our full being, beyond all habitual patterns. Our lives are lived in intense and anxious struggle, in a swirl of speed and aggression, in competing, grasping, possessing, and achieving, forever burdening ourselves with extraneous activities and preoccupations. Meditation is the exact opposite. To meditate is to make a complete break with how we "normally" operate, for it is a state free of all cares and concerns, in which there is no competition, no desire to possess or grasp at anything, no intense and anxious struggle, and no hunger to achieve: an ambitionless state where there is neither acceptance nor rejection, neither hope nor fear, a state in which we slowly begin to release all those emotions and concepts that have imprisoned us into the space of natural simplicity.

The Buddhist meditation masters know how flexible and workable the mind is. If we train it, anything is possible. In fact, we are already perfectly trained by and for samsara, trained to get jealous, trained to grasp, trained to be anxious and sad and desperate and greedy, trained to react angrily to whatever provokes us. We are trained, in fact, to such an extent that these negative emotions rise spontaneously, without our even trying to generate them. So everything is a question of training and the power of habit. Devote the mind to confusion and we know only too well, if we're honest, that it will become a dark master of confusion, adept in its addictions, subtle and perversely supple in its slaveries. Devote it in meditation to the task of freeing itself from illusion, and we will find that with time, patience, discipline, and the right training, our mind will begin to unknot itself and know its essential bliss and clarity.

"Training" the mind does not in any way mean forcibly subjugating or brainwashing the mind. To train the mind is first to see directly and concretely how the mind functions, a knowledge that you derive from spiritual teachings and through personal experience in meditation practice. Then you can use that understanding to tame the mind and work with it skillfully, to make it more and more pliable, so that you can become master of your own mind and employ it to its fullest and most beneficial end.

The eighth-century Buddhist master Shantideva said:

*If this elephant of mind is bound on all sides by the cord of
    mindfulness,
All fear disappears and complete happiness comes.
All enemies: all the tigers, lions, elephants, bears, serpents
    [of our emotions];[2]
And all the keepers of hell; the demons and the horrors,
All of these are bound by the mastery of your mind,
And by the taming of that one mind, all are subdued,
Because from the mind are derived all fears and immeasurable sorrows.[3]*

Just as a writer only learns a spontaneous freedom of expression after years of often grueling study, and just as the simple grace of a dancer is achieved only with enormous, patient effort, so when you begin to understand where meditation will lead you, you will approach it as the greatest endeavor of your life, one that demands of you the deepest perseverance, enthusiasm, intelligence, and discipline.

THE HEART OF MEDITATION

The purpose of meditation is to awaken in us the sky-like nature of mind, and to introduce us to that which we really are, our unchanging pure awareness, which underlies the whole of life and death.

In the stillness and silence of meditation, we glimpse and return to that deep inner nature that we have so long ago lost sight of amid the busyness and distraction of our minds. Isn't it extraordinary that our minds cannot stay still for longer than a few moments without grasping after distraction; they are so restless and preoccupied that sometimes I think that living in a city in the modern world, we are already like the tormented beings in the intermediate state after death, where the consciousness is said to be agonizingly restless. According to some authorities, up to 13 percent of people in the United States suffer from some kind of mental disorder. What does that say about the way we live?

We are fragmented into so many different aspects. We don't know who we really are, or what aspects of ourselves we should identify with or believe in. So many contradictory voices, dictates, and feelings fight for control over our inner lives that we find ourselves scattered everywhere, in all directions, leaving nobody at home.

Meditation, then, is bringing the mind home.

In the teaching of Buddha, we say there are three things that make all the difference between your meditation being merely a way of bringing temporary relaxation, peace, and bliss, or of becoming a powerful cause for your enlightenment and the enlightenment of others. We call them: "Good in the Beginning, Good in the Middle, and Good at the End."

Good in the Beginning springs from the awareness that we and all sentient beings fundamentally have the buddha nature as our innermost essence, and that to realize it is to be free of ignorance and to put an end, finally, to suffering. So each time

we begin our practice of meditation, we are moved by this,
and inspire ourselves with the motivation to dedicate our
practice, and our life, to the enlightenment of all beings in
the spirit of this prayer, which all the buddhas of the past
have prayed:

By the power and the truth of this practice:
May all beings have happiness, and the causes of happiness;
May all be free from sorrow, and the causes of sorrow;
May all never be separated from the sacred happiness which is
*   sorrowless;*
And may all live in equanimity, without too much attachment and too
*   much aversion,*
And live believing in the equality of all that lives.

Good in the Middle is the frame of mind with which we
enter into the heart of the practice, one inspired by the realization of the nature of mind, from which arises an attitude of
non-grasping, free of any conceptual reference whatsoever,
and an awareness that all things are inherently "empty,"
illusory, and dream-like.

Good at the End is the way in which we bring our meditation to a close by dedicating all its merit, and praying
with real fervor: "May whatever merit that comes from this
practice go toward the enlightenment of all beings; may it
become a drop in the ocean of the activity of all the buddhas
in their tireless work for the liberation of all beings." Merit
is the positive power and benefit, the peace and happiness
that radiate from your practice. You dedicate this merit for the
long-term, ultimate benefit of beings, for their enlightenment.
On a more immediate level, you dedicate it so that there may
be peace in the world, so that everyone may be entirely free
of want and illness, and experience total well-being and lasting happiness. Then, realizing the illusory and dream-like
nature of reality, you reflect on how, in the deepest sense, you
who are dedicating your practice, those to whom you are
dedicating it, and even the very act of dedication are all inherently "empty" and illusory. This is said in the teachings to
seal the meditation and ensure that none of its pure power
can leak or seep away, and so ensure that none of the merit of
your practice is ever wasted.

These three sacred principles—the skillful *motivation,* the
attitude of non-grasping that secures the practice, and the *dedication* that seals it—are what make your meditation truly

enlightening and powerful. They have been beautifully described by the great Tibetan master Longchenpa as "the heart, the eye, and the life-force of true practice." As Nyoshul Khenpo says: "To accomplish complete enlightenment, more than this is not necessary: but less than this is incomplete."

THE PRACTICE OF MINDFULNESS

Meditation is bringing the mind back home, and this is first achieved through the practice of mindfulness.

Once an old woman came to Buddha and asked him how to meditate. He told her to remain aware of every movement of her hands as she drew the water from the well, knowing that if she did, she would soon find herself in that state of alert and spacious calm that is meditation.

The practice of mindfulness, of bringing the scattered mind home, and so of bringing the different aspects of our being into focus, is called "Peacefully Remaining" or "Calm Abiding." "Peacefully Remaining" accomplishes three things. First, all the fragmented aspects of ourselves, which have been at war, settle and dissolve and become friends. In that settling we begin to understand ourselves more, and sometimes even have glimpses of the radiance of our fundamental nature.

Second, the practice of mindfulness defuses our negativity, aggression, and turbulent emotions, which may have been gathering power over many lifetimes. Rather than suppressing emotions or indulging in them, here it is important to view them, and your thoughts, and whatever arises with an acceptance and generosity that are as open and spacious as possible. Tibetan masters say that this wise generosity has the flavor of boundless space, so warm and cozy that you feel enveloped and protected by it, as if by a blanket of sunlight.

Gradually, as you remain open and mindful, and use one of the techniques that I will explain later to focus your mind more and more, your negativity will slowly be defused; you begin to feel well in your being, or as the French say, être bien dans sa peau (well in your own skin). From this comes release and a profound ease. I think of this practice as the most effective form of therapy and self-healing.

Third, this practice unveils and reveals your essential Good Heart, because it dissolves and removes the unkindness or the harm in you. Only when we have removed the harm in ourselves do we become truly useful to others. Through the practice, then, by slowly removing the unkindness and harm from ourselves, we allow our true Good Heart, the fundamental goodness and kindness that are our real nature, to shine out and become the warm climate in which our true being flowers.

You will see now why I call meditation the true practice of peace, the true practice of nonaggression and nonviolence, and the real and greatest disarmament.

NATURAL GREAT PEACE

When I teach meditation, I often begin by saying: "Bring your mind home. And release. And relax."

The whole of meditation practice can be essentialized into these three crucial points: bring your mind home, and release, and relax. Each phrase contains meanings that resonate on many levels.

To *bring your mind home* means to bring the mind into the state of Calm Abiding through the practice of mindfulness. In its deepest sense, to bring your mind home is to turn your mind inward and to rest in the nature of mind. This itself is the highest meditation.

To *release* means to release mind from its prison of grasping, since you recognize that all pain and fear and distress arise from the craving of the grasping mind. On a deeper level, the realization and confidence that arise from your growing understanding of the nature of mind inspire the profound and natural generosity that enables you to release all grasping from your heart, letting it free itself, to melt away in the inspiration of meditation.

Finally, to *relax* means to be spacious and to relax the mind of its tensions. More deeply, you relax into the true nature of your mind, the state of Rigpa. The Tibetan words that evoke this process suggest the sense of "relaxing *upon* the Rigpa." It is like pouring a handful of sand onto a flat surface; each grain settles of its own accord. This is how you relax into your true nature, letting all thoughts and emotions naturally subside and dissolve into the state of the nature of mind.

When I meditate, I am always inspired by this poem by Nyoshul Khenpo:

> Rest in natural great peace
> This exhausted mind
> Beaten helpless by karma and neurotic thought,
> Like the relentless fury of the pounding waves
> In the infinite ocean of samsara.

Rest in natural great peace.

Above all, be at ease, be as natural and spacious as possible. Slip quietly out of the noose of your habitual anxious self, release all grasping, and relax into your true nature. Think of your ordinary, emotional, thought-ridden self as a block of ice or a slab of butter left out in the sun. If you are feeling hard and cold, let this aggression melt away in the sunlight of your meditation. Let peace work on you and enable you to gather your scattered mind into the mindfulness of Calm Abiding, and awaken in you the awareness and insight of Clear Seeing. And you will find all your negativity disarmed, your aggression dissolved, and your confusion evaporating slowly, like mist into the vast and stainless sky of your absolute nature.[4]

Quietly sitting, body still, speech silent, mind at peace, let thoughts and emotions, whatever rises, come and go, without clinging to anything.

What does this state feel like? Dudjom Rinpoche used to say, imagine a man who comes home after a long, hard day's work in the fields, and sinks into his favorite chair in front of the fire. He has been working all day and he knows that he has achieved what he wanted to achieve; there is nothing more to worry about, nothing left unaccomplished, and he can let go completely of all his cares and concerns, content, simply, to be.

So when you meditate, it is essential to create the right inner environment of the mind. All effort and struggle come from not being spacious, and so creating that right environment is vital for your meditation truly to happen. When humor and spaciousness are present, meditation arises effortlessly.

Sometimes when I meditate, I don't use any particular method. I just allow my mind to rest, and find, especially when I am inspired, that I can bring my mind home and relax very quickly. I sit quietly and rest in the nature of mind; I don't question or doubt whether I am in the "correct" state or not. There is no effort, only rich understanding, wakefulness, and unshakable certainty. When I am in the nature of mind, the ordinary mind is no longer there. There is no need to sustain or confirm a sense of being: I simply am. A fundamental trust is present. There is nothing in particular to do.

METHODS IN MEDITATION

If your mind is able to settle naturally of its own accord, and if you find you are inspired simply to rest in its pure awareness, then you do not need any method of meditation. In fact, it might even be unskillful when you're in such a state to try to employ one. However, the vast majority of us find it difficult to arrive at that state straight away. We simply do not know how to awaken it, and our minds are so wild and so distracted that we need a skillful means, a method to evoke it.

By "skillful" I mean that you bring together your understanding of the essential nature of your mind, your knowledge of your own various, shifting moods, and the insight you have developed through your practice into how to work with yourself, from moment to moment. By bringing these together, you learn the art of applying whatever method is appropriate for any particular situation or problem, to transform that environment of your mind.

But remember: A method is only a means, *not* the meditation itself. It is through practicing the method skillfully that you reach the perfection of that pure state of total presence, which is the real meditation.

There is a revealing Tibetan saying, *"Gompa ma yin, kompa yin,"* which means literally: "'Meditation' is not; 'getting used to' is." It means that meditation is nothing other than getting used to the *practice* of meditation. As it is said, "Meditation is not striving, but naturally becoming assimilated into it." As you continue to practice the method, then meditation slowly arises. Meditation is not something that you can "do," it is something that has to happen spontaneously, only when we have perfected the practice.

However, for meditation to happen, calm and auspicious conditions have to be created. Before we have mastery over our mind, we need first to calm its environment. At the moment, mind is like a candle flame: unstable, flickering, constantly changing, fanned by the violent winds of our thoughts and emotions. The flame will only burn steadily when we can calm the air around it; so we can only begin to glimpse and rest in the nature of mind when we have stilled the turbulence of our thoughts and emotions. On the other hand, once we have found a stability in our meditation, noises and disturbances of every kind will have far less impact.

In the west, people tend to be absorbed by what I would call "the technology of meditation." The modern world, after all, is fascinated by mechanisms and machines, and addicted to purely practical formulae. But by far the most important feature of meditation is not the technique, but the spirit: the skillful, inspired, and creative way in which we practice, which could also be called "the posture."

THE POSTURE

The masters say: "If you create an auspicious condition in your body and your environment, then meditation and realization will automatically arise." Talk about posture is not esoteric pedantry; the whole point of assuming a correct posture is to create a more inspiring environment for meditation, for the awakening of Rigpa. There is a connection between the posture of the body and the attitude of the mind. Mind and body are interrelated, and meditation arises naturally once your posture and attitude are inspired.

If you are sitting, and your mind is not wholly in tune with your body—if you are, for instance, anxious and preoccupied with something—then your body will experience physical discomfort and difficulties arise more easily. Whereas if your mind is in a calm, inspired state, it will influence your whole posture, and you can sit much more naturally and effortlessly. So it is very important to unite the posture of your body and the confidence that arises from your realization of the nature of mind.

The posture I am going to explain to you may differ slightly from others you may be used to. It comes from the ancient teachings of Dzogchen and is the one my masters taught me, and I have found it extremely powerful.

In the Dzogchen teachings it is said that *your View and your posture* should be like a mountain. Your View is the summation of your whole understanding and insight into the nature of mind, which you bring to your meditation. So your View translates into and inspires your posture, expressing the core of your being in the way you sit.

Sit, then, as if you were a mountain, with all the unshakable, steadfast majesty of a mountain. A mountain is completely natural and at ease with itself, however strong the winds that batter it, however thick the dark clouds that swirl around its peak. Sitting like a mountain, let your mind rise and fly and soar.

The most essential point of this posture is to keep the back straight, like "an arrow" or "a pile of golden coins." The "inner energy" or *prana* will then flow easily through the subtle channels of the body, and your mind will find its true state of rest. Don't force anything. The lower part of the spine has a natural curve; it should be relaxed but upright. Your head should be balanced comfortably on your neck. It is your shoulders and the upper part of your torso that carry the strength and grace of the posture, and they should be held in strong poise, but without any tension.

Sit with your legs crossed. You do not have to sit in the full-lotus posture, which is emphasized more in advanced yoga practice. The crossed legs express the unity of life and death, good and bad, skillful means and wisdom, masculine and feminine principles, samsara and *nirvana;* the humor of non-duality. You may also choose to sit on a chair, with your legs relaxed, but be sure always to keep your back straight.[5]

In my tradition of meditation, your eyes should be kept open: this is a very important point. If you are sensitive to disturbances from outside, when you begin to practice you may find it helpful to close your eyes for a while and quietly turn within.

Once you feel established in calm, gradually open your eyes, and you will find your gaze has grown more peaceful and tranquil. Now look downwards, along the line of your nose, at an angle of about 45 degrees in front of you. One practical tip in general is that whenever your mind is wild, it is best to lower your gaze, and whenever it is dull and sleepy, to bring the gaze up.

Once your mind is calm and the clarity of insight begins to arise, you will feel free to bring your gaze up, opening your eyes more and looking into the space directly in front of you. This is the gaze recommended in the Dzogchen practice.

In the Dzogchen teachings it is said that *your meditation and your gaze* should be like the vast expanse of a great ocean: all-pervading, open, and limitless. Just as your View and posture are inseparable, so your meditation inspires your gaze, and they now merge as one.

Do not focus then on anything in particular; instead, turn back into yourself slightly, and let your gaze expand and become more and more spacious and pervasive. You will dis-cover now that your vision itself becomes more expansive, and that there is more peace, more compassion in your gaze, more equanimity, and more poise.

The Tibetan name of the Buddha of Compassion is Chenrézig. *Chen* is the eye, *ré* is the corner of the eye, and *zig* means see. This signifies that with his compassionate eyes Chenrézig sees the needs of all beings. So direct the compas-sion that radiates from your meditation, softly and gently, through your eyes, so that your gaze becomes the very gaze of compassion itself, all-pervasive and ocean-like.

There are several reasons for keeping the eyes open. With the eyes open, you are less likely to fall asleep. Then, meditation is not a means of running away from the world, or of escaping from it into a trance-like experience of an altered state of consciousness. On the contrary, it is a direct way to help us truly understand ourselves, and relate to life and the world.

Therefore, in meditation, you keep your eyes open, not closed. Instead of shutting out life, you remain open and at peace with everything. You leave all your senses—hearing, seeing, feeling—just open, naturally, as they are, without grasping after their perceptions. As Dudjom Rinpoche said: "Though different forms are perceived, they are in essence empty; yet in the emptiness one perceives forms. Though different sounds are heard, they are empty; yet in the emptiness one perceives sounds. Also different thoughts arise; they are empty, yet in the emptiness one perceives thoughts." Whatever you see, whatever you hear, leave it as it is, without grasping. Leave the hearing in the hearing, leave the seeing in the seeing, without letting your attachment enter into the perception.

According to the special luminosity practice of Dzogchen, all the light of our wisdom-energy resides in the heart center, which is connected through "wisdom channels" to the eyes. The eyes are the "doors" of the luminosity, so you keep them open, in order not to block these wisdom channels.[6]

When you meditate keep your mouth slightly open, as if about to say a deep, relaxing "Aaaah." By keeping the mouth slightly open and breathing mainly through the mouth, it is said that the "karmic winds" that create discursive thoughts are normally less likely to arise, and create obstacles in your mind and meditation.

Rest your hands comfortably covering your knees. This is called the "mind in comfort and ease" posture.

There is a spark of hope, a playful humor, about this posture, which lies in the secret understanding that we all have the buddha nature. So when you assume this posture, you are playfully imitating a buddha, acknowledging and giving real encouragement to the emergence of your own buddha nature. You begin in fact to respect yourself as a potential buddha.

At the same time, you still recognize your relative condition. But because you have let yourself be inspired by a joyful trust in your own true buddha nature, you can accept your negative aspects more easily and deal with them more kindly and with more humor. When you meditate, then, invite yourself to feel the self-esteem, the dignity, and strong humility of the buddha that you are. I often say that if you simply let yourself be inspired by this joyful trust, it is enough: out of this understanding and confidence meditation will naturally arise.

THREE METHODS OF MEDITATION

The Buddha taught 84,000 different ways to tame and pacify the negative emotions, and in Buddhism there are countless methods of meditation. I have found three meditation techniques that are particularly effective in the modern world, and which anyone can use and benefit from. They are "watching" the breath, using an object, and reciting a mantra.

1. "Watching" the Breath

The first method is very ancient and found in all schools of Buddhism. It is to rest your attention, lightly and mindfully, on the breath.

Breath *is* life, the basic and most fundamental expression of our life. In Judaism *ruah,* the breath, means the spirit of God that infuses the creation; in Christianity also there is a profound link between the Holy Spirit, without which nothing could have life, and the breath. In the teaching of Buddha, the breath, or *prana* in Sanskrit, is said to be "the vehicle of the mind," because it is the prana that makes our mind move. So when you calm the mind by working skillfully with the breath, you are simultaneously and automatically taming and training the mind. Haven't we all experienced how relaxing it can be when life becomes stressful, to be alone for a few minutes and just breathe, in and out, deeply and quietly? Even such a simple exercise can help us a great deal.

So when you meditate, breathe naturally, just as you always do. Focus your awareness lightly on the outbreath. When you breathe out, just flow out with the outbreath. Each time you breathe out, you are letting go and releasing all your grasping. Imagine your breath dissolving into the all-pervading expanse of truth. Each time you breathe out, and before you breathe in again, you will find that there will be a natural gap, as the grasping dissolves.

Rest in that gap, in that open space. And when, naturally, you breathe in, don't focus especially on the inbreath but go on resting your mind in the gap that has opened up.

When you are practicing, it's important not to get involved in mental commentary, analysis, or internal gossip. Do not mistake the running commentary in your mind ("Now I'm breathing in, now I'm breathing out") for mindfulness; what is important is pure presence.

Don't concentrate too much on the breath; give it about 25 percent of your attention, with the other 75 percent quietly and spaciously relaxed. As you become more mindful of your breathing, you will find that you become more and more present, gather all your scattered aspects back into yourself, and become whole.

Rather than "watching" the breath, let yourself gradually identify with it, as if you were becoming it. Slowly the breath, the breather, and the breathing become one; duality and separation dissolve.

You will find that this very simple process of mindfulness filters your thoughts and emotions. Then, as if you were shedding an old skin, something is peeled off and freed.

Some people, however, are not relaxed or at ease with watching the breathing; they find it almost claustrophobic. For them, the next technique might be more helpful.

2. Using an Object

A second method, which many people find useful, is to rest the mind lightly on an object. You can use an object of natural beauty that invokes a special feeling of inspiration for you, such as a flower or crystal. But something that embodies the truth, such as an image of the Buddha, or Christ, or particularly your master, is even more powerful. Your master is your living link with the truth; and because of your personal connection to your master, just seeing his or her face connects you to the inspiration and truth of your own nature.

Many people have found a particular connection with the picture of the statue of Padmasambhava called "Looks Like Me," which was made from life and blessed by him in the eighth century in Tibet. Padmasambhava, by the enormous power of his spiritual personality, brought the teaching of Buddha to Tibet. He is known as the "second Buddha," and affectionately called "Guru Rinpoche," meaning "Precious Master," by the Tibetan people. Dilgo Khyentse Rinpoche

Padmasambhava: "Looks Like Me." Padmasambhava, the "Precious Master," "Guru Rinpoche," is the founder of Tibetan Buddhism, and the Buddha of our time. It is believed that, on seeing this statue at Samye in Tibet, where it was made in the eighth century, he remarked, "It looks like me," and then blessed it, saying, "Now it is the same as me!"

said: "There have been many incredible and incomparable masters from the noble land of India and Tibet, the Land of Snows, yet of them all, the one who has the greatest compassion and blessing toward beings in this difficult age is Padmasambhava, who embodies the compassion and wisdom of all the buddhas. One of his qualities is that he has the power to give his blessing instantly to whoever prays to him, and whatever we may pray for, he has the power to grant our wish immediately."

Inspired by this, fix a copy of this picture at your eye level, and lightly set your attention on his face, especially on the gaze of his eyes. There is a deep stillness in the immediacy of that gaze, which almost bursts out of the photograph to carry you into a state of awareness without clinging, the state of meditation. Then leave your mind quietly, at peace, with Padmasambhava.

3. Reciting a Mantra

A third technique, used a great deal in Tibetan Buddhism (and also in Sufism, Orthodox Christianity, and Hinduism), is uniting the mind with the sound of a *mantra*. The definition of mantra is "that which protects the mind." That which protects the mind from negativity, or that which protects you from your own mind, is called mantra.

When you are nervous, disoriented, or emotionally fragile, chanting or reciting a mantra inspiringly can change the state of your mind completely, by transforming its energy and atmosphere. How is this possible? Mantra is the essence of sound, and the embodiment of the truth in the form of sound. Each syllable is impregnated with spiritual power, condenses a spiritual truth, and vibrates with the blessing of the speech of the buddhas. It is also said that the mind rides on the subtle energy of the breath, the prana, which moves through and purifies the subtle channels of the body. So when you chant a mantra, you are charging your breath and energy with the energy of the mantra, and so working directly on your mind and subtle body.

The mantra I recommend to my students is OM AH HUM VAJRA GURU PADMA SIDDHI HUM (Tibetans say: Om Ah Hung Benza Guru Péma Siddhi Hung), which is the mantra of Padmasambhava, the mantra of all the buddhas, masters, and realized beings, and so uniquely powerful for peace, for healing, for transformation and for protection in this violent, chaotic age.[7] Recite the mantra quietly, with deep attention, and let your breath, the mantra, and your awareness become slowly one. Or chant it in an inspiring way, and rest in the profound silence that sometimes follows.

Even after a lifetime of being familiar with the practice, I am still sometimes astonished by the power of mantra. A few years ago, I was conducting a workshop for three hundred people in Lyons, France, mostly housewives and therapists. I had been teaching all day, but they seemed really to want to make the most of their time with me and kept on asking me questions, relentlessly, one after another. By the end of the afternoon I was completely drained, and a dull and heavy atmosphere had descended over the whole room. So I chanted a mantra, this mantra I have taught you here. I was amazed by the effect: In a few moments I felt all my energy was restored, the atmosphere around us was transformed, and the whole audience seemed once again bright and enchanting. I have had experiences like these time and time again, so I know it is not just an occasional "miracle"!

THE MIND IN MEDITATION

What, then, should we "do" with the mind in meditation? Nothing at all. Just leave it, simply, as it is. One master described meditation as "mind, suspended in space, nowhere."

There is a famous saying: "If the mind is not contrived, it is spontaneously blissful, just as water, when not agitated, is by nature transparent and clear." I often compare the mind in meditation to a jar of muddy water: The more we leave the water without interfering or stirring it, the more the particles of dirt will sink to the bottom, letting the natural clarity of the water shine through. The very nature of the mind is such that if you only leave it in its unaltered and natural state, it will find its true nature, which is bliss and clarity.

So take care not to impose anything on the mind, or to tax it. When you meditate there should be no effort to control, and no attempt to be peaceful. Don't be overly solemn or feel that you are taking part in some special ritual; let go even of the idea that you are meditating. Let your body remain as it is, and your breath as you find it. Think of yourself as the sky, holding the whole universe.

A DELICATE BALANCE

In meditation, as in all arts, there has to be a delicate balance between relaxation and alertness. Once a monk called Śhrona was studying meditation with one of the Buddha's closest disciples. He had difficulty finding the right frame of mind. He tried very hard to concentrate, and gave himself a headache. Then he relaxed his mind, but so much that he fell asleep. Finally he appealed to Buddha for help. Knowing that Shrona had been a famous musician before he became a monk, Buddha asked him: "Weren't you a *vina* player when you were a layperson?"

Shrona nodded.

"How did you get the best sound out of your vina? Was it when the strings were very tight or when they were very loose?"

"Neither. When they had just the right tension, neither too taut nor too slack."

"Well, it's exactly the same with your mind."

One of the greatest of Tibet's many woman masters, Ma Chik Lap Drön, said: "Alert, alert; yet relax, relax. This is a crucial point for the View in meditation." Alert your alertness, but at the same time be relaxed, so relaxed in fact that you don't even hold onto an idea of relaxation.

THOUGHTS AND EMOTIONS:
THE WAVES AND THE OCEAN

When people begin to meditate, they often say that their thoughts are running riot, and have become wilder than ever before. But I reassure them and say that this is a good sign. Far from meaning that your thoughts have become wilder, it shows that *you* have become quieter, and you are finally aware of just how noisy your thoughts have always been. Don't be disheartened or give up. Whatever arises, just keep being present, keep returning to the breath, even in the midst of all the confusion.

In the ancient meditation instructions, it is said that at the beginning thoughts will arrive one on top of another, uninterrupted, like a steep mountain waterfall. Gradually, as you perfect meditation, thoughts become like the water in a deep, narrow gorge, then a great river slowly winding its way down to the sea, and finally the mind becomes like a still and placid ocean, ruffled by only the occasional ripple or wave.

Sometimes people think that when they meditate there should be no thoughts and emotions at all; and when thoughts and emotions do arise, they become annoyed and exasperated with themselves and think they have failed. Nothing could be further from the truth. There is a Tibetan saying: "It's a tall order to ask for meat without bones, and tea without leaves." So long as you have a mind, there will be thoughts and emotions.

Just as the ocean has waves, or the sun has rays, so the mind's own radiance is its thoughts and emotions. The ocean has waves, yet the ocean is not particularly disturbed by them. The waves are the *very nature* of the ocean. Waves will rise, but *where* do they go? Back into the ocean. And where do the waves come from? The ocean. In the same manner, thoughts and emotions are the radiance and expression of the *very nature* of the mind. They rise from the mind, but where do they dissolve? Back into the mind. Whatever rises, do not see it as a particular problem. If you do not impulsively react, if you are only patient, it will once again settle into its essential nature.

When you have this understanding, then rising thoughts only enhance your practice. But when you do not understand what they intrinsically are—the radiance of the nature of your mind—then your thoughts become the seed of confusion. So have a spacious, open, and compassionate attitude toward your thoughts and emotions, because in fact your thoughts are your family, the family of your mind. Before them, as Dudjom Rinpoche used to say: "Be like an old wise man, watching a child play."

We often wonder what to do about negativity or certain troubling emotions. In the spaciousness of meditation, you can view your thoughts and emotions with a totally unbiased attitude. When your attitude changes, then the whole atmosphere of your mind changes, even the very nature of your thoughts and emotions. When *you* become more agreeable, then *they* do; if you have no difficulty with them, they will have no difficulty with you either.

So whatever thoughts and emotions arise, allow them to rise and settle, like the waves in the ocean. Whatever you find yourself thinking, let that thought rise and settle, without any constraint. Don't grasp at it, feed it, or indulge it; don't cling to it and don't try to solidify it. Neither follow thoughts nor invite them; be like the ocean looking at its own waves, or the sky gazing down on the clouds that pass through it.

You will soon find that thoughts are like the wind; they come and go. The secret is not to "think" about thoughts, but to allow them to flow through the mind, while keeping your mind free of afterthoughts.

In the ordinary mind, we perceive the stream of thoughts as continuous; but in reality this is not the case. You will discover for yourself that there is a gap between each thought. When the past thought is past, and the future thought not yet arisen, you will always find a gap in which the Rigpa, the nature of mind, is revealed. So the work of meditation is to allow thoughts to slow down, to make that gap become more and more apparent.

My master had a student called Apa Pant, a distinguished Indian diplomat and author, who served as Indian ambassador in a number of capital cities around the world. He had even been the representative of the Government of India in Tibet in Lhasa, and for a time he was their representative in Sikkim. He was also a practitioner of meditation and yoga, and each time he saw my master, he would always ask him "how to meditate." He was following an Eastern tradition, where the student keeps asking the master one simple, basic question, over and over again.

Apa Pant told me this story. One day our master Jamyang Khyentse was watching a "Lama Dance" in front of the Palace Temple in Gangtok, the capital of Sikkim, and he was chuckling at the antics of the *atsara,* the clown who provides light relief between dances. Apa Pant kept pestering him, asking him again and again how to meditate, so this time when my master replied, it was in such a way as to let him know that he was telling him once and for all: "Look, it's like this: When the past thought has ceased, and the future thought has not yet risen, isn't there a gap?"

"Yes," said Apa Pant.

"Well, prolong it: *That* is meditation."

EXPERIENCES

As you continue to practice, you may have all kinds of experiences, both good and bad. Just as a room with many doors and windows allows the air to enter from many directions, in the same way, when your mind becomes open, it is natural that all kinds of experiences can come into it. You might experience states of bliss, clarity, or absence of thoughts. In one way these are very good experiences, and signs of progress in meditation. For when you experience bliss, it's a sign that desire has temporarily dissolved. When you experience real clarity, it's a sign that aggression has temporarily ceased. When you experience a state of absence of thought, it's a sign that your ignorance has temporarily died. By themselves they are good experiences, but if you get attached to them they become obstacles. Experiences are not realization in themselves; but if we remain free of attachment to them, they become what they really are, that is, materials for realization.

Negative experiences are often the most misleading because we usually take them as a bad sign. But in fact the negative experiences in our practice are blessings in disguise. Try not to react to them with aversion as you might normally do, but recognize them instead for what they truly are, merely experiences, illusory and dream-like. The realization of the true nature of the experience liberates you from the harm or danger of the experience itself, and as a result even a negative experience can become a source of great blessing and accomplishment. There are innumerable stories of how masters worked like this with negative experiences and transformed them into catalysts for realization.

Traditionally it's said that for a real practitioner, it's not the negative experiences but the good ones that bring obstacles. When things are going well, you have got to be especially careful and mindful so that you don't become complacent or over-confident. Remember what Dudjom Rinpoche said to me when I was in the middle of a very powerful experience: "Don't get too excited. In the end, it's neither good nor bad." He knew I was becoming attached to the experience: *that* attachment, like any other, has to be cut through. What we have to learn, in both meditation and in life, is to be free of attachment to the good experiences, and free of aversion to the negative ones.

Dudjom Rinpoche warns us of another pitfall: "On the other hand, in meditation practice, you might experience a muddy, semiconscious, drifting state, like having a hood over your head: a dreamy dullness. This is really nothing more than a kind of blurred and mindless stagnation. How do you get out of this state? Alert yourself, straighten your back, breathe the stale air out of your lungs, and direct your awareness into clear space to freshen your mind. If you remain in this stagnant state, you will not evolve; so whenever this setback arises, clear it again and again. It is important to be as watchful as possible, and to stay as vigilant as you can."

Whatever method you use, drop it, or simply let it dissolve on its own, when you find you have arrived naturally at a state of alert, expansive, and vibrant peace. Then continue to remain there quietly, undistracted, without necessarily using any particular method. The method has already achieved its purpose. However, if you do stray or become distracted, then return to whatever technique is most appropriate to call you back.

The real glory of meditation lies not in any method but in its continual living experience of presence, in its bliss, clarity, peace, and most important of all, complete absence of grasping. The diminishing of grasping in yourself is a sign that you are becoming freer of yourself. And the more you experience this freedom, the clearer the sign that the ego and the hopes and fears that keep it alive are dissolving, and the closer you will come to the infinitely generous "wisdom of egolessness." When you live in that wisdom home, you'll no longer find a barrier between "I" and "you," "this" and "that," "inside" and "outside"; you'll have come, finally, to your true home, the state of non-duality.[8]

TAKING BREAKS

Often people ask: "How long should I meditate? And when? Should I practice twenty minutes in the morning and in the evening, or is it better to do several short practices during the day?" Yes, it is good to meditate for twenty minutes, though that is not to say that twenty minutes is the limit. I have not found that it says twenty minutes anywhere in the scriptures; I think it is a notion that has been contrived in the West, and I call it "Meditation Western Standard Time." The point is not how long you meditate; the point is whether the practice actually brings you to a certain state of mindfulness and presence, where you are a little open and able to connect with your heart essence. And five minutes of wakeful sitting practice is of far greater value than twenty minutes of dozing!

Dudjom Rinpoche used to say that a beginner should practice in short sessions. Practice for four or five minutes, and then take a short break of just one minute. During the break let go of the method, but do not let go of your mindfulness altogether. Sometimes when you have been struggling to practice, curiously, the very moment when you take a break from the method—if you are still mindful and present—is the moment when meditation actually happens. That is why the break is just as important a part of meditation as the sitting itself. Sometimes I say to students who are having problems with their practice to practice during the break and take a break during their meditation!

Sit for a short time; then take a break, a very short break of about thirty seconds or a minute. But be mindful of whatever you do, and do not lose your presence and its natural ease. Then alert yourself and sit again. If you do many short sessions like this, your breaks will often make your meditation more real and more inspiring; they will take the clumsy, irksome rigidity and solemnity and unnaturalness out of your practice, and bring you more and more focus and ease. Gradually, through this interplay of breaks and sitting, the barrier between meditation and everyday life will crumble, the contrast between them will dissolve, and you will find yourself increasingly in your natural pure presence, without distraction. Then, as Dudjom Rinpoche used to say, "Even though the meditator may leave the meditation, the meditation will not leave the meditator."

INTEGRATION: MEDITATION IN ACTION

I have found that modern spiritual practitioners lack the knowledge of how to integrate their meditation practice with everyday life. I cannot say it strongly enough: to integrate meditation in action is the whole ground and point and purpose of meditation. The violence and stress, the challenges and distractions of modern life make this integration even more urgently necessary.

People complain to me, "I have meditated for twelve years, but somehow I haven't changed. I am still the same. Why?" Because there is an abyss between their spiritual practice and their everyday life. They seem to exist in two separate worlds, and not to inspire each other at all. I am reminded of a teacher I knew when I was at school in Tibet. He was brilliant at expounding the rules of Tibetan grammar, but he could hardly write one correct sentence!

How, then, do we achieve this integration, this permeation of everyday life with the calm humor and spacious detachment of meditation? There is no substitute for regular practice, for only through real practice will we begin to taste unbrokenly the calm of our nature of mind and so be able to sustain the experience of it in our everyday life.

I always tell my students not to come out of meditation too quickly: Allow a period of some minutes for the peace of the practice of meditation to infiltrate your life. As my master, Dudjom Rinpoche, said: "Don't jump up and rush off, but mingle your mindfulness with everyday life. Be like a man who's fractured his skull, always careful in case someone will touch him."

Then, after meditation, it's important not to give in to the tendency we have to solidify the way we perceive things. When you do reenter everyday life, let the wisdom, insight, compassion, humor, fluidity, spaciousness, and detachment that meditation brought you pervade your day-to-day experience. Meditation awakens in you the realization of how the nature of everything is illusory and dream-like; maintain that awareness even in the thick of samsara. One great master has said: "After meditation practice, one should become a child of illusion."

Dudjom Rinpoche advised: "In a sense everything is dream-like and illusory, but even so, humorously you go on doing things. For example, if you are walking, without unnecessary solemnity or self-consciousness, lightheartedly walk toward the open space of truth. When you sit, be the stronghold of truth. As you eat, feed your negativities and illusions into the belly of emptiness, dissolving them into all-pervading space. And when you go to the toilet, consider all your obscurations and blockages are being cleansed and washed away."

So what really matters is not just the practice of sitting but far more the state of mind you find yourself in after meditation. It is this calm and centered state of mind you should prolong through everything you do. I like the Zen story in which the disciple asked his master:

"Master, how do you put enlightenment into action? How do you practice it in everyday life?"

"By eating and by sleeping," replied the master.

"But Master, everybody sleeps and everybody eats."

"But not everybody eats when they eat, and not everybody sleeps when they sleep."

From this comes the famous Zen saying, "When I eat, I eat; when I sleep, I sleep."

To eat when you eat and sleep when you sleep means to be completely present in all your actions, with none of the distractions of ego to stop you being there. This is integration.

And if you really wish to achieve this, what you need to do is not just practice as an occasional medicine or therapy, but as if it were your daily sustenance or food. That is why one excellent way to develop this power of integration is to practice it in a retreat environment, far from the stresses of modern city life.

All too often people come to meditation in the hope of extraordinary results, like visions, lights, or some supernatural miracle. When no such thing occurs, they feel extremely disappointed. But the real miracle of meditation is more ordinary and much more useful. It is a subtle transformation, and this transformation happens not only in your mind and your emotions, but also actually in your body. It is very healing. Scientists and doctors have discovered that when you are in a good humor, then even the cells in your body are more joyful; and when your mind is in a more negative state, then your cells can become malignant. The whole state of your health has a lot to do with your state of mind and your way of being.

INSPIRATION

I have said that meditation is the road to enlightenment and the greatest endeavor of this life. Whenever I talk about meditation to my students, I always stress the necessity to practice it with resolute discipline and one-pointed devotion; at the same time, I always tell them how important it is to do it in as inspired and as richly creative a way as possible. In one sense meditation is an art, and you should bring to it an artist's delight and fertility of invention.

Become as resourceful in inspiring yourself to enter your own peace as you are at being neurotic and competitive in the world. There are so many ways of making the approach to meditation as joyful as possible. You can find the music that most exalts you and use it to open your heart and mind. You can collect pieces of poetry, or quotations or lines of teachings that over the years have moved you, and keep them always at hand to elevate your spirit. I have always loved Tibetan *thangka* paintings, and derive strength from their beauty. You too can find reproductions of paintings that arouse a sense of sacredness, and hang them on the walls of your room. Listen to a cassette tape of a teaching by a great master, or a sacred chant. You can make of the place where you meditate a simple paradise, with one flower, one stick of incense, one candle, one photograph of an enlightened master, or one statue of a deity or a buddha. You can transform the most ordinary of rooms into an intimate sacred space, into an environment where every day you come to the meeting with your true self with all the joy and happy ceremony of one old friend greeting another.

And if you find that meditation does not come easily in your city room, be inventive and go out into nature. Nature is always an unfailing fountain of inspiration. To calm your mind, go for a walk at dawn in the park, or watch the dew on a rose in a garden. Lie on the ground and gaze up into the sky, and let your mind expand into its spaciousness. Let the sky outside awake a sky inside your mind. Stand by a stream and mingle your mind with its rushing; become one with its ceaseless sound. Sit by a waterfall and let its healing laughter purify your spirit. Walk on a beach and take the sea wind full and sweet against your face. Celebrate and use the beauty of moonlight to poise your mind. Sit by a lake or in a garden and, breathing quietly, let your mind fall silent as the moon comes up majestically and slowly in the cloudless night.

Everything can be used as an invitation to meditation. A smile, a face in the subway, the sight of a small flower growing in the crack of a cement pavement, a fall of rich cloth in a shop window, the way the sun lights up flower pots on a window sill. Be alert for any sign of beauty or grace. Offer up every joy, be awake at all moments, to "the news that is always arriving out of silence."[9]

Slowly you will become a master of your own bliss, a chemist of your own joy, with all sorts of remedies always at hand to elevate, cheer, illuminate, and inspire your every breath and movement. What is a great spiritual practitioner? A person who lives always in the presence of his or her own true self, someone who has found and who uses continually the springs and sources of profound inspiration. As the modern English writer Lewis Thompson wrote: "Christ, supreme poet, lived truth so passionately that every gesture of his, at once pure Act and perfect Symbol, embodies the transcendent."[10]

To embody the transcendent is why we are here.

SIX

Evolution, Karma, and Rebirth

ON THAT MOMENTOUS NIGHT when the Buddha attained enlightenment, it is said that he went through several different stages of awakening. In the first, with his mind "collected and purified, without blemish, free of defilements, grown soft, workable, fixed and immovable," he turned his attention to the recollection of his previous lives. This is what he tells us of that experience:

> I remembered many, many former existences I had passed through: one, two births, three, four, five . . . fifty, one hundred . . . a hundred thousand, in various world-periods. I knew everything about these various births: where they had taken place, what my name had been, which family I had been born into, and what I had done. I lived through again the good and bad fortune of each life and my death in each life, and came to life again and again. In this way I recalled innumerable previous existences with their exact characteristic features and circumstances. This knowledge I gained in the first watch of the night.[1]

Since the dawn of history, reincarnation and a firm faith in life after death have occupied an essential place in nearly all the world's religions. Belief in rebirth existed amidst Christians in the early history of Christianity, and persisted in various forms well into the Middle Ages. Origen, one of the most influential of the church fathers, believed in the "pre-existence of souls" and wrote in the third century: "Each soul comes to this world reinforced by the victories or enfeebled by the defeats of its previous lives." Although Christianity eventually rejected the belief in reincarnation, traces of it can be found throughout Renaissance thought, in the writings of major romantic poets like Blake and Shelley, and even in so unlikely a figure as the novelist Balzac. Since the advent of interest in Eastern religions that began at the end of the last century, a remarkable number of Westerners have come to accept the Hindu and Buddhist knowledge of rebirth. One of them, the great American industrialist and philanthropist Henry Ford, wrote:

> I adopted the theory of reincarnation when I was twenty-six. Religion offered nothing to the point. Even work could not give me complete satisfaction. Work is futile if we cannot utilize the experience we collect in one life in the next. When I discovered reincarnation . . . time was no longer limited. I was no longer a slave to the hands of the clock . . . I would like to communicate to others the calmness that the long view of life gives to us.[2]

A Gallup poll taken in 1982 showed that nearly one in four Americans believe in reincarnation.[3] This is an astonishing statistic considering how dominant the materialist and scientific philosophy is in almost every aspect of life.

However, most people still have only the most shadowy idea about life after death, and no idea of what it might be like. Again and again, people tell me they cannot bring themselves to believe in something for which there is no evidence. But that is hardly proof, is it, that it does not exist? As Voltaire said: "After all, it is no more surprising to be born twice than it is to be born once."

"If we have lived before," I'm often asked, "why don't we remember it?" But why should the fact that we cannot remember our past lives mean that we have never lived before? After all, experiences of our childhood, or of yesterday, or even of what we were thinking an hour ago were vivid as they occurred, but the memory of them has almost totally eroded, as though they had never taken place. If we cannot remember what we were doing or thinking last Monday, how on earth do we imagine it would be easy, or normal, to remember what we were doing in a previous lifetime?

Sometimes I tease people and ask: "What makes you so adamant that there's no life after death? What proof do you have? What if you found there was a life after this one, having died denying its existence? What would you do then? Aren't you limiting yourself with your conviction that it doesn't exist? Doesn't it make more sense to give the possibility of a life after death the benefit of the doubt, or at least be open to it, even if there is not what you would call 'concrete evidence'? What *would* constitute concrete evidence for life after death?"

I then like to ask people to ask themselves: Why do you imagine all the major religions believe in a life after this one, and why have hundreds of millions of people throughout history, including the greatest philosophers, sages, and creative geniuses of Asia, lived this belief as an essential part of their lives? Were they all simply deluded?

Let us get back to this point about concrete evidence. Just because we have never heard of Tibet, or just because we have never been there, does not mean that Tibet does not exist. Before the huge continent of America was "discovered," who in Europe had any idea that it was there? Even after it had been discovered, people disputed the fact that it had. It is, I believe, our drastically limited vision of life that prevents us from accepting or even beginning seriously to think about the possibility of rebirth.

Fortunately this is not the end of the story. Those of us who undertake a spiritual discipline—of meditation, for example—come to discover many things about our own mind that we did not know before. For as our mind opens more and more to the extraordinary, vast, and hitherto unsuspected existence of the nature of mind, we begin to glimpse a completely different dimension, one in which all of our assumptions about our identity and reality we thought we knew so well start to dissolve, and in which the possibility of lives other than this one becomes at least likely. We begin to understand that everything we are being told by the masters about life and death, and life after death, is real.

SOME SUGGESTIVE "PROOFS" OF REBIRTH

There is by now a vast modern literature dealing with the testimonies of those who claim to be able to remember past lives. I suggest that if you really want to come to some serious understanding of rebirth, you investigate this open-mindedly but with as much discrimination as possible.

Of the hundreds of stories about reincarnation that could be told here, there is one that particularly fascinates me. It is the story of an elderly man from Norfolk in England called Arthur Flowerdew, who from the age of twelve experienced inexplicable but vivid mental pictures of what seemed like some great city surrounded by desert. One of the images that came most frequently to his mind was of a temple apparently carved out of a cliff. These strange images kept coming back to him, especially when he played with the pink and orange pebbles on the seashore near his home. As he grew older, the details of the city in his vision grew clearer, and he saw more buildings, the layout of the streets, soldiers, and the approach to the city itself through a narrow canyon.

Arthur Flowerdew much later in his life, quite by chance, saw a television documentary film on the ancient city of Petra in Jordan. He was astounded to see, for the very first time, the place he had carried around for so many years in those pictures in his mind. He claimed afterward that he had never even seen a book about Petra. However, his visions became well-known, and an appearance in a BBC television program brought him to the attention of the Jordanian government, who proposed to fly him to Jordan along with a BBC producer to film his reactions to Petra. His only previous trip abroad had been a brief visit to the French coast.

Before the expedition left, Arthur Flowerdew was introduced to a world authority on Petra and author of a book on the ancient city, who questioned him in detail, but was baffled by the precision of his knowledge, some of which he said could only have been known by an archaeologist specializing in this area. The BBC recorded Arthur Flowerdew's pre-visit description of Petra, so as to compare it with what would be seen in Jordan. Flowerdew singled out three places in his vision of Petra: a curious volcano-shaped rock on the outskirts of the city, a small temple where he believed he had been killed in the first century B.C., and an unusual structure in the city that was well-known to archaeologists, but for which they could find no function. The Petra expert could recall no such rock and doubted that it was there. When he showed Arthur Flowerdew a photograph of the part of the city where the temple had stood, he astounded him by pointing to almost the exact site. Then the elderly man calmly explained the purpose of the structure, one that had not been considered before, as the guard room in which he had served as a soldier two thousand years before.

A significant number of his predictions proved accurate. On the expedition's approach to Petra, Arthur Flowerdew pointed out the mysterious rock; and once in the city he went straight to the guard room, without a glance at the map, and demonstrated how its peculiar check-in system for guards was used. Finally he went to the spot where he said he had been killed by an enemy spear in the first century B.C. He also indicated the location and purpose of other unexcavated structures on the site.

The expert and archaeologist of Petra who accompanied Arthur Flowerdew could not explain this very ordinary English man's uncanny knowledge of the city. He said:

He's filled in details and a lot of it is very consistent with known archaeological and historical facts and it would require a mind very different from his to be able to sustain a fabric of deception on the scale of his memories—at least those which he's reported to me. I don't think he's a fraud. I don't think he has the capacity to be a fraud on this scale.[4]

What else could explain Arthur Flowerdew's extraordinary knowledge except rebirth? You could say that he might have read books about Petra, or that he might have even received his knowledge by telepathy; yet the fact remains that some of the information he was able to give was unknown even to the experts.

Then there are fascinating cases of children who can spontaneously remember details of a previous life. Many of these cases have been collected by Dr. Ian Stevenson of the University of Virginia.[5] One startling account of a child's memories of a past life came to the attention of the Dalai Lama, who sent a special representative to interview her and verify her account.[6]

Her name was Kamaljit Kour, and she was the daughter of a schoolteacher in a Sikh family in the Punjab in India. One day, on a visit to a fair in a local village with her father, she suddenly asked him to take her to another village, some distance away. Her father was surprised and asked her why. "I have nothing here," she told him. "This is not my home. Please take me to that village. One of my school-friends and I were riding on our bicycles when suddenly we were hit by a bus. My friend was killed instantly. I was injured in the head, ear, and nose. I was taken from the site of the accident and laid on the bench in front of a small courthouse nearby. Then I was taken to the village hospital. My wounds were bleeding profusely and my parents and relatives joined me there. Since there were no facilities to cure me in the local hospital, they decided to take me to Ambala. As the doctors said I could not be cured, I asked my relatives to take me home." Her father was shocked, but when she insisted, he finally agreed to take her to the village, though he thought that it was just a child's whim.

They went to the village together as promised, and she recognized it as they approached, pointing out the place where the bus had hit her, and asking to be put in a rickshaw, whereupon she gave directions to the driver. She stopped the rickshaw when they arrived at a cluster of houses where she claimed she had lived. The little girl and her bewildered father made their way to the house she said belonged to her former family, and her father, who still did not believe her, asked the neighbors whether there was a family like the one Kamaljit Kour had described, who had lost their daughter. They confirmed the story, and told the girl's astonished father that Rishma, the daughter of the family, had been sixteen years old when she was killed; she had died in the car on the way home from the hospital.

The father felt extremely unnerved at this, and told Kamaljit that they should go home. But she went right up to the house, asked for her school photo, and gazed at it with delight. When Rishma's grandfather and her uncles arrived, she recognized them and named them without mistake. She pointed out her own room, and showed her father each of the other rooms in the house. Then she asked for her school books, her two silver bangles and her two ribbons, and her new maroon suit. Her aunt explained that these were all things Rishma had owned. Then she led the way to her uncle's house, where she identified some more items. The next day she met all of her former relatives, and when it was time to catch the bus home, she refused to go, announcing to her father that she was going to stay. Eventually he persuaded her to leave with him.

The family started to piece the story together. Kamaljit Kour was born ten months after Rishma died. Although the little girl had not yet started school, she often pretended to read, and she could remember the names of all her school friends in Rishma's school photograph. Kamaljit Kour had also always asked for maroon-colored clothes. Her parents discovered that Rishma had been given a new maroon suit of which she was very proud, but she had never had time to wear it. The last thing Kamaljit Kour remembers of her former life was the lights of the car going out on the way home from the hospital; that must have been when she died.

I can think of ways that one might try to discredit this account. You might say that perhaps this little girl's family had put her up to claiming she was the reincarnation of Rishma for some reason of their own. Rishma's family were wealthy farmers, but Kamaljit Kour's own family were not poor, and had one of the better houses in their village, with a courtyard and garden. What is intriguing about this story is that in fact her family in this life felt rather uneasy about the whole business, and worried about "what the neighbors might think." However, what I find most telling is that Rishma's own family admitted that, although they did not know much about their religion, or even whether reincarnation is accepted or not by Sikhs, they were convinced beyond any doubt that Kamaljit Kour was in fact their Rishma.

To anyone who wants to study seriously the possibility of life after death, I suggest that they look at the very moving testimonies of the near-death experience. A startling number of those who have survived this experience have been left with a conviction that life continues after death. Many of these had no previous religious belief at all, or any spiritual experience:

> Now, my entire life through, I am thoroughly convinced that there is life after death, without a shadow of a doubt, and I am not afraid to die. I am not. Some people I have known are so afraid, so scared. I always smile to myself when I hear people doubt there is an afterlife, or say, "When you're dead, you're gone." I think to myself, "They really don't know."[7]

> What happened to me at that time is the most unusual experience I have ever had. It has made me realize that there is life after death.[8]

> I know there is life after death! Nobody can shake my belief. I have no doubt—it's peaceful and nothing to be feared. I don't know what's beyond what I experienced, but it's plenty for me . . .
>   It gave me an answer to what I think everyone really must wonder about at one time or another in this life. Yes, there is an afterlife! More beautiful than anything we can begin to imagine! Once you know it, there is nothing that can equal it. You just know![9]

The studies on this subject also show that the near-death experiencers tend afterward to be more open and inclined toward accepting reincarnation.

Then again, could not the amazing talents for music or mathematics that certain child prodigies display be attributed to their development in other lives? Think of Mozart, composing minuets at the age of five, and publishing sonatas at eight.[10]

If life after death does exist, you may ask, why is it so difficult to remember? In the "Myth of Er," Plato suggests an "explanation" for this lack of memory. Er was a soldier who was taken for dead in battle, and seems to have had a near-death experience. He saw many things while "dead," and was instructed to return to life in order to tell others what the after-death state is like. Just before he returned, he saw those who were being prepared to be born moving in terrible, stifling heat through the "Plain of Oblivion," a desert bare of all trees and plants. "When evening came," Plato tells us, "they encamped beside the River Unmindfulness, whose water no vessel can hold. All are requested to drink a certain measure of this water, and some have not the wisdom to save them from drinking more. Every man, as he drinks, forgets everything."[11] Er himself was not permitted to drink the water, and awoke to find himself on the funeral pyre, able to remember all that he had heard and seen.

Is there some universal law that makes it almost impossible for us to remember where and what we have lived before? Or is it just the sheer volume, range, and intensity of our experiences that have erased any memory of past lives? How much would it help us, I sometimes wonder, if we did remember them? Couldn't that just confuse us even more?

THE CONTINUITY OF MIND

From the Buddhist point of view, the main argument that "establishes" rebirth is one based on a profound understanding of the continuity of mind. Where does consciousness come from? It cannot arise out of nowhere. A moment of consciousness cannot be produced without the moment of consciousness that immediately preceded it. His Holiness the Dalai Lama explains this complex process in this way:

The basis on which Buddhists accept the concept of rebirth is principally the continuity of consciousness. Take the material world as an example: all the elements in our present universe, even down to a microscopic level, can be traced back, we believe, to an origin, an initial point where all the elements of the material world are condensed into what are technically known as "space particles." These particles, in turn, are the state which is the result of the disintegration of a previous universe. So there is a constant cycle, in which the universe evolves and disintegrates, and then comes back again into being.

Now mind is very similar. The fact that we possess something called "mind or consciousness" is quite obvious, since our experience testifies to its presence. Then it is also evident, again from our own experience, that what we call "mind or consciousness" is something which is subject to change when it is exposed to different conditions and circumstances. This shows us its moment to moment nature, its susceptibility to change.

Another fact that is obvious is that gross levels of "mind or consciousness" are intimately linked with physiological states of the body, and are in fact dependent on them. But there must be some basis, energy, or source which allows mind, when interacting with material particles, to be capable of producing conscious living beings.

Just like the material plane, this too must have its continuum in the past. So if you trace our present mind or consciousness back, then you will find that you are tracing the origin of the continuity of mind, just like the origin of the material universe, into an infinite dimension; it is, as you will see, beginningless.

Therefore there must be successive rebirths that allow that continuum of mind to be there.

Buddhism believes in universal causation, that everything is subject to change, and to causes and conditions. So there is no place given to a divine creator, nor to beings who are self-created; rather everything arises as a consequence of causes and conditions. So mind, or consciousness, too comes into being as a result of its previous instants.

When we talk of causes and conditions, there are two principal types: substantial causes, the stuff from which something is produced, and cooperative factors, which contribute towards that causation. In the case of mind and body, although one can affect the other, one cannot become the substance of the other . . . Mind and matter, although dependent on one another, cannot serve as substantial causes for each other.

This is the basis on which Buddhism accepts rebirth.[12]

Most people take the word "reincarnation" to imply there is some "thing" that reincarnates, which travels from life to life. But in Buddhism we do not believe in an independent and unchanging entity like a soul or ego that survives the death of the body. What provides the continuity between lives is not an entity, we believe, but the ultimately subtlest level of consciousness. The Dalai Lama explains:

According to the Buddhist explanation, the ultimate creative principle is consciousness. There are different levels of consciousness. What we call innermost subtle consciousness is always there. The continuity of that consciousness is almost like something permanent, like the space-particles. In the field of matter, that is the space-particles; in the field of consciousness, it is the Clear Light . . . The Clear Light, with its special energy, makes the connection with consciousness.[13]

The exact way in which rebirth takes place has been well illustrated with the following example:

> *The successive existences in a series of rebirths are not like the pearls in a pearl necklace, held together by a string, the "soul," which passes through all the pearls; rather they are like dice piled one on top of the other. Each die is separate, but it supports the one above it, with which it is functionally connected. Between the dice there is no identity, but conditionality.*[14]

There is in the Buddhist scriptures a very clear account of this process of conditionality. The Buddhist sage Nagasena explained it to the King Milinda in a set of famous answers to questions that the King posed him.

The King asked Nagasena: "When someone is reborn, is he the same as the one who just died, or is he different?"

Nagasena replied: "He is neither the same, nor different . . . Tell me, if a man were to light a lamp, could it provide light the whole night long?"

"Yes."

"Is the flame then which burns in the first watch of the night the same as the one that burns in the second . . . or the last?"

"No."

"Does that mean there is one lamp in the first watch of the night, another in the second, and another in the third?"

"No, it's because of that one lamp that the light shines all night."

"Rebirth is much the same: one phenomenon arises and another stops, simultaneously. So the first act of consciousness in the new existence is neither the same as the last act of consciousness in the previous existence, nor is it different."

The King asks for another example to explain the precise nature of this dependence, and Nagasena compares it to milk: the curds, butter, or *ghee* that can be made from milk are never the same as the milk, but they depend on it entirely for their production.

The King then asks: "If there is no being that passes on from body to body, wouldn't we then be free of all the negative actions we had done in past lives?"

Nagasena gives this example: A man steals someone's mangoes. The mangoes he steals are not exactly the same mangoes that the other person had originally owned and planted, so how can he possibly deserve to be punished?

The reason he does, Nagasena explains, is that the stolen mangoes only grew because of those that their owner had planted in the first place. In the same way, it is because of our actions in one life, pure or impure, that we are linked with another life, and we are not free from their results.

KARMA

In the second watch of the night when Buddha attained enlightenment, he gained another kind of knowledge, which complemented his knowledge of rebirth: that of *karma,* the natural law of cause and effect.

"With the heavenly eye, purified and beyond the range of human vision, I saw how beings vanish and come to be again. I saw high and low, brilliant and insignificant, and how each obtained according to his karma a favorable or painful rebirth."[15]

The truth and the driving force behind rebirth is what is called karma. Karma is often totally misunderstood in the West as fate or predestination; it is best thought of as the infallible law of cause and effect that governs the universe. The word *karma* literally means "action," and karma is both the power latent within actions, and the results our actions bring.

There are many kinds of karma: international karma, national karma, the karma of a city, and individual karma. All are intricately interrelated, and only understood in their full complexity by an enlightened being.

In simple terms, what does karma mean? It means that whatever we do, with our body, speech, or mind, will have a corresponding result. Each action, even the smallest, is preg-nant with its consequences. It is said by the masters that even a little poison can cause death, and even a tiny seed can become a huge tree. And as Buddha said: "Do not overlook negative actions merely because they are small; however small a spark may be, it can burn down a haystack as big as a mountain." Similarly he said: "Do not overlook tiny good actions, thinking they are of no benefit; even tiny drops of water in the end will fill a huge vessel." Karma does not decay like external things, or ever become inoperative. It can-not be destroyed "by time, fire, or water." Its power will never disappear, until it is ripened.

Although the results of our actions may not have matured yet, they will inevitably ripen, given the right conditions. Usually we forget what we do, and it is only long afterward that the results catch up with us. By then we are unable to connect them with their causes. Imagine an eagle, says Jikmé Lingpa. It is flying, high in the sky. It casts no shadow. Nothing shows that it is there. Then suddenly it spies its prey, dives, and swoops to the ground. And as it drops, its menacing shadow appears.

The results of our actions are often delayed, even into future lifetimes; we cannot pin down one cause, because any event can be an extremely complicated mixture of many karmas ripening together. So we tend to assume now that things happen to us "by chance," and when everything goes well, we simply call it "good luck."

And yet what else but karma could really begin to explain satisfyingly the extreme and extraordinary differences between each of us? Even though we may be born in the same family or country, or in similar circumstances, we all have different characters, totally different things happen to us, we have different talents, inclinations, and destinies.

As Buddha said, "What you are is what you have been, what you will be is what you do now." Padmasambhava went further: "If you want to know your past life, look into your present condition; if you want to know your future life, look at your present actions."

THE GOOD HEART

The kind of birth we will have in the next life is determined, then, by the nature of our actions in this one. And it is important never to forget that the effect of our actions depends entirely upon the intention or motivation behind them, and not upon their scale.

At the time of Buddha, there lived an old beggar woman called "Relying on Joy." She used to watch the kings, princes, and people making offerings to Buddha and his disciples, and there was nothing she would have liked more than to be able to do the same. So she went out begging, but at the end of a whole day all she had was one small coin. She took it to the oil-merchant to try to buy some oil. He told her that she could not possibly buy anything with so little. But when he heard that she wanted it to make an offering to Buddha, he took pity on her and gave her the oil she wanted. She took it to the monastery, where she lit a lamp. She placed it before Buddha, and made this wish: "I have nothing to offer but this tiny lamp. But through this offering, in the future may I be blessed with the lamp of wisdom. May I free all beings from their darkness. May I purify all their obscurations, and lead them to enlightenment."

That night the oil in all the other lamps went out. But the beggar woman's lamp was still burning at dawn, when Buddha's disciple Maudgalyayana came to collect all the lamps. When he saw that one was still alight, full of oil and with a new wick, he thought, "There's no reason why this lamp should still be burning in the daytime," and he tried to blow it out. But it kept on burning. He tried to snuff it out with his fingers, but it stayed alight. He tried to smother it with his robe, but still it burned on. The Buddha had been watching all along, and said, "Maudgalyayana, do you want to put out that lamp? You cannot. You could not even move it, let alone put it out. If you were to pour the water from all the oceans over this lamp, it still wouldn't go out. The water in all the rivers and lakes of the world could not extinguish it. Why not? Because this lamp was offered with devotion, and with purity of heart and mind. And that motivation has made it of tremendous benefit." When Buddha had said this, the beggar woman approached him, and he made a prophecy that in the future she would become a perfect buddha, called "Light of the Lamp."

So it is our motivation, good or bad, that determines the fruit of our actions. Shantideva said:

Whatever joy there is in this world
All comes from desiring others to be happy,
And whatever suffering there is in this world
All comes from desiring myself to be happy.[16]

Because the law of karma is inevitable and infallible, whenever we harm others, we are directly harming ourselves, and whenever we bring them happiness, we are bringing ourselves future happiness. So the Dalai Lama says:

If you try to subdue your selfish motives—anger and so forth—and
develop more kindness and compassion for others, ultimately you
yourself will benefit more than you would otherwise. So sometimes I
say that the wise selfish person should practice this way. Foolish
selfish people are always thinking of themselves, and the result is
negative. Wise selfish people think of others, help others as much as
they can, and the result is that they too receive benefit.[17]

The belief in reincarnation shows us that there is some kind of ultimate justice or goodness in the universe. It is that goodness that we are all trying to uncover and to free.

Whenever we act positively, we move toward it; whenever we act negatively, we obscure and inhibit it. And whenever we cannot express it in our lives and actions, we feel miserable and frustrated.

So if you were to draw one essential message from the fact of reincarnation, it would be: Develop this good heart, that longs for other beings to find lasting happiness, and acts to secure that happiness. Nourish and practice kindness. The Dalai Lama has said: "There is no need for temples; no need for complicated philosophy. Our own brain, our own heart is our temple; my philosophy is kindness."

CREATIVITY

Karma, then, is not fatalistic or predetermined. Karma means *our* ability to create and to change. It is creative because we *can* determine how and why we act. We *can* change. The future is in our hands, and in the hands of our heart. Buddha said:

> *Karma creates all, like an artist,*
> *Karma composes, like a dancer.*[18]

As everything is impermanent, fluid, and interdependent, how we act and think inevitably change the future. There is no situation, however seemingly hopeless or terrible, such as a terminal disease, which we cannot use to evolve. And there is no crime or cruelty that sincere regret and real spiritual practice cannot purify.

Milarepa is considered Tibet's greatest yogin, poet, and saint. I remember as a child the thrill of reading his life story, and poring over the little painted illustrations in my handwritten copy of his life. As a young man Milarepa trained to be a sorcerer, and out of revenge killed and ruined countless people with his black magic. And yet through his remorse, and the ordeals and hardships he had to undergo with his great master Marpa, he was able to purify all these negative actions. He went on to become enlightened, a figure who has been the inspiration of millions down through the centuries.

In Tibet we say: "Negative action has one good quality, it can be purified." So there is always hope. Even murderers and the most hardened criminals can change and overcome the conditioning that led them to their crimes. Our present condition, if we use it skillfully and with wisdom, can be an inspiration to free ourselves from the bondage of suffering.

Whatever is happening to us now mirrors our past karma. If we know that, and know it really, whenever suffering and difficulties befall us, we do not view them particularly as a failure or a catastrophe, or see suffering as a punishment in any way. Nor do we blame ourselves, or indulge in self-hatred. We see the pain we are going through as the completion of the effects, the fruition, of a past karma. Tibetans say that suffering is "a broom that sweeps away all our negative karma." We can even be grateful that one karma is coming to an end. We know that "good fortune," a fruit of good karma, may soon pass if we do not use it well, and "misfortune," the result of negative karma, may in fact be giving us a marvelous opportunity to evolve.

For Tibetan people, karma has a really vivid and practical meaning in their everyday lives. They live out the principle of karma, in the knowledge of its truth, and this is the basis of Buddhist ethics. They understand it to be a natural and just process. So karma inspires in them a sense of personal responsibility in whatever they do. When I was young, my family had a wonderful servant called A-pé Dorje who loved me very much. He really was a holy man, and never harmed anyone in his whole life. Whenever I said or did anything harmful in my childhood, he would immediately say gently, "Oh, that's not right," and so instilled in me a deep sense of the omnipresence of karma, and an almost automatic habit of transforming my responses should any harmful thought arise.

Is karma really so hard to see in operation? Don't we only have to look back at our own lives to see clearly the consequences of some of our actions? When we upset or hurt someone, didn't it rebound on us? Were we not left with a bitter and dark memory, and the shadows of self-disgust? That memory and those shadows are karma. Our habits and our fears too are also due to karma, the result of actions, words, or thoughts we have done in the past. If we examine our actions, and become really mindful of them, we will see that there is a pattern that repeats itself in our actions. *Whenever we act negatively, it leads to pain and suffering; whenever we act positively, it eventually results in happiness.*

RESPONSIBILITY

I have been very moved by how the near-death experience reports confirm, in a very precise and startling way, the truth about karma. One of the common elements of the near-death experience, an element that has occasioned a great deal of thought, is the "panoramic life review." It appears that people who undergo this experience not only review in the most vivid detail the events of their past life, but also can witness the fullest possible implications of what they have done. They experience, in fact, the complete range of effects their actions had on others and all the feelings, however disturbing or shocking, they aroused in them[19]:

> Everything in my life went by for review—I was ashamed of a lot of the things I experienced because it seemed I had a different knowledge . . . Not only what I had done, but how I had affected other people . . . I found out that not even your thoughts are lost.[20]

> My life passed before me . . . what occurred was every emotion I have ever felt in my life, I felt. And my eyes were showing me the basis of how that emotion affected my life. What my life had done so far to affect other people's lives . . .[21]

> I was the very people that I hurt, and I was the very people I helped to feel good.[22]

> It was a total reliving of every thought I had thought, every word I had ever spoken, and every deed I had ever done; plus the effect of each thought, word, and deed on everyone and anyone who had ever come within my environment or sphere of influence whether I knew them or not . . . ; plus the effect of each thought, word, and deed on weather, plants, animals, soil, trees, water, and air.[23]

I feel that these testimonies should be taken very seriously. They will help all of us to realize the full implications of our actions, words, and thoughts, and impel us to become increasingly responsible. I have noticed that many people feel menaced by the reality of karma, because they are beginning to understand they have no escape from its natural law. There are some who profess complete contempt for karma, but deep inside they have profound doubts about their own denial. During the daytime they may act with fearless contempt for all morality, an artificial, careless confidence, but alone at night their minds are often dark and troubled.

Both the East and the West have their characteristic ways of evading the responsibilities that come from understanding karma. In the East people use karma as an excuse not to give anyone a helping hand, saying that, whatever they suffer, it is "their karma." In the "free-thinking" Western world, we do the opposite. Westerners who believe in karma can be exaggeratedly "sensitive" and "careful," and say that actually to help someone would be to interfere with something they have to "work out for themselves." What an evasion and betrayal of our humanity! Perhaps it is just as likely that it is our karma to find a way to help. I know several rich people: Their wealth could be their destruction, in encouraging sloth and selfishness; or they could seize the chance that money offers really to help others, and by doing so help themselves.

We must never forget that it is through our actions, words, and thoughts that we have a choice. And if we choose we can put an end to suffering and the causes of suffering, and help our true potential, our buddha nature, to awaken in us. Until this buddha nature is completely awakened, and we are freed from our ignorance and merge with the deathless, enlightened mind, there can be no end to the round of life and death. So, the teachings tell us, if we do not assume the fullest possible responsibility for ourselves now in this life, our suffering will go on not only for a few lives but for thousands of lives.

It is this sobering knowledge that makes Buddhists consider that future lives are more important even than this one, because there are many more that await us in the future. This long-term vision governs how they live. They know if we were to sacrifice the whole of eternity for this life, it would be like spending our entire life savings on one drink, madly ignoring the consequences.

But if we do observe the law of karma and awaken in ourselves the good heart of love and compassion, if we purify our mindstream and gradually awaken the wisdom of the nature of our mind, then we can become a truly human being, and ultimately enlightened.

Albert Einstein said:

> A human being is part of a whole, called by us the "Universe," a part limited in time and space. He experiences himself, his thoughts and feelings, as something separated from the rest—a kind of optical delusion of his consciousness. This delusion is a kind of prison for us, restricting us to our personal desires and to affection for a few persons nearest us. Our task must be to free ourselves from this prison by widening our circles of compassion to embrace all living creatures and the whole of nature in its beauty.[24]

REINCARNATIONS IN TIBET

Those who master the law of karma and achieve realization can choose to return in life after life to help others. In Tibet a tradition of recognizing such incarnations or *tulkus* began in the thirteenth century and continues to the present day. When a realized master dies, he (or she) may leave precise indications of where he will be reborn. One of his closest disciples or spiritual friends may then have a vision or dream foretelling his imminent rebirth. In some cases his former disciples might approach a master known and revered for having the ability to recognize tulkus, and this master might have a dream or vision that would enable him to direct the search for the tulku. When a child is found, it will be this master who authenticates him.

The true purpose of this tradition is that it ensures that the wisdom memory of realized masters is not lost. The most important feature of the life of an incarnation is that in the course of training, his or her original nature—the wisdom memory the incarnation has inherited—awakens, and this is the true sign of his or her authenticity. His Holiness the Dalai Lama, for example, admits he was able to understand at an early age, without much difficulty, aspects of Buddhist philosophy and teaching that are difficult to grasp, and usually take many years to master.

Great care is taken in the upbringing of tulkus. Even before their training begins, their parents are instructed to take special care of them. Their training is much more strict and intensive than that of ordinary monks, for so much more is expected of them.

Sometimes they remember their past lives or demonstrate remarkable abilities. As the Dalai Lama says: "It is common for small children who are reincarnations to remember objects and people from their previous lives. Some can also recite scriptures, although they have not yet been taught them."[25] Some incarnations need to practice or study less than others. This was the case with my own master, Jamyang Khyentse.

When my master was young he had a very demanding tutor. He had to live with him in his hermitage in the mountains. One morning his tutor left for a neighboring village to conduct a ritual for someone who had just died. Just before he left he gave my master a book called *Chanting the Names of Manjushri,* an extremely difficult text about fifty pages long, which would ordinarily take months to memorize. His parting words were: "Memorize this by this evening!"

The young Khyentse was like any other child, and once his tutor had left he began to play. He played and he played, until the neighbors became increasingly anxious. They pleaded with him, "You'd better start studying, otherwise you'll get a beating." They knew just how strict and wrathful his tutor was. Even then he paid no attention, and kept on playing. Finally just before sunset, when he knew his tutor would be returning, he read through the whole text once. When his tutor returned and tested him, he was able to recite the entire work from memory, word perfect.

Ordinarily, no tutor in his right mind would set such a task for an infant. In his heart of hearts, he knew that Khyentse was the incarnation of Manjushri, the Buddha of Wisdom, and it was almost as if he were trying to lure him into "proving" himself. The child himself, by accepting such a difficult task without protest, was tacitly acknowledging who he was. Later Khyentse wrote in his autobiography that although his tutor did not admit it, even he was quite impressed.

What continues in a tulku? Is the tulku exactly the same person as the figure he reincarnates? He both is and he isn't. His motivation and dedication to help all beings is the same, but he is not actually the same person. What continues from life to life is a blessing, what a Christian would call "grace." This transmission of a blessing and grace is exactly tuned and appropriate to each succeeding age, and the incarnation appears in a way potentially best suited to the karma of the people of his time, to be able most completely to help them.

Perhaps the most moving example of the richness, effectiveness, and subtlety of this system is His Holiness the Dalai Lama. He is revered by Buddhists as the incarnation of Avalokiteshvara, the Buddha of Infinite Compassion.

Brought up in Tibet as its god-king, the Dalai Lama received all the traditional training and major teachings of all the lineages, and became one of the very greatest living masters in the Tibetan tradition. Yet the whole world knows him as a being of direct simplicity and the most practical outlook. The Dalai Lama has a keen interest in all aspects of contemporary physics, neurobiology, psychology, and politics, and his views and message of universal responsibility are embraced not only by Buddhists but by people of all persuasions all over the world. His dedication to nonviolence in the forty-year-long, agonizing struggle of the Tibetan people for their independence from the Chinese won him the Nobel Peace Prize in 1989; in a particularly violent time, his example has inspired people in their aspirations for freedom in countries in every part of the globe. The Dalai Lama has become one of the leading spokesmen for the preservation of the world's environment, tirelessly trying to awaken his fellow human beings to the dangers of a selfish, materialistic philosophy. He is honored by intellectuals and leaders everywhere, and yet I have known hundreds of quite ordinary people of all kinds and nations whose lives have been changed by the beauty, humor, and joy of his holy presence. The Dalai Lama is, I believe, nothing less than the face of the Buddha of Compassion turned toward an endangered humanity, the incarnation of Avalokiteshvara not only for Tibet and not only for Buddhists, but for the whole world—in need, as never before, of healing compassion and of his example of total dedication to peace.

It may be surprising for the West to learn how very many incarnations there have been in Tibet, and how the majority have been great masters, scholars, authors, mystics, and saints who made an outstanding contribution both to the teaching of Buddhism and to society. They played a central role in the history of Tibet. I believe that this process of incarnation is not limited to Tibet, but can occur in all countries and at all times. Throughout history there have been figures of artistic genius, spiritual strength, and humanitarian vision who have helped the human race to go forward. I think of Gandhi, Einstein, Abraham Lincoln, Mother Teresa, of Shakespeare, of St. Francis, of Beethoven, of Michelangelo. When Tibetans hear of such people, they immediately say they are bodhisattvas. And whenever I hear of them, of their work and vision, I am moved by the majesty of the vast evolutionary process of the buddhas and masters that emanate to liberate beings and better the world.

SEVEN

Bardos and Other Realities

BARDO IS A TIBETAN WORD that simply means a "transition" or a gap between the completion of one situation and the onset of another. *Bar* means "in between," and *do* means "suspended" or "thrown." Bardo is a word made famous by the popularity of the *Tibetan Book of the Dead*. Since its first translation into English in 1927, this book has aroused enormous interest among psychologists, writers, and philosophers in the West, and has sold millions of copies.

The title *Tibetan Book of the Dead* was coined by its translator, the American scholar W. Y. Evans-Wentz, in imitation of the famous (and equally mistitled) *Egyptian Book of the Dead*.[1] The actual name of the book is *Bardo Tödrol Chenmo*, which means "the Great Liberation through Hearing in the Bardo." Bardo teachings are extremely ancient, and found in what are called the Dzogchen Tantras.[2] These teachings have a lineage stretching back beyond human masters to the Primordial Buddha (called in Sanskrit Samantabhadra, and in Tibetan Kuntuzangpo), who represents the absolute, naked, sky-like primordial purity of the nature of our mind. But the *Bardo Tödrol Chenmo* itself is part of one large cycle of teachings handed down by the master Padmasambhava and revealed in the fourteenth century by the Tibetan visionary Karma Lingpa.

The *Great Liberation through Hearing in the Bardo,* the *Tibetan Book of the Dead,* is a unique book of knowledge. It is a kind of guidebook or a travelogue of the after-death states, which is designed to be read by a master or spiritual friend to a person as the person dies, and after death. In Tibet there are said to be "Five Methods for Attaining Enlightenment without Meditation": on *seeing* a great master or sacred object; on *wearing* specially blessed drawings of mandalas with sacred mantras; on *tasting* sacred nectars, consecrated by the masters through special intensive practice; on *remembering* the transference of consciousness, the *phowa,* at the moment of death; and on *hearing* certain profound teachings, such as the *Great Liberation through Hearing in the Bardo.*

The *Tibetan Book of the Dead* is destined for a practitioner or someone who is familiar with its teachings. For a modern reader it is extremely difficult to penetrate, and raises a lot of questions that simply cannot be answered without some knowledge of the tradition that gave birth to it. This is especially the case since the book cannot be fully understood and used without knowing the unwritten oral instructions that a master transmits to a disciple, and which are the key to its practice.

In this book, then, I am setting the teachings, which the West has become familiar with through the *Tibetan Book of the Dead,* in a very much larger and more comprehensive context.

BARDOS

Because of the popularity of the *Tibetan Book of the Dead,* people usually associate the word bardo with death. It is true that "bardo" is used in everyday speech among Tibetans for the intermediate state between death and rebirth, but it has a much wider and deeper meaning. It is in the bardo teachings, perhaps more than anywhere else, that we can see just how profound and all-encompassing the buddhas' knowledge of life and death is, and how inseparable what we have called "life" and what we have called "death" truly are, when seen and understood clearly from the perspective of enlightenment.

We can divide the whole of our existence into four realities: life, dying and death, after-death, and rebirth. These are the Four Bardos:

- the "natural" bardo of this life
- the "painful" bardo of dying
- the "luminous" bardo of dharmata
- the "karmic" bardo of becoming

1. The natural bardo of this life spans the entire period between birth and death. In our present state of knowledge, this may seem more than just a bardo, a transition. But if we think about it, it will become clear that, compared to the enormous length and duration of our karmic history, the time we spend in this life is in fact relatively short. The teachings tell us emphatically that the bardo of this life is the only, and

therefore the best, time to prepare for death: by becoming familiar with the teaching and stabilizing the practice.

2. The painful bardo of dying lasts from the beginning of the process of dying right up until the end of what is known as the "inner respiration"; this, in turn, culminates in the dawning of the nature of mind, what we call the "Ground Luminosity," at the moment of death.

3. The luminous bardo of dharmata encompasses the after-death experience of the radiance of the nature of mind, the luminosity or "Clear Light," which manifests as sound, color, and light.

4. The karmic bardo of becoming is what we generally call the Bardo or intermediate state, which lasts right up until the moment we take on a new birth.

What distinguishes and defines each of the bardos is that they are all gaps or periods in which the possibility of awakening is particularly present. Opportunities for liberation are occurring continuously and uninterruptedly throughout life and death, and the bardo teachings are the key or tool that enables us to discover and recognize them, and to make the fullest possible use of them.

UNCERTAINTY AND OPPORTUNITY

One of the central characteristics of the bardos is that they are periods of deep uncertainty. Take this life as a prime example. As the world around us becomes more turbulent, so our lives become more fragmented. Out of touch and disconnected from ourselves, we are anxious, restless, and often paranoid. A tiny crisis pricks the balloon of the strategies we hide behind. A single moment of panic shows us how precarious and unstable everything is. To live in the modern world is to live in what is clearly a bardo realm; you don't have to die to experience one.

This uncertainty, which already pervades everything now, becomes even more intense, even more accentuated after we die, when our clarity or confusion, the masters tell us, will be "multiplied by seven."

Anyone looking honestly at life will see that we live in a constant state of suspense and ambiguity. Our minds are perpetually shifting in and out of confusion and clarity. If only we were confused all the time, that would at least make for some kind of clarity. What is really baffling about life is that sometimes, despite all our confusion, we can also be really wise! This shows us what the bardo is: a continuous, unnerving oscillation between clarity and confusion, bewilderment and insight, certainty and uncertainty, sanity and insanity. In our minds, as we are now, wisdom and confusion arise simultaneously, or, as we say, are "co-emergent." This means that we face a continuous state of choice between the two, and that everything depends on which we will choose.

This constant uncertainty may make everything seem bleak and almost hopeless; but if you look more deeply at it, you will see that its very nature creates gaps, spaces in which profound chances and opportunities for transformation are continuously flowering—if, that is, they can be seen and seized.

Because life is nothing but a perpetual fluctuation of birth, death, and transition, so bardo experiences are happening to us all the time and are a basic part of our psychological makeup. Normally, however, we are oblivious to the bardos and their gaps, as our mind passes from one so-called "solid" situation to the next, habitually ignoring the transitions that are always occurring. In fact, as the teachings can help us to understand, every moment of our experience is a bardo, as each thought and each emotion arises out of, and dies back into, the essence of mind. It is in moments of strong change and transition especially, the teachings make us aware, that the true sky-like, primordial nature of our mind will have a chance to manifest.

Let me give you an example. Imagine that you come home one day after work to find your door smashed open, hanging on its hinges. You have been robbed. You go inside and find that everything you own has vanished. For a moment you are paralyzed with shock, and in despair you frantically go through the mental process of trying to recreate what is gone. It hits you: You've lost everything. Your restless, agitated mind is then stunned, and thoughts subside. And there's a sudden, deep stillness, almost an experience of bliss. No more struggle, no more effort, because both are hopeless. Now you just have to give up; you have no choice.

So one moment you have lost something precious, and then, in the very next moment, you find your mind is resting in a deep state of peace. When this kind of experience occurs, do not immediately rush to find solutions. Remain for a while in that state of peace. Allow it to be a gap. And if you really rest in that gap, looking into the mind, you will catch a glimpse of the deathless nature of the enlightened mind.

The deeper our sensitivity and the more acute our alertness to the amazing opportunities for radical insight offered by gaps and transitions like these in life, the more inwardly prepared we will be for when they occur in an immensely more powerful and uncontrolled way at death.

This is extremely important, because the bardo teachings tell us that there are moments when the mind is far freer than usual, moments far more powerful than others, which carry a far stronger karmic charge and implication. The supreme one of these is the moment of death. For at that moment the body is left behind, and we are offered the greatest possible opportunity for liberation.

However consummate our spiritual mastery may be, we are limited by the body and its karma. But with the physical release of death comes the most marvelous opportunity to fulfill everything we have been striving for in our practice and our life. Even in the case of a supreme master who has reached the highest realization, the ultimate release, called *parinirvana,* dawns only at death. That is why in the Tibetan tradition we do not celebrate the birthdays of masters; we celebrate *their death,* their moment of final illumination.

In my childhood in Tibet, and years afterward, I have heard account after account of great practitioners, and even of seemingly ordinary yogins and laypeople, who died in an amazing and dramatic way. Not until that very last moment did they finally display the depth of their realization and the power of the teaching that they had come to embody.[3]

The Dzogchen Tantras, the ancient teachings from which the bardo instructions come, speak of a mythical bird, the *garuda,* which is born fully grown. This image symbolizes our primordial nature, which is already completely perfect. The garuda chick has all its wing feathers fully developed inside the egg, but it cannot fly before it hatches. Only at the moment when the shell cracks open can it burst out and soar up into the sky. Similarly, the masters tell us, the qualities of buddhahood are veiled by the body, and as soon as the body is discarded, they will be radiantly displayed.

The reason why the moment of death is so potent with opportunity is because it is then that the fundamental nature of mind, the Ground Luminosity or Clear Light, will naturally manifest, and in a vast and splendid way. If at this crucial moment we can recognize the Ground Luminosity, the teachings tell us, we will attain liberation.

This is not, however, possible unless you have become acquainted and really familiar with the nature of mind in your lifetime through spiritual practice. And this is why, rather surprisingly, it is said in our tradition that a person who is liberated at the moment of death is considered to be liberated in *this* lifetime, and *not* in one of the bardo states after death; for it is within this lifetime that the essential recognition of the Clear Light has taken place and been established. This is a crucial point to understand.

OTHER REALITIES

I have said that the bardos are opportunities, but what is it exactly about the bardos that makes it possible for us to seize the opportunities they offer? The answer is simple: They are all different states, and different realities, of mind.

In the Buddhist training we prepare, through meditation, to discover precisely the various interrelated aspects of mind, and skillfully enter different levels of consciousness. There is a distinct and exact relation between the bardo states and the levels of consciousness we experience throughout the cycle of life and death. So as we move from one bardo to another, both in life and death, there is a corresponding change in consciousness which, through spiritual practice, we can intimately acquaint ourselves with, and come, in the end, completely to comprehend.

Since the process that unfolds in the bardos of death is embedded in the depths of our mind, it manifests in life also at many levels. There is, for example, a vivid correspondence between the degrees in subtlety of consciousness we move through in sleep and dream, and the three bardos associated with death:

- Going to sleep is similar to the bardo of dying, where the elements and thought processes dissolve, opening into the experience of the Ground Luminosity.
- Dreaming is akin to the bardo of becoming, the intermediate state where you have a clairvoyant and highly mobile "mental body" that goes through all kinds of experiences. In the dream state too we have a similar kind of body, the dream body, in which we undergo all the experiences of dream life.
- In between the bardo of dying and the bardo of becoming is a very special state of luminosity or Clear Light called,

as I have said, the "bardo of dharmata." This is an experience that occurs to everyone, but there are very few who can even notice it, let alone experience it completely, as it can only be recognized by a trained practitioner. This bardo of dharmata corresponds to the period after falling asleep and before dreams begin.

Of course the bardos of death are much deeper states of consciousness than the sleep and dream states, and far more powerful moments, but their relative levels of subtlety correspond and show the kind of links and parallels that exist between all the different levels of consciousness. Masters often use this particular comparison to show just how difficult it is to maintain awareness during the bardo states. How many of us are aware of the change in consciousness when we fall asleep? Or of the moment of sleep before dreams begin? How many of us are aware even when we dream that we are dreaming? Imagine, then, how difficult it will be to remain aware during the turmoil of the bardos of death.

How your mind is in the sleep and dream state indicates how your mind will be in the corresponding bardo states; for example, the way in which you react to dreams, nightmares, and difficulties now shows how you might react after you die.

This is why the yoga of sleep and dream plays such an important part in the preparation for death. What a real practitioner seeks to do is to keep, unfailing and unbroken, his or her awareness of the nature of mind throughout day and night, and so use directly the different phases of sleep and dream to recognize and become familiar with what will happen in the bardos during and after death.

So we find two other bardos often included *within* the natural bardo of this life: the bardo of sleep and dream, and the bardo of meditation. Meditation is the practice of the daytime, and sleep and dream yoga the practices of the night. In the tradition to which the *Tibetan Book of the Dead* belongs, these two are added to the Four Bardos to make a series of Six Bardos.

LIFE AND DEATH IN THE PALM OF THEIR HAND

Each of the bardos has its own unique set of instructions and meditation practices, which are directed precisely to those realities and their particular states of mind. This is how the spiritual practices and training designed for each of the bardo states can enable us to make the fullest possible use of them and of their opportunities for liberation. The essential point to understand about the bardos is this: By following the training of these practices, *it is actually possible to realize these states of mind while we are still alive.* We can actually experience them while we are here now.

This kind of complete mastery of the different dimensions of mind may seem very hard for a Westerner to comprehend, but it is by no means impossible to attain.

Kunu Lama Tenzin Gyaltsen was an accomplished master, who came originally from the Himalayan region of northern India. When he was young he met a Lama in Sikkim, who advised him to go to Tibet to pursue his studies of Buddhism. So he went to Kham in eastern Tibet, where he received teachings from some of the greatest Lamas, including my master Jamyang Khyentse. Kunu Lama's knowledge of Sanskrit earned him respect and opened many doors for him. The masters were keen to teach him, in the hope that he would take these teachings back to India and pass them on there, where they knew the teachings had almost disappeared. During his time in Tibet, Kunu Lama became exceptionally learned and realized.

Eventually he did return to India, where he lived as a true ascetic. When my master and I came to India on pilgrimage after leaving Tibet, we searched for him everywhere in Benares. Finally we found him staying in a Hindu temple. No one knew who he was, or even that he was a Buddhist, let alone that he was a master. They knew him as a gentle, saintly yogin, and they offered him food. Whenever I think of him, I always say to myself, "This is what St. Francis of Assisi must have been like."

When the Tibetan monks and Lamas first came into exile, Kunu Lama was chosen to teach them grammar and Sanskrit at a school founded by the Dalai Lama. Many learned Lamas attended and studied with him, and they all considered him an excellent language teacher. But then one day someone happened to ask him a question regarding the teaching of Buddha. The answer he gave was extremely profound. So they went on asking him questions, and they found that whatever they asked, he knew the answer. He could in fact give any teaching that was asked for. So his reputation spread far and wide, and in no time at all he was teaching members of each of the different schools their own unique traditions.

His Holiness the Dalai Lama then took him as his spiritual guide. He acknowledged Kunu Lama as the inspiration for his teaching and practice of compassion. In fact, he was a living example of compassion. Yet even when he became well known he did not change. He still wore the same simple old clothes, and he lived in one small room. When anyone came and offered him a gift, he would make a present of it to his next visitor. And if someone cooked for him, he would eat; if not, he would go without.

One day a master whom I know well went to visit Kunu Lama, to ask him some questions about the bardos. This master is a professor, extremely well-versed in the tradition of the *Tibetan Book of the Dead,* and experienced in the practices connected with it. He told me how he asked his questions, and then listened, spellbound, to Kunu Lama's reply. He had never heard anything like it before. As he described the bardos, it was so vivid and precise that it was as if he were giving someone directions to go to Kensington High Street, or Central Park, or the Champs Elysées. It was as if he was actually there.

Kunu Lama was pointing out the bardos directly from his own experience. A practitioner of his caliber has journeyed through all the different dimensions of reality. And it is because the bardo states are all contained within our minds that they can be revealed and freed through the bardo practices.

These teachings come from the wisdom mind of the buddhas, who can see life and death like looking in the palm of their hand.

We too are buddhas. So if we can practice in the bardo of this life, and go deeper and deeper into the nature of our mind, then we can discover this knowledge of the bardos, and the truth of these teachings will unfold in us by itself. That is why the natural bardo of this life is of the utmost importance. It is here and now that the whole preparation for all the bardos takes place. "The supreme way of preparing," it is said, "is now—to become enlightened in this lifetime."

EIGHT

This Life: The Natural Bardo

LET US EXPLORE the first of the Four Bardos, the natural bardo of this life, and all its many implications; then we will proceed to explore the other three bardos in the appropriate time and order. The natural bardo of this life spans the whole of our lifetime between birth and death. Its teachings make clear to us why this bardo is such a precious opportunity, what it really means to be a human being, and what is the most important and only truly essential thing for us to do with the gift of this human life.

The masters tell us that there is an aspect of our minds that is its fundamental basis, a state called "the ground of the ordinary mind." Longchenpa, the outstanding fourteenth-century Tibetan master, describes it in this way: "It is unenlightenment and a neutral state, which belongs to the category of mind and mental events, and it has become the foundation of all karmas and 'traces' of samsara and nirvana."[1] It functions like a storehouse, in which the imprints of past actions caused by our negative emotions are all stored like seeds. When the right conditions arise, they germinate and manifest as circumstances and situations in our lives.

Imagine this ground of the ordinary mind as being like a bank in which karma is deposited as imprints and habitual tendencies. If we have a habit of thinking in a particular pattern, positive or negative, then these tendencies will be triggered and provoked very easily, and recur and go on recurring. With constant repetition our inclinations and habits become steadily more entrenched, and go on continuing, increasing and gathering power, even when we sleep. This is how they come to determine our life, our death, and our rebirth.

We often wonder: "How will I be when I die?" The answer to that is that whatever state of mind we are in *now*, whatever kind of person we are *now*: that's what we will be like at the moment of death, if we do not change. This is why it is so absolutely important to use *this* lifetime to purify our mind-stream, and so our basic being and character, while we can.

KARMIC VISION

How is it that we come to be alive as human beings? All beings who have similar karma will have a common vision of the world around them, and this set of perceptions they share is called "a karmic vision." That close correspondence between our karma and the kind of realm in which we find ourselves also explains how different forms arise: You and I, for example, are human beings because of the basic common karma that we share.

Yet even within the human realm, all of us have our own individual karma. We are born in different countries, cities, or families; we each have different upbringings, education, influences and beliefs, and all this conditioning comprises that karma. Each one of us is a complex summation of habits and past actions, and so we cannot but see things in our own uniquely personal way. Human beings look much the same but perceive things utterly differently, and we each live in our own unique and separate individual worlds. As Kalu Rinpoche says:

> *If a hundred people sleep and dream, each of them will experience a different world in his dream. Everyone's dream might be said to be true, but it would be meaningless to ascertain that only one person's dream was the true world and all others were fallacies. There is truth for each perceiver according to the karmic patterns conditioning his perceptions.*[2]

SIX REALMS

Our human existence is not the only kind of karmic vision. Six realms of existence are identified in Buddhism: gods, demigods, humans, animals, hungry ghosts, and hells. They are each the result of one of the six main negative emotions: pride, jealousy, desire, ignorance, greed, and anger.

Do these realms actually exist externally? They may, in fact, exist beyond the range of the perception of our karmic vision. Let's never forget: *What we see is what our karmic vision allows us to see, and no more.* Just as we, in the present, unpurified, and unevolved state of our perception, can only be aware of *this* universe, an insect might see one of our fingers as a whole landscape in itself. We are so arrogant that we believe only "seeing is believing." Yet the great Buddhist teachings speak of innumerable worlds in different dimensions—there may even be many worlds very like, or just like ours—and several modern astrophysicists have developed theories about the existence of parallel universes. How can we possibly say definitively what does or does not exist beyond the bounds of our limited vision?

Looking at the world around us, and into our own minds, we can see that the six realms definitely do exist. They exist in the way we unconsciously allow our negative emotions to project and crystallize entire realms around us, and to define the style, form, flavor, and context of our life in those realms. And they exist also inwardly as the different seeds and tendencies of the various negative emotions within our psychophysical system, always ready to germinate and grow, depending on what influences them and how we choose to live.

Let's look at how some of these realms are projected into and crystallized in the world around us. The main feature of the realm of the gods, for example, is that it is devoid of suffering, a realm of changeless beauty and sensual ecstasy. Imagine the gods: tall, blond surfers, lounging on beaches and in gardens flooded by brilliant sunshine, listening to any kind of music they choose, intoxicated by every kind of stimulant, high on meditation, yoga, bodywork, and ways of improving themselves, but never taxing their brains, never confronting any complex or painful situation, never conscious of their true nature, and so anesthetized that they are never aware of what their condition really is.

If some parts of California and Australia spring to mind as the realm of the gods, you can see the demigod realm being acted out every day perhaps in the intrigue and rivalry of Wall Street, or in the seething corridors of Washington and Whitehall. And the hungry ghost realms? They exist wherever people, though immensely rich, are never satisfied, craving to take over this company or that one, or endlessly playing out their greed in court cases. Switch on any television channel and you have entered immediately the world of demigods and hungry ghosts.

The quality of life in the realm of the gods may look superior to our own, yet the masters tell us that human life is infinitely more valuable. Why? Because of the very fact that we have the awareness and intelligence that are the raw materials for enlightenment, and because the very suffering that pervades this human realm is itself the spur to spiritual transformation. Pain, grief, loss, and ceaseless frustration of every kind are there for a real and dramatic purpose: to wake us up, to enable and almost to force us to break out of the cycle of samsara and so release our imprisoned splendor.

Every spiritual tradition has stressed that this human life is unique, and has a potential that ordinarily we hardly even begin to imagine. If we miss the opportunity this life offers us for transforming ourselves, they say, it may well be an extremely long time before we have another. Imagine a blind turtle, roaming the depths of an ocean the size of the universe. Up above floats a wooden ring, tossed to and fro on the waves. Every hundred years the turtle comes, once, to the surface. To be born a human being is said by Buddhists to be *more* difficult than for that turtle to surface accidentally with its head poking through the wooden ring. And even among those who have a human birth, it is said, those who have the great good fortune to make a connection with the teachings are rare; and those who really take them to heart and embody them in their actions even rarer, as rare, in fact, "as stars in broad daylight."

THE DOORS OF PERCEPTION

As I have said, how we perceive the world depends entirely on our karmic vision. The masters use a traditional example: six different kinds of being meet by the banks of a river. The human being in the group sees the river as water, a substance to wash in or to quench his thirst; for an animal such as a fish, the river is its home; the god sees it as nectar that brings bliss; the demigod as a weapon; the hungry ghost as pus and putrid blood; and the being from the hell realm as molten lava. The water is the same, but it is perceived in totally different, even contradictory, ways.

This profusion of perceptions shows us that all karmic visions are illusions; for if one substance can be perceived in so many different ways, how can anything have any one true, inherent reality? It also shows us how it is possible that some people feel this world as heaven, and others as hell.

The teachings tell us that there are essentially three kinds of vision: the "impure, karmic vision" of ordinary beings; the "vision of experience," which opens to practitioners in meditation and is the path or medium of transcendence; and the "pure vision" of realized beings. A realized being, or a buddha, will perceive this world as spontaneously perfect, a completely and dazzlingly pure realm. Since they have purified all the causes of karmic vision, they see everything directly in its naked, primordial sacredness.

Everything that we see around us is seen as it is because we have been repeatedly solidifying our experience of inner and outer reality in the same way, lifetime after lifetime, and this has led to the mistaken assumption that what we see is objectively real. In fact, as we go further along the spiritual path, we learn how to work directly with our fixed perceptions. All our old concepts of the world or matter or even ourselves are purified and dissolved, and an entirely new, what you could call "heavenly" field of vision and perception opens up. As Blake says:

> If the doors of perception were cleansed,
> Everything would appear . . . as it is, infinite.[3]

I shall never forget when Dudjom Rinpoche, in a moment of intimacy, leaned toward me and said in his soft, hoarse, slightly high-pitched voice: "You know, don't you, that actually all these things around us go away, just go away . . ."

With most of us, however, karma and negative emotions obscure the ability to see our own intrinsic nature, and the nature of reality. As a result we clutch onto happiness and suffering as real, and in our unskillful and ignorant actions go on sowing the seeds of our next birth. Our actions keep us bound to the continuous cycle of worldly existence, to the endless round of birth and death. So everything is at risk in how we live now, at this very moment: How we live now can cost us our entire future.

This is the real and urgent reason why we must prepare now to meet death wisely, to transform our karmic future, and to avoid the tragedy of falling into delusion again and again and repeating the painful round of birth and death. This life is the only time and place we can prepare in, and we can only truly prepare through spiritual practice: This is the inescapable message of the natural bardo of this life. As Padmasambhava says:

> Now when the bardo of this life is dawning upon me,
> I will abandon laziness for which life has no time,
> Enter, undistracted, the path of listening and hearing, reflection and
>   contemplation, and meditation,

Making perceptions and mind the path, and realize the "three
    kayas": the enlightened mind;[4]
Now that I have once attained a human body,
There is no time on the path for the mind to wander.

THE WISDOM OF EGOLESSNESS

I sometimes wonder what a person from a little village in
Tibet would feel if you suddenly brought him to a modern city
with all its sophisticated technology. He would probably think
he had already died and was in the Bardo state. He would
gape incredulously at the planes flying in the sky above him,
or at someone talking on the telephone to another person on
the other side of the world. He would assume he was witnessing miracles. And yet all this seems normal to someone
living in the modern world with a Western education, which
explains the scientific background to these things, step by step.

In just the same way, in Tibetan Buddhism there is a basic,
normal, elementary spiritual education, a complete spiritual
training for the natural bardo of this life, which gives you
the essential vocabulary, the ABC of the mind. The bases of
this training are what are called the "three wisdom tools":
the wisdom of listening and hearing; the wisdom of contemplation and reflection; and the wisdom of meditation.
Through them we are brought to reawaken to our true nature,
through them we uncover and come to embody the joy and
freedom of what we truly are, what we call "the wisdom of
egolessness."

Imagine a person who suddenly wakes up in hospital after
a road accident to find she is suffering from total amnesia.
Outwardly, everything is intact: she has the same face and
form, her senses and her mind are there, but she doesn't have
any idea or any trace of a memory of who she really is. In
exactly the same way, we cannot remember our true identity,
our original nature. Frantically, and in real dread, we cast
around and improvise another identity, one we clutch onto
with all the desperation of someone falling continuously into
an abyss. This false and ignorantly assumed identity is "ego."

So ego, then, is the absence of true knowledge of who we
really are, together with its result: a doomed clutching on, at
all costs, to a cobbled together and makeshift image of ourselves, an inevitably chameleon charlatan self that keeps
changing and has to, to keep alive the fiction of its existence.
In Tibetan ego is called *dak dzin,* which means "grasping to a
self." Ego is then defined as incessant movements of grasping

at a delusory notion of "I" and "mine," self and other, and all the concepts, ideas, desires, and activity that will sustain that false construction. Such a grasping is futile from the start and condemned to frustration, for there is no basis or truth in it, and what we are grasping at is by its very nature ungraspable. The fact that we need to grasp at all and go on and on grasping shows that in the depths of our being we know that the self does not inherently exist. From this secret, unnerving knowledge spring all our fundamental insecurities and fear.

So long as we haven't unmasked the ego, it continues to hoodwink us, like a sleazy politician endlessly parading bogus promises, or a lawyer constantly inventing ingenious lies and defenses, or a talk show host going on and on talking, keeping up a stream of suave and emptily convincing chatter, which actually says nothing at all.

Lifetimes of ignorance have brought us to identify the whole of our being with ego. Its greatest triumph is to inveigle us into believing its best interests are our best interests, and even into identifying our very survival with its own. This is a savage irony, considering that ego and its grasping are at the root of all our suffering. Yet ego is so convincing, and we have been its dupe for so long, that the thought that we might ever become egoless terrifies us. To be egoless, ego whispers to us, is to lose all the rich romance of being human, to be reduced to a colorless robot or a brain-dead vegetable.

Ego plays brilliantly on our fundamental fear of losing control, and of the unknown. We might say to ourselves: "I should really let go of ego, I'm in such pain; but if I do, what's going to happen to me?"

Ego will chime in, sweetly: "I know I'm sometimes a nuisance, and believe me, I quite understand if you want me to leave. But is that really what you want? Think: If I do go, what's going to happen to you? Who will look after you? Who will protect and care for you like I've done all these years?"

And even if we were to see through ego's lies, we are just too scared to abandon it; for without any true knowledge of the nature of our mind, or true identity, we simply have no other alternative. Again and again we cave in to its demands with the same sad self-hatred as the alcoholic feels reaching for the drink that he knows is destroying him, or the drug addict groping for the drug that she knows after a brief high will only leave her flat and desperate.

EGO ON THE SPIRITUAL PATH

To end the bizarre tyranny of ego is why we go on the spiritual path, but the resourcefulness of ego is almost infinite and it can at every stage sabotage and pervert our desire to be free of it. The truth is simple, and the teachings are extremely clear; but I have seen again and again, with great sadness, that as soon as they begin to touch and move us, ego tries to complicate them because it knows it is fundamentally threatened.

At the beginning, when we first become fascinated by the spiritual path and all its possibilities, ego may even encourage us and say: "This is really wonderful. Just the thing for you! This teaching makes total sense!"

Then when we say we want to try meditation practice, or go on a retreat, ego will croon: "What a marvelous idea! Why don't I come with you. We can both learn something." All through the honeymoon period of our spiritual development, ego will keep urging us on: "This is wonderful—it's so amazing, so inspiring . . ."

But as soon as we enter what I call the "kitchen sink" period of the spiritual path, and the teachings begin to touch us deeply, unavoidably we are faced with the truth of our selves. As the ego is revealed, its sore spots are touched, and all sorts of problems will start arising. It's as if a mirror we cannot look away from were stuck in front of us. The mirror is totally clear, but there is an ugly, glowering face in it, our own, staring back at us. We begin to rebel because we hate what we see; we may strike out in anger and smash the mirror, but it will only shatter into hundreds of identical ugly faces, all still staring at us.

Now is the time we begin to rage and complain bitterly; and where is our ego? Standing staunchly by our side, egging us on: "You're quite right, this is outrageous and unbearable. Don't stand for it!" As we listen enthralled, ego goes on to conjure up all sorts of doubts and demented emotions, throwing fuel on the fire: "Can't you see now this is not the right teaching for you? I told you so all along! Can't you see he is not your teacher? After all, you are an intelligent, modern, sophisticated Western person, and exotic things like Zen, Sufism, meditation, Tibetan Buddhism belong to foreign, Eastern cultures. What possible use could a philosophy made up in the Himalayas a thousand years ago be to you?"

As ego watches us gleefully become more and more ensnared in its web, it will even blame all the pain, loneliness, and difficulties we are going through as we come to know ourselves on the teaching, and even on the teacher: "These gurus don't care anyway, whatever you're going through. They are only out to exploit you. They just use words like 'compassion' and 'devotion' to get you in their power . . ."

Ego is so clever that it can twist the teachings for its own purposes; after all, "The devil can quote scriptures for his own ends." Ego's ultimate weapon is to point its finger hypocritically at the teacher and his followers, and say: "No one around here seems to be living up to the truth of the teachings!" Now ego poses as the righteous arbiter of all conduct: the shrewdest position of all from which to undermine your faith, and erode whatever devotion and commitment to spiritual change you have.

Yet however hard ego may try to sabotage the spiritual path, if you really continue on it, and work deeply with the practice of meditation, you will begin slowly to realize just how gulled you have been by ego's promises: false hopes and false fears. Slowly you begin to understand that both hope and fear are enemies of your peace of mind; hopes deceive you, and leave you empty and disappointed, and fears paralyze you in the narrow cell of your false identity. You begin to see also just how all-encompassing the sway of ego has been over your mind, and in the space of freedom opened up by meditation, when you are momentarily released from grasping, you glimpse the exhilarating spaciousness of your true nature. You realize that for years, your ego, like a crazy con artist, has been swindling you with schemes and plans and promises that have never been real and have only brought you to inner bankruptcy. When, in the equanimity of meditation, you see this, without any consolation or desire to cover up what you've discovered, all the plans and schemes reveal themselves as hollow and start to crumble.

This is not a purely destructive process. For alongside an extremely precise and sometimes painful realization of the fraudulence and virtual criminality of your ego, and everyone else's, grows a sense of inner expansiveness, a direct knowledge of the "egolessness" and interdependence of all things, and that vivid and generous humor that is the hallmark of freedom.

Because you have learned through discipline to simplify your life, and so reduced the opportunities for ego to seduce you; and because you have practiced the mindfulness of meditation, and through it loosened the hold of aggression, clinging, and negativity on your whole being, the wisdom of insight can slowly dawn. And in the all-revealing clarity of its sunlight this insight can show you, distinctly and directly, both the subtlest workings of your own mind and the nature of reality.

THE WISE GUIDE

Two people have been living in you all your life. One is the ego, garrulous, demanding, hysterical, calculating; the other is the hidden spiritual being, whose still voice of wisdom you have only rarely heard or attended to. As you listen more and more to the teachings, contemplate them, and integrate them into your life, your inner voice, your innate wisdom of discernment, what we call in Buddhism "discriminating awareness," is awakened and strengthened, and you start to begin to distinguish between its guidance and the various clamorous and enthralling voices of ego. The memory of your real nature, with all its splendor and confidence, begins to return to you.

You will find, in fact, that you have uncovered in yourself your own wise guide. Because he or she knows you through and through, since he or she *is* you, your guide can help you, with increasing clarity and humor, negotiate all the difficulties of your thoughts and emotions. Your guide can also be a continual, joyful, tender, sometimes teasing presence, who knows always what is best for you and will help you find more and more ways out of your obsession with your habitual responses and confused emotions. As the voice of your discriminating awareness grows stronger and clearer, you will start to distinguish between its truth and the various deceptions of the ego, and you will be able to listen to it with discernment and confidence.

The more often you listen to this wise guide, the more easily you will be able to change your negative moods yourself, see through them, and even laugh at them for the absurd dramas and ridiculous illusions that they are. Gradually you will find yourself able to free yourself more and more quickly from the dark emotions that have ruled your life, and this ability to do so is the greatest miracle of all. Tertön Sogyal, the Tibetan mystic, said that he was not really impressed by someone who could turn the floor into the ceiling or fire into water. A real miracle, he said, was if someone could liberate just one negative emotion.

More and more, then, instead of the harsh and fragmented gossip that ego has been talking to you all your life, you will find yourself hearing in your mind the clear directions of the teachings, which inspire, admonish, guide, and direct you at every turn. The more you listen, the more guidance you will receive. If you follow the voice of your wise guide, the voice of your discriminating awareness, and let ego fall silent, you come to experience that presence of wisdom and joy and bliss that you really are. A new life, utterly different from that when you were masquerading as your ego, begins in you. And when death comes, you will have learned already in life how to control those emotions and thoughts that in the states of death, the bardos, would otherwise take on an overwhelming reality.

When your amnesia over your identity begins to be cured, you will realize finally that dak dzin, grasping at self, is the root cause of all your suffering. You will understand at last how much harm it has done both to yourself and to others, and you will realize that both the noblest and the wisest thing to do is to cherish others instead of cherishing yourself. This will bring healing to your heart, healing to your mind, and healing to your spirit.

It is important to remember always that the principle of egolessness does not mean that there was an ego in the first place, and the Buddhists did away with it. On the contrary, it means there was never any ego at all to begin with. To realize that is called "egolessness."

THE THREE WISDOM TOOLS

The way to discover the freedom of the wisdom of egolessness, the masters advise us, is through the process of listening and hearing, contemplation and reflection, and meditation. They advise us to begin by *listening* repeatedly to the spiritual teachings. As we listen, they will keep on and on reminding us of our hidden wisdom nature. It is as if we were that person I asked you to imagine, lying in the hospital bed suffering from amnesia, and someone who loved and cared for us were whispering our real name in our ear, and showing us photos of our family and old friends, trying to bring back our knowledge of our lost identity. Gradually, as we listen to the teachings, certain passages and insights in them will strike a strange chord in us, memories of our true nature will start to trickle back, and a deep feeling of something homely and uncannily familiar will slowly awaken.

Listening is a far more difficult process than most people imagine; really to listen in the way that is meant by the masters is to let go utterly of ourselves, to let go of all the information, all the concepts, all the ideas, and all the prejudices that our heads are stuffed with. If you really listen to the teachings, those concepts that are our real hindrance, the one thing that stands between us and our true nature, can slowly and steadily be washed away.

In trying really to listen, I have often been inspired by the Zen master Suzuki-roshi, who said: "If your mind is empty, it is always ready for anything; it is open to everything. In the beginner's mind there are many possibilities, in the expert's mind there are few."[5] The beginner's mind is an open mind, an empty mind, a ready mind, and if we really listen with a beginner's mind, we might really begin to hear. For if we listen with a silent mind, as free as possible from the clamor of preconceived ideas, a possibility will be created for the truth of the teachings to pierce us, and for the meaning of life and death to become increasingly and startlingly clear. My master Dilgo Khyentse Rinpoche said: "The more and more you listen, the more and more you hear; the more and more you hear, the deeper and deeper your understanding becomes."

The deepening of understanding, then, comes through *contemplation* and reflection, the second tool of wisdom. As we contemplate what we've heard, it gradually begins to permeate our mindstream and saturate our inner experience of our lives. Everyday events start to mirror and more and more subtly and directly to confirm the truths of the teachings, as contemplation slowly unfolds and enriches what we have begun to understand intellectually and carries that understanding down from our head into our heart.

The third tool of wisdom is *meditation*. After listening to the teachings and reflecting on them, we put into action the insights we have gained and apply them directly, through the process of meditation, to the needs of everyday life.

DOUBTS ON THE PATH

Once, it seems, there was a time when an exceptional master could give one teaching to an exceptional student, and the student could attain liberation. Dudjom Rinpoche used to tell the story of a powerful bandit in India, who after countless successful raids, realized the terrible suffering he had been causing. He yearned for some way of atoning for what he had done, and visited a famous master. He asked him: "I am a sinner, I am in torment. What's the way out? What can I do?"

The master looked the bandit up and down and then asked him what he was good at.

"Nothing," replied the bandit.

"Nothing?" barked the master. "You must be good at something!" The bandit was silent for a while, and eventually admitted: "Actually, there is one thing I have a talent for, and that's stealing."

The master chuckled: "Good! That's exactly the skill you'll need now. Go to a quiet place and rob all your perceptions, and steal all the stars and planets in the sky, and dissolve them into the belly of emptiness, the all-encompassing space of the nature of mind." Within twenty-one days the bandit had realized the nature of his mind, and eventually came to be regarded as one of the great saints of India.

In ancient times, then, there were extraordinary masters and students as receptive and single-minded as that bandit, who could, by just practicing with unswerving devotion one single instruction, attain liberation. Even now, if we were to put our mind to one powerful wisdom method and work with it directly, there is a real possibility we would become enlightened.

Our minds, however, are riddled and confused with doubt. I sometimes think that doubt is an even greater block to human evolution than desire and attachment. Our society promotes cleverness instead of wisdom, and celebrates the most superficial, harsh, and least useful aspects of our intelligence. We have become so falsely "sophisticated" and neurotic that we take doubt itself for truth, and the doubt that is nothing more than ego's desperate attempt to defend itself from wisdom is deified as the goal and fruit of true knowledge. This form of mean-spirited doubt is the shabby emperor of samsara, served by a flock of "experts" who teach us not the open-souled and generous doubt that Buddha assured us was necessary for testing and proving the worth of the teachings, but a destructive form of doubt that leaves us nothing to believe in, nothing to hope for, and nothing to live by.

Our contemporary education, then, indoctrinates us in the glorification of doubt, has created in fact what could almost be called a religion or theology of doubt, in which to be seen to be intelligent we have to be seen to doubt everything, to always point to what's wrong and rarely to ask what's right or good, cynically to denigrate all inherited spiritual ideals and philosophies, or anything that is done in simple goodwill or with an innocent heart.

The Buddha summons us to another kind of doubt, "like analyzing gold, scorching, cutting, and rubbing it to test its purity." For that form of doubt that really would expose us to the truth if we followed it to the end, we have neither the insight, the courage, nor the training. We have been schooled in a sterile addiction to contradiction that has robbed us repeatedly of all real openness to any more expansive and ennobling truth.

In the place of our contemporary nihilistic form of doubt, then, I would ask you to put what I call a "noble doubt," the kind of doubt that is an integral part of the path toward enlightenment. The vast truth of the mystical teachings handed down to us is not something that our endangered world can afford to dismiss. Instead of doubting *them,* why don't we doubt ourselves: our ignorance, our assumption that we understand everything already, our grasping and evasion, our passion for so-called explanations of reality that have about them nothing of the awe-inspiring and all-encompassing wisdom of what the masters, the messengers of Reality, have told us?

This kind of noble doubt spurs us onward, inspires us, tests us, makes us more and more authentic, empowers us, and draws us more and more within the exalting energy field of the truth. When I am with my masters, I ask them again and again the questions I need answers to. Sometimes I don't get clear answers, but I do not doubt them or the truth of the teachings. Sometimes I may doubt my own spiritual maturity or my ability to really hear the truth in a way that I could fully understand, and more often I press on asking and asking, until I do get a clear answer. And when that answer comes, and rings strongly and purely in my mind, and my heart responds to it with a shock of gratitude and recognition, then a conviction is inspired in me that the derision of a world of doubters could not destroy.

I remember one winter, when I was driving with one of my students from Paris down to Italy on a clear and moonlit night. She worked as a therapist, and had undergone many different kinds of training. What she had realized, she told me, was that the more knowledge you have, the more doubts it gives rise to, and the subtler the excuses for doubting whenever the truth begins to touch you deeply. She had tried many times, she said, to run away from the teachings, but finally she realized that there was nowhere to run to, because what she was really trying to run away from was herself.

I told her that doubt is not a disease, but merely a symptom of a lack of what we in our tradition call "the View," which is the realization of the nature of mind, and so of the nature of reality. When that View is there completely, there will be no possibility for the slightest trace of doubt, for then we'll be looking at reality with its own eyes. But until we reach enlightenment, I said, there will inevitably be doubts, because doubt is a fundamental activity of the unenlightened mind, and the only way to deal with doubts is neither to suppress nor indulge them.

Doubts demand from us a real skillfulness in dealing with them, and I notice how few people have any idea how to pursue doubts or to use them. Isn't it ironic that in a civilization that so worships the power of deflation and doubt, hardly anyone has the courage to deflate the claims of doubt itself, to do as one Hindu master said: turn the dogs of doubt on doubt itself, to unmask cynicism and to uncover what fear, despair, hopelessness, and tired conditioning it springs from? Then doubt would no longer be an obstacle but a door to realization, and whenever doubt appeared in the mind, a seeker would welcome it as a means of going deeper into the truth.

There is a story I love about a Zen master. This master had a faithful but very naive student, who regarded him as a living buddha. Then one day the master accidentally sat down on a needle. He screamed, "Ouch!" and jumped into the air. The student instantly lost all his faith and left, saying how disappointed he was to find that his master was not fully enlightened. Otherwise, he thought, how would he jump up and scream out loud like that? The master was sad when he realized his student had left, and said: "Alas, poor man! If only he had known that in reality neither me, nor the needle, nor the 'ouch' really existed."

Don't let us make the same impulsive mistake as that Zen student. Don't let us take doubts with exaggerated seriousness, or let them grow out of proportion, or become black-and-white or fanatical about them. What we need to learn is how slowly to change our culturally conditioned and passionate involvement with doubt into a free, humorous, and compassionate one. This means giving doubts time, and giving ourselves time to find answers to our questions that are not merely intellectual or "philosophical," but living and real and genuine and workable. Doubts cannot resolve themselves immediately; but if we are patient a space can be created within us, in which doubts can be carefully and objectively examined, unraveled, dissolved, and healed. What we lack, especially in this culture, is the right undistracted and richly spacious environment of the mind, which can only be created through sustained meditation practice, and in which insights can be given the chance slowly to mature and ripen.

Don't be in too much of a hurry to solve all your doubts and problems; as the masters say, "Make haste slowly." I always tell my students not to have unreasonable expectations, because it takes time for spiritual growth. It takes years to learn Japanese properly or become a doctor: Can we really expect to have all the answers, let alone become enlightened, in a few weeks? The spiritual journey is one of continuous learning and purification. When you know this, you become humble. There is a famous Tibetan saying: "Do not mistake understanding for realization, and do not mistake realization for liberation." And Milarepa said: "Do not entertain hopes for realization, but practice all your life." One of the things I have come to appreciate most about my own tradition is its down-to-earth, no-nonsense practicality, and its acute sense that the greatest achievements take the deepest patience and the longest time.

NINE

The Spiritual Path

IN THE SUFI MASTER RUMI'S *Table Talk*, there is this fierce and pointed passage:

The master said there is one thing in this world which must never be forgotten. If you were to forget everything else, but were not to forget this, there would be no cause to worry, while if you remembered, performed and attended to everything else, but forgot that one thing, you would in fact have done nothing whatsoever. It is as if a king had sent you to a country to carry out one special, specific task. You go to the country and you perform a hundred other tasks, but if you have not performed the task you were sent for, it is as if you have performed nothing at all. So man has come into the world for a particular task, and that is his purpose. If he doesn't perform it, he will have done nothing.

All the spiritual teachers of humanity have told us the same thing, that the purpose of life on earth is to achieve union with our fundamental, enlightened nature. The "task" for which the "king" has sent us into this strange, dark country is to realize and embody our true being. There is only one way to do this, and that is to undertake the spiritual journey, with all the ardor and intelligence, courage and resolve for transformation that we can muster. As Death says to Nachiketas in the Katha Upanishad:

There is the path of wisdom and the path of ignorance. They are far apart and lead to different ends . . . Abiding in the midst of ignorance, thinking themselves wise and learned, fools go aimlessly hither and thither like the blind led by the blind. What lies beyond life shines not to those who are childish, or careless, or deluded by wealth.

FINDING THE WAY

At other times and in other civilizations, this path of spiritual transformation was confined to a relatively select number of people; now, however, a large proportion of the human race must seek the path of wisdom if the world is to be preserved from the internal and external dangers that threaten it. In this time of violence and disintegration, spiritual vision is not an elitist luxury but vital to our survival.

To follow the path of wisdom has never been more urgent or more difficult. Our society is dedicated almost entirely to the celebration of ego, with all its sad fantasies about success and power, and it celebrates those very forces of greed and ignorance that are destroying the planet. It has never been more difficult to hear the unflattering voice of the truth, and never more difficult, once having heard it, to follow it: because there is nothing in the world around us that supports our choice, and the entire society in which we live seems to negate every idea of sacredness or eternal meaning. So at the time of our most acute danger, when our very future is in doubt, we as human beings find ourselves at our most bewildered, and trapped in a nightmare of our own creation.

Yet there is one significant source of hope in this tragic situation, and that is that the spiritual teachings of all the great mystical traditions are still available. Unfortunately, however, there are very few masters to embody them, and an almost total lack of discrimination in those searching for the truth. The West has become a heaven for spiritual charlatans. In the case of a scientist, you can verify who is genuine and who is not, because other scientists can check their background and test their findings. Yet in the West, without the guidelines and criteria of a thriving and full-fledged wisdom culture, the authenticity of so-called "masters" is almost impossible to establish. Anyone, it seems, can parade as a master and attract a following.

This was not the case in Tibet, where choosing a particular path or teacher to follow was far safer. People coming to Tibetan Buddhism for the first time often wonder why such great importance is placed on lineage, on the unbroken chain of transmission from master to master. Lineage serves as a crucial safeguard: It maintains the authenticity and purity of the teaching. People know who a master is from who *his* master is. It is not a question of preserving some fossilized, ritualistic knowledge, but of transmitting from heart to heart, from mind to mind, an essential and living wisdom and its skillful and powerful methods.

Recognizing who is and who is not a true master is a very subtle and demanding business; and in an age like ours, addicted to entertainment, easy answers, and quick fixes, the more sober and untheatrical attributes of spiritual mastery might very well go unnoticed. Our ideas about what holiness is, that it is pious, bland, and meek, may make us blind to the dynamic and sometimes exuberantly playful manifestation of the enlightened mind.

As Patrul Rinpoche wrote: "The extraordinary qualities of great beings who hide their nature escapes ordinary people like us, despite our best efforts in examining them. On the other hand, even ordinary charlatans are expert at deceiving others by behaving like saints." If Patrul Rinpoche could write that in the last century in Tibet, how much more true must it be in the chaos of our contemporary spiritual supermarket?

So how are we today, in an extremely distrustful age, to find the trust that is so necessary in following the spiritual path? What criteria can we use to assess whether or not a master is genuine?

I remember vividly being with a master whom I know when he asked his students what had drawn them to him, and why they had trusted him. One woman said: "I've come to see how you really want, more than anything, for us to understand and apply the teachings, and how skillfully you direct them to help us do so." A man in his fifties said: "It's not what you know that moves me, but that you really do have an altruistic and a good heart."

A woman in her late thirties confessed: "I've tried to make you into my mother, my father, my therapist, my husband, my lover; you have calmly sat through the drama of all these projections and never ever turned away from me."

An engineer in his twenties said: "What I have found in you is that you are genuinely humble, that you really wish the very best for all of us, that as well as being a teacher you have never stopped being a student of your great masters." A young lawyer said: "For you it's the teachings that are the most important thing. Sometimes I even think that your ideal would be almost for *you* to become completely obsolete, simply to pass on the teachings as selflessly as possible."

Another student said shyly: "At first I was terrified at opening myself up to you. I've been hurt so often. But as I began to do so, I started to notice real changes in myself, and slowly I became more and more grateful to you, because I realized how much you were helping me. And then I discovered in myself a trust in you so deep, deeper than I'd ever imagined possible."

Finally a computer operator in his forties said: "You have been such a wonderful mirror for me, and you show me two things: the relative aspect of who I am, and the absolute aspect of who I am. I can look at you and see—not because of who you are but because of what you are mirroring back to me—all of my relative confusion, very clearly. But I can also look at you and I can see, reflected in you, the nature of mind, out of which everything is arising, moment by moment."

These replies show us that true teachers are kind, *compassionate,* tireless in their desire to share whatever wisdom they have acquired from their masters, never abuse or manipulate their students under any circumstances, never under any circumstances abandon them, serve not their own ends but the greatness of the teachings, and always remain humble. Real trust can and should only grow toward someone whom you come to know, over time, embodies all these qualities. You will find that this trust becomes the ground of your life, there to support you through all the difficulties of life and death.

In Buddhism we establish whether a teacher is authentic by whether or not the guidance he or she is giving accords with the teaching of Buddha. It cannot be stressed too often that it is *the truth of the teaching* which is all-important, and never the personality of the teacher. This is why Buddha reminded us in the "Four Reliances":

Rely on the message of the teacher, not on his personality;
Rely on the meaning, not just on the words;
Rely on the real meaning, not on the provisional one;
Rely on your wisdom mind, not on your ordinary, judgmental mind.

So it is important to remember that the true teacher, as we shall see, *is* the spokesman of the truth: its compassionate "wisdom display." All the buddhas, masters, and prophets, in fact, are the emanations of this truth, appearing in countless skillful, compassionate guises in order to guide us, through their teaching, back to our true nature. At first, then, more important than finding the teacher is finding and following the truth of the teaching, for it is through making a connection with the truth of the teaching that you will discover your living connection with a master.

HOW TO FOLLOW THE PATH

We all have the karma to meet one spiritual path or another, and I would encourage you, from the bottom of my heart, to follow with complete sincerity the path that inspires you most.

Read the great spiritual books of all the traditions, come to some understanding of what the masters might mean by liberation and enlightenment, and find out which approach to absolute reality really attracts and suits you most. Exercise in your search as much discernment as you can; the spiritual path demands more intelligence, more sober understanding, more subtle powers of discrimination than any other discipline, because the highest truth is at stake. Use your common sense at every moment. Come to the path as humorously aware as possible of the baggage you will be bringing with you: your lacks, fantasies, failings, and projections. Blend, with a soaring awareness of what your true nature might be, a down-to-earth and level-headed humility, and a clear appreciation of where you are on your spiritual journey and what still remains to be understood and accomplished.

The most important thing is not to get trapped in what I see everywhere in the West, a "shopping mentality": shopping around from master to master, teaching to teaching, without any continuity or real, sustained dedication to any one discipline. Nearly all the great spiritual masters of all traditions agree that the essential thing is to master one way, one path to the truth, by following one tradition with all your heart and mind to the end of the spiritual journey, while remaining open and respectful toward the insights of all others. In Tibet we used to say, "Knowing one, you accomplish all." The modern faddish idea that we can always keep all our options open and so never need commit ourselves to any thing is one of the greatest and most dangerous delusions of our culture, and one of ego's most effective ways of sabotaging our spiritual search.

When you go on searching all the time, the searching itself becomes an obsession and takes you over. You become a spiritual tourist, bustling about and never getting anywhere. As Patrul Rinpoche says, "You leave your elephant at home and look for its footprints in the forest." Following one teaching is not a way of confining you or jealously monopolizing you. It's a compassionate and skillful way of keeping you centered and always on the path, despite all the obstacles that you and the world will inevitably present.

So when you have explored the mystical traditions, choose one master and follow him or her. It's one thing to set out on the spiritual journey, its quite another to find the patience and endurance, the wisdom, courage, and humility to follow it to the end. You may have the karma to find a teacher, but you must then create the karma to follow your teacher. For very few of us know how truly to follow a master, which is an art in itself. So however great the teaching or master may be, what is essential is that you find in yourself the insight and skill to learn how to love and follow the master and the teaching.

This is not easy. Things will never be perfect. How could they be? We are still in samsara. Even when you have chosen your master and are following the teachings as sincerely as you can, you will often meet difficulties and frustrations, contradictions and imperfections. Don't succumb to obstacles and tiny difficulties. These are often only ego's childish emotions. Don't let them blind you to the essential and enduring value of what you have chosen. Don't let your impatience drag you away from your commitment to the truth. I have been saddened, again and again, to see how many people take up a teaching or master with enthusiasm and promise, only to lose heart when the smallest, unavoidable obstacles arise, then tumble back into samsara and old habits and waste years or perhaps a lifetime.

As the Buddha said in his first teaching, the root of all our suffering in samsara is *ignorance*. Ignorance, until we free ourselves from it, can seem endless, and even when we have embarked on the spiritual path our search is fogged by it. However, if you remember this, and keep the teachings in your heart, you will gradually develop the discernment to recognize the innumerable confusions of ignorance for what they are, and so never jeopardize your commitment or lose your perspective.

Life, as the Buddha told us, is as brief as a lightning flash; yet as Wordsworth said, "The world is too much with us: getting and spending, we lay waste our powers." It is that laying waste of our powers, that betrayal of our essence, that abandonment of the miraculous chance that this life, the natural bardo, gives us of knowing and embodying our enlightened nature, that is perhaps the most heartbreaking thing about human life. What the masters are essentially telling us is to stop fooling ourselves: What will we have learned, if at the moment of death we do not know who we really are? As the *Tibetan Book of the Dead* says:

> With mind far off, not thinking of death's coming,
> Performing these meaningless activities,
> Returning empty-handed now would be complete confusion;

The need is recognition, the spiritual teachings,
So why not practice the path of wisdom at this very moment?
From the mouths of the saints come these words:
If you do not keep your master's teaching in your heart
Will you not become your own deceiver?

THE MASTER

The Buddha says in one of the Tantras[1]: "Of all the buddhas who have ever attained enlightenment, not a single one accomplished this without relying upon a master, and of all the thousand buddhas that will appear in this eon, none of them will attain enlightenment without relying on a master."

In 1987, after my beloved master Dudjom Rinpoche passed away in France, I was sitting in a train, returning back to Paris from the south of France where he had lived. Images of his thousands of acts of generosity, tenderness, and compassion passed through my mind; I found myself in tears, saying to myself over and over again: "Had it not been for you, how could I possibly have understood?"

I realized, with an intimacy and poignancy that I had never experienced before, just why such a sacred emphasis is placed in our tradition on the relationship between master and disciple, and just how essential this relationship is to the living transmission of the truth, from mind to mind, from heart to heart. Without my masters, I would have had no possibility at all of realizing the truth of the teachings: I cannot imagine even having been able to reach the humble level of understanding that I have.

Many people in the West are suspicious of masters—often, unfortunately, for good reasons. I do not have to catalogue here the many dreadful and disappointing cases of folly, greed, and charlatanry that have occurred in the modern world since the opening to Eastern wisdom in the 1950s and 1960s. However, all the great wisdom traditions, whether Christian, Sufi, Buddhist, or Hindu, rely for their force on the master-disciple relationship. And so what the world needs urgently now is as clear as possible an understanding of what a real master is, and what a real student or disciple is, and what is the true nature of the transformation that takes place through devotion to the master, what you might call "the alchemy of discipleship."

Perhaps the most moving and accurate account of the true nature of the master I have ever heard comes from my master Jamyang Khyentse. He said that although our true nature is buddha, it has been obscured from beginningless time by a dark cloud of ignorance and confusion. This true nature, however, our buddha nature, has never completely surrendered to the tyranny of ignorance; somewhere it is always rebelling against its domination.

Our buddha nature, then, has an active aspect, which is our "inner teacher." From the very moment we became obscured, this inner teacher has been working tirelessly for us, tirelessly trying to bring us back to the radiance and spaciousness of our true being. Not for one second, Jamyang Khyentse said, has the inner teacher given up on us. In its infinite compassion, one with the infinite compassion of all the buddhas and all the enlightened beings, it has been ceaselessly working for our evolution—not only in this life but in all our past lives also—using all kinds of skillful means and all types of situations to teach and awaken us, and to guide us back to the truth.

When we have prayed and aspired and hungered for the truth for a long time, for many, many lives, and when our karma has become sufficiently purified, a kind of miracle takes place. And this miracle, if we can understand and use it, can lead to the ending of ignorance forever: The inner teacher, who has been with us always, manifests in the form of the "outer teacher," whom, almost as if by magic, we actually encounter. This encounter is the most important of any lifetime.

Who is this outer teacher? None other than the embodiment and voice and representative of our inner teacher. The master whose human shape and human voice and wisdom we come to love with a love deeper than any other in our lives is none other than the external manifestation of the mystery of our own inner truth. What else could explain why we feel so strongly connected to him or her?

At the deepest and highest level, the master and the disciple are not and cannot ever be in any way separate; for the master's task is to teach us to receive, without any obscuration of any kind, the clear message of our own inner teacher, and to bring us to realize the continual presence of this ultimate teacher within us. I pray that all of you may taste, in this life, the joy of this most perfect kind of friendship.

Not only is the master the direct spokesman of your own inner teacher, he or she is also the bearer, channel, and transmitter of all the blessings of all the enlightened beings. That is what gives your master the extraordinary power to illumine your mind and heart. He or she is nothing less than the human face of the absolute, the telephone, if you like, through which all the buddhas and all the enlightened beings can call you. He or she is the crystallization of the wisdom of all the buddhas, and the embodiment of their compassion directed always toward you: the rays of their universal sunlight aimed directly at your heart and mind in order to liberate you.

In my tradition we revere the master for being even kinder than the buddhas themselves. Although the compassion and power of the buddhas are always present, our obscurations prevent us from meeting the buddhas face to face. But we *can* meet the master; he or she is here, living, breathing, speaking, acting, before us to show us, in all the ways possible, the path of the buddhas: the way to liberation. For me, my masters have been the embodiment of living truth, undeniable signs that enlightenment is possible in a body, in this life, in this world, even here and even now, the supreme inspirations in my practice, in my work, in my life, and in my journey toward liberation. My masters are for me the embodiments of my sacred commitment to keep enlightenment foremost in my mind until I actually achieve it. I know enough to know that only when I reach enlightenment will I have a complete understanding of who they really are and of their infinite generosity, love, and wisdom.

I would like to share with you this beautiful prayer, the words of Jikmé Lingpa, a prayer we say in Tibet to invoke the presence of the master in our heart:

From the blossoming lotus of devotion, at the center of my heart,
Rise up, O compassionate master, my only refuge!
I am plagued by past actions and turbulent emotions:
To protect me in my misfortune
Remain as the jewel-ornament on the crown of my head, the mandala
*   of great bliss,*
Arousing all my mindfulness and awareness, I pray!

THE ALCHEMY OF DEVOTION

Just as Buddha said that of all the buddhas who attained enlightenment, not one accomplished this without relying on the master, he also said: "It is only through devotion, and devotion alone, that you will realize the absolute truth."

The absolute truth cannot be realized within the domain of the ordinary mind. And the path beyond the ordinary mind, all the great wisdom traditions have told us, is through the heart. This path of the heart is devotion.

Dilgo Khyentse Rinpoche wrote:

> There is only one way of attaining liberation and of obtaining the omniscience of enlightenment: following an authentic spiritual master. He is the guide that will help you to cross the ocean of samsara.
>
> The sun and the moon are reflected in clear, still water instantly. Similarly, the blessings of all the buddhas are always present for those who have complete confidence in them. The sun's rays fall everywhere uniformly, but only where they are focused through a magnifying glass can they set dry grass on fire. When the all-pervading rays of the Buddha's compassion are focused through the magnifying glass of your faith and devotion, the flame of blessings blazes up in your being.

So then, it is essential to know what real devotion is. It is not mindless adoration; it is not abdication of your responsibility to yourself, nor undiscriminating following of another's personality or whim. Real devotion is an unbroken receptivity to the truth. Real devotion is rooted in an awed and reverent gratitude, but one that is lucid, grounded, and intelligent.

When the master is able to open your innermost heart, and offers you an undeniably powerful glimpse of the nature of your mind, a wave of joyful gratitude surges up in you toward the one who helped you to see, and the truth that you now realize the master embodies in his or her being, teachings, and wisdom mind. That uncontrived, genuine feeling is always rooted in repeated, undeniable, inner experience—a repeated clarity of direct recognition—and *this,* and this only, is what we call devotion, *mö gü* in Tibetan. *Mö gü* means "longing and respect": *respect* for the master, which grows deeper and deeper as you understand more and more who he or she really is, and *longing* for what he or she can introduce in you, because you have come to know the master is your heart link with the absolute truth and the embodiment of the true nature of your mind.

Dilgo Khyentse Rinpoche tells us,

> At first this devotion may not be natural or spontaneous, so we must employ a variety of techniques to help us to achieve this. Chiefly we

must always remember the excellent qualities of the teacher, especially
his kindness to us. By repeatedly generating confidence, appreciation
to the guru, and devotion toward him, a time will come when the
mere mention of his name or the thought of him will stop all our
ordinary perceptions, and we will see him as the Buddha himself.[2]

To see the master not as a human being, but as the Buddha
himself, is the source of the highest blessing. For as Padmasambhava says: "Complete devotion brings complete blessing;
absence of doubts brings complete success." The Tibetans
know that if you relate to your teacher as a buddha, you will
receive the blessing of a buddha, but if you relate to your master as a human being, you will only get the blessing of a
human being. So to receive the full transformative power of
the blessing of his or her teaching, the complete unfolding of
its glory, you must try and unfold in yourself the richest possible kind of devotion. Only if you come to see your master
as a buddha can a buddha-like teaching come through to you
from your master's wisdom mind. If you cannot recognize
your master as a buddha, but see him or her as a human
being, the full blessing can never be there, and even the greatest teaching will leave you somewhere unreceptive.

The more I come to reflect on devotion and its place and
role in the overall vision of the teachings, the more deeply I
realize that it is essentially a skillful and powerful means of
making us more receptive to the truth of the master's teaching. Masters themselves do not need our adoration, but seeing
them as living buddhas will enable us to listen to and hear
their message and to follow their instructions with the
greatest possible fidelity. Devotion, then, is in one sense the
most practical way of ensuring a total respect for, and therefore openness to, the teachings, as embodied by the master
and transmitted through him or her. The more devoted you
are, the more open you are to the teachings; the more open
you are to the teachings, the more chance there is for them to
penetrate your heart and mind, and so bring about a complete
spiritual transformation.

So it is only by seeing your master as a living buddha that
the process of transformation of yourself into a living buddha
can be truly begun and truly accomplished. When your
mind and heart are fully open in joy and wonder and recognition and gratitude to the mystery of the living presence of
enlightenment in the master, then slowly, over many years,

transmission from the master's wisdom mind and heart to yours can take place, revealing to you the full splendor of your own buddha nature, and with it the perfect splendor of the universe itself.

This most intimate relationship between disciple and master becomes a mirror, a living analogy for the disciple's relationship to life and the world in general. The master becomes the pivotal figure in a sustained practice of "pure vision," which culminates when the disciple sees directly and beyond any doubt: the master as the living buddha, his or her every word as buddha speech, his or her mind the wisdom mind of all the buddhas, his or her every action an expression of buddha activity, the place where he or she lives as nothing less than a buddha realm, and even those around the master as a luminous display of his or her wisdom.

As these perceptions become more and more stable and actual, the inner miracle disciples have longed for over so many lives can gradually take place: They begin to see naturally that they, the universe, and all beings without exception are spontaneously pure and perfect. They are looking at last at reality with its own eyes. The master, then, is the path, the magical touchstone for a total transformation of the disciple's every perception.

Devotion becomes the purest, quickest, and simplest way to realize the nature of our mind and all things. As we progress in it, the process reveals itself as wonderfully interdependent: We, from our side, try continually to generate devotion, the devotion we arouse itself generates glimpses of the nature of mind, and these glimpses only enhance and deepen our devotion to the master who is inspiring us. So in the end devotion springs out of wisdom: devotion and the living experience of the nature of mind become inseparable, and inspire one another.

The teacher of Patrul Rinpoche was called Jikmé Gyalwé Nyugu. For many years he had been doing a solitary retreat in a cave in the mountains. One day when he came outside, the sun was pouring down; he gazed out into the sky and saw a cloud moving in the direction of where his master, Jikmé Lingpa, lived. The thought rose in his mind, "Over there is where my master is," and with that thought a tremendous feeling of longing and devotion surged up in him. It was so strong, so shattering, that he fainted. When Jikmé Gyalwé Nyugu came to, the entire blessing of his master's wisdom mind had been transmitted to him, and he had reached the highest stage of realization, what we call "the exhaustion of phenomenal reality."

THE STREAM OF BLESSINGS

Such stories about the power of devotion and the blessing of the master do not merely belong to the past. In a figure like Khandro Tsering Chödrön, the greatest woman master of our day, who was the wife of my master Jamyang Khyentse, you see very clearly what years of the deepest devotion and practice can create out of the human spirit. Her humility and beauty of heart, and the shining simplicity, modesty, and lucid, tender wisdom of her presence are honored by all Tibetans, even though she herself has tried as far as possible to remain in the background, never to push herself forward, and to live the hidden and austere life of an ancient contemplative.

Jamyang Khyentse has been the inspiration of Khandro's entire life. It was her spiritual marriage to him that transformed her from a very beautiful and slightly rebellious young woman into the radiant *dakini*³ that other great masters hold in the highest regard. Dilgo Khyentse Rinpoche looked to her as a "spiritual mother," and always used to say how privileged he felt that of all the Lamas she revered and loved him most deeply. Whenever he used to see Khandro, he would take her hand and tenderly caress it, and then slowly place it on his head; he knew that was the only way he could ever get Khandro to bless him.

Jamyang Khyentse gave Khandro all the teachings, and trained her and inspired her to practice. Her questions to him would be in the form of songs, and he would write songs back to her, in an almost teasing and playful way. Khandro has demonstrated her undying devotion to her master by continuing to live after his death in the place in Sikkim where he lived toward the end of his life, and where he died, and where his relics are kept, enshrined in a *stupa*.⁴ There, near him, she carries on her clear, independent life, devoted to constant prayer. She has read the whole *Word of the Buddha* and hundreds of volumes of commentaries, slowly, word by word. Dilgo Khyentse Rinpoche used to say that every time he went back to the stupa of Jamyang Khyentse, he felt as if he were coming home, because Khandro's presence made the atmosphere so rich and warm. It was as if, he implied, my master Jamyang Khyentse was still present and still alive, in her devotion and her being.

Again and again, I have heard Khandro say that if your link with your master is kept really pure, then everything will go well in your life. Her own life is the most moving and exquisite example of this. Devotion has enabled her to embody the heart of the teachings and radiate their warmth to others. Khandro does not teach in a formal way, in fact, she does not speak a great deal; but what she does say can often be so penetratingly clear that it becomes prophetic. To listen to her fervent and blissful chanting, or to practice with her, is to be inspired to the depths of your being. Even to walk with her, or shop, or simply sit with her is to bathe in the powerful, quiet happiness of her presence.

Because Khandro is so retiring, and because her greatness is in her ordinariness, only those with real insight see who she is. We live in a time when those who thrust themselves forward are frequently admired the most, but it is in the humble, like Khandro, that the truth really lives. And if Khandro were ever to teach in the West, she would be a perfect master: the very greatest kind of woman master, one who incarnates with a mysterious completeness the love and healing wisdom of Tara, enlightened compassion in its female form. If I were to die, and Khandro were there next to me, I would feel more confident and more at peace than if any other master were by my side.

All that I have realized I have realized through devotion to my masters. Increasingly, as I go on teaching, I become aware, humbly and with real awe, of how their blessings are beginning to work through me. I am nothing without their blessing, and if there is anything I feel I can do, it is acting as a bridge between you and them. Again and again, I notice that when I speak of my masters in my teaching, my devotion to them inspires a vision of devotion in those listening; and in those marvelous moments I feel my masters are present, blessing and opening the hearts of my students to the truth.

I remember in Sikkim in the 1960s, not long after my master Jamyang Khyentse had died, Dilgo Khyentse Rinpoche was giving a long set of initiations, the visionary teachings of Padmasambhava, which can take several months to bestow. Many masters were there in a monastery in the hills behind Gangtok, the capital, and I was sitting with Khandro Tsering

Chödrön and Lama Chokden, Jamyang Khyentse's assistant and master of ceremonies.

It was then that I experienced, in the most vivid way, the truth of how a master can transmit the blessing of his wisdom mind to a student. One day Dilgo Khyentse Rinpoche gave a teaching about devotion and about our master Jamyang Khyentse, which was extraordinarily moving; the words flowed from him in a torrent of eloquence and the purest spiritual poetry. Again and again, as I listened to Dilgo Khyentse Rinpoche and watched him, I was reminded in the most mysterious way of Jamyang Khyentse himself, and how he had been able simply to speak and pour out, as if from a hidden inexhaustible source, the most exalted teaching. Slowly I realized, with wonder, what had happened: the blessing of the wisdom mind of Jamyang Khyentse had been transmitted completely to his heart-son Dilgo Khyentse Rinpoche, and was now, before us all, speaking effortlessly through him.

At the end of the teaching, I turned to Khandro and Chokden, and I saw that tears were streaming down their faces. "We knew that Dilgo Khyentse was a great master," they said, "and we know how it is said that a master will transmit the entire blessing of his wisdom mind to his heart-son. But it is only now, only today, only here, that we realize what this truly means."

Thinking again of that wonderful day in Sikkim, and of those great masters I have known, these words of a Tibetan saint that have always inspired me return to me: "When the sun of fierce devotion shines on the snow mountain of the master, the stream of his blessings will pour down," and I remember the words of Dilgo Khyentse Rinpoche himself, which express perhaps more eloquently than any other passage I know the vast and noble qualities of the master:

He is like a great ship for beings to cross the perilous ocean of existence, an unerring captain who guides them to the dry land of liberation, a rain that extinguishes the fire of the passions, a bright sun and moon that dispel the darkness of ignorance, a firm ground that can bear the weight of both good and bad, a wish-fulfilling tree that bestows temporal happiness and ultimate bliss, a treasury of vast and deep instructions, a wish-fulfilling jewel granting all the qualities of realization, a father and a mother giving their love equally to all sentient beings, a great river of compassion, a mountain rising above worldly concerns unshaken by the winds of emotions, and a great cloud filled with rain to soothe the torments of the passions. In brief,

he is the equal of all the buddhas. To make any connection with him,
whether through seeing him, hearing his voice, remembering him, or
being touched by his hand, will lead us toward liberation. To have
full confidence in him is the sure way to progress toward enlighten-
ment. The warmth of his wisdom and compassion will melt the ore of
our being and release the gold of the buddha-nature within.[5]

I have become aware of the blessings of my masters trick-
ling down to me almost imperceptibly and informing my
mind. Ever since Dudjom Rinpoche died, my students tell me
my teachings became more flowing, more lucid. Not long
ago, after hearing Dilgo Khyentse Rinpoche give a particularly
astonishing teaching, I expressed my deep admiration for him
and said: "It's almost miraculous how effortlessly and spontaneously these teachings flow from your wisdom mind." He
leaned toward me tenderly, with a teasing glint in his eye.
"And may your teachings in English flow in exactly the same
way," he said. Since then, through no doing of my own, I
have felt my ability to express the teachings grow more and
more natural. I consider this book to be a manifestation of the
blessing of my masters, transmitted through the wisdom
mind of the ultimate master and supreme guide, Padmasambhava. This book, then, is their gift to you.

It is my devotion to my masters that gives me the strength
to teach, and the openness and receptivity to learn, and go on
learning. Dilgo Khyentse Rinpoche himself never stopped
humbly receiving teachings from other masters, and often
those who were his own disciples. The devotion that gives
the inspiration to teach, then, is also the devotion that gives
the humility to go on learning. Gampopa, Milarepa's greatest
disciple, asked him, at the moment of their parting, "When
will be the time for me to start guiding students?" Milarepa
replied, "When you are not like you are now, when your
whole perception has been transformed, and you are able to
see, really see, this old man before you as nothing less than
the Buddha himself. When devotion has brought you to that
moment of recognition, that moment will be the sign that
the time for you to teach has come."

These teachings have been brought to you from Padmasambhava's enlightened heart, across centuries, over a thousand years, by an unbroken lineage of masters, each one of
whom only became masters because they had learned
humbly to be disciples, and remained, in the deepest sense,

disciples of their masters all their lives. Even at the age of eighty-two, when Dilgo Khyentse Rinpoche spoke of his master Jamyang Khyentse, tears of gratitude and devotion came to his eyes. In his last letter to me before he died, he signed himself "the worst disciple." That showed me how endless true devotion is, how with the greatest possible realization comes the greatest devotion and the most complete, because the most humble, gratitude.

GURU YOGA: MERGING WITH THE WISDOM MIND OF THE MASTER

All the buddhas, bodhisattvas, and enlightened beings are present at all moments to help us, and it is through the presence of the master that all of their blessings are focused directly at us. Those who know Padmasambhava know the living truth of the promise he made over a thousand years ago: "I am never far from those with faith, or even from those without it, though they do not see me. My children will always, always, be protected by my compassion."

All we need to do to receive direct help is to ask. Didn't Christ also say: "Ask, and it shall be given you; seek and ye shall find; knock and it shall be opened unto you. Everyone that asketh receiveth; and he that seeketh findeth"?[6] And yet asking is what we find hardest. Many of us, I feel, hardly know *how* to ask. Sometimes it is because we are arrogant, sometimes because we are unwilling to seek for help, sometimes because we are lazy, sometimes our minds are so busy with questions, distractions, and confusion that the simplicity of asking does not occur to us. The turning point in any healing of alcoholics or drug addicts is when they admit their illness and ask for aid. In one way or another, we are all addicts of samsara; the moment when help can come for us is when we admit our addiction and simply ask.

What most of us need, almost more than anything, is the courage and humility really to ask for help, from the depths of our hearts: to ask for the compassion of the enlightened beings, to ask for purification and healing, to ask for the power to understand the meaning of our suffering and transform it; at a *relative* level to ask for the growth in our lives of clarity, of peace, of discernment, and to ask for the realization of the *absolute* nature of mind that comes from merging with the deathless wisdom mind of the master.

There is no swifter, more moving, or more powerful practice for invoking the help of the enlightened beings, for arousing devotion and realizing the nature of mind, than the practice of Guru Yoga. Dilgo Khyentse Rinpoche wrote, "The words Guru Yoga mean 'union with the nature of the guru,' and in this practice we are given methods by which we can blend our own minds with the enlightened mind of the master."[7] Remember that the master—the guru—embodies the crystallization of the blessings of all buddhas, masters, and enlightened beings. So to invoke him or her is to invoke them all; and to merge your mind and heart with your master's wisdom mind is to merge your mind with the truth and very embodiment of enlightenment.

The outer teacher introduces you directly to the truth of your inner teacher. The more it is revealed through his or her teaching and inspiration, the more you begin to realize that outer and inner teacher are indivisible. As you gradually discover the truth of this for yourself, by invoking it again and again in the practice of Guru Yoga, a deepening confidence, gratitude, joy, and devotion are born in you, through which your mind and the wisdom mind of the master do actually become indivisible. In a Guru Yoga practice he composed at my request, Dilgo Khyentse Rinpoche wrote:

> *That which accomplishes the great purity of perception*
> *Is devotion, which is the radiance of Rigpa . . .*
> *Recognizing and remembering that my own Rigpa is the master—*
> *Through this, may your mind and mine merge as one.*

This is why all the wisdom traditions of Tibet have placed so much importance on the practice of Guru Yoga, and all the foremost Tibetan masters have treasured it as their innermost heart practice. Dudjom Rinpoche wrote:

> *It is vital to put all your energy into the Guru Yoga, holding onto it as the life and heart of the practice. If you do not, then your meditation will be very dull, and even if you do make a little progress, there will be no end to obstacles, and no possibility of true, genuine realization being born within the mind. So by fervently praying with uncontrived devotion, after a while the direct blessing of the wisdom mind of the master will be transmitted, empowering you with a unique realization, beyond words, born deep within your mind.*

What I would like to give you now is a simple practice of Guru Yoga that anyone, whatever their religion or spiritual belief, can do.

This wonderful practice is my main practice, the heart and inspiration of my whole life, and whenever I do the Guru

Yoga, it is Padmasambhava that I focus on. As Buddha himself was passing away, he prophesied that Padmasambhava would be born not long after his death in order to spread the teaching of the Tantras. It was Padmasambhava, as I have said, who established Buddhism in Tibet in the eighth century. For us Tibetans, Padmasambhava, Guru Rinpoche, embodies a cosmic, timeless principle; he is the universal master. He has appeared countless times to the masters of Tibet, and these meetings and visions have been precisely recorded: the date, the place, and manner in which they occurred, along with the teachings and prophecies Padmasambhava gave. He also left thousands of visionary teachings for future times, which have been revealed again and again by the many great masters who have been his emanations; one of these visionary treasures, or *termas,* is the *Tibetan Book of the Dead.*

I have always turned to Padmasambhava in times of difficulty and crisis, and his blessing and power have never failed me. When I think of him, all my masters are embodied in him. To me he is completely alive at all moments, and the whole universe, at each moment, shines with his beauty, strength, and presence.

> *O Guru Rinpoche, Precious One,*
> *You are the embodiment of*
> *The compassion and blessings of all the buddhas,*
> *The only protector of beings.*
> *My body, my possessions, my heart and soul*
> *Without hesitation, I surrender to you!*
> *From now until I attain enlightenment,*
> *In happiness or sorrow, in circumstances good or bad, in situations*
>   *high or low:*
> *I rely on you completely, O Padmasambhava, you who know me:*
>   *think of me, inspire me, guide me, make me one with you!*[8]

I consider Padmasambhava as the embodiment of all my masters, and so when I merge my mind with him in Guru Yoga, all of them are included within him. You can, however, use any enlightened being, saint, or master from any religion or mystical tradition for whom you feel devotion, whether they are alive or not.

This practice of Guru Yoga has four main phases: invocation; merging your mind with the master through his heart essence, the mantra; receiving the blessing or empowerment; and uniting your mind with the master and resting in the nature of Rigpa.

1. Invocation

Sit quietly. From the depths of your heart, invoke in the sky in front of you the embodiment of the truth in the person of your master, a saint, or an enlightened being.

Try to visualize the master or buddha as alive, and as radiant and translucent as a rainbow. Believe, with complete trust, that all the blessings and qualities of the wisdom, compassion, and power of all the buddhas and enlightened beings are embodied in him or her.

If you have difficulty visualizing the master, imagine this embodiment of truth simply as a being of light, or try to feel his or her perfect presence there in the sky before you: the presence of all the buddhas and masters. Let all the inspiration, joy, and awe you then feel take the place of visualization. Trust, simply, that the presence you are invoking *is* really there. The Buddha himself said: "Whoever thinks of me, I am in front of them." My master Dudjom Rinpoche used to say that it does not matter if at the beginning you cannot visualize; what is more important is to feel the presence in your heart, and know that this presence embodies the blessings, compassion, energy, and wisdom of all the buddhas.

Then, relaxing and filling your heart with the master's presence, invoke him or her very strongly with all your heart and mind; with total trust, call upon him or her inwardly: "Help me, inspire me to purify all my karma and negative emotions, and to realize the true nature of my mind!"

Then, with deep devotion, merge your mind with the master, and rest your mind in his or her wisdom mind. And as you do so, give yourself up to the master completely, saying to yourself something like: "Help me, now. Take care of me. Fill me with your joy and energy, your wisdom and compassion. Gather me into the loving heart of your wisdom mind. Bless my mind; inspire my understanding." Then, Dilgo Khyentse Rinpoche says: "There is *no doubt* that the blessing will enter your heart."

When we undertake this practice, it is a direct, skillful, and powerful way to carry us beyond our ordinary mind and into the pure realm of the wisdom of Rigpa. There, we recognize, come to discover, and acknowledge that all buddhas are present.

So, feeling the living presence of Buddha, of Padmasambhava, of your master, and simply opening your heart and mind to the embodiment of truth, really does bless and transform your mind. As you invoke the Buddha, your own buddha nature is inspired to awaken and blossom, as naturally as a flower in sunlight.

2. Maturing and Deepening the Blessing

When I come to this part of the practice, merging my mind with the master through the mantra, I recite the mantra OM AH HUM VAJRA GURU PADMA SIDDHI HUM (pronounced by Tibetans: Om Ah Hung Benza Guru Péma Siddhi Hung), which I think of as actually *being* Padmasambhava, and the blessing of all the masters, in the form of sound. I imagine my whole being filled with him, and I feel, as I recite the mantra—which is his heart essence—that it vibrates and pervades me, as if hundreds of little Padmasambhavas in the form of sound were circulating inside me, transforming my whole being.

Using the mantra, then, offer your heart and soul in fervent and one-pointed devotion, and merge and mix and blend your mind with Padmasambhava or your master. Gradually you will feel yourself coming closer to Padmasambhava, and closing the gap between you and his wisdom mind. Slowly, through the blessing and power of this practice, you will find you actually experience your mind being transformed into the wisdom mind of Padmasambhava and the master: You begin to recognize their indivisibility. Just as if you put your finger into water, it will get wet, and if you put it into fire, it will burn, so if you invest your mind in the wisdom mind of the buddhas, it will transform into their wisdom nature. What happens is that gradually your mind begins to find itself in the state of Rigpa, as the innermost nature of mind *is* nothing other than the wisdom mind of all the buddhas. It is as if your ordinary mind gradually dies and dissolves, and your pure awareness, your buddha nature, your inner teacher, is revealed. This is the true meaning of "blessing"—a transformation in which your mind transcends into the state of the absolute.

This "maturing of the blessing" is the heart and main part of the practice, to which you should devote the most time when you do the Guru Yoga practice.

3. Empowerment

Imagine now that from the master thousands of brilliant rays of light stream out toward you, and penetrate you, purifying, healing, blessing, empowering, and sowing in you the seeds of enlightenment.

To make the practice as rich and inspiring as possible, you could imagine it unfolding in these three phases:

First, dazzling light, crystal white in color, bursts out from the forehead of the master and enters the energy center in your forehead and fills your whole body. This white light represents the blessing of the body of all the buddhas: It cleanses all the negative karma you have accumulated through negative actions of the body; it purifies the subtle channels of your psycho-physical system; it gives you the blessing of the body of the buddhas; it empowers you for visualization practice; and it opens you to the realization of that compassionate energy of Rigpa, the nature of mind, that is manifesting in everything.

Second, a stream of ruby red light shines out from the throat of the master into the energy center at your throat, filling your entire body. This red light represents the blessing of the speech of all the buddhas: it cleanses all the negative karma you have accumulated through harmful speech; it purifies the inner air of your psycho-physical system; it gives you the blessing of the speech of the buddhas; it empowers you for mantra practice; and it opens you to the realization of the radiance of the nature of Rigpa.

Third, a stream of shimmering blue light, the color of lapis lazuli, bursts out from the heart of the master into the energy center at your heart, and fills your whole body. This blue light represents the blessing of the mind of the buddhas: It cleanses all the negative karma you have accumulated through negative activity of your mind; it purifies the creative essence, or energy, within your psycho-physical system; it gives you the blessing of the mind of the buddhas; it empowers you for advanced yoga practices; and it opens you to the realization of the primordial purity of the essence of Rigpa.

Know and feel that you are now empowered, through the blessing, with the indestructible body, speech, and mind of Padmasambhava, of all the buddhas.

4. Resting in the Rigpa

Now let the master dissolve into light and become one with you, in the nature of your mind. Recognize beyond any doubt that this sky-like nature of your mind is the absolute master. Where else would all the enlightened beings be but in the Rigpa, in the nature of your mind?

Secure in that realization, in a state of spacious and carefree ease, you rest in the warmth, glory, and blessing of your absolute nature. You have arrived at the original ground: the primordial purity of natural simplicity. As you rest in this state of Rigpa, you recognize the truth of Padmasambhava's words: "Mind itself is Padmasambhava; there is no practice or meditation apart from that."

I have given this practice here, as part of the natural bardo of this life, because this is the most important practice in life and so the most important practice at the moment of death. Guru Yoga, as you will see in chapter 13, "Spiritual Help for the Dying," forms the basis of the practice of phowa, the transference of consciousness at the moment of death. For if, at the moment of death, you can unite your mind confidently with the wisdom mind of the master and die in that peace, then all, I promise and assure you, will be well.

Our task in life, then, is to practice this merging with the wisdom mind of the master again and again, so that it becomes so natural that every activity—sitting, walking, eating, drinking, sleeping, dreaming, and waking—starts to be increasingly permeated by the master's living presence. Slowly, over years of focused devotion, you begin to know and realize all appearances to be the display of the wisdom of the master. All the situations of life, even those that once seemed tragic, meaningless, or terrifying, reveal themselves more and more transparently to be the direct teaching and blessing of the master, and the inner teacher. As Dilgo Khyentse Rinpoche says:

> Devotion is the essence of the path, and if we have in mind nothing but the guru and feel nothing but fervent devotion, whatever occurs is perceived as his blessing. If we simply practice with this constantly present devotion, this is prayer itself.
>
> When all thoughts are imbued with devotion to the guru, there is a natural confidence that this will take care of whatever may happen. All forms are the guru, all sounds are prayer, and all gross and subtle thoughts arise as devotion. Everything is spontaneously liberated in the absolute nature, like knots untied in the sky.[9]

TEN

The Innermost Essence

NO ONE CAN DIE FEARLESSLY and in complete security until they have truly realized the nature of mind. For only this realization, deepened over years of sustained practice, can keep the mind stable during the molten chaos of the process of death. Of all the ways I know of helping people to realize the nature of mind, that of the practice of Dzogchen, the most ancient and direct stream of wisdom within the teachings of Buddhism, and the source of the bardo teachings themselves, is the clearest, most effective, and most relevant to the environment and needs of today.

The origins of Dzogchen are traced to the Primordial Buddha, Samantabhadra, from whom it has been handed down in an unbroken line of great masters to the present. Hundreds of thousands of individuals in India, the Himalayas, and Tibet have attained realization and enlightenment through its practice. There is a wonderful prophecy that "in this dark age, the heart essence of Samantabhadra will blaze like fire." My life, my teachings, and this book are dedicated to lighting this fire in the hearts and minds of the world.

My constant support and inspiration and guide in this is the supreme master Padmasambhava. He is the essential spirit of Dzogchen, its greatest exponent and its human embodiment, with his glorious qualities of magnanimity, miraculous power, prophetic vision, awakened energy, and boundless compassion.

Dzogchen was not widely taught in Tibet, and for a while many of the greatest masters did not teach it in the modern world. Why then am I teaching it now? Some of my masters have told me that this *is* the time for Dzogchen to spread, the time alluded to in the prophecy. I feel too that it would be uncompassionate not to share with people the existence of such an extraordinary wisdom. Human beings have come to a critical place in their evolution, and this age of extreme confusion demands a teaching of comparably extreme power and clarity. I have also found that modern people want a path shorn of dogma, fundamentalism, exclusivity, complex metaphysics, and culturally exotic paraphernalia, a path at once simple and profound, a path that does not need to be practiced in ashrams or monasteries but one that can be integrated with ordinary life and practiced anywhere.

So what, then, is Dzogchen? Dzogchen is not simply a teaching, not another philosophy, not another elaborate system, not a seductive clutch of techniques. Dzogchen is a state, *the* primordial state, that state of total awakening that is the heart-essence of all the buddhas and all spiritual paths, and the summit of an individual's spiritual evolution. Dzogchen is often translated as "Great Perfection." I prefer to leave it untranslated, for Great Perfection carries a sense of a perfectness we have to strive to attain, a goal that lies at the end of a long and grueling journey. Nothing could be further from the true meaning of Dzogchen: the *already* self-perfected state of our primordial nature, which needs no "perfecting," for it has always been perfect from the very beginning, just like the sky.

All the Buddhist teachings are explained in terms of "Ground, Path, and Fruition." The Ground of Dzogchen is this fundamental, primordial state, our absolute nature, which is already perfect and always present. Patrul Rinpoche says: "It is neither to be sought externally, nor is it something you did not have before and that now has to be newly born in your mind." So from the point of view of the Ground—the absolute—our nature is the same as the buddhas', and there is no question at this level, "not a hair's breadth," the masters say, of teaching or practice to do.

Yet, we have to understand, the buddhas took one path and we took another. The buddhas recognize their original nature and become enlightened; we do not recognize that nature and so become confused. In the teachings, this state of affairs is called "One Ground, Two Paths." Our relative condition is that our intrinsic nature *is* obscured, and we need to follow the teachings and practice in order to return us to the truth: This is the Path of Dzogchen. Finally, to realize our original nature is to attain complete liberation and become a buddha. This is the Fruition of Dzogchen and is actually possible, if a practitioner really puts his or her heart and mind to it, in one lifetime.

The Dzogchen masters are acutely aware of the dangers of confusing the absolute with the relative. People who fail to understand this relationship can overlook and even disdain the relative aspects of spiritual practice and the karmic law of cause and effect. However, those who truly seize the meaning of Dzogchen will have only a deeper respect for karma, as well as a keener and more urgent appreciation of the need for purification and for spiritual practice. This is because they will understand the vastness of what it is in them that has been obscured, and so endeavour all the more fervently, and with an always fresh, natural discipline, to remove whatever stands between them and their true nature.

The Dzogchen teachings are like a mirror that reflects the Ground of our original nature with such a soaring and liberating purity, and such a stainless clarity, that we are inherently safeguarded from being imprisoned in any form of conceptually fabricated understanding, however subtle, or convincing, or seductive.

What, then, for me is the wonder of Dzogchen? All of the teachings lead to enlightenment, but the uniqueness of Dzogchen is that even in the relative dimension of the teachings, the language of Dzogchen never stains the absolute with concepts; it leaves the absolute unspoiled in its naked, dynamic, majestic simplicity, and yet still speaks of it to anyone of an open mind in terms so graphic, so electric, that even before we become enlightened, we are graced with the strongest possible glimpse of the splendor of the awakened state.

THE VIEW

The practical training of the Dzogchen Path is traditionally, and most simply, described in terms of View, Meditation, and Action. To see directly the absolute state, the Ground of our being, is the View; the way of stabilizing that View and making it an unbroken experience is Meditation; and integrating the View into our entire reality, and life, is what is meant by Action.

What then is the View? It is nothing less than *seeing* the actual state of things as they are; it is *knowing* that the true nature of mind is the true nature of everything; and it is *realizing* that the true nature of our mind is the absolute truth. Dudjom Rinpoche says: "The View is the comprehension of the naked awareness, within which everything is contained: sensory perception and phenomenal existence, samsara and nirvana. This awareness has two aspects: 'emptiness' as the absolute, and appearances or perception as the relative."

What this means is that the entire range of all possible appearances, and all possible phenomena in all the different realities, whether samsara or nirvana, all of these without exception have always been and will always be perfect and complete, within the vast and boundless expanse of the nature of mind. Yet even though the essence of everything is empty and "pure from the very beginning," its nature is rich in noble qualities, pregnant with every possibility, a limitless, incessantly and dynamically creative field that is always spontaneously perfect.

You might ask: "If realizing the View is realizing the nature of mind, what then is the nature of mind like?" Imagine a sky, empty, spacious, and pure from the beginning; its *essence* is like this. Imagine a sun, luminous, clear, unobstructed, and spontaneously present; its *nature* is like this. Imagine that sun shining out impartially on us and all things, penetrating all directions; its *energy*, which is the manifestation of compassion, is like this: Nothing can obstruct it and it pervades everywhere.

You can also think of the nature of mind like a mirror, with five different powers or "wisdoms." Its openness and vastness is the "wisdom of all-encompassing space," the womb of compassion. Its capacity to reflect in precise detail whatever comes before it is the "mirror-like wisdom." Its fundamental lack of any bias toward any impression is the "equalizing wisdom." Its ability to distinguish clearly, without confusing in any way the various different phenomena that arise, is the "wisdom of discernment." And its potential of having everything already accomplished, perfected, and spontaneously present is the "all-accomplishing wisdom."

In Dzogchen the View is introduced to the student directly by the master. It is the directness of this introduction that characterizes Dzogchen and makes it unique.

What is transmitted to the student in the introduction is the direct experience of the wisdom mind of the buddhas, through the blessing of a master who embodies its complete realization. To be able to receive the introduction, students have to have arrived at a point where, as a result of past aspirations and purified karma, they have both the openness of mind and devotion to make them receptive to the true meaning of Dzogchen.

How can the wisdom mind of the buddhas be introduced? Imagine the nature of mind as your own face; it is always with you, but you cannot see it without help. Now imagine that you have never seen a mirror before. The introduction by the master is like holding up a mirror suddenly in which you can, for the first time, see your own face reflected. Just like your face, this pure awareness of Rigpa is not something "new" that the master is giving you which you did not have before, nor is it something you could possibly find outside of yourself. It has always been yours, and has always been with you, but up until that startling moment you have never actually seen it directly.

Patrul Rinpoche explains that, "According to the special tradition of the great masters of the practice lineage, the nature of mind, the face of Rigpa, is introduced upon the very dissolution of conceptual mind." In the moment of introduction, the master cuts through the conceptual mind altogether, laying bare the naked Rigpa and revealing explicitly its true nature.

In that powerful moment, a merging of minds and hearts takes place, and the student has an undeniable experience, or glimpse, of the nature of Rigpa. In one and the same moment, the master introduces and the student recognizes. As the master directs his blessing from the wisdom of his Rigpa into the heart of the Rigpa of his student, the master shows the student directly the original face of the nature of mind.

For the master's introduction to be fully effective, however, the right conditions or environment have to be created. Only a few special individuals in history, because of their purified karma, have been able to recognize and become enlightened in an instant; and so the introduction must almost always be preceded by the following preliminaries. It is these preliminaries that purify and peel away the ordinary mind and bring you to the state wherein your Rigpa can be revealed to you.

First, meditation, the supreme antidote to distraction, brings the mind home and enables it to settle into its natural state.

Second, deep practices of purification, and the strengthening of positive karma through the accumulation of merit and wisdom, start to wear away and dissolve the emotional and intellectual veils that obscure the nature of mind. As my master Jamyang Khyentse wrote: "If the obscurations are removed, the wisdom of one's own Rigpa will naturally shine." These purification practices, called *Ngöndro* in Tibetan, have been skillfully designed to effect a comprehensive inner transformation. They involve the entire being—body, speech, and mind—and begin with a series of deep contemplations on

- the uniqueness of human life
- the ever-presence of impermanence and death
- the infallibility of the cause and effect of our actions
- the vicious cycle of frustration and suffering that is samsara.

These reflections inspire a strong sense of "renunciation," an urgent desire to emerge from samsara and follow the path to liberation, which forms the foundation for the specific practices of

- taking refuge in the Buddha, the truth of his teaching and the example of its practitioners, and so awakening a confidence and trust in our own inner buddha nature
- giving birth to compassion (*Bodhicitta*—the heart of the enlightened mind, which I shall explain in detail in chapter 12) and training the mind to work with ourself and others, and the difficulties of life
- removing obscurations and "defilements" through the visualization and mantra practice of purification and healing
- accumulating merit and wisdom by developing universal generosity and creating auspicious circumstances.[1]

All these practices build up to and center around the Guru Yoga, which is the most crucial, moving and powerful practice of all, indispensable for opening the heart and mind to the realization of the state of Dzogchen.[2]

Third, a special meditative investigation into the nature of mind and phenomena exhausts the mind's restless hunger for thinking and research, and its dependence on endless conceptualizing, analysis, and references, and awakens a personal realization of the nature of emptiness.

I cannot stress strongly enough how important these preliminaries are. They have to work hand in hand systematically, to inspire the student to awaken the nature of mind, and to enable the student to be ready and prepared when the master chooses the time to show him or her the original face of Rigpa.

Nyoshul Lungtok, who later became one of the greatest Dzogchen masters of recent times, followed his teacher Patrul Rinpoche for about eighteen years. During all that time, they were almost inseparable. Nyoshul Lungtok studied and practiced extremely diligently, and accumulated a wealth of purification, merit, and practice; he was ready to recognize the Rigpa, but had not yet had the final introduction. Then, one famous evening, Patrul Rinpoche gave him the introduction. It happened when they were staying together in one of the hermitages high up in the mountains above Dzogchen Monastery.[3] It was a very beautiful night. The dark blue sky was clear and the stars shone brilliantly. The sound of their solitude was heightened by the distant barking of a dog from the monastery below.

Patrul Rinpoche was lying stretched out on the ground, doing a special Dzogchen practice. He called Nyoshul Lungtok over to him, saying: "Did you say you do not know the essence of the mind?"

Nyoshul Lungtok guessed from his tone that this was a special moment and nodded expectantly.

"There's nothing to it really," Patrul Rinpoche said casually, and added: "My son, come and lie down over here: be like your old father." Nyoshul Lungtok stretched out by his side.

Then Patrul Rinpoche asked him, "Do you see the stars up there in the sky?"

"Yes."

"Do you hear the dogs barking in Dzogchen Monastery?"

"Yes."

"Do you hear what I'm saying to you?"

"Yes."

"Well, the nature of Dzogchen is this: simply this."

Nyoshul Lungtok tells us what happened then: "At that instant, I arrived at a certainty of realization from within. I had been liberated from the fetters of "it is" and "it is not." I had realized the primordial wisdom, the naked union of emptiness and intrinsic awareness. I was introduced to this realization by his blessing, as the great Indian master Saraha said:

He in whose heart the words of the master have entered,
Sees the truth like a treasure in his own palm."[4]

At that moment everything fell into place; the fruit of all Nyoshul Lungtok's years of learning, purification, and practice was born. He attained the realization of the nature of mind. There was nothing extraordinary or esoteric or mystical about the words Patrul Rinpoche used; in fact, they were extremely ordinary. But beyond the words something else was being communicated. What he was revealing was the inherent nature of everything, which is the true meaning of Dzogchen.

At that moment he had already brought Nyoshul Lungtok directly into that state through the power and blessing of his realization.

But masters are very different, and they can use all kinds of skillful means to provoke that shift of consciousness. Patrul Rinpoche himself was introduced to the nature of mind in a very different way, by a highly eccentric master called Do Khyentse. This is the oral tradition that I heard of this story.

Patrul Rinpoche had been doing an advanced practice of yoga and visualization, and had become stuck; none of the mandalas of the deities would appear clearly in his mind.[5] One day he came upon Do Khyentse, who had made a fire out in the open and was sitting in front of it drinking tea. In Tibet when you see a master for whom you have deep devotion, traditionally you begin to prostrate your body on the ground as a mark of your respect. As Patrul Rinpoche started prostrating from a distance, Do Khyentse spotted him and growled menacingly, "Hey, you old dog! If you are brave, then come over here!" Do Khyentse was a very impressive master. He was like a samurai, with his long hair, his rakish clothes, and his passion for riding beautiful horses. As Patrul Rinpoche continued doing prostrations and began to approach closer, Do Khyentse, cursing him all the time, started to hurl pebbles at him, and gradually larger rocks and stones. When he finally came within reach, Do Khyentse started punching him and knocked him out altogether.

When Patrul Rinpoche came to, he was in an entirely different state of consciousness. The mandalas he had been trying so hard to visualize spontaneously manifested in front of him. Each of Do Khyentse's curses and insults had destroyed the last remnants of Patrul Rinpoche's conceptual mind, and each stone that hit him opened up the energy centers and subtle channels in his body. For two marvelous weeks the visions of the mandalas did not leave him.

I am going to attempt now to give some sense of what the View is like and how it feels when the Rigpa is directly revealed, even though all words and conceptual terms fail, really, to describe it.

Dudjom Rinpoche says: "That moment is like taking a hood off your head. What boundless spaciousness and relief! This is the supreme seeing: seeing what was not seen before." When you "see what was not seen before," everything opens, expands, and becomes crisp, clear, brimming with life, vivid with wonder and freshness. It is as if the roof of your mind were flying off, or a flock of birds suddenly took off from a dark nest. All limitations dissolve and fall away, as if, the Tibetans say, a seal were broken open.

Imagine you were living in a house on the top of a mountain, which was itself at the top of the whole world. Suddenly the entire structure of the house, which limited your view, just falls away and you can see all around you, both outside and inside. But there is not any "thing" to see; what happens has no ordinary reference whatsoever; it is total, complete, unprecedented, perfect seeing.

Dudjom Rinpoche says: "Your deadliest enemies, the ones who have kept you tied to samsara through countless lives from beginningless time up until the present, are the grasping and the grasped." When the master introduces and you recognize, "These two are burned away completely like feathers in a flame, leaving no trace." Both grasping and grasped, what is grasped and the grasper, are freed completely from their very basis. The roots of ignorance and suffering are severed utterly. And all things appear like a reflection in a mirror, transparent, shimmering, illusory, and dream-like.

When you naturally arrive at this state of meditation, inspired by the View, you can remain there for a long time without any distraction or special effort. Then there is nothing called "meditation" to protect or sustain, for you are in the natural flow of the wisdom of Rigpa. And you realize, when you are in it, that is how it has always been, and is. When the wisdom of Rigpa shines, not one shadow of doubt can remain, and a deep, complete understanding arises, effortlessly and directly.

All the images I have given and the metaphors I have tried to use you will discover to be fused in one all-comprehensive experience of truth. Devotion is in this state, and compassion is in this state, and all the wisdoms, and bliss, clarity, and absence of thoughts, but not separate from one another, all integrated and linked inextricably with each other in one taste. This moment is the moment of awakening. A profound sense of humor wells up from within, and you smile in amusement at how inadequate all your former concepts and ideas about the nature of mind were.

What springs from this is a growing sense of tremendous and unshakeable certainty and conviction that "this is it": There is nothing further to seek, nothing more that could possibly be hoped for. This certainty of the View is what has to be deepened through glimpse after glimpse of the nature of mind, and stabilized through the continuous discipline of meditation.

MEDITATION

What, then, is meditation in Dzogchen? It is simply resting, undistracted, in the View, once it has been introduced. Dudjom Rinpoche describes it: "Meditation consists of being attentive to such a state of Rigpa, free from all mental constructions, whilst remaining fully relaxed, without any distraction or grasping. For it is said that 'Meditation is not striving, but naturally becoming assimilated into it.'"

The whole point of Dzogchen meditation practice is to strengthen and stabilize Rigpa, and allow it to grow to full maturity. The ordinary, habitual mind with its projections is extremely powerful. It keeps returning, and takes hold of us easily when we are inattentive or distracted. As Dudjom Rinpoche used to say, "At present our Rigpa is like a little baby, stranded on the battlefield of strong arising thoughts." I like to say we have to begin by babysitting our Rigpa, in the secure environment of meditation.

If meditation is simply to continue the flow of Rigpa after the introduction, how do we know when it is Rigpa and when it is not? I asked Dilgo Khyentse Rinpoche this question, and he replied with his characteristic simplicity: "If you are in an unaltered state, it is Rigpa." If we are not contriving or manipulating the mind in any way, but simply resting in an unaltered state of pure and pristine awareness, then that *is* Rigpa. If there is any contriving on our part or any kind of manipulating or grasping, it is not. Rigpa is a state in which there is no longer any doubt; there is not really a mind to doubt: You see directly. If you are in this state, a complete, natural certainty and confidence surge up with the Rigpa itself, and that is how you know.[6]

The tradition of Dzogchen is one of extreme precision, since the deeper you go, the subtler the deceptions that can arise, and what is at stake is the knowledge of absolute reality. Even after the introduction, the masters clarify in detail the states that are not Dzogchen meditation and must not be confused with it. In one of these states you drift into a no-man's land of the mind, where there are no thoughts or memories; it is a dark, dull, indifferent state, where you are plunged into the ground of the ordinary mind. In a second state, there is some stillness and slight clarity, but the state of stillness is a stagnant one, still buried in the ordinary mind. In a third you experience an absence of thoughts, but are "spaced out" in a vacant state of wonder. In a fourth your mind wanders away, hankering after thoughts and projections. None of these are the true state of meditation, and the practitioner has to watch out skillfully to avoid being deluded in these ways.

The essence of meditation practice in Dzogchen is encapsulated by these four points:

- When one past thought has ceased and a future thought has not yet risen, in that gap, in between, isn't there a consciousness of the present moment; fresh, virgin, unaltered by even a hair's breadth of concept, a luminous, naked awareness?

  Well, that is what Rigpa is!

- Yet it doesn't stay in that state forever, because another thought suddenly arises, doesn't it?

  This is the self-radiance of that Rigpa.

- However, if you do not recognize this thought for what it really is, the very instant it arises, then it will turn into just another ordinary thought, as before. This is called the "chain of delusion," and is the root of samsara.

- If you are able to recognize the true nature of the thought as soon as it arises, and leave it alone without any follow-up, then whatever thoughts that arise all automatically dissolve back into the vast expanse of Rigpa and are liberated.

Clearly it takes a lifetime of practice to understand and realize the full richness and majesty of these four profound yet simple points, and here I can only give you a taste of the vastness of what is meditation in Dzogchen.

Perhaps the most important point is that Dzogchen meditation comes to be a continual flow of Rigpa, like a river constantly moving day and night without any interruption. This, of course, is an ideal state, for this undistracted resting in the View, once it has been introduced and recognized, is the reward of years of sustained practice.

Dzogchen meditation is subtly powerful in dealing with the arisings of the mind, and has a unique perspective on them. All the risings are seen in their true nature, not as separate from Rigpa, and not as antagonistic to it, but actually as none other—and this is very important—than its "self-radiance," the manifestation of its very energy.

Say you find yourself in a deep state of stillness; often it does not last very long and a thought or a movement always arises, like a wave in the ocean. Don't reject the movement or particularly embrace the stillness, but continue the flow of your pure presence. The pervasive, peaceful state of your meditation is the Rigpa itself, and all risings are none other than this Rigpa's self-radiance. This is the heart and the basis of Dzogchen practice. One way to imagine this is as if you were riding on the sun's rays back to the sun: You trace the risings back, at once, to their very root, the ground of Rigpa. As you embody the steadfast stability of the View, you are no longer deceived and distracted by whatever rises, and so cannot fall prey to delusion.

Of course there are rough as well as gentle waves in the ocean; strong emotions come, like anger, desire, jealousy. The real practitioner recognizes them not as a disturbance or obstacle, but as a great opportunity. The fact that you react to arisings such as these with habitual tendencies of attachment and aversion is a sign not only that you are distracted, but also that you do not have the recognition and have lost the ground of Rigpa. To react to emotions in this way empowers them and binds us even tighter in the chains of delusion. The great secret of Dzogchen is to see right through them as soon as they arise, to what they really are: the vivid and electric manifestation of the energy of Rigpa itself. As you gradually learn to do this, even the most turbulent emotions fail to seize hold of you and dissolve, as wild waves rise and rear and sink back into the calm of the ocean.

The practitioner discovers—and this is a revolutionary insight, whose subtlety and power cannot be overestimated—that not only do violent emotions not necessarily sweep you away and drag you back into the whirlpools of your own neuroses, they can actually be used to deepen, embolden, invigorate, and strengthen the Rigpa. The tempestuous energy becomes raw food of the awakened energy of Rigpa. The stronger and more flaming the emotion, the more Rigpa is strengthened. I feel that this unique method of Dzogchen has extraordinary power to free even the most inveterate, deeply rooted emotional and psychological problems.

Let me introduce you now, as simply as I can, to an explanation of how exactly this process works. This will be invaluable later on, when we come to look at what happens at the moment of death.

In Dzogchen the fundamental, inherent nature of everything is called the "Ground Luminosity" or the "Mother Luminosity." This pervades our whole experience, and is therefore the inherent nature of the thoughts and emotions that arise in our minds as well, although we do not recognize it. When the master introduces us to the true nature of mind, to the state of Rigpa, it is as if he or she gives us a master key. In Dzogchen we call this key, which is going to open to us the door to total knowledge, the "Path Luminosity" or "Child Luminosity." The Ground Luminosity and the Path Luminosity are fundamentally the same, of course, and it is only for the purposes of explanation and practice that they are categorized in this way. But once we have the key of the Path Luminosity through the introduction of the master, we can use it at will to open the door to the innate nature of reality. This opening of the door in Dzogchen practice is called the "meeting of the Ground and Path Luminosities" or the "meeting of Mother and Child Luminosities." Another way to say this is that as soon as a thought or emotion arises, the Path Luminosity—the Rigpa—recognizes it immediately for what it is, recognizes its inherent nature, the Ground Luminosity. In that moment of recognition, the two luminosities merge and thoughts and emotions are liberated in their very ground.

It is essential to perfect this practice of the merging of the two luminosities and the self-liberation of risings in life, because what happens at the moment of death, for everyone, is this: The Ground Luminosity dawns in vast splendor, and with it brings an opportunity for total liberation—if, and only if, you have learned how to recognize it.

It will be clear now, perhaps, that this merging of the luminosities and self-liberation of thoughts and emotions is meditation at its very deepest level. In fact, a term such as "meditation" is not really appropriate for Dzogchen practice, as ultimately it implies meditating "on" something, whereas in Dzogchen all is only and forever Rigpa. So there is no question of a meditation separate from simply abiding by the pure presence of Rigpa.

The only word that could possibly describe this is "non-meditation." In this state, the masters say, even if you look for delusion, there is none left. Even if you looked for ordinary pebbles on an island of gold and jewels, you wouldn't have a chance of finding any. When the View is constant, and the flow of Rigpa unfailing, and the merging of the two luminosities continuous and spontaneous, all possible delusion is liberated at its very root, and your entire perception arises, without a break, as Rigpa.

The masters stress that to stabilize the View in meditation, it is essential, first of all, to accomplish this practice in a *special environment* of retreat, where all the favorable conditions are present; amidst the distractions and busyness of the world, however much you meditate, true experience will not be born in your mind. Second, though there is no difference in Dzogchen between meditation and everyday life, until you have found true stability through doing the practice in *proper sessions,* you will not be able to integrate the wisdom of meditation into the experience of daily life. Third, even when you practice, you might be able to abide by the continual flow of Rigpa with the confidence of the View; but if you are unable to continue that flow *at all times and in all situations,* mixing your practice with everyday life, it will not serve as a remedy when unfavorable circumstances arise, and you will be led astray into delusion by thoughts and emotions.

There is a delightful story about a Dzogchen yogin who lived unostentatiously, surrounded, however, by a large following of disciples. A certain monk, who had an exaggerated opinion of his own learning and scholarship, was jealous of the yogin, whom he knew not to be very well read at all. He thought: "How does he, just an ordinary person, dare to teach? How dare he pretend to be a master? I will go and test his knowledge, show it up for the sham it is and humiliate him in front of his disciples, so that they will leave him and follow me."

One day, then, he visited the yogin and said scornfully: "You Dzogchen bunch, is meditate *all* you ever do?"

The yogin's reply took him completely by surprise: "What is there to meditate on?"

"You don't even meditate, then," the scholar brayed triumphantly.

"But when am I *ever* distracted?" said the yogin.

ACTION

As abiding by the flow of Rigpa becomes a reality, it begins to permeate the practitioner's everyday life and action, and breeds a deep stability and confidence. Dudjom Rinpoche says:

> *Action is being truly observant of your own thoughts, good or bad, looking into the true nature of whatever thoughts may arise, neither tracing the past nor inviting the future, neither allowing any clinging*

to experiences of joy, nor being overcome by sad situations. In so doing, you try to reach and remain in the state of great equilibrium, where all good and bad, peace and distress, are devoid of true identity.

Realizing the View subtly but completely transforms your vision of everything. More and more, I have come to realize how thoughts and concepts are all that block us from always being, quite simply, in the absolute. Now I see clearly why the masters so often say: "Try hard not to create too much hope and fear," for they only engender more mental gossip. When the View is there, thoughts are seen for what they truly are: fleeting and transparent, and only relative. You see through everything directly, as if you had X-ray eyes. You do not cling to thoughts and emotions or reject them, but welcome them all within the vast embrace of Rigpa. What you took so seriously before—ambitions, plans, expectations, doubts, and passions—no longer have any deep and anxious hold on you, for the View has helped you to see the futility and pointlessness of them all, and born in you a spirit of true renunciation.

Remaining in the clarity and confidence of Rigpa allows all your thoughts and emotions to liberate naturally and effort-lessly within its vast expanse, like writing in water or painting in the sky. If you truly perfect this practice, karma has no chance at all to be accumulated; and in this state of aimless, carefree abandon, what Dudjom Rinpoche calls "uninhibited, naked ease," the karmic law of cause and effect can no longer bind you in any way.

Don't assume, whatever you do, that this is, or could possibly be, easy. It is extremely hard to rest undistracted in the nature of mind, even for a moment, let alone to self-liberate a single thought or emotion as it rises. We often assume that simply because we understand something intellectually, or think we do, we have actually realized it. This is a great delusion. It requires the maturity that only years of listening, contemplation, reflection, meditation, and sustained practice can ripen. And it cannot be said too often that the practice of Dzogchen always requires the guidance and instruction of a qualified master.

Otherwise there is a great danger, called in the tradition "losing the Action in the View." A teaching as high and powerful as Dzogchen entails an extreme risk. Deluding your-self that you are liberating thoughts and emotions, when in fact you are nowhere near being able to do so, and thinking that you are acting with the spontaneity of a true Dzogchen yogin, all you are doing is simply accumulating vast amounts of negative karma. As Padmasambhava says, and this is the attitude we all should have:

> *Though my View is as spacious as the sky,*
> *My actions and respect for cause and effect are as fine as grains of*
>   *flour.*

Masters of the Dzogchen tradition have stressed again and again that without being thoroughly and deeply acquainted with the "essence and method of self-liberation" through long practice, meditation "only furthers the path of delusion." This may seem harsh, but it is the case, because only constant self-liberation of thoughts can really end the reign of delusion and really protect you from being plunged again into suffering and neurosis. Without the method of self-liberation, you will not be able to withstand misfortunes and evil circumstances when they arise, and even if you meditate you will find that still your emotions like anger and desire run as rampant as ever. The danger of other kinds of meditation that do not have this method is that they become like "the meditation of the gods," straying all too easily into sumptuous self-absorption or passive trance or vacancy of one kind or another, and none of them attack and dissolve delusion at its root.

The great Dzogchen master Vimalamitra spoke in the most precise way of the degrees of increasing naturalness in this liberation: When you first master this practice, liberation happens simultaneously with the rising, like recognizing an old friend in a crowd. Perfecting and deepening the practice, liberation will happen simultaneously with the arising of thought and emotion, like a snake uncoiling and unwinding its own knots. And in the final state of mastery, liberation is like a thief entering an empty house; whatever arises neither harms or benefits a true Dzogchen yogin.

Even in the greatest yogin, sorrow and joy still arise just as before. The difference between an ordinary person and the yogin is how they view their emotions and react to them. An ordinary person will instinctively accept or reject them, and so arouse the attachment or aversion that will result in the accumulation of negative karma. A yogin, however, perceives everything that rises in its natural, pristine state, without allowing grasping to enter his or her perception.

Dilgo Khyentse Rinpoche describes a yogin wandering through a garden. He is completely awake to the splendor and beauty of the flowers, and relishes their colors, shapes, and scents. But there is no trace of clinging nor any "afterthought" in his mind. As Dudjom Rinpoche says:

> *Whatever perceptions arise, you should be like a little child going into a beautifully decorated temple; he looks, but grasping does not enter into his perception at all. So you leave everything fresh, natural, vivid, and unspoiled. When you leave each thing in its own state, then its shape doesn't change, its color doesn't fade, and its glow does not disappear. Whatever appears is unstained by any grasping, so then all that you perceive arises as the naked wisdom of Rigpa, which is the indivisibility of luminosity and emptiness.*

The confidence, the contentment, the spacious serenity, the strength, the profound humor, and the certainty that arise from directly realizing the View of Rigpa is the greatest treasure of life, the ultimate happiness, which once attained, nothing can destroy, not even death. Dilgo Khyentse Rinpoche says:

> *Once you have the View, although the delusory perceptions of samsara may arise in your mind, you will be like the sky; when a rainbow appears in front of it, it's not particularly flattered, and when the clouds appear, it's not particularly disappointed either. There is a deep sense of contentment. You chuckle from inside as you see the facade of samsara and nirvana; the View will keep you constantly amused, with a little inner smile bubbling away all the time.*

As Dudjom Rinpoche says: "Having purified the great delusion, the heart's darkness, the radiant light of the unobscured sun continuously rises."

Someone who takes to heart the instruction of this book about Dzogchen and its message about dying, will, I hope, be inspired to seek, find, and follow a qualified master, and undertake to commit him- or herself to a complete training. The heart of the Dzogchen training is two practices, *Trekchö* and *Tögal,* which are indispensable for a deep understanding of what happens during the bardos. I can only give here the briefest of introductions to them. The complete explanation is only given from a master to disciple, when the disciple has made a wholehearted commitment to the teachings, and reached a certain stage of development. What I have explained in this chapter, "The Innermost Essence," is the heart of the practice of Trekchö.

Trekchö means cutting through delusion with fierce, direct thoroughness. Essentially delusion is cut through with the irresistible force of the view of Rigpa, like a knife cleaving through butter or a karate expert demolishing a pile of bricks. The whole fantastical edifice of delusion collapses, as if you were blasting its keystone away. Delusion is cut through, and the primordial purity and natural simplicity of the nature of mind is laid bare.

Only when the master has determined that you have a thorough grounding in the practice of Trekchö will he or she introduce you to the advanced practice of Tögal. The Tögal practitioner works directly with the Clear Light that dwells inherently, "spontaneously present," within all phenomena, using specific and exceptionally powerful exercises to reveal it within himself or herself.

Tögal has a quality of instantaneousness, of immediate realization. Instead of traveling over a range of mountains to reach a distant peak, the Tögal approach would be to leap there in one bound. The effect of Tögal is to enable a person to actualize all the different aspects of enlightenment within themselves in one lifetime.[7] Therefore it is regarded as the extraordinary, unique method of Dzogchen; whereas Trekchö is its wisdom, Tögal is its skillful means. It requires enormous discipline, and is generally practiced in a retreat environment.

Yet it cannot be stressed too often that the path of Dzogchen can only be followed under the direct guidance of a qualified master. As the Dalai Lama says: "One fact that you must bear in mind is that the practices of Dzogchen, such as Trekchö and Tögal, can only be achieved through the guidance of an experienced master, and through receiving the inspiration and blessing from a living person who has that realization."[8]

THE RAINBOW BODY

Through these advanced practices of Dzogchen, accomplished practitioners can bring their lives to an extraordinary and triumphant end. As they die, they enable their body to be reabsorbed back into the light essence of the elements that created it, and consequently their material body dissolves into light and then disappears completely. This process is known as the "rainbow body" or "body of light," because the dissolution is often accompanied by spontaneous manifestations of light and rainbows. The ancient Tantras of Dzogchen, and the writings of the great masters, distinguish different categories of this amazing, otherworldly phenomenon, for at one time, if at least not normal, it was reasonably frequent.

Usually a person who knows he or she is about to attain the rainbow body will ask to be left alone and undisturbed in a room or a tent for seven days. On the eighth day only the hair and nails, the impurities of the body, are found.

This may be very difficult for us now to believe, but the factual history of the Dzogchen lineage is full of examples of individuals who attained the rainbow body, and as Dudjom Rinpoche often used to point out, this is not just ancient history. Of the many examples, I would like to choose one of the most recent, and one with which I have a personal connection. In 1952 there was a famous instance of the rainbow body in the east of Tibet, witnessed by many people. The man who attained it, Sönam Namgyal, was the father of my tutor and the brother of Lama Tseten, whose death I described at the beginning of this book.

He was a very simple, humble person, who made his way as an itinerant stone carver, carving mantras and sacred texts. Some say he had been a hunter in his youth, and had received teaching from a great master. No one really knew he was a practitioner; he was truly what is called "a hidden yogin." Some time before his death, he would be seen to go up into the mountains and just sit, silhouetted against the skyline, gazing up into space. He composed his own songs and chants and sung them instead of the traditional ones. No one had any idea what he was doing. He then fell ill, or seemed to, but became, strangely, increasingly happy. When the illness got worse, his family called in masters and doctors. His son told him he should remember all the teachings he had heard, and he smiled and said, "I've forgotten them all and anyway, there's nothing to remember. Everything is illusion, but I am confident that all is well."

Just before his death at seventy-nine, he said: "All I ask is that when I die, don't move my body for a week." When he died his family wrapped his body and invited Lamas and monks to come and practice for him. They placed the body in a small room in the house, and they could not help noticing that although he had been a tall person, they had no trouble getting it in, as if he were becoming smaller. At the same time, an extraordinary display of rainbow-colored light was seen all around the house. When they looked into the room on the sixth day, they saw that the body was getting smaller and smaller. On the eighth day after his death, the morning on which the funeral had been arranged, the undertakers arrived to collect his body. When they undid its coverings, they found nothing inside but his nails and hair.

My master Jamyang Khyentse asked for these to be brought to him, and verified that this was a case of the rainbow body.

PART TWO

Dying

ELEVEN

Heart Advice
on Helping the Dying

IN A HOSPICE I KNOW, Emily, a woman in her late sixties, was dying of breast cancer. Her daughter would visit her every day and there seemed to be a happy relationship between the two. But when her daughter had left, Emily would nearly always sit alone and cry. After a while it became clear that the reason for this was that her daughter had refused completely to accept the inevitability of her death, but spent her whole time encouraging her mother to "think positively," hoping that by this her cancer would be cured. All that happened was that Emily had to keep her thoughts, deep fears, panic, and grief to herself, with no one to share them with, no one to help her explore them, no one to help her understand her life, and no one to help her find a healing meaning in her death.

The most essential thing in life is to establish an unafraid, heartfelt communication with others, and it is never more important than with a dying person, as Emily showed me.

Often the dying person feels reserved and insecure, and is not sure of your intentions when you first visit. So don't feel anything extraordinary is supposed to happen, just be natural and relaxed, be yourself. Often dying people do not say what they want or mean, and the people close to them do not know what to say or do. It's hard to find out what they might be trying to say, or even what they might be hiding. Sometimes not even they know. So the first essential thing is to relax any tension in the atmosphere in whatever way comes most easily and naturally.

Once trust and confidence have been established, the atmosphere becomes relaxed and this will allow the dying person to bring up the things he or she really wants to talk about. Encourage the person warmly to feel as free as possible to express thoughts, fears, and emotions about dying and death. This honest and unshrinking baring of emotion is central to any possible transformation—of coming to terms with life or dying a good death—and you must allow the person complete freedom, and give your full permission to say whatever he or she wants.

When the dying person is finally communicating his or her most private feelings, do not interrupt, deny, or diminish what the person is saying. The terminally ill or dying are in the most vulnerable situation of their lives, and you will need all your skill and resources of sensitivity, and warmth, and loving compassion to enable them to reveal themselves. Learn to listen, and learn to receive in silence: an open, calm silence that makes the other person feel accepted. Be as relaxed as you can, be at ease; sit there with your dying friend or relative as if you had nothing more important or enjoyable to do.

I have found that, as in all grave situations of life, two things are most useful: a common-sense approach and a sense of humor. Humor has a marvelous way of lightening the atmosphere, helping to put the process of dying in its true and universal perspective, and breaking the over-seriousness and intensity of the situation. Use humor, then, as skillfully and as gently as possible.

I have found also, from my own experience, that it is essential not to take anything too personally. When you least expect it, dying people can make you the target of all their anger and blame. As Elisabeth Kübler-Ross says, anger and blame can "be displaced in all directions, and projected onto the environment at times almost at random."[1] Do not imagine that this rage is really aimed at you; realizing what fear and grief it springs from will stop you from reacting to it in ways that might damage your relationship.

Sometimes you may be tempted to preach to the dying, or to give them your own spiritual formula. Avoid this temptation absolutely, especially when you suspect that it is not what the dying person wants! No one wishes to be "rescued" with someone else's beliefs. Remember your task is not to convert anyone to anything, but to help the person in front of you get in touch with his or her own strength, confidence, faith, and spirituality, whatever that might be. Of course, if the person is really open to spiritual matters, and really wants to know what you think about them, don't hold back either.

Do not expect too much from yourself, or expect your help to produce miraculous results in the dying person or "save" them. You will only be disappointed. People will die as they have lived, as themselves. For real communication to be established, you must make a determined effort to see the person in terms of his or her own life, character, background, and history, and to accept the person unreservedly. Also don't be distressed if your help seems to be having very little effect and the dying person does not respond. We cannot know the deeper effects of our care.

SHOWING UNCONDITIONAL LOVE

A dying person most needs to be shown as unconditional a love as possible, released from all expectations. Don't think you have to be an expert in any way. Be natural, be yourself, be a true friend, and the dying person will be reassured that you are really with them, communicating with them simply and as an equal, as one human being to another.

I have said, "Show the dying person unconditional love," but in some situations that is far from easy. We may have a long history of suffering with the person, we may feel guilty about what we have done to the person in the past, or anger and resentment at what the person has done to us.

So let me suggest two very simple ways in which you can release the love within you toward the dying person. I and my students who work with the dying have found both these ways to be powerful. First, look at the dying person in front of you and think of that person as just like you, with the same needs, the same fundamental desire to be happy and avoid suffering, the same loneliness, the same fear of the unknown, the same secret areas of sadness, the same half-acknowledged feelings of helplessness. You will find that if you really do this, your heart will open toward the person and love will be present between you.

The second way, and I have found this even more powerful, is to put yourself directly and unflinchingly in the dying person's place. Imagine that you are on that bed before you, facing your death. Imagine that you are there in pain and alone. Then really ask yourself: What would you most need? What would you most like? What would you really wish from the friend in front of you?

If you do these two practices, I think you would find that what the dying person wants is what *you* would most want: to be really loved and accepted.

I have often seen also that people who are very sick long to be touched, long to be treated as living people and not diseases. A great deal of consolation can be given to the very ill simply by touching their hands, looking into their eyes, gently massaging them or holding them in your arms, or breathing in the same rhythm gently with them. The body has its own language of love; use it fearlessly, and you will find you bring to the dying comfort and consolation.

Often we forget that the dying are losing their whole world: their house, their job, their relationships, their body, and their mind—they're losing everything. All the losses we could possibly experience in life are joined together in one overwhelming loss when we die, so how could anyone dying not be sometimes sad, sometimes panicked, sometimes angry? Elisabeth Kübler-Ross suggests five stages in the process of coming to terms with dying: denial, anger, bargaining, depression, and acceptance. Of course not everyone will go through all these stages, or necessarily in this order; and for some people the road to acceptance may be an extremely long and thorny one; others may not reach acceptance at all. Ours is a culture that does not give people very much true perspective on their thoughts, emotions, and experiences, and many people facing death and its final challenge find themselves feeling cheated by their own ignorance, and terribly frustrated and angry, especially since no one seems to want to comprehend them and their most heartfelt needs. As Cicely Saunders, the great pioneer of the hospice movement in Britain, writes: "I once asked a man who knew he was dying what he needed above all in those who were caring for him. He said, 'For someone to look as if they are trying to understand me.' Indeed, it is impossible to understand fully another person, but I never forgot that he did not ask for success but only that someone should care enough to try."[2]

It is essential that we care enough to try, and that we reassure that person that whatever he or she may be feeling, whatever his or her frustration and anger, it is normal. Dying will bring out many repressed emotions: sadness or numbness or guilt, or even jealousy of those who are still well. Help the person not to repress these emotions when they rise. Be with the person as the waves of pain and grief break; with acceptance, time, and patient understanding, the emotions slowly subside and return the dying person to that ground of serenity, calm, and sanity that is most deeply and truly theirs.

Don't try to be too wise; don't always try to search for something profound to say. You don't have to *do* or say anything to make things better. Just be there as fully as you can. And if you are feeling a lot of anxiety and fear, and don't know what to do, admit that openly to the dying person and ask his or her help. This honesty will bring you and the dying person closer together, and help in opening up a freer communication. Sometimes the dying know far better than we how they can be helped, and we need to know how to draw on their wisdom and let them give to us what they know. Cicely Saunders has asked us to remind ourselves that, in being with the dying, we are not the only givers. "Sooner or later all who work with dying people know they are receiving more than they are giving as they meet endurance, courage and often humor. We need to say so. . . . "[3] Acknowledging our recognition of their courage can often inspire the dying person.

I find too that I have been helped by remembering one thing: that the person in front of me dying is always, somewhere, inherently good. Whatever rage or emotion arises, however momentarily shocking or horrifying these may be, focusing on that inner goodness will give you the control and perspective you need to be as helpful as possible. Just as when you quarrel with a good friend, you do not forget the best parts of that person, do the same with the dying person: Don't judge them by whatever emotions arise. This acceptance of yours will release the dying person to be as uninhibited as he or she need to be. Treat the dying as if they were what they are sometimes capable of being: open, loving, and generous.

On a deeper, spiritual level, I find it extremely helpful always to remember the dying person has the true buddha nature, whether he or she realizes it or not, and the potential for complete enlightenment. As the dying come closer to death, this possibility is in many ways even greater. So they deserve even more care and respect.

TELLING THE TRUTH

People often ask me: "Should people be told they are dying?" And I always reply: "Yes, as quietly, as kindly, as sensitively, and as skillfully as possible." From my years of visiting ill and dying patients, I agree with Elisabeth Kübler-Ross, who has observed that: "Most, if not all of the patients know anyway. They sense it by the changed attention, by the new and different approach that people take to them, by the lowering of voices or avoidance of sounds, by the tearful face of a relative or ominous, unsmiling member of the family who cannot hide his true feelings."[4]

I have often found that people instinctively know they are dying, but count on others—their doctor or loved ones—to confirm it. If they don't, the dying person may think that it is because family members cannot cope with the news. And then the dying person won't bring up the subject either. This lack of honesty will make him or her feel only more isolated and more anxious. I believe it is essential to tell the dying person the truth; he or she at least deserves that much. If the dying are not told the truth, how can they prepare themselves for death? How can they carry the relationships of their lives to a true conclusion? How can they take care of the many practical issues they must resolve? How can they help those who are left when they are gone to survive?

From my point of view as a spiritual practitioner, I believe dying to be a great opportunity for people to come to terms with their whole lives; and I have seen many, many individuals take this opportunity, in the most inspiring way, to change themselves and come closer to their own deepest truth. So by kindly and sensitively telling people at the earliest opportunity that they are dying, we are really giving them the chance to prepare, and to find their own powers of strength, and the meaning of their lives.

Let me tell you a story I was told by Sister Brigid, a Catholic nurse working in an Irish hospice. Mr. Murphy was in his sixties, and he and his wife were told by their doctor that he did not have long to live. The following day Mrs. Murphy visited her husband at the hospice, and they talked and wept all day long. Sister Brigid watched as the old couple talked and frequently broke down into tears, and when this had gone on for three days, she wondered if she should intervene. Yet the next day the Murphys seemed suddenly very relaxed and peaceful, holding hands and showing each other great tenderness.

Sister Brigid stopped Mrs. Murphy in the corridor and asked her what had taken place between them to have had such a great change on their behavior. Mrs. Murphy told her that when they found out her husband was dying, they looked back over their years together, and many memories came back to them. They had been married almost forty years, and naturally they felt enormous sorrow, thinking and talking about all the things they would never be able to do together again. Mr. Murphy had then made out his will, and written final messages to his grown-up children. All of this was terribly sad, because it was so hard to let go, but they carried on, as Mr. Murphy wanted to end his life well.

Sister Brigid told me that for the next three weeks Mr. Murphy lived, the couple radiated peace and a simple, wonderful feeling of love. Even after her husband died, Mrs. Murphy continued to visit patients at the hospice, where she was an inspiration to everyone.

This story shows to me the importance of telling people early that they are going to die, and also the great advantage of facing squarely the pain of loss. The Murphys knew that they were going to lose many things, but by facing those losses and grieving together, they found what they could not lose, the deep love between them that would remain after Mr. Murphy's death.

FEARS ABOUT DYING

I am sure that one of the things that helped Mrs. Murphy help her husband was that she faced within herself her own fears of dying. You cannot help a dying person until you have acknowledged how their fear of dying disturbs you and brings up your most uncomfortable fears. Working with the dying is like facing a polished and fierce mirror of your own reality. You see in it the stark face of your own panic and of your terror of pain. If you don't look at and accept that face of panic and fear in yourself, how will you be able to bear it in the person in front of you? When you come to try and help the dying, you will need to examine your every reaction, since your reactions will be reflected in those of the person dying and will contribute a great deal to their help or detriment.

Looking at your fears honestly will also help you in your own journey to maturity. Sometimes I think there could be no more effective way of speeding up our growth as human beings than working with the dying. Caring for the dying is itself a deep contemplation and reflection on your own death. It is a way to face and work with it. When you work with the dying, you can come to a kind of resolution, a clear understanding of what is the most important focus of life.

To learn really to help those who are dying is to begin to become fearless and responsible about our own dying, and to find in ourselves the beginnings of an unbounded compassion that we may never have suspected.

Being aware of your own fears about dying will help you immeasurably to be aware of the fears of the dying person. Just imagine deeply what those might be: fear of increasing, uncontrolled pain, fear of suffering, fear of indignity, fear of dependence, fear that the lives we have led have been meaningless, fear of separation from all we love, fear of losing control, fear of losing respect; perhaps our greatest fear of all is fear of fear itself, which grows more and more powerful the more we evade it.

Usually when you feel fear, you feel isolated and alone, and without company. But when somebody keeps company with you and talks of his or her own fears, then you realize fear is universal and the edge, the personal pain, is taken off it. Your fears are brought back to the human and universal context. Then you are able to understand, be more compassionate, and deal with your own fears in a much more positive and inspiring way.

As you grow to confront and accept your own fears, you will become increasingly sensitive to those of the person before you, and you will find you develop the intelligence and insight to help that person to bring his or her fears out into the open, deal with them, and begin skillfully to dispel them. For facing your fears, you will find, will not only make you more compassionate and braver and clearer; it will also make you more skillful, and that skillfulness will open to you all kinds of ways of enabling the dying to understand and face themselves.

One of the fears that we can most easily dispel is the anxiety we all have about unmitigated pain in the process of dying. I would like to think that everyone in the world could know that this is now unnecessary. Physical suffering should be kept to a minimum; there is enough suffering in death anyway. A study at St. Christopher's Hospice in London, which I know well and where my students have died, has shown that given the right care, 98 percent of patients can have a peaceful death. The hospice movement has developed a variety of ways of managing pain by using various combinations of drugs, and not simply narcotics. The Buddhist masters speak of the need to die consciously with as lucid, unblurred, and serene a mental mastery as possible. Keeping pain under control without clouding the dying person's consciousness is the first prerequisite for this, and now it can be done: Everyone should be entitled to that simple help at this most demanding moment of passage.

UNFINISHED BUSINESS

Another anxiety the dying person often has is that of leaving unfinished business. The masters tell us that we should die peacefully, "without grasping, yearning, and attachment." This cannot fully happen if the unfinished business of a lifetime, as far as possible, is not cleared. Sometimes you will find that people hold onto life and are afraid to let go and die, because they have not come to terms with what they have been and done. And when a person dies harboring guilt or bad feelings toward others, those who survive him suffer even more deeply in their grief.

Sometimes people ask me: "Isn't it too late to heal the pain of the past? Hasn't there been too much suffering between me and my dying friend or relative for healing to be possible?" It is my belief, and has been my experience, that it is never too late; even after enormous pain and abuse, people can find a way to forgive each other. The moment of death has a grandeur, solemnity, and finality that can make people reexamine all their attitudes, and be more open and ready to forgive, when before they could not bear to. Even at the very end of a life, the mistakes of a life can be undone.

There is a method for helping to complete unfinished business that I and my students who work with the dying find very helpful. It was formulated from the Buddhist practice of equalizing and exchanging the self with others, and from the Gestalt technique, by Christine Longaker, one of my earliest students, who came to the field of death and dying after the death of her husband from leukemia.[5] Usually unfinished business is the result of blocked communication; when we have been wounded, we often become very defensive, always arguing from a position of being in the right and blindly refusing to see the other person's point of view. This is not only unhelpful, it freezes any possibility of real exchange. So when you do this exercise, begin it with the strong motivation that you are bringing up all your negative thoughts and feelings to try and understand them, to work with them and resolve them, and finally now to let go of them.

Then visualize in front of you the person with whom you have the problem. See this person in your mind's eye, exactly as he or she has always looked to you.

Consider now that a real change takes place, so the person is far more open and receptive to listen to what you have to say, more willing than ever before to share honestly, and resolve the problem between you. Visualize vividly the person in this new state of openness. This will also help you feel more open to him or her. Then really feel, deep in your heart, what it is you most need to say to the person. Tell him or her what the problem is, tell the person all your feelings, your difficulties, your hurt, your regret. Tell him or her what you haven't felt safe, or comfortable enough, to say before.

Now take a piece of paper and write what you would say, all of it. Then, when you have finished, immediately begin to write what he or she might say in response to you. Don't stop to think about what the person used to say: Remember that now, as you have visualized, he or she has truly heard you and is more open. So just write, see what comes spontaneously; and allow the person, in your mind, to express completely his or her side of the problem as well.

Search yourself and see if there is anything else you need to say to the person—any other hurt feelings or regrets from the past that you have been holding back or have never aired. Again, each time after you have stated your feelings, write a response by the other person, writing down just whatever comes into your mind. Continue this dialogue until you really feel there is nothing more you are holding back, or nothing more that needs to be said.

To see if you are truly ready to conclude the dialogue, ask yourself deeply if you are now able to let go of the past wholeheartedly, really able, satisfied by the insight and healing that this written dialogue has given you, to forgive this person, or to feel that he or she would forgive you. When you feel you have accomplished this, remember to express any last feelings of love or appreciation you may have been holding back, and say goodbye. Visualize the person turning away and leaving now; and even though you must let go of him or her, remember that you can keep his or her love, and the warm memories of the best aspects of your relationship, always in your heart.

To come to an even clearer reconciliation with the past, find a friend to whom you can read your written dialogue, or read it out loud by yourself at home. Once you have read this dialogue aloud, you will be surprised to notice a change in yourself, as though you have *actually* communicated with the other person, and *actually* cleared with them all the problems you have been having. Afterward you will find it far easier to let go, to speak directly with the other person about your difficulties. And when you have really let go, a subtle shift in the chemistry between you and the other person will take place, and the tension in the relationship that has lasted so long will often dissolve. Sometimes, amazingly, you can even become the best of friends. Never forget, as the famous Tibetan master Tsongkhapa once said, "A friend can turn into an enemy, and so an enemy can turn into a friend."

SAYING GOODBYE

It is not only the tensions that you have to learn to let go of, but the dying person as well. If you are attached and cling to the dying person, you can bring him or her a lot of unnecessary heartache and make it very hard for the person to let go and die peacefully.

Sometimes the dying person can linger on many months or weeks longer than doctors expected and experience tremendous physical suffering. Christine Longaker has discovered that for such a person to be able to let go and die peacefully, he or she needs to hear two explicit verbal assurances from loved ones. First, they must give the person permission to die, and second they must reassure the person they will be all right after he or she has gone, and that there is no need to worry about them.

When people ask me how best to give someone permission to die, I tell them to imagine themselves standing by the bedside of the person they love and saying with the deepest and most sincere tenderness: "I am here with you and I love you. You are dying, and that is completely natural; it happens to everyone. I wish you could stay here with me, but I don't want you to suffer any more. The time we have had together has been enough, and I shall always cherish it. Please now don't hold onto life any longer. Let go. I give you my full and heartfelt permission to die. You are not alone, now or ever. You have all my love."

A student of mine who works in a hospice told me of an elderly Scottish woman, Maggie, whom she visited after her husband, close to death, had already fallen into a coma.

Maggie felt inconsolably sad, for she had never spoken to her husband about her love for him, nor said goodbye, and now she felt it was too late. The hospice worker encouraged her, saying that although he seemed unresponsive, perhaps he could actually still hear her. She had read that many people who appear to be unconscious can in fact perceive what is going on. She urged her to spend some time with her husband, telling him all she wanted to say. Maggie would not have thought of doing this, but she went ahead and spoke to her husband of all the good times they had shared, of how she would miss him, and of how much she loved him. At the end, once she had said her goodbyes, she told him, "It is hard for me to be without you, but I don't want to see you suffer any more, so it is all right for you to let go." Once she had finished, her husband let out a long sigh and peacefully died.

Not only the one who is dying, but his or her whole family has to learn how to let go. Each member of the family may be at a different stage of acceptance, and this will have to be taken into account. One of the great achievements of the hospice movement is to recognize how important it is to help the whole family to face their own grief and insecurity about the future. Some families resist letting their loved one go, thinking that to do so is a betrayal, and a sign that they don't love them enough. Christine Longaker tells these families to imagine that they are in the place of the one who is dying. "Imagine you are standing on the deck of an ocean liner, about to set sail. You look back on the shore and see all your family and friends waving goodbye. You have no choice about leaving, and the ship is already moving away. How would you want the people you loved to be saying goodbye to you? What would help you most on your journey?"

Even a simple exercise like this can help so much in enabling each member of the family in their own way to deal with the sadness of saying goodbye.

Sometimes people ask me, "What should I say to my child about the death of her relative?" I say to them to be sensitive but tell the truth. Don't let the child think that death is something strange or terrifying. Let her take part as far as possible in the life of the dying person, and answer honestly any questions the child might pose. A child's directness and innocence can actually bring a sweetness, lightness, even sometimes a humor into the pain of dying. Encourage the child to pray for the dying person, and so feel that he or she is really doing something to help. And after the death has taken place, make sure that you give the child special attention and affection.

TOWARD A PEACEFUL DEATH

When I think back to Tibet and the deaths that I witnessed there, I am struck by what a calm and harmonious environment many of them occurred in. This kind of environment, alas, is often lacking in the West, but my experience over the last twenty years has shown that it can, with imagination, be created. I feel that wherever possible, people should die at home, because it is at home that the majority of people are likely to feel most comfortable. And the peaceful death that the Buddhist masters advise is easiest to obtain in familiar surroundings. But if someone has to die in hospital, there is a great deal that you the loved ones can do to make that death as easy and inspiring as possible. Bring in plants, flowers, pictures, photographs of loved ones, drawings by children and grandchildren, or a cassette player with musical tapes, or if it is possible, home-cooked meals. You might even get permission for children to visit or for loved ones to stay overnight.

If the dying person is a Buddhist or a member of another faith, friends could make a small shrine in his or her room, with inspiring pictures or images. I remember a student of mine, Reiner, who was dying in a private ward in a hospital in Munich. A shrine had been created for him with pictures of his masters on it. I was very moved by it, and realized how profoundly Reiner was being helped by the atmosphere it created. The Buddhist teachings tell us to make a shrine with offerings when a person is dying. Seeing Reiner's devotion and peace of mind made me understand just how empowering this can be, and how it can help inspire people to make their dying a sacred process.

When a person is very close to death, I suggest that you request that the hospital staff do not disturb him or her so often, and that they stop taking tests. I'm often asked what is my attitude to death in intensive care units. I have to say that being in an intensive care unit will make a peaceful death very difficult, and hardly allow for spiritual practice at the moment of death. As the person is dying, there is no privacy: They are hooked up to monitors, and attempts to resuscitate them will be made when they stop breathing or their heart fails. There will be no chance of leaving the body undisturbed for a period of time after death, as the masters advise.

If you can, you should arrange with the doctor to be told when there is no possibility of the person recovering, and then request to have them moved to a private room, if the dying person wishes it, with the monitors disconnected. Make sure that the staff knows and respects the dying person's wishes, especially if he or she does not wish to be resuscitated, and make sure that the staff knows too to leave the body undisturbed after death for as long as possible. In a modern hospital, of course, it is not possible to leave the body alone for the three-day period that was customary in Tibet, but every support of silence and peace should be given to the dead to help them begin their journey after death.

Try and make certain also that while the person is actually in the final stages of dying, all injections and all invasive procedures of any kind are discontinued. These can cause anger, irritation, and pain, and for the mind of the dying person to be as calm as possible in the moments before death is, as I will explain in detail later, absolutely crucial.

Most people die in a state of unconsciousness. One fact we have learned from the near-death experience is that comatose and dying patients may be much more aware of things around them than we realize. Many of the near-death experiencers reported out-of-the-body experiences, from which they were able to give surprisingly accurate detailed accounts of their surroundings and even, in some cases, of other rooms in the same hospital. This clearly shows the importance of talking positively and frequently to a dying person or to a person in a coma. Conscious, alert, and actively loving care for the dying person must go on until the last moments of his or her life, and as I will show, even beyond.

One of the things I hope for from this book is that doctors all over the world will take *extremely seriously* the need to allow the dying person to die in silence and serenity. I want to appeal to the goodwill of the medical profession, and hope to inspire it to find ways to make the very difficult transition of death as easy, painless, and peaceful as possible. Peaceful death is really an essential human right, more essential perhaps even than the right to vote or the right to justice; it is a right on which, all religious traditions tell us, a great deal depends for the well-being and spiritual future of the dying person.

There is no greater gift of charity you can give than helping a person to die well.

TWELVE

Compassion:
The Wish-Fulfilling Jewel

CARING FOR THE DYING makes you poignantly aware
not only of their mortality, but also of your own. So many
veils and illusions separate us from the stark knowledge that
we are dying; when we finally know we are dying, and all
other sentient beings are dying with us, we start to have a
burning, almost heartbreaking sense of the fragility and
preciousness of each moment and each being, and from this
can grow a deep, clear, limitless compassion for all beings.
Sir Thomas More, I heard, wrote these words just before his
beheading: "We are all in the same cart, going to execution;
how can I hate anyone or wish anyone harm?" To feel the
full force of your mortality, and to open your heart entirely to it,
is to allow to grow in you that all-encompassing, fearless
compassion that fuels the lives of all those who wish truly to
be of help to others.

So everything that I have been saying up until now about
caring for the dying could perhaps be summed up in two
words: love and compassion. What is compassion? It is not
simply a sense of sympathy or caring for the person suffering,
not simply a warmth of heart toward the person before you,
or a sharp clarity of recognition of their needs and pain, it is
also a sustained and practical determination to do whatever is
possible and necessary to help alleviate their suffering.

Compassion is not true compassion unless it is active.
Avalokiteshvara, the Buddha of Compassion, is often represented in Tibetan iconography as having a thousand eyes that
see the pain in all corners of the universe, and a thousand
arms to reach out to all corners of the universe to extend
his help.

THE LOGIC OF COMPASSION

We all feel and know something of the benefits of compassion. But the particular strength of the Buddhist teaching is that it shows you clearly a "logic" of compassion. Once you have grasped it, this logic makes your practice of compassion at once more urgent and all-embracing, and more stable and grounded, because it is based on the clarity of a reasoning whose truth becomes ever more apparent as you pursue and test it.

We may say, and even half-believe, that compassion is marvelous, but in practice our actions are deeply uncompassionate and bring us and others mostly frustration and distress, and not the happiness we are all seeking for.

Isn't it absurd, then, that we all long for happiness, yet nearly all our actions and feelings lead us directly away from that happiness? Could there be any greater sign that our whole view of what real happiness is, and of how to attain it, is radically flawed?

What do we imagine will make us happy? A canny, self-seeking, resourceful selfishness, the selfish protection of ego, which can, as we all know, make us at moments extremely brutal. But in fact the complete reverse is true: Self-grasping and self-cherishing are seen, when you really look at them, to be the root of all harm to others, and also of all harm to ourselves.[1]

Every single negative thing we have ever thought or done has ultimately arisen from our grasping at a false self, and our cherishing of that false self, making it the dearest and most important element in our lives. All those negative thoughts, emotions, desires, and actions that are the cause of our negative karma are engendered by self-grasping and self-cherishing. They are the dark, powerful magnet that attracts to us, life after life, every obstacle, every misfortune, every anguish, every disaster, and so they are the root cause of all the sufferings of samsara.

When we have really grasped the law of karma in all its stark power and complex reverberations over many, many lifetimes, and seen just how our self-grasping and self-cherishing, life after life, have woven us repeatedly into a net of ignorance that seems only to be ensnaring us more and more tightly; when we have really understood the dangerous and doomed nature of the self-grasping mind's enterprise; when we have really pursued its operations into their most subtle hiding

places; when we have really understood just how our whole
ordinary mind and actions are defined, narrowed, and dark-
ened by it, how almost impossible it makes it for us to uncover
the heart of unconditional love, and how it has blocked in us
all sources of real love and real compassion, then there comes
a moment when we understand, with extreme and poignant
clarity, what Shantideva said:

> If all the harms
> Fears and sufferings in the world
> Arise from self-grasping,
> What need have I for such a great evil spirit?

and a resolution is born in us to destroy that evil spirit, our
greatest enemy. With that evil spirit dead, the cause of all our
suffering will be removed, and our true nature, in all its spaciousness and dynamic generosity, will shine out.

You can have no greater ally in this war against your
greatest enemy, your own self-grasping and self-cherishing,
than the practice of compassion. It is compassion, dedicating
ourselves to others, taking on their suffering instead of
cherishing ourselves, that hand in hand with the wisdom of
egolessness destroys most effectively and most completely
that ancient attachment to a false self that has been the cause
of our endless wandering in samsara. That is why in our tradition we see compassion as the source and essence of
enlightenment, and the heart of enlightened activity. As
Shantideva says:

> What need is there to say more?
> The childish work for their own benefit,
> The buddhas work for the benefit of others.
> Just look at the difference between them.
>
> If I do not exchange my happiness
> For the suffering of others,
> I shall not attain the state of buddhahood
> And even in samsara I shall have no real joy.[2]

To realize what I call the wisdom of compassion is to see
with complete clarity its benefits, as well as the damage that
its opposite has done to us. We need to make a very clear distinction between what is in our *ego's self-interest* and what is
in *our ultimate interest*; it is from mistaking one for the other
that all our suffering comes. We go on stubbornly believing

that self-cherishing is the best protection in life, but in fact the opposite is true. Self-grasping creates self-cherishing, which in turn creates an ingrained aversion to harm and suffering. However, harm and suffering have no objective existence; what gives them their existence and their power is only our aversion to them. When you understand this, you understand then that it is our aversion, in fact, that attracts to us every negativity and obstacle that can possibly happen to us, and fills our lives with nervous anxiety, expectation, and fear. Wear down that aversion by wearing down the self-grasping mind and its attachment to a nonexistent self, and you will wear down any hold on you that any obstacle and negativity can have. For how can you attack someone or something that is just not there?

It is compassion, then, that is the best protection; it is also, as the great masters of the past have always known, the source of all healing. Suppose you have a disease such as cancer or AIDS. By taking on the sickness of those suffering like you, in addition to your own pain, with a mind full of compassion you will—beyond any doubt— purify the past negative karma that is the cause, now and in the future, of the continuation of your suffering.

In Tibet, I remember hearing, there were many extraordinary cases of people, who when they heard they were dying of a terminal illness, gave away everything they had and went to the cemetery to die. There they practiced taking on the suffering of others; and what is amazing is that instead of dying, they returned home, fully healed.

Working with the dying, I have experienced again and again, gives all who do so a direct opportunity to practice compassion in action, and in the situation where it is probably most deeply needed of all.

Your compassion can have perhaps three essential benefits for the dying person: First, because it is opening your heart, you will find it easier to show the dying person the kind of unconditional love I have spoken about, and which they need so much. On a deeper, spiritual level, I have seen again and again how, if you try to embody compassion and act out of the heart of compassion, you will create an atmosphere in which the other person can be inspired to imagine the spiritual dimension or even take up spiritual practice. On the deepest level of all, if you do constantly practice compassion for the dying person and in turn inspire them to do the same, you might not only heal them spiritually, but perhaps even physically too. And you will discover for yourself, with wonder, what all the spiritual masters know, that *the power of compassion has no bounds.*

Asanga was one of the most famous Indian Buddhist saints, and lived in the fourth century. He went to the mountains to do a solitary retreat, concentrating all his meditation practice on the Buddha Maitreya, in the fervent hope that he would be blessed with a vision of this Buddha and receive teachings from him.

For six years Asanga meditated in extreme hardship, but did not even have one auspicious dream. He was disheartened and thought he would never succeed with his aspiration to meet the Buddha Maitreya, and so he abandoned his retreat and left his hermitage. He had not gone far down the road when he saw a man rubbing an enormous iron bar with a strip of silk. Asanga went up to him and asked him what he was doing. "I haven't got a needle," the man replied, "so I'm going to make one out of this iron bar." Asanga stared at him, astounded; even if the man were able to manage it in a hundred years, he thought, what would be the point? He said to himself: "Look at the trouble people give themselves over things that are totally absurd. You are doing something really valuable, spiritual practice, and you're not nearly so dedicated." He turned around and went back to his retreat.

Another three years went by, still without the slightest sign from the Buddha Maitreya. "Now I know for certain," he thought "I'm never going to succeed." So he left again, and soon came to a bend in the road where there was a huge rock, so tall it seemed to touch the sky. At the foot of the rock was a man busily rubbing it with a feather soaked in water. "What are you doing?" Asanga asked.

"This rock is so big it's stopping the sun from shining on my house, so I'm trying to get rid of it." Asanga was amazed at the man's indefatigable energy, and ashamed at his own lack of dedication. He returned to his retreat.

Three more years passed, and still he had not even had a single good dream. He decided, once and for all, that it was hopeless, and he left his retreat for good. The day wore on, and in the afternoon he came across a dog lying by the side of the road. It had only its front legs, and the whole of the lower part of its body was rotting and covered with maggots. Despite its pitiful condition, the dog was snapping at passers-by, and pathetically trying to bite them by dragging itself along the ground with its two good legs.

Asanga was overwhelmed with a vivid and unbearable feeling of compassion. He cut a piece of flesh off his own body and gave it to the dog to eat. Then he bent down to take off the maggots that were consuming the dog's body. But he suddenly thought he might hurt them if he tried to pull them out with his fingers, and realized that the only way to remove them would be on his tongue. Asanga knelt on the ground, and looking at the horrible festering, writhing mass, closed his eyes. He leant closer and put out his tongue . . . The next thing he knew, his tongue was touching the ground. He opened his eyes and looked up. The dog was gone; there in its place was the Buddha Maitreya, ringed by a shimmering aura of light.

"At last," said Asanga, "why did you never appear to me before?"

Maitreya spoke softly: "It is not true that I have never appeared to you before. I was with you all the time, but your negative karma and obscurations prevented you from seeing me. Your twelve years of practice dissolved them slightly, so that you were at last able to see the dog. Then, thanks to your genuine and heartfelt compassion, all those obscurations were completely swept away, and you can see me before you with your very own eyes. If you don't believe that this is what happened, put me on your shoulder and try and see if anyone else can see me."

Asanga put Maitreya on his right shoulder and went to the marketplace, where he began to ask everyone: "What have I got on my shoulder?" "Nothing," most people said, and hurried on. Only one old woman, whose karma had been slightly purified, answered: "You've got the rotting corpse of an old dog on your shoulder, that's all." Asanga at last understood the boundless power of compassion that had purified and transformed his karma, and so made him a vessel fit to receive the vision and instruction of Maitreya. Then the Buddha Maitreya, whose name means "loving kindness," took Asanga to a heavenly realm, and there gave him many sublime teachings that are among the most important in the whole of Buddhism.

THE STORY OF TONGLEN
AND THE POWER OF COMPASSION

My students often come to me and ask: "My friend's or my relative's suffering is disturbing me very much, and I really want to help. But I find I cannot feel enough love actually to be able to help. The compassion I want to show is blocked. What can I do?" Haven't all of us surely known the sad frustration of not being able to find in our hearts enough love and compassion for the people who are suffering around us, and so not enough strength to help them?

One of the great qualities of the Buddhist tradition is its development of an array of practices that can really help you in situations like this, that can truly nourish you and fill you with the power and the joyful resourcefulness and enthusiasm that will enable you to purify your mind and unblock your heart, so that the healing energies of wisdom and compassion can play upon and transform the situation you find yourself in.

Of all the practices I know, the practice of *Tonglen,* which in Tibetan means "giving and receiving," is one of the most useful and powerful. When you feel yourself locked in upon yourself, Tonglen opens you to the truth of the suffering of others; when your heart is blocked, it destroys those forces that are obstructing it; and when you feel estranged from the person who is in pain before you, or bitter or despairing, it helps you to find within yourself and then to reveal the loving, expansive radiance of your own true nature. No other practice I know is as effective in destroying the self-grasping, self-cherishing, self-absorption of the ego, which is the root of all our suffering and the root of all hard-heartedness.

One of the greatest masters of Tonglen in Tibet was Geshe Chekhawa, who lived in the eleventh century. He was extremely learned and accomplished in many different forms of meditation. One day when he happened to be in his teacher's room, he came across a book lying open at the following lines:

> Give all profit and gain to others,
> Take all loss and defeat on yourself.

The vast and almost unimaginable compassion of these lines astounded him, and he set out to find the master who had written them. One day on his journey he met a leper, who told him that this master had died. But Geshe Chekhawa persevered, and his long efforts were rewarded when he found the dead master's principal disciple. Geshe Chekhawa asked this disciple: "Just how important do you think the teachings contained in these two lines are?" The disciple replied: "Whether you like it or not, you will have to practice this teaching if you truly wish to attain buddhahood."

This reply astonished Geshe Chekhawa almost as much as his first reading of the two lines, and he stayed with this disciple for twelve years, to study this teaching and to take to heart the practice of Tonglen, which is its practical application. During that time, Geshe Chekhawa had to face many different kinds of ordeals: all sorts of difficulties, criticism, hardships, and abuse. And the teaching was so effective, and his perseverance in its practice so intense, that after six years he had completely eradicated any self-grasping and self-cherishing. The practice of Tonglen had transformed him into a master of compassion.

At first Geshe Chekhawa taught Tonglen to only a few close disciples, thinking that it would only work for those who had great faith in it. Then he began to teach it to a group of lepers. Leprosy at that time was common in Tibet, and ordinary doctors were unable to treat or cure it. But many of the lepers who did Tonglen practice were cured. The news of this spread fast, and other lepers flocked to his house, which began to seem like a hospital.

Still Geshe Chekhawa didn't teach Tonglen widely. It was only when he noticed the effect it had on his brother that he began to give it out more publicly. Geshe Chekhawa's brother was an inveterate skeptic, who derided all forms of spiritual practice. However, when he saw what was happening to the lepers who were practicing Tonglen, this brother could not help being impressed and intrigued. One day he hid behind a door and listened to Geshe Chekhawa teaching Tonglen, and then, in secret, started doing the practice on his own. When Geshe Chekhawa noticed that his brother's hard character was beginning to soften, he guessed what had happened.

If this practice could work on his brother, he thought, and transform him, then it could work on and transform any other human being. This convinced Geshe Chekhawa to teach Tonglen far more widely. He himself never ceased to practice it. Toward the end of his life, Geshe Chekhawa told his students that for a long time he had been praying fervently to be reborn in the hell realms, so as to be of help to all the beings suffering there. Unfortunately, he added, he had recently had several clear dreams that indicated he was to be reborn in one of the realms of the buddhas. He was bitterly disappointed and begged his students, with tears in his eyes, to pray to the buddhas that this would not happen, and that his passionate wish to help the beings in hell would be fulfilled.

HOW TO AWAKEN LOVE AND COMPASSION

Before you can truly practice Tonglen, you have to be able to evoke compassion in yourself. That is harder than we often imagine, because the sources of our love and compassion are sometimes hidden from us, and we may have no ready access to them. Fortunately there are several special techniques that the Buddhist "training of the mind" in compassion has developed to help us evoke our own hidden love. Out of the enormous range of methods available, I have selected the following ones, and have ordered them in a particular way so as to be of the greatest possible use to people in the modern world.

1. Loving Kindness: Unsealing the Spring

When we believe that we don't have enough love in us, there is a method for discovering and invoking it. Go back in your mind and recreate, almost visualize, a love that someone gave you that really moved you, perhaps in your childhood. Traditionally you are taught to think of your mother and her lifelong devotion to you, but if you find that problematic, you could think of your grandmother or grandfather, or anyone who had been deeply kind to you in your life. Remember a particular instance when they really showed you love, and you felt their love vividly.

Now let that feeling arise again in your heart, and infuse you with gratitude. As you do so, your love will go out naturally to that person who evoked it. You will remember then that even though you may not always feel that you have been loved enough, you were loved genuinely once. Knowing that now will make you feel again that you are, as that person made you feel then, worthy of love and really lovable.

Let your heart open now, and let love flow from it; then extend this love to all beings. Begin with those who are closest to you, then extend your love to friends and to acquaintances, then to neighbors, to strangers, then even to those whom you don't like or have difficulties with, even those whom you might consider as your "enemies," and finally to the whole universe. Let this love become more and more boundless. Equanimity is one of the four essential facets, with loving kindness, compassion, and joy, of what the teachings say form the entire aspiration of compassion. The all-inclusive, unbiased view of equanimity is really the starting point and the basis of the path of compassion.

You will find that this practice unseals a spring of love, and by that unsealing in you of your own loving kindness, you will find that it will inspire the birth of compassion. For as Maitreya said in one of the teachings he gave Asanga: "The water of compassion courses through the canal of loving kindness."

2. Compassion: Considering Yourself the Same as Others

One powerful way to evoke compassion, as I have described in the previous chapter, is to think of others as exactly the same as you. "After all," the Dalai Lama explains, "all human beings are the same—made of human flesh, bones, and blood. We all want happiness and want to avoid suffering. Further, we have an equal right to be happy. In other words, it is important to realize our sameness as human beings."[3]

Say, for example, you are having difficulties with a loved one, such as your mother or father, husband or wife, lover or friend. How helpful and revealing it can be to consider the other person not in his or her "role" of mother or father or husband, but simply as another "you," another human being, with the same feelings as you, the same desire for happiness, the same fear of suffering. Thinking of the person as a real person, exactly the same as you, will open your heart to him or her and give you more insight into how to help.

If you consider others just the same as yourself, it will help you to open up your relationships and give them a new and richer meaning. Imagine if societies and nations began to view each other in the same way; at last we would have the beginnings of a solid basis for peace on earth and the happy coexistence of all peoples.

3. Compassion: Exchanging Yourself for Others

When someone is suffering and you find yourself at a loss to know how to help, put yourself unflinchingly in his or her place. Imagine as vividly as possible what you would be going through if you were suffering the same pain. Ask yourself: "How would I feel? How would I want my friends to treat me? What would I most want from them?"

When you exchange yourself for others in this way, you are directly transferring your cherishing from its usual object, yourself, to other beings. So exchanging yourself for others is a very powerful way of loosening the hold on you of the self-cherishing and the self-grasping of ego, and so of releasing the heart of your compassion.

4. Using a Friend to Generate Compassion

Another moving technique for arousing compassion for a person who is suffering is to imagine one of your dearest friends, or someone you really love, in that person's place.

Imagine your brother or daughter or parent or best friend in the same kind of painful situation. Quite naturally your heart will open, and compassion will awaken in you: What more would you want than to free them from their torment? Now take this compassion released in your heart and transfer it to the person who needs your help: You will find that your help is inspired more naturally, and that you can direct it more easily.

People sometimes ask me: "If I do this, will the friend or relative whom I am imagining in pain come to some harm?" On the contrary, thinking about them with such love and compassion can only be of help to them, and will even bring about the healing of whatever suffering and pain they may have gone through in the past, may be going through now, or have yet to go through.

For the fact that they are the instrument of your arousing compassion, even if it is only for an instant, will bring them tremendous merit and benefit. Because they have been responsible, in part, for the opening of your heart, and for allowing you to help the sick or dying person with your compassion, then the merit from that action will naturally return to them.

You can also mentally dedicate the merit of that action to your friend or relative who helped you to open your heart. And you can wish the person well, and pray that in the future he or she will be free of suffering. You will be grateful toward your friend, and your friend might feel inspired and grateful too, if you tell the person that he or she helped you to evoke your compassion.

So to ask, "Will my friend or relative I am imagining in place of the sick or dying person come to some harm?"

shows that we have not really understood how powerful and miraculous the working of compassion is. It blesses and heals all those involved: the person who generates compassion, the person through whom that compassion is generated, and the person to whom that compassion is directed. As Portia says in Shakespeare's *Merchant of Venice:*

The quality of mercy is not strained,
It droppeth as the gentle rain from heaven
Upon the place beneath: it is twice bless'd;
It blesseth him that gives, and him that takes . . .

Compassion is the wish-fulfilling gem whose light of healing spreads in all directions.

There is a very beautiful story that I love that illustrates this. Buddha once recounted one of his previous lives, before he became enlightened. A great emperor had three sons, and the Buddha had been the youngest, who was called Mahasattva. Mahasattva was by nature a loving and compassionate little boy, and thought of all living things as his children.

One day the emperor and his court went to picnic in a forest, and the princes went off to play in the woods. After a while they came across a tigress who had given birth, and was so exhausted with hunger that she was on the point of eating her little cubs. Mahasattva asked his brothers: "What would the tigress need to eat now to revive her?"

"Only fresh meat or blood," they replied.

"Who could give his own flesh and blood to see that she is fed and save the lives of her and her cubs?" he asked.

"Who, indeed?" they replied.

Mahasattva was deeply moved by the plight of the tigress and her cubs, and started to think: "For so long I have been wandering uselessly through samsara, life after life, and because of my desire, anger, and ignorance, have done little to help other beings. Here at last is a great opportunity."

The princes were walking back to join their family, when Mahasattva said: "You two go on ahead. I will catch you up later." Quietly he crept back to the tigress, went right up to her, and lay down on the ground in front of her, to offer himself to her as food. The tigress looked at him, but was so weak that she could not even open her mouth. So the prince found a sharp stick and cut a deep gash in his body; the blood flowed out, the tigress licked it, and grew strong enough to open her jaws and eat him.

Mahasattva had given his body to the tigress in order to save her cubs, and through the great merit of his compassion, he was reborn in a higher realm, and progressed toward his enlightenment and his rebirth as the Buddha. But it was not only himself he had helped through his action: The power of his compassion had also purified the tigress and her cubs of their karma, and even of any karmic debt they might have owed to him for saving their lives in the way he did. Because it was so strong, in fact, his compassionate act created a karmic link between them that was to continue far into the future. The tigress and her cubs, who received the flesh of Mahasattva's body, were reborn, it is said, as the Buddha's first five disciples, the very first to receive his teaching after his enlightenment. What a vision this story gives us of how vast and mysterious the power of compassion truly is!

5. How to Meditate on Compassion

Yet, as I have said, evoking this power of compassion in us is not always easy. I find myself that the simplest ways are the best and the most direct. Every day, life gives us innumerable chances to open our hearts, if we can only take them. An old woman passes you with a sad and lonely face, swollen veins on her legs, and two heavy plastic bags full of shopping she can hardly carry; a shabbily-dressed old man shuffles in front of you in line at the post office; a boy on crutches looks harried and anxious as he tries to cross the street in the afternoon traffic; a dog lies bleeding to death on the road; a young girl sits alone, sobbing hysterically in the subway. Switch on a television, and there on the news perhaps is a mother in Beirut kneeling above the body of her murdered son; or an old grandmother in Moscow pointing to the soup that is her food for today, not knowing if she'll even have that tomorrow; or one of the AIDS children in Romania staring out at you with eyes drained of any living expression.

Any one of these sights could open the eyes of your heart to the fact of vast suffering in the world. Let it. Don't waste the love and grief it arouses; in the moment you feel compassion welling up in you, don't brush it aside, don't shrug it off and try quickly to return to "normal," don't be afraid of your feeling or embarrassed by it, or allow yourself to be distracted from it or let it run aground in apathy. Be vulnerable: use that quick, bright uprush of compassion; focus on it, go deep into your heart and meditate on it, develop it, enhance, and deepen it. By doing this you will realize how blind you have been to suffering, how the pain that you are experiencing or seeing now is only a tiny fraction of the pain of the world.

All beings, everywhere, suffer; let your heart go out to them all in spontaneous and immeasurable compassion, and direct that compassion, along with the blessing of all the Buddhas, to the alleviation of suffering everywhere.

Compassion is a far greater and nobler thing than pity. Pity has its roots in fear, and a sense of arrogance and condescension, sometimes even a smug feeling of "I'm glad it's not me." As Stephen Levine says: "When your fear touches someone's pain it becomes pity; when your love touches someone's pain, it becomes compassion."[4] To train in compassion, then, is to know all beings are the same and suffer in similar ways, to honor all those who suffer, and to know you are neither separate from nor superior to anyone.   .

So your first response on seeing someone suffer becomes not mere pity, but deep compassion. You feel for that person respect and even gratitude, because you now know that whoever prompts you to develop compassion by their suffering is in fact giving you one of the greatest gifts of all, because they are helping you to develop that very quality you need most in your progress toward enlightenment. That is why we say in Tibet that the beggar who is asking you for money, or the sick old woman wringing your heart, may be the buddhas in disguise, manifesting on your path to help you grow in compassion and so move towards buddhahood.

6. How to Direct Your Compassion

When you meditate deeply enough on compassion, there will arise in you a strong determination to alleviate the suffering of all beings, and an acute sense of responsibility toward that noble aim. There are two ways, then, of mentally directing this compassion and making it active.

The first way is to pray to all the buddhas and enlightened beings, from the depths of your heart, that everything you do, all your thoughts, words, and deeds, should only benefit beings and bring them happiness. In the words of one great prayer: "Bless me into usefulness." Pray that you benefit all who come in contact with you, and help them transform their suffering and their lives.

The second and universal way is to direct whatever compassion you have to all beings, by dedicating all your positive actions and spiritual practice to their welfare and especially toward their enlightenment. For when you meditate deeply on compassion, a realization dawns in you that the only way for you to be of *complete* help to other beings is for you to gain enlightenment. From that a strong sense of determination and universal responsibility is born, and the compassionate wish arises in you at that moment to attain enlightenment for the benefit of all others.

This compassionate wish is called Bodhicitta in Sanskrit; *bodhi* means our enlightened essence, and *citta* means heart. So we could translate it as "the heart of our enlightened mind." To awaken and develop the heart of the enlightened mind is to ripen steadily the seed of our buddha nature, that seed that in the end, when our practice of compassion has become perfect and all-embracing, will flower majestically into buddhahood. Bodhicitta, then, is the spring and source and root of the entire spiritual path. That is why in our tradition we pray with such urgency:

> *Those who haven't yet given birth to precious Bodhicitta,*
> *May they give birth,*
> *Those who have given birth,*
> *May their Bodhicitta not lessen but*
> *Increase further and further.*

And this is why Shantideva could praise Bodhicitta with such joy:

> *It is the supreme elixir*
> *That overcomes the sovereignty of death.*
> *It is the inexhaustible treasure*
> *That eliminates poverty in the world.*
> *It is the supreme medicine*
> *That quells the world's disease.*
> *It is the tree that shelters all beings*
> *Wandering and tired on the path of conditioned existence.*
> *It is the universal bridge*
> *That leads to freedom from unhappy states of birth.*
> *It is the dawning moon of the mind*
> *That dispels the torment of disturbing conceptions.*
> *It is the great sun that finally removes*
> *The misty ignorance of the world.*[5]

THE STAGES OF TONGLEN

Now that I have introduced you to the various methods of evoking compassion, and to the importance and power of compassion itself, I can give you the noble practice of Tonglen most effectively; for now you will have the motivation, the understanding, and the tools to do it for your greatest benefit and the greatest benefit of others. Tonglen is a Buddhist practice, but I strongly believe that anyone—anyone at all—can do it. Even if you have no religious faith, I urge you simply to try it. I have found Tonglen to be of the greatest possible help.

Put very simply, the Tonglen practice of giving and receiving is to take on the suffering and pain of others, and give them your happiness, well-being, and peace of mind. Like one of the methods of meditation practice I explained earlier, Tonglen uses the medium of the breath. As Geshe Chekhawa wrote: "Giving and receiving should be practiced alternately. This alternation should be placed on the medium of the breath."

I know from my own experience how hard it is to imagine taking on the sufferings of others, and especially of sick and dying people, without first building in yourself a strength and confidence of compassion. It is this strength and this confidence that will give your practice the power to transmute their suffering.

This is why I always recommend that you begin the Tonglen practice for others by first practicing it on yourself. Before you send out love and compassion to others, you uncover, deepen, create, and strengthen them in yourself, and heal yourself of any reticence or distress or anger or fear that might create an obstacle to practicing Tonglen wholeheartedly.

Over the years a way of teaching Tonglen has developed that many of my students have found very helpful and therapeutic. It has four stages.

THE PRELIMINARY TONGLEN PRACTICE

The best way to do this practice, and any practice of Tonglen, is to begin by evoking and resting in the nature of mind. When you rest in the nature of mind and see all things directly as "empty," illusory, and dream-like, you are resting in the state of what is known as "ultimate" or "absolute Bodhicitta," the true heart of the enlightened mind. The teachings compare absolute Bodhicitta to an inexhaustible treasury of generosity; and compassion, when understood in its profoundest sense, is known and seen as the natural radiance of the nature of mind, the skillful means that rises from the heart of wisdom.

Begin by sitting and bringing the mind home. Allow all your thoughts to settle, neither inviting them nor following them. Close your eyes if you wish. When you feel really calm and centered, alert yourself slightly, and begin the practice.

1. Environmental Tonglen

We all know how the moods and atmospheres of our mind have a great hold on us. Sit with your mind and feel its mood and atmosphere. If you feel your mood is uneasy, or the atmosphere is dark, then as you breathe in, mentally absorb whatever is unwholesome; and as you breathe out, mentally give out calm, clarity, and joy, so purifying and healing the atmosphere and environment of your mind. This is why I call this first stage of the practice "environmental Tonglen."

2. Self Tonglen

For the purposes of this exercise, divide yourself into two aspects, A and B. A is the aspect of you that is whole, compassionate, warm, and loving, like a true friend, really willing to be there for you, responsive and open to you, without ever judging you, whatever your faults or shortcomings.

B is the aspect of you that has been hurt, that feels misunderstood and frustrated, bitter or angry, who might have been, for example, unjustly treated or abused as a child, or has suffered in relationships or been wronged by society.

Now, as you breathe in, imagine that A opens his or her heart completely, and warmly and compassionately accepts and embraces all of B's suffering and negativity and pain and hurt. Moved by this, B opens his or her heart and all pain and suffering melt away in this compassionate embrace.

As you breathe out, imagine A sending out to B all his or her healing love, warmth, trust, comfort, confidence, happiness, and joy.

3. Tonglen in a Living Situation

Imagine vividly a situation where you have acted badly, one about which you feel guilty, and which you wince to even think about.

Then, as you breathe in, accept total responsibility for your actions in that particular situation, without in any way trying to justify your behavior. Acknowledge exactly what you have done wrong, and wholeheartedly ask for forgiveness. Now, as you breathe out, send out reconciliation, forgiveness, healing, and understanding.

So you breathe in blame, and breathe out the undoing of harm; you breathe in responsibility, breathe out healing, forgiveness, and reconciliation.

This exercise is particularly powerful, and may give you the courage to go to see the person whom you have wronged, and the strength and willingness to talk to them directly and actually ask for forgiveness from the depths of your heart.

4. Tonglen for Others

Imagine someone to whom you feel very close, particularly someone who is suffering and in pain. As you breathe in, imagine you take in all their suffering and pain with compassion, and as you breathe out, send your warmth, healing, love, joy, and happiness streaming out to them.

Now, just as in the practice of loving kindness, gradually widen the circle of your compassion to embrace first other people whom you also feel very close to, then those whom you feel indifferent about, then those you dislike or have difficulty with, then even those whom you feel are actively monstrous and cruel. Allow your compassion to become universal, and to fold in its embrace all sentient beings, all beings, in fact, without any exception:

> Sentient beings are as limitless as the whole of space:
> May they each effortlessly realize the nature of their mind,
> And may every single being of all the six realms, who has each been
>   in one life or another my father or mother,
> Attain all together the ground of primordial perfection.

What I have been giving in this section is a complete preliminary practice to the main Tonglen, which, as you will see, involves a much richer process of visualization. This preliminary practice works with your attitude of mind and heart, and prepares, opens, and inspires you. Not only does it, in its own right, enable you to heal the environment of your mind, your own suffering, and the pain of the past, and to begin to help, through your compassion, all sentient beings; but it also establishes and makes you intimate and familiar with the process of giving and receiving that finds its complete expression in the main practice of Tonglen.

THE MAIN TONGLEN PRACTICE

In the Tonglen practice of giving and receiving, we *take on, through compassion,* all the various mental and physical sufferings of all beings: their fear, frustration, pain, anger, guilt, bitterness, doubt, and rage, and we *give* them, *through love,* all our happiness, and well-being, peace of mind, healing, and fulfillment.

1. Before you begin with this practice, sit quietly and bring your mind home. Then, making use of any of the exercises or methods I have described, whichever one you find really inspires you and works for you, meditate deeply on compassion. Summon and invoke the presence of all the buddhas, bodhisattvas, and enlightened beings, so that, through their inspiration and blessing, compassion may be born in your heart.

2. Imagine in front of you, as vividly and as poignantly as possible, someone you care for who is suffering. Try and imagine every aspect of the person's pain and distress. Then, as you feel your heart opening in compassion toward the person, imagine that all of his or her sufferings manifest together and gather into a great mass of hot, black, grimy smoke.

3. Now, as you breathe in, visualize that this mass of black smoke dissolves, with your in-breath, into the very core of your self-grasping at your heart. There it destroys completely all traces of self-cherishing, thereby purifying all your negative karma.

4. Imagine now that your self-cherishing has been destroyed, so that the heart of your enlightened mind, your Bodhicitta, is fully revealed. As you breathe out, then, imagine that you are sending out its brilliant, cooling light of peace, joy, happiness, and ultimate well-being to your friend in pain, and that its rays are purifying all their negative karma.

Here I find it inspiring to imagine, as Shantideva suggests, that your Bodhicitta has transformed your heart, or your whole body and being itself, into a dazzling, wish-fulfilling jewel, a jewel that can grant the desires and wishes of anyone, and provide exactly what he or she longs for and needs. True compassion *is* the wish-fulfilling jewel because it has the inherent power to give precisely to each being whatever that being most needs, and so alleviate his or her suffering, and bring about his or her true fulfillment.

5. So at the moment the light of your Bodhicitta streams out to touch your friend in pain, it is essential to feel a firm conviction that all of his or her negative karma *has* been

purified, and a deep, lasting joy that he or she has been totally freed of suffering and pain.

Then, as you go on breathing normally, in and out, continue steadily with this practice.

Practicing Tonglen on one friend in pain helps you to begin the process of gradually widening the circle of compassion to take on the suffering and purify the karma of all beings, and to give them all your happiness, well-being, joy, and peace of mind. This is the wonderful goal of Tonglen practice, and in a larger sense, of the whole path of compassion.

TONGLEN FOR A DYING PERSON

Now I think you can begin to see how Tonglen could be directed specifically toward helping the dying, how much strength and confidence it could give you when you come to help them, and how much actual, transforming help it could offer them.

I have given you the main Tonglen practice. Imagine now, in the place of your friend in pain, the person who is dying. Go through exactly the same stages as in the main Tonglen. In the visualization in part 3, imagine every aspect of the dying person's suffering and fear gathering into the mass of hot, black, grimy smoke, which you then breathe in; and consider too that by so doing, as before, you are destroying your self-grasping and self-cherishing, and purifying all your negative karma.

Now, as before, imagine, as you are breathing out, the light of the heart of your enlightened mind is filling the dying person with its peace and well-being, and purifying all his or her negative karma.

At every moment in our lives we need compassion, but what more urgent moment could there be than when we are dying? What more wonderful and consoling gift could you give to the dying than the knowledge that they are being prayed for, and that you are taking on their suffering and purifying their negative karma through your practice for them?

Even if they don't know that you are practicing for them, you are helping them and in turn they are helping you. They are *actively* helping you to develop your compassion, and so purify and heal yourself. For me, every dying person is a teacher, giving all those who help them a chance to transform themselves through developing their compassion.[6]

THE HOLY SECRET

You may be asking yourself this question: "If I take in the sufferings and pain of others, won't I risk harming myself?" If you feel at all hesitant, and feel that you don't yet have the strength or courage of compassion to do the practice of Tonglen wholeheartedly, don't worry. Just *imagine* yourself doing it, saying in your mind, "As I breathe in, I am taking on the suffering of my friend or others, and as I breathe out, I am giving him or them happiness and peace." Just simply doing this might create the climate in your mind that could inspire you to begin practicing Tonglen directly.

If you feel at all hesitant or unable to do the full practice, you can also do Tonglen in the form of a simple *prayer,* deeply aspiring to help beings. You might pray for example: "May I be able to take on the suffering of others; may I be able to give my well-being and happiness to them." This prayer will create auspicious conditions for the awakening of your power to do Tonglen in the future.

The one thing you should know for certain is that the only thing that Tonglen *could* harm is the one thing that has been harming you the most: your own ego, your self-grasping, self-cherishing mind, which is the root of suffering. For if you practice Tonglen as often as possible, this self-grasping mind will get weaker and weaker, and your true nature, compassion, will be given a chance to emerge more and more strongly. The stronger and greater your compassion, the stronger and greater your fearlessness and confidence. So compassion reveals itself yet again as your greatest resource and your greatest protection. As Shantideva says:

> Whoever wishes to quickly afford protection
> To both himself and others
> Should practice that holy secret:
> The exchanging of self for others.[7]

This holy secret of the practice of Tonglen is one that the mystic masters and saints of every tradition know; and living it and embodying it, with the abandon and fervor of true wisdom and true compassion, is what fills their lives with joy. One modern figure who has dedicated her life to serving the sick and dying and who radiates this joy of giving and receiving is Mother Teresa. I know of no more inspiring statement of the spiritual essence of Tonglen than these words of hers:

We all long for heaven where God is, but we have it in our power to be in heaven with Him at this very moment. But being happy with Him now means:

Loving as He loves,
Helping as He helps,
Giving as He gives,
Serving as He serves,
Rescuing as He rescues,
Being with Him twenty-four hours,
Touching Him in his distressing disguise.

A love as vast as this cured Geshe Chekhawa's lepers of their leprosy; it could also perhaps cure us of a disease even more dangerous: of that ignorance, which life after life has hindered us from realizing the nature of our mind, and so of attaining liberation.

THIRTEEN

Spiritual Help for the Dying

I FIRST CAME TO THE WEST at the beginning of the 1970s, and what disturbed me deeply, and has continued to disturb me, is the almost complete lack of spiritual help for the dying that exists in modern culture. In Tibet, as I have shown, everyone had some knowledge of the higher truths of Buddhism and some relationship with a master. No one died without being cared for, in both superficial and profound ways, by the community. I have been told many stories of people dying alone and in great distress and disillusion in the West without any spiritual help, and one of my main motivations in writing this book is to extend the healing wisdom of the world I was brought up in to all men and women. Do we not all have a right, as we are dying, not only to have our bodies treated with respect, but also, and perhaps even more important, our spirits? Shouldn't one of the main rights of any civilized society, extended to everyone in that society, be the right to die surrounded by the best spiritual care? Can we really call ourselves a "civilization" until this becomes an accepted norm? What does it really mean to have the technology to send people to the moon, when we do not know how to help our fellow humans die with dignity and hope?

Spiritual care is not a luxury for a few; it is *the* essential right of every human being, as essential as political liberty, medical assistance, and equality of opportunity. A real democratic ideal would include knowledgeable spiritual care for everyone as one of its most essential truths.

Wherever I go in the West, I am struck by the great mental suffering that arises from the fear of dying, whether or not this fear is acknowledged. How reassuring it would be for people if they knew that when they lay dying they would be cared for with loving insight! As it is, our culture is so heartless in its expediency and its denial of any real spiritual value

that people, when faced with terminal illness, feel terrified
that they are simply going to be thrown away like useless
goods. In Tibet it was a natural response to pray for the dying
and to give them spiritual care; in the West the only spiritual
attention that the majority pay to the dying is to go to their
funeral.

At the moment of their greatest vulnerability, then, people
in our world are abandoned and left almost totally without
support or insight. This is a tragic and humiliating state of
affairs, which must change. All of the modern world's preten-
sions to power and success will ring hollow until everyone
can die in this culture with some measure of true peace, and
until at least some effort is made to ensure this is possible.

BY THE BEDSIDE OF THE DYING

A friend of mine, who had just graduated from a famous
medical school, started work at one of the larger London
hospitals. On her very first day on the ward, four or five
people died. It was a terrible shock for her; nothing in her
training had equipped her to deal with it at all. Isn't this
astonishing, considering she was being trained to be a doctor?
One old man was lying in his bed, staring at the wall. He
was alone, with no family or friends to visit him, and he was
desperate for someone to talk to. She went over to him. His
eyes filled with tears and his voice trembled as he asked her
the last question she expected to hear: "Do you think God
will ever forgive me for my sins?" My friend had no idea at
all how to respond; her training had left her completely
unprepared for any spiritual questions. She had nothing to
say; all she had to hide behind was her professional status as a
doctor. There was no chaplain close by, and she just stood
there, paralyzed, unable to answer her patient's desperate call
for help and for reassurance about the meaning of his life.

She asked me, in her pain and bewilderment: "What
would you have done?" I said to her I would have sat by his
side, held his hand, and let him talk. I have been amazed
again and again by how, if you just let people talk, giving
them your complete and compassionate attention, they will
say things of a surprising spiritual depth, even when they
think they don't have any spiritual beliefs. Everyone has their
own life wisdom, and when you let a person talk you allow
this life wisdom to emerge. I have often been very moved by
how you can help people *to help themselves* by helping them to
discover their own truth, a truth whose richness, sweetness,

and profundity they may never have suspected. The sources of healing and awareness are deep within each of us, and your task is never under any circumstances to impose your beliefs but to enable them to find these within themselves.

Believe as you sit by the dying person that you are sitting by someone who has the true potential to be a buddha. Imagine their buddha nature as a shining and stainless mirror, and all their pain and anxiety a thin, gray mist on it that can quickly clear. This will help you to see them as lovable and forgivable, and draw out of you your unconditional love; you will find this attitude will allow the dying person to open remarkably to you.

My master Dudjom Rinpoche used to say that to help a dying person is like holding out a hand to someone who is on the point of falling over, to lift them up. Through the strength and peace and deep compassionate attention of your presence, you will help them awaken their own strength. The quality of your *presence* at this most vulnerable and extreme moment is all-important. As Cicely Saunders wrote: "The dying have shed the masks and superficialities of everyday living and they are all the more open and sensitive because of this. They see through all unreality. I remember one man saying, 'No, no reading. I only want what is in your mind and in your heart.'"[1]

I never go to the bedside of a dying person without practicing beforehand, without steeping myself in the sacred atmosphere of the nature of mind. Then I do not have to struggle to find compassion and authenticity, for they will be there and radiate naturally.

Remember, you can do nothing to inspire the person in front of you if you do not inspire yourself first. So when you don't know what to do, when you feel hardly able to do anything to help, then pray and meditate, invoke the Buddha or any other figure whose sacred power you believe in. When I'm faced with someone going through terrible suffering, I call down with fervor the help of all the buddhas and enlightened beings, with my heart completely open to the person dying in front of me, and compassion for their pain filling my being. I invoke as intensely as possible the presence of my masters, the buddhas, of those enlightened beings with whom I have a particular connection. Summoning all my powers of devotion and faith, I see them in glory above the dying person, gazing down at them with love, and pouring down light and blessing on them, purifying them of all their past karma and present agony. And as I do this, I keep praying that the person in front of me should be spared further suffering, and find peace and liberation.

I do this with the deepest concentration and earnestness, and then I try to rest in the nature of my mind and allow its peace and radiance to permeate the atmosphere of the room. Many, many times I have been awed by the sense of sacred presence that then establishes itself very naturally, and which in turn inspires the dying person.

I'm now going to say something that may surprise you. *Death can be very inspiring.* In my experiences with dying people, I have found that I have surprised myself by the way in which my prayer and invocation transformed the atmosphere, and I myself have had my faith deepened by seeing how effective this invocation and prayer and this presence of the buddhas are. I have found that being by the bedside of a dying person has made my own practice far more powerful.

Sometimes I see that the dying person also feels this atmosphere of deep inspiration, and is grateful to have provided the opportunity for our reaching, together, a moment of real and transformative rapture.

GIVING HOPE AND FINDING FORGIVENESS

I would like to single out two points in giving spiritual help to the dying: giving hope, and finding forgiveness.

Always when you are with a dying person, dwell on what they have accomplished and done well. Help them to feel as constructive and as happy as possible about their lives. Concentrate on their virtues and not their failings. People who are dying are frequently extremely vulnerable to guilt, regret, and depression; allow the person to express these freely, listen to the person and acknowledge what he or she says. At the same time, where appropriate, be sure to remind the person of his or her buddha nature, and encourage the person to try to rest in the nature of mind through the practice of meditation. Especially remind the person that pain and suffering are not all that he or she is. Find the most skillful and sensitive way possible to inspire the person and give him or her hope. So rather than dwelling on his or her mistakes, the person can die in a more peaceful frame of mind.

To the man who cried out: "Do you think God will ever forgive me for my sins?" I would say: "Forgiveness already exists in the nature of God; it is already there. God has already forgiven you, for God is forgiveness itself. 'To err is human, and to forgive divine.' But can you truly forgive yourself? That's the real question.

"Your feeling of being unforgiven and unforgivable *is* what makes you suffer so. But it only exists in your heart or mind. Haven't you read how in some of the near-death experiences a great golden presence of light arrives that is all-forgiving? And it is very often said that it is finally *we* who judge ourselves.

"In order to clear your guilt, ask for purification from the depths of your heart. If you really ask for purification, and go through it, forgiveness will be there. God will forgive you, just as the father in Christ's beautiful parable forgives the prodigal son. To help yourself to forgive yourself, remember the good things you have done, forgive everyone else in your life, and ask for forgiveness from anyone you may have harmed."

Not everyone believes in a formal religion, but I think nearly everyone believes in forgiveness. You can be of immeasurable help to the dying by enabling them to see the approach of death as the time for reconciliation and reckoning.

Encourage them to make up with friends or relatives, and to clear their heart, so as not to keep even a trace of hatred or the slightest grudge. If they cannot meet the person from whom they feel estranged, suggest they phone them or leave a taped message or letter and ask for forgiveness. If they suspect that the person they want to pardon them cannot do so, it is not wise to encourage them to confront the person directly; a negative response would only add to their already great distress. And sometimes people need time to forgive. Let them leave a message of some kind asking for forgiveness, and they will at least die knowing that they have done their best. They will have cleared the difficulty or anger from their heart. Time and time again, I have seen people whose hearts have been hardened by self-hatred and guilt find, through a simple act of asking for pardon, unsuspected strength and peace.

All religions stress the power of forgiveness, and this power is never more necessary, nor more deeply felt, than when someone is dying. Through forgiving and being forgiven, we purify ourselves of the darkness of what we have done, and prepare ourselves most completely for the journey through death.

FINDING A SPIRITUAL PRACTICE

If your dying friend or relative is familiar with some kind of meditation practice, encourage him or her to rest in meditation as much as possible, and meditate with the person as death approaches. If the dying person is at all open to the idea of spiritual practice, help the person find a suitable, simple practice, do it with him or her as often as possible, and keep reminding the person gently of it as death nears.

Be resourceful and inventive in how you help at this crucial moment, for a great deal depends on it: The whole atmosphere of dying can be transformed if people find a practice they can do wholeheartedly before and as they die. There are so many aspects of spiritual practice; use your acumen and sensitivity to find the one they might be most connected with: it could be forgiveness, purification, dedication, or feeling the presence of light or love. And as you help them begin, pray for the success of their practice with all your heart and mind; pray for them to be given every energy and faith to follow the path they choose. I have known people even at the latest stages of dying make the most startling spiritual progress by using one prayer or one mantra or one simple visualization with which they really made a connection in their heart.

Stephen Levine tells the story of a woman he was counseling who was dying of cancer.[2] She felt lost because, although she had a natural devotion to Jesus Christ, she had left the church. Together they explored what she might do to strengthen that faith and devotion. She came to the realization that what would help her renew her connection with Christ, and to find some trust and confidence while dying, would be to repeat continuously the prayer, "Lord Jesus Christ, have mercy on me." Saying this prayer opened her heart, and she began to feel Christ's presence with her at all times.

THE ESSENTIAL PHOWA PRACTICE

The most valuable and powerful of all practices I have found in caring for the dying, one which I have seen an astonishing number of people take to with enthusiasm, is a practice from the Tibetan tradition called *phowa* (pronounced "po-wa"), which means the transference of consciousness.

Phowa for dying people has been performed by friends, relatives, or masters, quite simply and naturally, all over the modern world—in Australia, America, and Europe. Thousands of people have been given the chance to die serenely because of its power. It gives me joy to make the *heart* of the phowa practice now available to anyone who wishes to use it.

I want to emphasize that this is a practice that anyone at all can do. It is simple, but it is also the most essential practice we can do to prepare for our own death, and it is the main practice I teach my students for helping their dying friends and relatives, and their loved ones who have already died.

Practice One

First make sure you are comfortable, and assume the meditative posture. If you are doing this practice as you are coming close to death, just sit as comfortably as you are able, or practice lying down.

Then bring your mind home, release, and relax completely.

1. In the sky in front of you, invoke the embodiment of whatever truth you believe in, in the form of radiant light. Choose whichever divine being or saint you feel close to. If you are a Buddhist, invoke a buddha with whom you feel an intimate connection. If you are a practicing Christian, feel with all your heart the vivid, immediate presence of God, the Holy Spirit, Jesus, or the Virgin Mary. If you don't feel linked with any particular spiritual figure, simply imagine a form of pure golden light in the sky before you. The important point is that you consider the being you are visualizing or whose presence you feel *is* the embodiment of the truth, wisdom, and compassion of all the buddhas, saints, masters, and enlightened beings. Don't worry if you cannot visualize them very clearly, just fill your heart with their presence and trust that they are there.

2. Then focus your mind, heart, and soul on the presence you have invoked, and pray:

> *Through your blessing, grace, and guidance, through the power of the light that streams from you:*
> *May all my negative karma, destructive emotions, obscurations, and blockages be purified and removed,*
> *May I know myself forgiven for all the harm I may have thought and done,*
> *May I accomplish this profound practice of phowa, and die a good and peaceful death,*
> *And through the triumph of my death, may I be able to benefit all other beings, living or dead.*

3. Now imagine that the presence of light you have invoked is so moved by your sincere and heartfelt prayer that he or she responds with a loving smile and sends out love and compassion in a stream of rays of light from his or her heart. As these touch and penetrate you, they cleanse and purify all your negative karma, destructive emotions, and obscurations, which are the causes of suffering. You see and feel that you are totally immersed in light.

4. You are now completely purified and completely healed by the light streaming from the presence. Consider that your very body, itself created by karma, now dissolves completely into light.

5. The body of light you are now soars up into the sky and merges, inseparably, with the blissful presence of light.

6. Remain in that state of oneness with the presence for as long as possible.

Practice Two

1. To do this practice even more simply, begin as before by resting quietly, and then invoke the presence of the embodiment of truth.

2. Imagine your consciousness as a sphere of light at your heart, which flashes out from you like a shooting star, and flies into the heart of the presence in front of you.

3. It dissolves and merges with the presence.

Through this practice you are investing your mind in the wisdom mind of the Buddha or enlightened being, which is the same as surrendering your soul into the nature of God. Dilgo Khyentse Rinpoche says this is like casting a pebble into a lake; think of it plummeting down into the water, deeper and deeper. Imagine that through the blessing your mind is transformed into the wisdom mind of this enlightened presence.

Practice Three

The most essential way to do the practice is this: Simply merge your mind with the wisdom mind of the pure presence. Consider: "My mind and the mind of the Buddha are one."

Choose whichever one of these versions of the phowa feels more comfortable, or has most appeal for you at any particular moment. Sometimes the most powerful practices can be the most simple. But whichever one you choose, remember that it is essential to take the time now to become familiar with this practice. How else will you have the confidence to do it for yourself or others at the moment of death? My master Jamyang Khyentse wrote, "If you meditate and practice in this manner always, at the moment of death it will come easier."[3]

In fact you should be so familiar with the practice of phowa that it becomes a natural reflex, your second nature. If you have seen the film *Gandhi,* you will know that when he was shot, his immediate response was to call out: "Ram . . . Ram!" which is, in the Hindu tradition, the sacred name of God. Remember that we never know how we will die, or if we will be given the time to recall any kind of practice at all. What time will we have, for example, if we smash our car into a truck at 100 mph on the freeway? There won't be a second then to think about how to do phowa, or to check the instructions in this book. Either we are familiar with the phowa or we are not. There is a simple way to gauge this: Just look at your reactions when you are in a critical situation or in a moment of crisis, such as an earthquake, or in a nightmare. Do you respond with the practice or don't you? And if you do, how stable and confident is your practice?

I remember a student of mine in America who went out riding one day. The horse threw her; her foot got stuck in the stirrup, and she was dragged along the ground. Her mind went blank. She tried desperately to recall some practice, but nothing at all would come. She grew terrified. What was good about that terror was that it made her realize that her practice had to become her second nature. This was the lesson she had to learn; it is the lesson, in fact, we all have to learn. Practice phowa as intensively as you can, until you can be sure you will react with it to any unforeseen event. This will make certain that whenever death comes, you will be as ready as you can be.

USING THE ESSENTIAL PHOWA PRACTICE
TO HELP THE DYING

How can we use this practice to help someone who is dying?

The principle and the sequence of the practice are exactly the same; the only difference is that you visualize the Buddha or spiritual presence above the head of the dying person:

Imagine that the rays of light pour down onto the dying person, purifying his or her whole being, and then he or she dissolves into light and merges into the spiritual presence.

Do this practice throughout your loved one's illness, and especially (and most important) when the person is breathing their last breath, or as soon as possible after breathing stops and before the body is touched or disturbed in any way. If the dying person knows you are going to do this practice for them, and knows what it is, it can be a great source of inspiration and comfort.

Sit quietly with the dying person, and offer a candle or light in front of a picture or statue of Buddha or Christ or the Virgin Mary. Then do the practice for them. You can be doing the practice quietly, and the person need not even know about it; on the other hand, if he or she is open to it, as sometimes dying people are, share the practice and explain how to do it.

People often ask me: "If my dying relative or friend is a practicing Christian and I am a Buddhist, is there any conflict?" How could there be? I tell them: You are invoking the truth, and Christ and Buddha are both compassionate manifestations of truth, appearing in different ways to help beings.

I strongly suggest to doctors and nurses that they can also do phowa for their dying patients. Imagine how marvelously it could change the atmosphere in a hospital if those who were ministering to the dying were also doing this practice. I remember the death of Samten in my childhood, when my master and the monks were all practicing for him. How powerful and uplifting it was! My deepest prayer is for everyone to die with the same grace and peace that he did.

I have formulated this essential phowa specially from the traditional Tibetan practice for dying, and it incorporates all the most important principles. So it is not only a practice for dying, but it can also be used both to purify and to heal; it is important for the living, and for the sick as well. If a person is going to be healed, it will assist that healing; if a person is dying, it will help them and heal their spirit in death; and if the person has died, it will continue to purify them.

If you are not sure whether a person who is seriously ill is going to live or die, then whenever you visit them you can do this phowa practice for them. And when you go home, do it again. The more you do it, the more your dying friend will be purified. You never know if you will see your friend again, or if you will be present when he or she actually dies. So seal each visit with this practice, just as a preparation, and go on doing the practice in whatever spare moments you have.[4]

DEDICATING OUR DEATH

From the *Tibetan Book of the Dead*:

O son/daughter of an enlightened family,[5] what is called "death" has now arrived, so adopt this attitude: "I have arrived at the time of death, so now, by means of this death, I will adopt only the attitude of the enlightened state of mind, loving kindness and compassion, and attain perfect enlightenment for the sake of all sentient beings who are as limitless as space . . ."

Recently one of my students came to me and said: "My friend is only twenty-five. He's in pain, and dying of leukemia. He is already frighteningly bitter; I'm terrified that he'll drown in bitterness. He keeps asking me: 'What can I do with all this useless, horrible suffering?'"

My heart went out to her and her friend. Perhaps nothing is as painful as believing that there is no use to the pain you are going through. I told my student that there was a way that her friend could transform his death even now, and even in the great pain he was enduring: to dedicate, with all his heart, the suffering of his dying, and his death itself, to the benefit and ultimate happiness of others.

I told her to tell him: "I know how much pain you're in. Imagine now all the others in the world who are in a pain like yours, or even greater. Fill your heart with compassion for them. And pray to whomever you believe in and ask that your suffering should help alleviate theirs. Again and again dedicate your pain to the alleviation of their pain. And you will quickly discover in yourself a new source of strength, a compassion you'll hardly be able now to imagine, and a certainty, beyond any shadow of a doubt, that your suffering is not only not being wasted, but has now a marvelous meaning."

What I was describing to my student was in fact the practice of Tonglen, which I have already shared with you, but which takes on a very special significance when someone is terminally ill or dying:

If you have an illness like cancer or AIDS, try as intensely as you can to imagine every other person in the world who has the same disease as you.

Say to yourself with deep compassion: "May I take on the suffering of everyone who has this terrible illness. May they be free from this affliction and from all their suffering."

Then imagine that their illness and tumors leave their body in the form of smoke, and dissolve into your illness and tumors. When you breathe in, you breathe in all their suffering, and when you breathe out, you breathe out total healing and well-being. Each time you do this practice, believe, with complete conviction, that they are now healed.

As you approach death, think continually to yourself: "May I take on the suffering, the fear, and loneliness of all others all over the world who are dying or will die. May they be all freed from pain and confusion; may they all find comfort and peace of mind. May whatever suffering I am enduring now and will endure in the future help them toward a good rebirth and ultimate enlightenment."

I knew an artist in New York who was dying from AIDS. He was a sardonic character and hated institutional religion, although secretly some of us suspected he had more spiritual curiosity than he admitted. Friends persuaded him to see a Tibetan master, who immediately understood that the greatest source of his frustration and suffering was that he felt his pain was of no use to himself or to anyone else. So he taught him one thing, and one thing only: the Tonglen practice. Despite some initial skepticism, he did practice it; and all his friends saw he went through an extraordinary change. He told many of them that, through Tonglen, the pain that before had been pointless and horrific was now infused with an almost glorious purpose. Everyone who knew him experienced firsthand how this new sense of meaning transformed his dying. He died in peace, reconciled to himself and his suffering.

If the practice of taking on the suffering of others can transform someone who has little experience of practice before, then imagine what power it has in the hands of a great master. When Gyalwang Karmapa died in Chicago in 1981, one of his Tibetan disciples wrote:

By the time that I saw him, His Holiness had already had many operations, some parts of his body removed, things put inside him, his blood transfused, and so on. Every day the doctors discovered the symptoms of some new disease, only to find them gone the next day and replaced by another illness, as if all the diseases in the world were finding room in his flesh. For two months he had taken no solid food, and finally his doctors gave up hope. It was impossible for him to live, and the doctors thought the life-supporting systems should be disconnected.

But the Karmapa said, "No, I'm going to live. Leave them in place." And he did live, astonishing the doctors, and remaining seemingly at ease in his situation—humorous, playful, smiling, as if he were rejoicing at everything his body suffered. Then I thought, with the clearest possible conviction, that the Karmapa had submitted himself to all this cutting, to the manifestation of all those diseases in his body, to the lack of food, in a quite intentional and voluntary way: He was deliberately suffering all of these diseases to help minimize the coming pains of war, disease, and famine, and in this way he was deliberately working to avert the terrible suffering of this dark age. For those of us present, his death was an unforgettable inspiration. It profoundly revealed the efficacy of the Dharma,[6] *and the fact that enlightenment for the sake of others can actually be achieved.*[7]

I know and I firmly believe that there is no need for anyone on earth to die in resentment and bitterness. No suffering, however dreadful, is or can be meaningless if it is dedicated to the alleviation of the suffering of others.

We have before us the noble and exalting examples of the supreme masters of compassion, who, it is said, live and die in the practice of Tonglen, taking on the pain of all sentient beings while they breathe in, and pouring out healing to the whole world when they breathe out, all their lives long, and right up until their very last breath. So boundless and powerful is their compassion, the teachings say, that at the moment of their death, it carries them immediately to rebirth in a buddha realm.

How transformed the world and our experience of it would be if each of us, while we live and as we die, could say this prayer, along with Shantideva and all the masters of compassion:

May I be a protector to those without protection,
A leader for those who journey,
And a boat, a bridge, a passage
For those desiring the further shore.

May the pain of every living creature
Be completely cleared away.
May I be the doctor and the medicine

And may I be the nurse
For all sick beings in the world
Until everyone is healed.

Just like space
And the great elements such as earth,
May I always support the life
Of all the boundless creatures.

And until they pass away from pain
May I also be the source of life
For all the realms of varied beings
That reach unto the ends of space.[8]

FOURTEEN

The Practices for Dying

I REMEMBER HOW PEOPLE would often come to see my master, Jamyang Khyentse, simply to ask for his guidance for the moment of death. He was so loved and revered throughout Tibet, especially in the eastern province of Kham, that some would travel for months on end to meet him and get his blessing just once before they died. All my masters would give this as their advice, for this is the essence of what is needed as you come to die: "Be free of attachment and aversion. Keep your mind pure. And unite your mind with the Buddha."

The whole Buddhist attitude to the moment of death can be summed up in this one verse by Padmasambhava from the cycle of the *Tibetan Book of the Dead:*

Now when the bardo of dying dawns upon me,
I will abandon all grasping, yearning and attachment,
Enter undistracted into clear awareness of the teaching,
And eject my consciousness into the space of unborn Rigpa;
As I leave this compound body of flesh and blood
I will know it to be a transitory illusion.

At the moment of death, there are two things that count: Whatever we have done in our lives, and what state of mind we are in at that moment. Even if we have accumulated a lot of negative karma, if we are able really to make a change of heart at the moment of death, it can decisively influence our future and transform our karma, for the moment of death is an exceptionally powerful opportunity for purifying karma.

THE MOMENT OF DEATH

Remember that all the habits and tendencies that are stored in the ground of our ordinary mind are lying ready to be activated by any influence. Even now we know how it only takes the slightest provocation to prompt our instinctive, habitual reactions to surface. This is especially true at the moment of death. The Dalai Lama explains:

> At the time of death attitudes of long familiarity usually take precedence and direct the rebirth. For this same reason, strong attachment is generated for the self, since one fears that one's self is becoming nonexistent. This attachment serves as the connecting link to the intermediate state between lives, the liking for a body in turn acts as a cause establishing the body of the intermediate (bardo) being.[1]

Therefore our state of mind at death is all-important. If we die in a positive frame of mind, we can improve our next birth, despite our negative karma. And if we are upset and distressed, it may have a detrimental effect, even though we may have used our lives well. This means that *the last thought and emotion that we have before we die has an extremely powerful determining effect on our immediate future.* Just as the mind of a mad person is usually entirely occupied by one obsession, which returns again and again, so at the moment of death our minds are totally vulnerable and exposed to whatever thoughts then preoccupy us. That last thought or emotion we have can be magnified out of all proportion and flood our whole perception. This is why the masters stress that the quality of the atmosphere around us when we die is crucial. With our friends and relatives, we should do all we can to inspire positive emotions and sacred feelings, like love, compassion, and devotion, and all we can to help them to "let go of grasping, yearning, and attachment."

LETTING GO OF ATTACHMENT

The ideal way for a person to die is having given away everything, internally and externally, so that there is as little as possible yearning, grasping, and attachment for the mind at that essential moment to latch onto. So before we die we should try to free ourselves of attachment to all our possessions, friends, and loved ones. We cannot take anything with us, so we should make plans to give away all our belongings beforehand as gifts or offerings to charity.

In Tibet the masters, before they left their bodies, would indicate what they would like to offer to other teachers. Sometimes a master who was intending to reincarnate in the future would leave a particular group of objects for his reincarnation, giving a clear indication of what he wanted to leave. I am convinced that we should also be exact about who is going to receive our possessions or our money. These wishes should be expressed as lucidly as possible. If they are not, then after you die, if you are in the bardo of becoming, you will see your relatives squabbling over your goods or misusing your money, and this will disturb you. State precisely just how much of your money should be dedicated to charity, or different spiritual purposes, or given to each of your relatives. Making everything clear, down to the final details, will reassure you and help you truly to let go.

As I have said, it is essential that the atmosphere around us when we die should be as peaceful as possible. The Tibetan masters therefore advise that grieving friends and relatives should not be present at a dying person's bedside, in case they provoke a disturbing emotion at the moment of death. Hospice workers have told me that dying people sometimes request that their close family do not visit them just as they are dying, because of this very fear of evoking painful feelings and strong attachment. Sometimes this may be extremely difficult for families to understand; they may feel they are no longer loved by the dying person. However, they should bear in mind that the mere presence of loved ones may provoke strong feelings of attachment in the dying person, which make it harder than ever for him or her to let go.

It is extremely hard not to cry when we are at the bedside of someone we love who is dying. I advise everyone to do their best to work out attachment and grief with the dying person before death comes: Cry together, express your love, and say goodbye, but try to finish with this process before the actual moment of death arrives. If possible, it is best if friends and relatives do not show excessive grief at the moment of death, because the consciousness of the dying person is at that moment exceptionally vulnerable. The *Tibetan Book of the Dead* says that your crying and tears around a person's bedside are experienced like thunder and hail. But don't worry if you have found yourself weeping at a deathbed; it can't be helped, and there is no reason to upset yourself and to feel guilty.

One of my great-aunts, Ani Pelu, was an extraordinary spiritual practitioner. She had studied with some of the legendary masters of her time, especially with Jamyang Khyentse, and he blessed her by writing for her a special "heart advice." She was sturdy and round, very much the boss of our household, with a beautiful and noble face and a yogin's uninhibited, even temperamental nature. She seemed to be a very practical woman, and she took direct charge of administering the family's affairs. Yet a month before she died she changed completely, in the most moving way. She who had been so busy let everything drop, with a calm and care-free abandon. She seemed to be continually in a state of meditation, and kept singing out her favorite passages from the writings of Longchenpa, the Dzogchen saint. She had enjoyed eating meat; yet just before she died, she didn't want to touch meat at all. She had been the queen of her world, and few people had thought of her as a *yogini*. In her dying she showed who she really was, and I shall never forget the profound peace that radiated from her in those days.

Ani Pelu, in many ways, was my guardian angel; I think she loved me specially because she had no children of her own. My father was always very busy being Jamyang Khyentse's administrator, and my mother was also busy with her huge household; she did not think of things that Ani Pelu never forgot. Ani Pelu would often ask my master: "What's going to happen to this boy when he grows up? Is he going to be all right? Is he going to have obstacles?" and sometimes he would reply to her and say things he would never have said about my future if she had not been there to badger him.

At the end of her life, Ani Pelu had tremendous serenity in her being and stability in her spiritual practice, yet even she, when she was at the point of death, made a request that I should not be present, just in case her love for me might cause her an instant's attachment. This shows how seriously she took her beloved master Jamyang Khyentse's heart advice: "At the moment of death, abandon all thoughts of attachment and aversion."

ENTERING THE CLEAR AWARENESS

Her sister Ani Rilu had also spent her whole life practicing, and had met the same great masters. She had a thick volume of prayers, and she would recite prayers and practice all day long. From time to time she would doze off, and when she woke up again she would carry on practicing from where she had left off. All day and all night she did the same thing, so that she hardly ever slept the whole night through, and often she ended up doing her morning practice in the evening and her evening practice in the morning. Her elder sister, Pelu, was a much more decisive and orderly person, and toward the end of her life she could not stand this endless disruption of normal routine. She would say: "Why don't you do the morning practice in the morning and the evening practice in the evening, and switch the light off and go to bed like everybody else does?" Ani Rilu would murmur, "Yes . . . yes," but go on just the same.

In those days I would have been rather on Ani Pelu's side, but now I see the wisdom of what Ani Rilu was doing. She was immersing herself in a stream of spiritual practice, and her whole life and being became one continuous flow of prayer. In fact, I think her practice was so strong that she continued praying even in her dreams, and anyone who does that will have a very good chance of liberation in the bardos.

Ani Rilu's dying had the same peaceful and passive quality as her life. She had been ill for some time, and it was nine o'clock one winter morning when the wife of my master sensed that death was approaching quickly. Although by that time Ani Rilu could not speak, she was still alert. Someone was sent immediately to ask Dodrupchen Rinpoche, a remarkable master who lived nearby, to come to give the last guidance and to effect the phowa, the practice of the transference of consciousness at the moment of death.

In our family there was an old man called A-pé Dorje, who died in 1989 at the age of eighty-five. He had been with my family for five generations, and was a man whose grandfatherly wisdom and common sense, exceptional moral strength and good heart, and gift for reconciling quarrels made him for me the embodiment of everything good that is Tibetan: a rugged, earthy, ordinary person who lives spontaneously by the spirit of the teachings.[2] He taught me so much as a child, most especially, how important it is to be kind to others and never to harbor negative thoughts even if someone harms you. He had a natural gift of imparting spiritual values in the most simple way; he almost charmed you into being your best self. A-pé Dorje was a born storyteller, and he would keep me enthralled as a child with fairy stories and tales from the Gesar epic, or accounts of the struggles in the eastern provinces, when China invaded Tibet in the early 1950s. Wherever he went he brought a lightness and joy, and a humor that would make any difficult situation seem less complicated. Even when he was nearing his eighties, I remember, he was sprightly and active, and went shopping every day almost till his death.

A-pé Dorje used to go shopping every morning around nine. He had heard that Ani Rilu was on the verge of death, and came to her room. He had a habit of speaking rather loudly, almost shouting. "Ani Rilu," he called out. She opened her eyes. "My dear girl," he beamed at her affectionately with his enchanting smile, "now is the moment to show your true mettle. Don't falter. Don't waver. You have been so blessed to have met so many wonderful masters and received teachings from all of them. Not only that, but you have had the price-less opportunity to practice as well. What more could you ask for? Now, the only thing you need to do is to keep the essence of the teachings in your heart, and especially the instruction for the moment of death that your masters have given you. Keep that in your mind, and do not be distracted.

"Don't worry about us, we'll be fine. I'm going shopping now, and perhaps when I come back, I won't see you. So, goodbye." He said this with a huge grin. Ani Rilu was still alert and the way he said it made her smile in recognition, and give a little nod.

A-pé Dorje knew that it is vital, as we come near to death, to essentialize all our spiritual practice into one "heart prac-tice" that embodies everything. What he said to Ani Rilu sums up the third line in the verse by Padmasambhava, which tells us, at the moment of death, to: "Enter, undistracted, into clear awareness of the teaching."

For someone who has gained recognition of the nature of mind and stabilized it in his or her practice, this means to rest in the state of Rigpa. If you do not have that stability, remem-ber, in your innermost heart, the essence of your master's teaching, especially the most essential instructions for the moment of death. *Hold that in your mind and heart, and think of your master, and unite your mind as one with him or her as you die.*

THE INSTRUCTIONS FOR DYING

An image that is often given to characterize the bardo of dying is that of a beautiful actress sitting in front of her mir-ror. Her final performance is about to begin, and she is putting on her makeup and checking her appearance for the last time before going out on stage. In just the same way, at the mo-ment of death the master reintroduces us to the essential truth of the teachings—in the mirror of the nature of mind—and points us directly to the heart of our practice. If our master is not present, spiritual friends who have a good karmic connec-tion with us should be there to help remind us.

It is said that the best time for this introduction is after the outer breathing has ceased and before the end of the "inner respiration," though it is safest to begin during the dissolution process, before the senses have completely failed. If you will not have the opportunity to see your master just before your death, you will need to receive and acquaint yourself with these instructions well beforehand.

If the master is present at the deathbed, what he or she does then in our tradition follows this sequence. The master first declares words like: "O son/ daughter of an enlightened family, listen without distraction . . ." and then leads us through the stages of the dissolution process, one by one. Then he or she will essentialize the heart of the introduction powerfully and explicitly, in a few pungent words, so that it creates a strong impression on our mind, and ask us to rest in the nature of mind. In case this is beyond our capacity, the master will remind us of the phowa practice, if we are familiar with it; if not, he or she will effect the phowa practice for us. Then, as a further precaution, the master might also explain the nature of the experiences of the bardos after death, and how they are all, without exception, the projections of our own mind, and inspire us with the confidence to recognize this at every moment. "O son or daughter, whatever you see, however terrifying it is, recognize it as your own projection; recognize it as the luminosity, the natural radiance of your mind."[3] Finally the master will instruct us to remember the pure realms of the buddhas, to generate devotion, and to pray to be reborn there. The master will repeat the words of the introduction three times, and remaining in the state of Rigpa, direct his or her blessing toward the dying disciple.

THE PRACTICES FOR DYING

There are three essential practices for dying:

- At best, resting in the nature of mind, or evoking the heart-essence of our practice
- Next, the phowa practice, the transference of consciousness
- Last, relying on the power of prayer, devotion, aspiration, and the blessings of enlightened beings.

Supreme practitioners of Dzogchen, as I have said, have completely realized the nature of mind during their lifetime. So when they die, they need only to continue to rest and abide in that state of Rigpa, as they make the transition through death. They have no need to transfer their consciousness into any buddha or enlightened realm, for they have already made real the wisdom mind of the buddhas within themselves. Death, for them, is the moment of ultimate liberation—the crowning moment of their realization, and the consummation of their practice. The *Tibetan Book of the Dead* has only these few words to remind such a practitioner: "O Sir! Now the Ground Luminosity is dawning. Recognize it, and rest in the practice."

Those who have completely accomplished the practice of Dzogchen are said to die *"like a new-born child,"* free of all care and concern about death. They do not need to concern themselves with when or where they will die, nor do they have any need of teachings, instructions, or reminders.

"Medium practitioners of the best capacity" die *"like beggars in the street."* No one notices them and nothing disturbs them. Because of the stability of their practice, they are absolutely unaffected by the environment around them. They could die with the same ease in a busy hospital, or at home in the middle of a nagging and squabbling family.

I shall never forget an old yogin I knew in Tibet. He used to be like a Pied Piper, and all the children would follow him around. Everywhere he went, he would chant and sing, drawing the whole community around him, and he would tell them all to practice and to say "OM MANI PADME HUM," the mantra of the Buddha of Compassion.[4] He had a big prayer wheel; and whenever anyone gave him something, he would sew it onto his clothes, so that he ended up looking like a prayer wheel himself as he turned about. Also, I remember, he had a dog who followed him everywhere. He treated the dog like a human being, ate the same food as the dog from the same bowl, slept next to him, looked on him as his best friend, and regularly even talked to him.

Not many people took him seriously, and some called him a "crazy yogin," but many Lamas spoke highly of him and said we should not look down on him. My grandfather and my family would always treat him with respect, and would invite him into the shrine-room and offer him tea and bread. In Tibet it was the custom never to visit someone's home empty-handed, and one day, in the middle of drinking his tea, he stopped: "Oh! I'm sorry, I almost forgot . . . this is my gift for you!" He picked up the very bread and white scarf my grandfather had just offered him, and gave them back to him as if they were a present.

Often he used to sleep outside in the open air. One day, in the precincts of the Dzogchen monastery, he passed away: with his dog by his side, right in the middle of the street, and in a pile of garbage. No one expected what happened next, but it was witnessed by many people. All around his body appeared a dazzling sphere of rainbow-colored light.

It is said that "medium practitioners of middling capacity die *like wild animals or lions, on snow mountains, in mountain caves and empty valleys.*" They can take care of themselves completely, and prefer to go to deserted places and die quietly, without being disturbed or fussed over by friends and relatives.

Accomplished practitioners such as these are reminded by the master of the practices they would employ as they approach death. Here are two examples, which come from the tradition of Dzogchen. In the first, practitioners are advised to lie down in the "sleeping lion position." Then they are told to focus their awareness in their eyes, and fix their gaze in the sky in front of them. Simply leaving their mind unaltered, they rest in that state, allowing their Rigpa to mix with the primordial space of truth. As the Ground Luminosity of death arises, they flow into it quite naturally and attain enlightenment.

But this is only possible for a person who has already stabilized his or her realization of the nature of mind through the practice. For those who have not reached this level of perfection, and need a more formal method to focus on, there is another practice: To visualize their consciousness as a white syllable "A," and eject it through the central channel and out through the crown of their heads into the buddha realm. This is a practice of phowa, the transference of consciousness, and it is the method my master helped Lama Tseten to do when he died.

People who successfully accomplish either of these two practices will still go through the physical processes of dying, it is said, but they will not go through the subsequent bardo states.

PHOWA: THE TRANSFERENCE OF THE CONSCIOUSNESS

Now that the bardo of dying dawns upon me,
I will abandon all grasping, yearning, and attachment,
Enter undistracted into clear awareness of the teaching,

And eject my consciousness into the space of unborn Rigpa,
As I leave this compound body of flesh and blood
I will know it to be a transitory illusion.

"Ejecting the consciousness into the space of unborn Rigpa" refers to the transference of consciousness, the phowa practice, which is the most commonly used practice for dying, and the special instruction associated with the bardo of dying. Phowa is a practice of yoga and meditation that has been used for centuries to help the dying and to prepare for death. The principle is that at the moment of death, the practitioner ejects his or her consciousness and merges it with the wisdom mind of the Buddha, in what Padmasambhava calls "the space of unborn Rigpa." This practice can be carried out by the individual, or effected by a qualified master or good practitioner on the individual's behalf.

There are many categories of phowa, which correspond to the capacities, experience, and training of different individuals. But the phowa practice that is most commonly used is known as the "phowa of three recognitions": *recognition of our central channel[5] as the path; recognition of our consciousness as the traveler; and recognition of the environment of a buddha realm as the destination.*

Ordinary Tibetan people with responsibilities of work and family are not able to devote all their lives to study and practice, yet they have tremendous faith and trust in the teachings. When their children grow up and they approach the end of their lives—what in the West would be called "retirement"—Tibetans often go on pilgrimage or meet masters and concentrate on spiritual practice; frequently they will undertake a training in phowa to prepare for death. Phowa is often referred to in the teachings as a method of attaining enlightenment without a lifelong experience of meditation practice.

In the phowa practice, the central presence invoked is that of the Buddha Amitabha, the Buddha of Limitless Light. Amitabha enjoys widespread popularity among ordinary people in China and Japan, as well as in Tibet and the Himalayas. He is the primordial Buddha of the Lotus or Padma family, which is the buddha family to which human beings belong; he represents our pure nature, and symbolizes the transmutation of desire, the predominant emotion of the human realm. More intrinsically, Amitabha is the limitless, luminous nature of our mind. At death the true nature of mind will manifest at the moment of the dawning of the Ground Luminosity, yet not all of us may have the familiarity with it to recognize it. How skillful and compassionate the buddhas are to have handed down to us a method for invoking the very embodiment of the luminosity, in the radiant presence of Amitabha!

It would be inappropriate here to explain the details of the traditional phowa practice, which must, always and in all circumstances, be carried out under the guidance of a qualified master. Never try to do this practice on your own without the proper guidance.

At death, the teachings explain, our consciousness, which is mounted on a "wind" and so needs an aperture through which to leave the body, can leave it through any one of nine openings. The route it takes determines exactly which realm of existence we are to be reborn in. When it leaves through the opening at the fontanel, at the crown of the head, we are reborn, it is said, in a pure land, where we can gradually proceed toward enlightenment.[6]

This practice, I must stress again, can only be carried out under the supervision of a qualified master, who has the blessing to give the proper transmission. It does not require extensive intellectual knowledge or depth of realization to accomplish the phowa successfully, only devotion, compassion, one-pointed visualization, and a deep feeling of the presence of the Buddha Amitabha. The student receives the instructions and then practices them until the signs of accomplishment appear. These include an itching at the top of the head, headaches, the emergence of a clear fluid, a swelling or a softness around the area of the fontanel, or even the opening of a small hole there, into which traditionally the tip of a stalk of grass is inserted as a test or measure of how successful the practice has been.

Recently a group of elderly Tibetan lay people settled in Switzerland trained under a well-known phowa master. Their children, who had been brought up in Switzerland, were skeptical about the effectiveness of this practice. But they were astounded at how their parents had been transformed and actually showed some of the signs of accomplishment mentioned above after a ten-day phowa retreat.

Research into the psychophysiological effects of phowa has been carried out by the Japanese scientist Dr. Hiroshi Motoyama. Precise physiological changes in the nervous, metabolic, and acupuncture meridian systems were detected to take place during phowa practice.[7] One of Dr. Motoyama's findings was that the patterns of the flow of energy through the meridians of the body of the phowa master he was studying were very similar to those measured in psychics with strong ESP abilities. He also found, from EEG (electroencephalograph) measurements, that brain waves during the phowa practice were quite different from those found in yogins practicing other kinds of meditation. They showed that phowa involves the stimulation of a certain part of the brain, the hypothalamus, as well as the stopping of ordinary conscious mental activity, in order to allow a deep state of meditation to be experienced.

Sometimes it is the case that through the blessing of the phowa, ordinary people will have strong visionary experiences. Their glimpses of the peace and light of the Buddha realm, and their visions of Amitabha, are reminiscent of certain aspects of the near-death experience. And, as in the near-death experience, success in the phowa practice also brings confidence and fearlessness in facing the moment of death.

The essential phowa practice I have explained in the previous chapter is as much a healing practice for the living as a practice for the moment of death, and can be done *at any time without danger.* However, the timing of the traditional phowa practice is of paramount importance. For example, it is said that if one were actually to transfer one's consciousness successfully, before the moment of natural death, it would be equivalent to suicide. The point when the phowa is done is when the outer respiration has ceased, and the inner breathing still continues; but perhaps it is safest to begin the phowa practice during the dissolution process (described in the next chapter), and to repeat the practice several times.

So when a master who has perfected the traditional phowa performs it for a dying person, visualizing the consciousness of the person and ejecting it out through the fontanel, it is essential that the timing is right and it is not done too early. An advanced practitioner, however, with knowledge of the process of death, can check details such as the channels, the movement of the winds, and the heat of the body to see when the moment for phowa has come. If a master is requested to do the transference for someone who is dying, he or she should be contacted as soon as possible, because even from a distance phowa can still be effected.

A number of obstacles to a successful phowa can present themselves. As any unwholesome frame of mind, or even the smallest longing for any possession, will be a hindrance when the time of death arrives, you should try not to be dominated by even the slightest negative thought or hankering. In Tibet they used to believe that phowa would be very difficult to accomplish if there were any materials made of animal skins or furs in the same room as the dying person. Finally as smoking—or any kind of drug—has the effect of blocking the central channel, it will render the phowa more difficult.

"Even a great sinner," it is said, can be liberated at the moment of death if a realized and powerful master transfers the person's consciousness into a buddha realm. And even if the dying person lacks merit and practice, and the master is not completely successful in effecting the phowa, the master can still effect the dying person's future, and this practice can help him or her take rebirth in a higher realm. For a successful phowa, however, the conditions do have to be perfect. Phowa can help a person with strong negative karma, but only if that person has a close and pure connection with the master who performs it, if he or she has faith in the teachings, and if he or she has truly asked, from the heart, for purification.

In an ideal setting in Tibet, members of the family would normally invite many Lamas to come and do the phowa again and again, until the signs of accomplishment appeared. They might do it for hours on end, hundreds of times, or even the whole day long. Some dying persons would take only one or two sessions of phowa to manifest a sign, whereas for others not even a whole day was enough. This, it goes without saying, depends very much on the karma of the person dying.

In Tibet there were practitioners who, even though they were not renowned for their practice, had special power to effect the phowa, and the signs would readily appear. There are various signs in the dying person of a successful phowa carried out by a practitioner. Sometimes a bunch of hair falls out near the fontanel, or a warmth or vapor is felt or seen to rise from the crown of the head. In some exceptional cases, the masters or practitioners have been so powerful that when they uttered the syllable that effects the transference, everyone in the room would faint, or a piece of bone would fly off the dead person's skull as the consciousness was propelled out with immense force.[8]

THE GRACE OF PRAYER
AT THE MOMENT OF DEATH

In all religious traditions it is held that to die in a state of prayer is enormously powerful. So what I hope you can do, as you die, is to invoke wholeheartedly all the buddhas and your master. Pray that, through regretting all your negative actions in this and other lives, they may be purified, and that you may die consciously and at peace, gain a good rebirth, and ultimately achieve liberation.

Make a one-pointed and concentrated wish that you will be reborn either in a pure realm or as a human being, but in order to protect, nurture, and help others. To die with such love and such tender compassion in your heart until your last breath is said in the Tibetan tradition to be another form of phowa, and it will ensure that you will at least attain another precious human body.

To create the most positive possible imprint on the mind-stream before death is essential. The most effective practice of all to achieve this is a simple practice of Guru Yoga, where the dying person merges his or her mind with the wisdom mind of the master, or Buddha, or any enlightened being. Even if you cannot visualize your master at this moment, try at least to remember him, think of him in your heart, and die in a state of devotion. When your consciousness awakens again after death, this imprint of the master's presence will awaken with you, and you will be liberated. If you die remembering the master, then the possibilities of his or her grace are limit-less: even the display of sound, light, and color in the bardo of dharmata may arise as the master's blessing and the radi-ance of his or her wisdom nature.

If the master is present at the deathbed, he or she will ensure that the mindstream of the dying person is imprinted with his or her presence. The master may, to distract the dying person from other distractions, make some striking and significant remark. He or she might say in a loud voice: "Remember me!" The master will draw the dying person's attention in whatever way is necessary, and create an indelible impression that will return as a memory of the master in the bardo state. When one well-known teacher's mother was dying and slipping into a coma, Dilgo Khyentse Rinpoche was present at her bedside and did something very unusual. He slapped her on the leg. If she did not forget Dilgo Khyentse

THE PRACTICES FOR DYING

Rinpoche as she entered into death, she would have been blessed indeed.

In our tradition ordinary practitioners will also pray to whichever buddha they feel devotion for, and with whom they feel a karmic connection. If it is Padmasambhava, they will pray to be born in his glorious pure realm, the Palace of Lotus Light on the Copper Colored Mountain; and if it is Amitabha they love and revere, they will pray to be reborn in his "Blissful" heaven, the marvelous Pure Land of Dewachen.[9]

THE ATMOSPHERE FOR DYING

How then do we most sensitively help ordinary spiritual practitioners who are dying? All of us will need the love and care that comes with emotional and practical support, but for spiritual practitioners the atmosphere, intensity, and dimension of spiritual help take on a special meaning. It would be ideal, and a great blessing, if their master were with them; but if this is not possible, their spiritual friends can be of enormous help in reminding the dying person of the essence of the teachings and the practice that has been closest to their heart during life. For a practitioner who is dying, spiritual inspiration, and the atmosphere of trust and faith and devotion that will naturally arise from it, are essential. The loving and unflagging presence of the master or spiritual friends, the encouragement of the teachings, and the strength of their own practice, all combine together to create and sustain this inspiration, as precious in the last weeks and days almost as breath itself.

A beloved student of mine was dying of cancer, and asked me how best she should practice as she came nearer to death, particularly when she no longer had the strength to concentrate on any formal practice.

"Remember just how very fortunate you have been," I told her, "to have met so many masters, received so many teachings, and had the time and possibility to practice. I promise you, the benefit of all that will never leave you: The good karma you have created by it will stay with you and help you. Even to hear the teaching once, or meet a master like Dilgo Khyentse Rinpoche and have a strong connection with him as you did, is liberating in itself. Never forget that, and never forget also how many people there are in your position who did not have that marvelous opportunity.

"If the time comes when you cannot practice actively any more, the only really important thing for you to do is to relax, as deeply as possible, in the confidence of the View, and rest in the nature of mind. It does not matter whether your body or your brain are still functioning: the nature of your mind is always there, sky-like, radiant, blissful, limitless and unchanging . . . Know that beyond all doubt, and let that knowledge give you the strength to say with carefree abandon to all your pain, however great it is: 'Go away now, and leave me alone!' If there is anything that irritates you or makes you feel uncomfortable in any way, don't waste your time trying to change it; keep returning to the View.

"Trust in the nature of your mind, trust it deeply, and relax completely. There is nothing new you need to learn or acquire or understand; just allow what you have already been given to blossom in you and open at greater and greater depths.

"Rely on whatever for you is the most inspiring of all the practices. And if it is difficult for you to visualize or follow a formal kind of practice, remember what Dudjom Rinpoche always used to say: that to feel the presence is more important than getting the details of the visualization clear. Now is the time to feel, as intensely as you can, to feel with your whole being the presence of your masters, of Padmasambhava, of the buddhas. Whatever may be happening to your body, remember that your heart is never sick or crippled.

"You have loved Dilgo Khyentse Rinpoche: Feel his presence, and really ask him for help and purification. Put yourself entirely in his hands: heart and mind, body and soul. The simplicity of total trust is one of the most powerful forces in the world.

"Did I ever tell you that beautiful story about Ben of Kongpo? He was a very simple man, with immense faith, who came from Kongpo, a province in southeastern Tibet. He had heard a lot about the Jowo Rinpoche, the 'Precious Lord,' a beautiful statue of Buddha as a prince at the age of twelve that is kept in the central cathedral in Lhasa. It is said to have been made while the Buddha was alive, and is the most holy statue in the whole of Tibet. Ben could not make out whether it was a buddha or a human being, and he was determined to go and visit the Jowo Rinpoche to see what all the talk was about. So he put on his boots and walked, week after week, to get to Lhasa in central Tibet.

"He was hungry when he arrived, and when he entered the cathedral, he saw the great statue of Buddha, and in front of it a row of butter-lamps and special cakes made as offerings to the shrine. He assumed at once that these cakes were what the Jowo Rinpoche ate: 'The cakes,' he said to himself, 'must be for dipping into the butter in the lamps, and the lamps must be kept alight to stop the butter from going hard. I'd better do what Jowo Rinpoche does.' So he dipped one in the butter and ate it, looking up at the statue, which seemed to be smiling down benignly just at him.

"'What a nice Lama you are,' he said. 'The dogs come in and steal the food people offer you, and all you do is smile. The wind blows out the lamps, and still you keep on smiling . . . Anyway, I am going to walk all around the temple in prayer, to show my respect. Would you mind looking after my boots till I get back?' Taking off his dirty old boots, he placed them on the altar in front of the statue, and left.

"While Ben was walking around the huge temple, the caretaker returned and saw to his horror that someone had been eating the offerings and had left a filthy pair of boots on the altar. He was outraged, and furiously seized the boots to throw them outside, when a voice came from the statue, saying: 'Stop! Put those boots back. I'm watching them for Ben of Kongpo.'

"Soon Ben came back to collect his boots, and gazed up at the face of the statue, still calmly smiling at him. 'You really are what I'd call a good Lama. Why don't you come down to our place next year? I will roast a pig and brew some beer . . .' The Jowo Rinpoche spoke for a second time, and promised he would visit Ben.

"Ben went home to Kongpo, told his wife everything that had happened, and instructed her to keep an eye open for the Jowo Rinpoche, because he didn't know exactly when he was coming. The year went by, and one day his wife came rushing back to the house to tell him she had seen something glowing like the sun, under the surface of the river. Ben told her to put the water on for tea, and raced down to the river. He saw the Jowo Rinpoche glittering in the water, and immediately thought he must have fallen in and was drowning. He leapt into the water, took hold of him and carried him out.

"As they went back to Ben's house, chatting all the way, they came to a huge rock face. The Jowo Rinpoche said:

'Well, actually I'm afraid I cannot come into the house,' and with that he dissolved into the rock. To this day there are two famous places of pilgrimage in Kongpo: one is the Rock Jowo, the rock face where a form of Buddha can be seen, and the other is the River Jowo, where the shape of Buddha can be seen in the river. People say that the blessing and the healing power of these places are identical to the Jowo Rinpoche in Lhasa. And it was all because of Ben's immense faith and simple trust.

"I want you to have the same kind of pure trust as Ben. Let your heart fill with devotion for Padmasambhava and Dilgo Khyentse Rinpoche, and simply feel you are in his presence, that the whole space around you is him. Then invoke him and go over in your mind every moment you spent with him. Merge your mind with his and say, from the depths of your heart, in your own words, 'You see how helpless I am, how I can no longer practice intensively. Now I must rely totally on you. I trust you completely. Take care of me. Make me one with you.' Do the Guru Yoga practice, imagining with special intensity the rays of light streaming out from your master and purifying you, burning away all your impurities, your illness too, and healing you; your body melting into light; and merging your mind, in the end, with his wisdom mind, in complete confidence.

"When you practice, don't worry if you feel it is not flowing easily; simply trust and feel it in your heart. Everything now depends on inspiration, because only that will relax your anxiety and dissolve your nervousness. So keep a wonderful photograph of Dilgo Khyentse Rinpoche, or Padmasambhava, in front of you. Focus on it gently at the beginning of your practice, and then just relax into its radiance. Imagine it was sunny outside, and that you could take off all your clothes and bask in the warmth: slip out of all your inhibitions and relax in the glow of the blessing, when you really feel it. And deeply, deeply let go of everything.

"Don't worry about anything. Even if you find your attention wandering, there is no particular 'thing' you have to hold onto. Just let go, and drift in the awareness of the blessing. Don't let small, niggling, questions distract you, like 'Is this Rigpa? Is it not?' Just let yourself be more and more natural. Remember, your Rigpa is always there, always in the nature of your mind. Remember Dilgo Khyentse Rinpoche's words: 'If your mind is unaltered, you are in the state of Rigpa.' So as you have received the teachings, you received the introduction to the nature of mind, just relax in the Rigpa, without doubting.

"You are lucky enough to have some good spiritual friends near you now. Encourage them to create an environment of practice around you, and to go on practicing around you up until and after your death. Get them to read you a poem you love, or a guidance from your master, or an inspiring teaching. Ask them to play you a tape of Dilgo Khyentse Rinpoche, a chant of the practice, or an exalting piece of music. What I pray is that your every waking moment should mingle with the blessing of the practice, in an atmosphere alive and luminous with inspiration.

"As the music or the tape of the teaching goes on playing, drift off to sleep in it, wake up in it, doze in it, eat in it . . . Let the atmosphere of practice totally pervade this last part of your life, just as my aunt Ani Rilu did. Do nothing but practice, so that it even continues in your dreams. And just as she did, let the practice be the last and strongest memory and influence on your mind, replacing in your mindstream a lifetime's ordinary habits.

"And as you feel yourself nearing the end, think only of Dilgo Khyentse Rinpoche, with every breath and heartbeat. Whatever thought you die with, remember, is the one that will return most potently when you reawaken in the bardos after death."

LEAVING THE BODY

Now that the bardo of dying dawns upon me,
I will abandon all grasping, yearning and attachment,
Enter undistracted into clear awareness of the teaching,
And eject my consciousness into the space of unborn Rigpa;
As I leave this compound body of flesh and blood
I will know it to be a transitory illusion.

At present, our body is undoubtedly the center of our whole universe. We associate it, without thinking, with our self and our ego, and this thoughtless and false association continually reinforces our illusion of their inseparable, concrete existence. Because our body seems so convincingly to exist, our "I" seems to exist and "you" seem to exist, and the entire illusory, dualistic world we never stop projecting around us looks ultimately solid and real. When we die this whole compound construction falls dramatically to pieces.

What happens, to put it extremely simply, is that consciousness, at its subtlest level, continues without the body and goes through the series of states called "bardos." The teachings tell us that it is precisely because we no longer have a body in the bardos that there is no ultimate reason to fear any experience, however terrifying, that may happen to us after death. How can any harm, after all, ever come to a "nobody"? The problem, however, is that in the bardos, most people go on grasping at a false sense of self, with its ghostly grasping at physical solidity; and this continuation of that illusion, which has been at the root of all suffering in life, exposes them in death to more suffering, especially in the "bardo of becoming."

What is essential, you can see, is to realize now, in life, when we still have a body, that its apparent, so convincing solidity is a mere illusion. The most powerful way to realize this is to learn how, after meditation, to "become a child of illusion": to refrain from solidifying, as we are always tempted to do, the perceptions of ourselves and our world; and to go on, like the "child of illusion," seeing directly, as we do in meditation, that all phenomena are illusory and dreamlike. The realization that this deepens of the body's illusory nature is one of the most profound and inspiring we can have to help us to let go.

Inspired by and armed with this knowledge, when we are faced at death with the *fact* that our body is an illusion, we will be able to recognize its illusory nature without fear, to calmly free ourselves from all attachment to it, and to leave it behind willingly, even gratefully and joyfully, knowing it now for what it is. In fact, you could say, we will be able, really and completely, *to die when we die,* and so achieve ultimate freedom.

Think, then, of the moment of death as a strange border zone of the mind, a no-man's land in which on the one hand, if we do not understand the illusory nature of our body, we might suffer vast emotional trauma as we lose it; and on the other hand, we are presented with the possibility of limitless freedom, a freedom that springs precisely from the absence of that very same body.

When we are at last freed from the body that has defined and dominated our understanding of ourselves for so long, the karmic vision of one life is completely exhausted, but any karma that might be created in the future has not yet begun to crystallize. So what happens in death is that there is a "gap" or space that is fertile with vast possibility; it is a moment of tremendous, pregnant power where the only thing that matters, or could matter, is how exactly our mind *is*. Stripped of a physical body, mind stands naked, revealed startlingly for what it has always been: the architect of our reality.

So if, at the moment of death, we have already a stable realization of the nature of mind, in one instant we can purify all our karma. And if we continue that stable recognition, we will actually be able to end our karma altogether, by entering the expanse of the primordial purity of the nature of mind, and attaining liberation. Padmasambhava explained this:

> *Why is it, you might wonder, that during the bardo state you can find stability by merely recognizing the nature of mind for a single instant? The answer is this: at present our mind is encased in a net, the net of the "wind of karma." And the "wind of karma" is encased itself in a net, the net of our physical body. The result is that we have no independence or freedom.*
>
> *But as soon as our body has separated into mind and matter, in the gap before it has been encased once again in the net of a future body, the mind,*[10] *along with its magical display, has no concrete, material support. For as long as it lacks such a material basis, we are independent—and we can recognize.*

This power to attain stability by just recognizing the nature of mind is like a torch which in one instant can clear away the darkness of eons. *So if we can recognize the nature of mind in the bardo in the same way as we can now when it is introduced by the master, there is not the slightest doubt that we will attain enlightenment. This is why, from this very moment on, we must become familiar with the nature of mind through practice.*[11]

FIFTEEN

The Process of Dying

IN THE WORDS OF PADMASAMBHAVA,

Human beings face two causes of death: untimely death and death due to the exhaustion of their natural lifespan. Untimely death can be averted through the methods taught for prolonging life. However, when the cause of death is the exhaustion of the natural lifespan, you are like a lamp which has run out of oil. There is no way of averting death by cheating it; you have to get ready to go.

Let us look now at the two causes of death: the exhaustion of our natural lifespan, and an obstacle or accident that brings our life to an untimely end.

THE EXHAUSTION OF OUR LIFESPAN

Because of our karma, we all have a certain lifespan; and when it is exhausted, it is extremely difficult to prolong our lives. However, a person who has perfected the advanced practices of yoga can overcome even this limit, and actually lengthen his or her life. There is a tradition that sometimes masters will be told by their teachers the length of their lifespan. Yet they know that through the strength of their own practice, the purity of their link with their students and their practice, and the benefit of their work, they can live longer. My master told Dilgo Khyentse Rinpoche he would live to the age of eighty, but beyond that depended on his own practice; he lived into his eighty-second year. Dudjom Rinpoche was told he had a lifespan of seventy-three, but he lived until the age of eighty-two.

UNTIMELY DEATH

It is said, on the other hand, that if it is only an obstacle of some kind that threatens us with untimely death, it can be more easily averted—provided, of course, that we have fore-knowledge. In the bardo teachings and Tibetan medical texts, we can find descriptions of signs warning of impending death, some foretelling death within years or months, and others in terms of weeks or days. They include physical signs, certain specific kinds of dreams, and special investigations using shadow images.[1] Unfortunately only someone with expert knowledge will be able to interpret these signs. Their purpose is to forewarn a person that his or her life is in danger, and to alert the person to the need for using practices that lengthen life, before these obstacles occur.

Any spiritual practice we do, since it accumulates "merit," will help prolong our lives and bring good health. A good practitioner, through the inspiration and power of his or her practice, comes to feel psychologically, emotionally, and spiritually whole, and this is both the greatest source of healing and the strongest protection against illness.

There are also special "long-life practices," which summon the life-energy from the elements and the universe through the power of meditation and visualization. When our energy is weak and unbalanced, these longevity practices strengthen and coordinate it, and this has the effect of extending our lifespan. There are also many other practices for enhancing life. One is to save the lives of animals that are due to be slaughtered, by buying them and setting them free. This practice is popular in Tibet and the Himalayan regions, where, for example, people often go to the fish market to buy fish and then release them. It is based on the natural karmic logic that taking the life of others or harming them will shorten your life, and giving life will lengthen it.

THE "PAINFUL" BARDO OF DYING

The bardo of dying falls between the moment we contract a terminal illness or condition that will end in death, and the ceasing of the "inner respiration." It is called "painful" because if we are not prepared for what will happen to us at death, it can be an experience of tremendous suffering.

Even for a practitioner the whole process of dying can still be a painful one, as losing the body and this life may be a very difficult experience. But if we have had instructions on the meaning of death, we will know what enormous hope there is when the Ground Luminosity dawns at the moment of death. However, there still remains the uncertainty of whether we will recognize it or not, and this is why it is so important to stabilize the recognition of the nature of mind through practice while we are still alive.

Many of us, however, have not had the good fortune to encounter the teachings, and we have no idea of what death really is. When we suddenly realize that our whole life, our whole reality, is disappearing, it is terrifying: We don't know what is happening to us, or where we are going. Nothing in our previous experience has prepared us for this. As anyone who has cared for the dying will know, our anxiety will even heighten the experience of physical pain. If we have not taken care of our lives, or our actions have been harmful and negative, we will feel regret, guilt, and fear. So just to have a measure of familiarity with these teachings on the bardos will bring us some reassurance, inspiration, and hope, even though we may never have practiced and realized them.

For good practitioners who know exactly what is happening, not only is death less painful and fearful but it is the very moment they have been looking forward to; they face it with equanimity, and even with joy. I remember how Dudjom Rinpoche used to tell the story of the death of one realized yogin. He had been ill for a few days, and his doctor came to read his pulse. The doctor detected that he was going to die, but he was not sure whether to tell him or not; his face fell, and he stood by the bedside looking solemn and serious. But the yogin insisted, with an almost childlike enthusiasm, that he tell him the worst. Finally the doctor gave in, but tried to speak as if to console him. He said gravely: "Be careful, the time has come." To the doctor's amazement the yogin was delighted, and as thrilled as a little child looking at a Christmas present that he is about to open. "Is it really true?" he asked. "What sweet words, what joyful news!" He gazed into the sky and passed away directly in a state of deep meditation.

In Tibet everyone knew that to die a spectacular death was the way to really make a name for yourself if you had not managed to do so already in life. One man I heard of was determined to die miraculously and in a grand style. He knew that often masters will indicate when they are going to die, and summon their disciples together to be present at their death. So this particular man gathered all his friends for a great feast around his deathbed. He sat there in meditation posture waiting for death, but nothing happened. After several hours his guests began to get tired of waiting and said to each other: "Let's start eating." They filled their plates, and then looked up at the prospective corpse and said: "He's dying, he doesn't need to eat." As time went by and still there was not a sign of death, the "dying" man became famished himself, and worried that there would soon be nothing left to eat. He got down from his deathbed and joined in the feast. His great deathbed scene had turned into a humiliating fiasco.

Good practitioners can take care of themselves when they die, but ordinary ones will need to have their teacher at their bedside, if possible, or otherwise a spiritual friend who can remind them of the essence of their practice and inspire them to the View.

Whoever we are, it can be a great help to be familiar with the process of dying. If we understand the stages of dying, we will know that all the strange and unfamiliar experiences we are passing through are part of a natural process. As this process begins, it signals the coming of death, and reminds us to alert ourselves. And for a practitioner each stage of dying will be a signpost, reminding us of what is happening to us, and of the practice to do at each point.

THE PROCESS OF DYING

The process of dying is explained in considerable detail in the different Tibetan teachings. Essentially it consists of two phases of dissolution: an outer dissolution, when the senses and elements dissolve, and an inner dissolution of the gross and subtle thought states and emotions. But first we need to understand the components of our body and mind, which disintegrate at death.

Our whole existence is determined by the elements: earth, water, fire, air, and space. Through them our body is formed and sustained, and when they dissolve, we die. We are familiar with the outer elements, which condition the way in which we live, but what is interesting is how these outer elements interact with the inner elements within our own physical body. And the potential and quality of these five elements also exist within our mind. Mind's ability to serve as the ground for all experience is the quality of earth; its continuity and adaptability is water; its clarity and capacity to perceive is fire; its continuous movement is air; and its unlimited emptiness is space.

The following explains how our physical body is formed. An ancient Tibetan medical text states:

*The sense consciousnesses arise from one's mind. The flesh, bones,
organ of smelling and odors are formed from the earth element. The
blood, organ of taste, tastes and liquids in the body arise from the
water element. The warmth, clear coloration, the organ of sight and
form are formed from the fire element. The breath, organ of
touch and physical sensations are formed from the air element.
The cavities in the body, the organ of hearing and sounds are
formed from the space element.*[2]

"In short," writes Kalu Rinpoche, "it is from mind, which
embodies the five elemental qualities, that the physical body
develops. The physical body itself is imbued with these
qualities, and it is because of this mind/body complex that
we perceive the outside world—which in turn is composed
of the five elemental qualities of earth, water, fire, wind and
space."[3]

The Tantric Buddhist tradition of Tibet offers an explanation of the body that is quite different from the one most of
us are used to. This is of a psycho-physical system, which
consists of a dynamic network of subtle channels, "winds" or
inner air, and essences. These are called respectively: *nadi,
prana,* and *bindu* in Sanskrit; and *tsa, lung,* and *tiklé* in Tibetan.
We are familiar with something similar in the meridians and
ch'i energy of Chinese medicine and acupuncture.

The human body is compared by the masters to a city, the
channels to its roads, the winds to a horse, and the mind to a
rider. There are 72,000 subtle channels in the body, but three
principal ones: the central channel, running parallel to the
spine, and the right and left channels, which run either side
of it. The right and left channels coil around the central one
at a number of points to form a series of "knots." Along the
central channel are situated a number of "channel wheels,"
the *chakras* or energy-centers, from which channels branch off
like the ribs of an umbrella.

Through these channels flow the winds, or inner air. There
are five root and five branch winds. Each of the root winds
supports an element and is responsible for a function of the
human body. The branch winds enable the senses to operate.
The winds that flow through all the channels except the central one are said to be impure and activate negative, dualistic
thought patterns; the winds in the central channel are called
"wisdom winds."[4]

The "essences" are contained within the channels. There
are red and white essences. The principal seat of the white

essence is the crown of the head, and of the red essence at the navel.

In advanced yoga practice, this system is visualized very precisely by a yogin. By causing the winds to enter and dissolve in the central channel through the force of meditation, a practitioner can have a direct realization of the luminosity or "Clear Light" of the nature of mind. This is made possible by the fact that the consciousness is mounted on the wind. So by directing his or her mind to any particular point in the body, a practitioner can bring the winds there. In this way the yogin is imitating what happens at death: when the knots in the channels are released, the winds flow into the central channel, and enlightenment is momentarily experienced.

Dilgo Khyentse Rinpoche tells the story of a retreat master at a monastery in Kham, who was close to his elder brothers. This master had perfected the yoga practice of channels, winds, and essences. One day he asked his attendant: "I am going to die now, so would you please look in the calendar for an auspicious date." The attendant was stunned, but did not dare contradict his master. He looked in the calendar and told him that the following Monday was a day when all the stars were auspicious. The master then said: "Monday is three days away. Well, I think I can make it." When his attendant came back into his room a few moments later, he found the master sitting upright in yogic meditation posture, so still that it looked as though he had passed away. There was no breathing, but a faint pulse was perceptible. He decided not to do anything, but to wait. At noon he suddenly heard a deep exhalation, and the master returned to his normal condition, talked with his attendant in a joyful mood, and asked for his lunch, which he ate with relish. He had been holding his breath for the whole of the morning session of meditation. The reason why he did this is that our lifespan is counted as a finite number of breaths, and the master, knowing he was near the end of these, held his breath so that the final number would not be reached till the auspicious day. Just after lunch, the master took a deep breath in again, and held it until the evening. He did the same the next day, and the day after. When Monday came, he asked: "Is today the auspicious day?" "Yes" replied the attendant. "Fine, I shall go today," concluded the master. And that day, without any visible illness or difficulty, the master passed away in his meditation.

Once we have a physical body, we also have what are known as the five *skandhas*—the aggregates that compose our

whole mental and physical existence. They are the constituents of our experience, the support for the grasping of ego,
and also the basis for the suffering of samsara. They are:
form, feeling, perception, intellect, and consciousness, also
translated as: form, sensation, recognition, formation, and
consciousness. "The five skandhas represent the constant
structure of the human psychology as well as its pattern of
evolution and the pattern of the evolution of the world.
The skandhas are also related to blockages of different
types—spiritual ones, material ones, and emotional ones."[5]
They are examined in great depth in Buddhist psychology.

All of these components will dissolve when we die. The
process of dying is a complex and interdependent one, in
which groups of related aspects of our body and mind disintegrate simultaneously. As the winds disappear, the bodily functions and the senses fail. The energy centers collapse, and
without their supporting winds the elements dissolve in
sequence from the grossest to the subtlest. The result is that
each stage of the dissolution has its physical and psychological
effect on the dying person, and is reflected by external, physical signs as well as inner experiences.

Friends sometimes ask me: Can people like us see these
external signs in a friend or relative who is dying? My students who care for the dying have told me that some of these
physical signs described below are observed in hospices and
hospitals. However, the stages of the outer dissolution may
take place extremely quickly and not very obviously, and
generally people caring for the dying in the modern world are
not looking for them. Often nurses in busy hospitals rely on
their intuition and many other factors, such as the behavior of
doctors or members of the patient's family, or the state of
mind of the dying person, to predict when someone might be
dying. They also observe, but not at all in a systematic way,
some physical signs, such as the change in skin color, a certain smell sometimes remarked on, and a noticeable change in
breathing. Modern drugs, however, may well mask the signs
that Tibetan teachings indicate, and there is as yet surprisingly little research in the West on this most important topic.
Doesn't this show how little the process of dying is understood or respected?

THE POSITION FOR DYING

Traditionally the position generally recommended for
dying is to lie down on the right side, taking the position of

"the sleeping lion," which is the posture in which Buddha died. The left hand rests on the left thigh; the right hand is placed under the chin, closing the right nostril. The legs are stretched out and very slightly bent. On the right side of the body are certain subtle channels that encourage the "karmic wind" of delusion. Lying on them in the sleeping lion's posture, and closing the right nostril, blocks these channels and facilitates a person's recognition of the luminosity when it dawns at death. It also helps the consciousness to leave the body through the aperture at the crown of the head, as all the other openings through which it could leave are blocked.

THE OUTER DISSOLUTION:
THE SENSES AND THE ELEMENTS

The outer dissolution is when the senses and elements dissolve. How exactly will we experience this when we die?

The first thing we may be aware of is how our senses cease to function. If people around our bed are talking, there will come a point where we can hear the sound of their voices but we cannot make out the words. This means that the ear consciousness has ceased to function. We look at an object in front of us, and we can only see its outline, not its details. This means that the eye consciousness has failed. And the same happens with our faculties of smell, taste, and touch. When the senses are no longer fully experienced, it marks the first phase of the dissolution process.

The next four phases follow the dissolution of the elements:

Earth
Our body begins to lose all its strength. We are drained of any energy. We cannot get up, stay upright, or hold anything. We can no longer support our head. We feel as though we are falling, sinking underground, or being crushed by a great weight. Some traditional texts say that it is as if a huge mountain were being pressed down upon us, and we were being squashed by it. We feel heavy and uncomfortable in any position. We may ask to be pulled up, to have our pillows made higher, or for the bed-covers to be taken off. Our complexion fades and a pallor sets in. Our cheeks sink, and dark stains appear on our teeth. It becomes harder to open and close our eyes. As the aggregate of form is dissolving, we become weak and frail. Our mind is agitated and delirious, but then sinks into drowsiness.

These are signs that the *earth* element is withdrawing into the water element. This means that the wind related to the earth element is becoming less capable of providing a base for consciousness, and the ability of the water element is more manifest. So the "secret sign" that appears in the mind is a vision of a shimmering mirage.

Water

We begin to lose control of our bodily fluids. Our nose begins to run, and we dribble. There can be a discharge from the eyes, and maybe we become incontinent. We cannot move our tongue. Our eyes start to feel dry in their sockets. Our lips are drawn and bloodless, and our mouth and throat sticky and clogged. The nostrils cave in, and we become very thirsty. We tremble and twitch. The smell of death begins to hang over us. As the aggregate of feeling is dissolving, bodily sensations dwindle, alternating between pain and pleasure, heat and cold. Our mind becomes hazy, frustrated, irritable, and nervous. Some sources say that we feel as if we were drowning in an ocean or being swept away by a huge river.

The *water* element is dissolving into fire, which is taking over in its ability to support consciousness. So the "secret sign" is a vision of a haze with swirling wisps of smoke.

Fire

Our mouth and nose dry up completely. All the warmth of our body begins to seep away, usually from the feet and hands toward the heart. Perhaps a steamy heat rises from the crown of our head. Our breath is cold as it passes through our mouth and nose. No longer can we drink or digest anything. The aggregate of perception is dissolving, and our mind swings alternately between clarity and confusion. We cannot remember the names of our family or friends, or even recognize who they are. It becomes more and more difficult to perceive anything outside of us as sound and sight are confused.

Kalu Rinpoche writes: "For the individual dying, the inner experience is of being consumed in a flame, being in the middle of a roaring blaze, or perhaps the whole world being consumed in a holocaust of fire."

The *fire* element is dissolving into air, and becoming less able to function as a base for consciousness, while the ability of the air element to do so is more apparent. So the secret sign is of shimmering red sparks dancing above an open fire, like fireflies.

Air

It becomes harder and harder to breathe. The air seems to be escaping through our throat. We begin to rasp and pant. Our inbreaths become short and labored, and our outbreaths become longer. Our eyes roll upward, and we are totally immobile. As the aggregate of intellect is dissolving, the mind becomes bewildered, unaware of the outside world. Everything becomes a blur. Our last feeling of contact with our physical environment is slipping away.

We begin to hallucinate and have visions: If there has been a lot of negativity in our lives, we may see terrifying forms. Haunting and dreadful moments of our lives are replayed, and we may even try to cry out in terror. If we have led lives of kindness and compassion, we may experience blissful, heavenly visions, and "meet" loving friends or enlightened beings. For those who have led good lives, there is peace in death instead of fear.

Kalu Rinpoche writes: "The internal experience for the dying individual is of a great wind sweeping away the whole world, including the dying person, an incredible maelstrom of wind, consuming the entire universe."[6]

What is happening is that the *air* element is dissolving into consciousness. The winds have all united in the "life-supporting wind" in the heart. So the "secret sign" is described as a vision of a flaming torch or lamp, with a red glow.

Our inbreaths continue to be more shallow, and our outbreaths longer. At this point blood gathers and enters the "channel of life" in the center of our heart. Three drops of blood collect, one after the other, causing three long, final outbreaths. Then, suddenly, our breathing ceases.

Just a slight warmth remains at our heart. All vital signs are gone, and this is the point where in a modern clinical situation we would be certified as "dead." But Tibetan masters talk of an internal process that still continues. The time between the end of the breathing and the cessation of the "inner respiration" is said to be approximately "the length of time it takes to eat a meal," roughly twenty minutes. But nothing is certain, and this whole process may take place very quickly.

THE INNER DISSOLUTION

In the inner dissolution, where gross and subtle thought states and emotions dissolve, four increasingly subtle levels of consciousness are to be encountered.

Here the process of death mirrors in reverse the process of conception. When our parents' sperm and ovum unite, our consciousness, impelled by its karma, is drawn in. During the development of the fetus, our father's essence, a nucleus that is described as "white and blissful," rests in the chakra at the crown of our head at the top of the central channel. The mother's essence, a nucleus that is "red and hot," rests in the chakra said to be located four finger-widths below the navel. It is from these two essences that the next phases of the dissolution evolve.

With the disappearance of the wind that holds it there, the white essence inherited from our father descends the central channel toward the heart. As an outer sign, there is an experience of "whiteness," like "a pure sky struck by moonlight." As an inner sign, our awareness becomes extremely clear, and all the thought states resulting from anger, thirty-three of them in all, come to an end. This phase is known as "Appearance."

Then the mother's essence begins to rise through the central channel, with the disappearance of the wind that keeps it in place. The outer sign is an experience of "redness," like a sun shining in a pure sky. As an inner sign, there arises a great experience of bliss, as all the thought states resulting from desire, forty in all, cease to function. This stage is known as "Increase."[7]

When the red and white essences meet at the heart, consciousness is enclosed between them. Tulku Urgyen Rinpoche, an outstanding master who lives in Nepal, says: "The experience is like the meeting of the sky and earth." As an outer sign, we experience a "blackness," like an empty sky shrouded in utter darkness. The inner sign is an experience of a state of mind free of thoughts. The seven thought states resulting from ignorance and delusion are brought to an end. This is known as "Full Attainment."[8]

Then, as we become slightly conscious again, the Ground Luminosity dawns, like an immaculate sky, free of clouds, fog, or mist. It is sometimes called "the mind of clear light of death." His Holiness the Dalai Lama says: "This consciousness is the innermost subtle mind. We call it the buddha nature, the real source of all consciousness. The continuum of this mind lasts even through Buddhahood."[9]

THE DEATH OF "THE POISONS"

What then is happening when we die? It is as if we are returning to our original state; everything dissolves, as body and mind are unraveled. The three "poisons"—anger, desire, and ignorance—all die, which means that all the negative emotions, the root of samsara, actually cease, and then there is a gap.

And where does this process take us? To the primordial ground of the nature of mind, in all its purity and natural simplicity. Now everything that obscured it is removed, and our true nature is revealed.

A similar enfolding can happen, as I explained in chapter 5, Bringing the Mind Home, when we practice meditation and have the experiences of bliss, clarity, and absence of thoughts, which indicate, in turn, that desire, anger, and ignorance have momentarily dissolved.

As anger, desire, and ignorance are dying, we are becoming purer and purer. Some masters explain that for a Dzogchen practitioner, the phases of appearance, increase, and attainment are signs of the gradual manifestation of Rigpa. As everything that obscures the nature of mind is dying, the clarity of Rigpa slowly begins to appear and increase. The whole process becomes a development of the state of luminosity, linked to the practitioner's recognition of the clarity of Rigpa.

In Tantra there is a different approach to practicing during the process of dissolution. In the yoga practice of channels, winds, and essences, the Tantric practitioner prepares in life for the process of dying, by simulating the changes of consciousness of the dissolution process, culminating in the experience of the luminosity or "Clear Light." The practitioner also seeks to maintain awareness of these changes as he or she falls asleep. Because what is important to remember is that this sequence of progressively deepening states of consciousness does not only happen when we die. It also occurs, usually unnoticed, as we fall asleep, or whenever we travel from the grosser to subtlest levels of consciousness. Some masters have even shown that it also happens in the very psychological processes of our everyday waking state.[10]

The detailed account of the dissolution process may seem complicated, yet if we become really familiar with this process, it can be of great benefit. For practitioners there is a range of specialized practices to do at each stage of the dissolution. For example, you can transform the process of dying into a practice of guru yoga. With each stage of the outer dissolution, you generate devotion and pray to the master, visualizing him in the different energy centers. When the earth element dissolves and the sign of the mirage appears, you visualize the master in your heart center. When the water element dissolves and the sign of smoke appears, you visualize the master in your navel center. When the fire element dissolves and the sign of fireflies appears, you visualize the master in the forehead center. And when the air element dissolves and the sign of the torch appears, you focus entirely on transferring your consciousness into the wisdom mind of your master.

There are many descriptions of the stages of dying, differing in small details and in their order. What I have explained here is a description of the general pattern, but it can unfold differently according to the makeup of the individual. I remember when Samten, my master's attendant, was dying, the sequence was most pronounced. But variations can occur owing to the effects of the particular illness of the dying person, and the state of the channels, winds, and essences. The masters say that all living beings, even the smallest insects, go through this process. In the case of a sudden death or an accident, it will still take place, but extremely quickly.

I have found that the easiest way to understand what is happening during the process of dying, with its outer and inner dissolution, is as *a gradual development and dawning of ever more subtle levels of consciousness.* Each one emerges upon the successive dissolution of the constituents of body and mind, as the process moves gradually toward the revelation of the very subtlest consciousness of all: the Ground Luminosity or Clear Light.

PART THREE

Death and Rebirth

SIXTEEN

The Ground

WE OFTEN HEAR STATEMENTS LIKE: "Death is the moment of truth," or "Death is the point when we finally come face to face with ourselves." And we have seen how those who go through a near-death experience sometimes report that as they witness their lives replayed before them, they are asked questions such as, "What have you done with your life? What have you done for others?" All of this points to one fact: that in death we cannot escape from who or what we really are. Whether we like it or not, our true nature is revealed. But it is important to know that there are two aspects of our being that are revealed at the moment of death: our absolute nature, and our relative nature—how we are, and have been, in this life.

As I have explained, in death all the components of our body and mind are stripped away and disintegrate. As the body dies, the senses and subtle elements dissolve, and this is followed by the death of the ordinary aspect of our mind, with all its negative emotions of anger, desire, and ignorance. Finally nothing remains to obscure our true nature, as everything that in life has clouded the enlightened mind has fallen away. And what is revealed is the primordial ground of our absolute nature, which is like a pure and cloudless sky.

This is called the dawning of the Ground Luminosity, or "Clear Light," where consciousness itself dissolves into the all-encompassing space of truth. The *Tibetan Book of the Dead* says of this moment:

The nature of everything is open, empty and naked like the sky.
Luminous emptiness, without center or circumference: the pure, naked
  Rigpa dawns.

Padmasambhava describes the luminosity:

This self-originated Clear Light, which from the very beginning was
  never born,

Is the child of Rigpa, which is itself without any parents—how amazing!

This self-originated wisdom has not been created by anyone—how amazing!

It has never experienced birth and has nothing in it that could cause it to die—how amazing!

Although it is evidently visible, yet there is no one there who sees it—how amazing!

Although it has wandered through samsara, no harm has come to it—how amazing!

Although it has seen buddhahood itself, no good has come to it—how amazing!

Although it exists in everyone everywhere, it has gone unrecognized—how amazing!

And yet you go on hoping to attain some other fruit than this elsewhere—how amazing!

Even though it is the thing that is most essentially yours, you seek for it elsewhere—how amazing!

Why is it that this state is called "luminosity" or Clear Light? The masters have different ways of explaining this. Some say that it expresses the radiant clarity of the nature of mind, its total freedom from darkness or obscuration: "free from the darkness of unknowing and endowed with the ability to cognize." Another master describes the luminosity or Clear Light as "a state of minimum distraction," because all the elements, senses, and sense-objects are dissolved. What is important is not to confuse it with the physical light that we know, nor with the experiences of light that will unfold presently in the next bardo; the luminosity that arises at death is the natural radiance of the wisdom of our own Rigpa, "the uncompounded nature present throughout all of samsara and nirvana."

The dawning of the Ground Luminosity, or Clear Light, at the moment of death is *the* great opportunity for liberation. But it is essential to realize on what terms this opportunity is given. Some modern writers and researchers on death have underestimated the profundity of this moment. Because they have read and interpreted the *Tibetan Book of the Dead* without the benefit of the oral instructions and training that fully explain its sacred meaning, they have oversimplified it and jumped to quick conclusions. One assumption they then make is that the dawning of the Ground Luminosity *is* enlightenment. We might all like to identify death with heaven or enlightenment; but more important than mere wishful thinking is to know that only if we have really been introduced to the nature of our mind, our Rigpa, and only if we have established and stabilized it through meditation and integrated it into our life, does the moment of death offer a real opportunity for liberation.

Even though the Ground Luminosity presents itself naturally to us all, most of us are totally unprepared for its sheer immensity, the vast and subtle depth of its naked simplicity. The majority of us will simply have no means of recognizing it, because we have not made ourselves familiar with ways of recognizing it in life. What happens, then, is that we tend to react instinctively with all our past fears, habits, and conditioning, all our old reflexes. Though the negative emotions may have died for the luminosity to appear, the habits of lifetimes still remain, hidden in the background of our ordinary mind. Though all our confusion dies in death, instead of surrendering and opening to the luminosity, in our fear and ignorance we withdraw and instinctively hold onto our grasping.

This is what obstructs us from truly using this powerful moment as an opportunity for liberation. Padmasambhava says: "All beings have lived and died and been reborn countless times. Over and over again they have experienced the indescribable Clear Light. But because they are obscured by the darkness of ignorance, they wander endlessly in a limitless samsara."

THE GROUND OF THE ORDINARY MIND

All these habitual tendencies, the results of our negative karma, which have sprung from the darkness of ignorance, are stored in the ground of the ordinary mind. I have often wondered what would be a good example to help describe the ground of the ordinary mind. You could compare it to a transparent glass bubble, a very thin elastic film, an almost invisible barrier or veil that obscures the whole of our mind; but perhaps the most useful image I can think of is of a glass door. Imagine you are sitting in front of a glass door that leads out into your garden, looking through it, gazing out into space. It seems as though there is nothing between you and the sky, because you cannot see the surface of the glass. You could even bang your nose if you got up and tried to walk through, thinking it wasn't there. But if you touch it you will see at once there is something there that holds your fingerprints, something that comes between you and the space outside.

In the same manner, the ground of the ordinary mind prevents us from breaking through to the sky-like nature of our mind, even if we can still have glimpses of it. As I have said, the masters explain how there is a danger that meditation practitioners can mistake the experience of the ground of the ordinary mind for the real nature of mind itself. When they rest in a state of great calm and stillness, all they could be doing in fact might be merely resting in the ground of the ordinary mind. It is the difference between looking up at the sky from within a glass dome, and standing outside in the open air. We have to break out of the ground of the ordinary mind altogether, to discover and let in the fresh air of Rigpa.

So the aim of all our spiritual practice, and the real preparation for the moment of death, is to purify this subtle barrier, and gradually weaken it and break it down. When you have broken it down completely, nothing comes between you and the state of omniscience.

The introduction by the master to the nature of mind breaks through the ground of the ordinary mind altogether, as it is through this dissolution of the conceptual mind that the enlightened mind is explicitly revealed. Then, each time we rest in the nature of mind, the ground of the ordinary mind gets weaker. But we will notice that how long we can stay in the state of the nature of mind depends entirely on the stability of our practice. Unfortunately, "Old habits die hard," and the ground of the ordinary mind returns; our mind is like an alcoholic who can kick the habit for a while, but relapses whenever tempted or depressed.

Just as the glass door picks up all the traces of dirt from our hands and fingers, the ground of the ordinary mind gathers and stores all our karma and habits. And just as we have to keep wiping the glass, so we have to keep purifying the ground of the ordinary mind. It is as if the glass slowly wears away as it gets thinner and thinner, little holes appear, and it begins to dissolve.

Through our practice we gradually stabilize the nature of mind more and more, so that it does not simply remain as our absolute nature but becomes our everyday reality. As it does so, the more our habits dissolve, and the less of a difference there is between meditation and everyday life. Gradually you become like someone who can walk straight out into the garden through the glass door, unobstructed. And the sign that the ground of the ordinary mind is weakening is that we are able to rest more and more effortlessly in the nature of mind.

When the Ground Luminosity dawns, the crucial issue will be how much we have been able to rest in the nature of mind, how much we have been able to unite our absolute nature and our everyday life, and how much we have been able to purify our ordinary condition into the state of primordial purity.

THE MEETING OF MOTHER AND CHILD

There is a way in which we can prepare completely to recognize the dawning of the Ground Luminosity at the moment of death. This is through the very highest level of meditation (as I have explained in chapter 10, The Innermost Essence), the final fruition of the practice of Dzogchen. It is called the "union of two luminosities," which is also known as "the merging of Mother and Child Luminosities."

The Mother Luminosity is the name we give to the Ground Luminosity. This is the fundamental, inherent nature of everything, which underlies our whole experience, and which manifests in its full glory at the moment of death.

The Child Luminosity, also called the Path Luminosity, is the nature of our mind, which, if introduced by the master, and if recognized by us, we can then gradually stabilize through meditation, and more and more completely integrate into our action in life. When the integration is complete, recognition is complete and realization occurs.

Even though the Ground Luminosity is our inherent nature and the nature of everything, we do not recognize it, and it remains as if hidden. I like to think of the Child Luminosity as a key the master gives us to help us open the door to the recognition of the Ground Luminosity, whenever the opportunity arises.

Imagine that you have to meet a woman arriving by plane. If you have no idea what she looks like, you might go to the airport and she could walk right past you and you would miss her. If you have a photo of her that is a good likeness, and you have a good picture of her in your mind, then you will recognize her as soon as she approaches you.

Once the nature of mind has been introduced and you recognize it, you have the key to recognizing it again. But just as you have to keep the photograph with you and keep looking at it again and again, to be sure of recognizing the person you are going to meet at the airport, so you have to keep deepening and stabilizing your recognition of the nature of mind through regular practice. Then the recognition becomes so ingrained in you, so much a part of you, that you have no further need of the photograph; when you meet the person recognition is spontaneous and immediate. So, after sustained practice of the recognition of the nature of mind, when at the moment of death the Ground Luminosity dawns, you will be able then to recognize it and merge with it—as instinctively, say the masters of the past, as a little child running eagerly into its mother's lap, like old friends meeting, or a river flowing into the sea.

Yet this is extremely difficult. The only way to ensure this recognition is through stabilizing and perfecting the practice of merging the two luminosities now, while we are still alive. This is only possible through a lifetime of training and endeavor. As my master Dudjom Rinpoche said, if we don't practice the merging of the two luminosities now, and from now on, there is no saying that recognition will happen naturally at death.

How exactly do we merge the luminosities? This is a very profound and advanced practice, and this is not the place to elaborate on it. But what we can say is this: When the master introduces us to the nature of mind, it is as if our sight has been restored, for we have been blind to the Ground Luminosity that is in everything. The master's introduction awakens in us a wisdom eye, with which we come to see clearly the true nature of whatever arises, the luminosity—Clear Light—nature of all our thoughts and emotions. Imagine that our recognition of the nature of mind comes, after stabilizing and perfecting the practice, to be like a steadily blazing sun. Thoughts and emotions go on arising; they are like waves of darkness. But each time the waves unfurl and meet the light, they dissolve immediately.

As we develop this ability to recognize more and more, it becomes part of our daily vision. When we are able to bring the realization of our absolute nature into our everyday experience, the more chance there is that we will actually recognize the Ground Luminosity at the moment of death.

The proof of whether we have this key will be how we view our thoughts and emotions as they arise; whether we are able to penetrate them directly with the View and recognize their inherent luminosity nature, or whether we obscure it with our instinctive habitual reactions.

If the ground of our ordinary mind is completely purified, it is as if we have shattered the storehouse of our karma and so emptied the karmic supply for future rebirths. However, if we have not been able to completely purify our mind, there will still be remnants of past habits and karmic tendencies resting in this storehouse of karma. Whenever suitable conditions materialize, they will manifest, propelling us into new rebirths.

THE DURATION OF THE GROUND LUMINOSITY

The Ground Luminosity dawns; for a practitioner, it lasts as long as he or she can rest, undistracted, in the state of the nature of mind. For most people, however, it lasts no longer than a snap of the fingers, and for some, the masters say, "as long as it takes to eat a meal." The vast majority of people do not recognize the Ground Luminosity at all, and instead they are plunged into a state of unconsciousness, which can last up to three and a half days. It is then that the consciousness finally leaves the body.

This has led to a custom in Tibet of making sure that the body is not touched or disturbed for three days after death. It is especially important in the case of a practitioner, who may have merged with the Ground Luminosity and be resting in that state of the nature of mind. I remember in Tibet how everyone took great care to maintain a silent and peaceful atmosphere around the body, particularly in the case of a great master or practitioner, to avoid causing the slightest disturbance.

But even the body of an ordinary person is often not moved before three days have elapsed, since you never know if a person is realized or not, and it is uncertain when the consciousness has separated from the body. It is believed that if the body is touched in a certain place—if, for example, an injection is given—it may draw the consciousness to that spot. Then the consciousness of the dead person may leave through the nearest opening instead of through the fontanel, and take on an unfortunate rebirth.

Some masters insist more than others on leaving the body for three days. Chadral Rinpoche, a Zen-like Tibetan master living in India and Nepal, told people who were complaining that a corpse might smell if it was kept in hot weather: "It's not as though you have to eat it, or try to sell it."

Strictly speaking, then, autopsies or cremations are best done after the three days' interval. However, these days, since it may not be at all practical or possible to keep a body this long without moving it, at least the phowa practice should be effected before the body is touched or moved in any way.

THE DEATH OF A MASTER

A realized practitioner continues to abide by the recognition of the nature of mind at the moment of death, and awakens into the Ground Luminosity when it manifests. He or she may even remain in that state for a number of days. Some practitioners and masters die sitting upright in meditation posture, and others in the "posture of the sleeping lion." Besides their perfect poise, there will be other signs that show they are resting in the state of the Ground Luminosity: There is still a certain color and glow in their face, the nose does not sink inward, the skin remains soft and flexible, the body does not become stiff, the eyes are said to keep a soft and compassionate glow, and there is still a warmth at the heart. Great care is taken that the master's body is not touched, and silence is maintained until he or she has arisen from this state of meditation.

Gyalwang Karmapa, a great master and head of one of the four main schools of Tibetan Buddhism, died in hospital in the United States in 1981. He was an extraordinary inspiration to all those around him because of his constant cheerfulness and compassion. Dr. Ranulfo Sanchez, chief of surgery, said:

> I personally felt that His Holiness was not just an ordinary man. When he looked at you, it was like he was searching inside you, as if he could see through you. I was very struck by the way he looked at me and seemed to understand what was going on. His Holiness affected practically everyone in the hospital who came in contact with him. Many times when we felt he was near death, he would smile at us and tell us we were wrong, and then he'd improve . . .
>
> His Holiness never took any pain medication. We the doctors would see him and realize he must be in a lot of pain, so we'd ask him, "Are you having a lot of pain today?" He'd say "No." Towards the end we knew he could sense our anxiety and it became a running joke. We'd ask him, "Are you having any pain?" He'd smile this extremely kind smile and say "No."
>
> All his vital signs were very low. I gave him a shot . . . so that he could communicate in his last minutes. I left the room for a few

minutes while he conversed with the tulkus, whom he assured he was not intending to die that day. When I returned five minutes later, he was sitting straight up, with his eyes wide open, and said clearly, "Hello, how are you?" All his vital signs had reversed and within half an hour he was sitting up in bed, talking and laughing. Medically this is unheard of; the nurses were all white. One of them lifted her sleeve to show me her arm, covered with goose-bumps.

The nursing staff noticed that Karmapa's body did not follow the usual progression of rigor mortis and decay, but seemed to remain just as it had been when he died. After a while they became aware that the area around his heart was still warm. Dr. Sanchez said:

They brought me into the room about thirty-six hours after he died. I felt the area right over his heart, and it was warmer than the surrounding area. It's something for which there is no medical explanation.[1]

Some masters pass away sitting in meditation, with the body supporting itself. Kalu Rinpoche died in 1989 in his monastery in the Himalayas, with a number of masters and a doctor and nurse present. His closest disciple wrote:

Rinpoche himself tried to sit up, and had difficulty to do so. Lama Gyaltsen, feeling that this was perhaps the time, and that not to sit up could create an obstacle for Rinpoche, supported Rinpoche's back as he sat up. Rinpoche extended his hand to me, and I also helped him to sit up. Rinpoche wanted to sit absolutely straight, both saying this and indicating with a gesture of his hand. The doctor and nurse were upset by this, and so Rinpoche relaxed his posture slightly. He, nevertheless, assumed meditation posture. . . . Rinpoche placed his hands in meditation posture, his open eyes gazed outwards in meditation gaze, and his lips moved softly. A profound feeling of peace and happiness settled on us all and spread through our minds. All of us present felt that the indescribable happiness that was filling us was the faintest reflection of what was pervading Rinpoche's mind . . . slowly Rinpoche's gaze and his eyelids lowered and the breath stopped.[2]

I shall always remember the death of my own beloved master, Jamyang Khyentse Chökyi Lodrö, in the summer of 1959. During the last part of his life, he would try and leave his monastery as little as possible. Masters of all traditions would flock to him for teachings, and holders of all lineages would look to him for instructions, as he was the source of their transmission. The monastery where he lived, Dzongsar, became one of the most vibrant centers of spiritual activity in Tibet, as all the great Lamas came and went. His word in the region was law; he was such a great master that almost everybody was his disciple, so much so that he had the power to stop civil wars by threatening to withdraw his spiritual protection from the fighters of both sides.

Unfortunately, as the grip of the Chinese invaders tightened, conditions in Kham deteriorated rapidly, and even as a young boy I could sense the impending menace of what was to come. In 1955 my master had certain signs that showed he should leave Tibet. First he went on a pilgrimage to the sacred sites of central and southern Tibet; and then, to fulfill a deep wish of his master, he made a pilgrimage to the holy places of India, and I went with him. We all hoped that the situation in the east might improve while we were away. It turned out, I was to realize later, that my master's decision to leave had been taken as a sign by many other Lamas and ordinary people that Tibet was doomed, and it allowed them to escape in good time.

My master had a longstanding invitation to visit Sikkim, a small country in the Himalayas and one of the sacred lands of Padmasambhava. Jamyang Khyentse was the incarnation of Sikkim's holiest saint, and the King of Sikkim had requested him to teach there and bless the land with his presence. Once they heard he had gone there, many masters came from Tibet to receive his teachings, and brought with them rare texts and scriptures that might not otherwise have survived. Jamyang Khyentse was a master of masters, and the Palace Temple where he lived became once again a great spiritual center. As the conditions in Tibet became more and more disastrous, more and more Lamas gathered around him.

Sometimes great masters who teach a lot, it is said, do not live very long; it is almost as if they attract toward them any obstacles there are to the spiritual teachings. There were prophecies that if my master had put aside teaching and traveled as an unknown hermit to remote corners of the country, he would have lived for many more years. In fact, he tried to do this: When we started on our last journey from Kham, he left all his possessions behind him and went in complete secrecy, not intending to teach but to travel on pilgrimage. Yet once they found out who he was, people everywhere requested him to give teachings and initiations. So vast was his compassion that, knowing what he was risking, he sacrificed his own life to keep on teaching.

It was in Sikkim, then, that Jamyang Khyentse fell ill; at that very same time, the terrible news came that Tibet had finally fallen. All the seniormost Lamas, the heads of the lineages, arrived one after another to visit him, and prayers and rituals for his long life went on day and night. Everybody took part. We all pleaded with him to continue living, for a master of his greatness has the power to decide when it is time to leave his body. He just lay there in bed, accepted all our offerings and laughed, and said with a knowing smile: "All right, just to be auspicious, I'll say I will live."

The first indication we had that my master was going to die was through Gyalwang Karmapa. He told Karmapa that he had completed the work he had come to do in this life, and he had decided to leave this world. One of Khyentse's close attendants burst into tears as soon as Karmapa revealed this to him, and then we knew. His death was eventually to occur just after we had heard that the three great monasteries of Tibet, Sera, Drepung, and Ganden, had been occupied by the Chinese. It seemed tragically symbolic that as Tibet collapsed, so this great being, the embodiment of Tibetan Buddhism, was passing away.

Jamyang Khyentse Chökyi Lodrö died at three o'clock in the morning, on the sixth day of the fifth Tibetan month. Ten days before, while we were doing a whole night's practice for his long life, suddenly the ground was shaken by an enormous earthquake. According to the Buddhist Sutras, this is a sign that marks the imminent passing of an enlightened being.[3]

For three days after he had passed away, complete secrecy was kept, and no one was allowed to know that Khyentse had died. I was told simply that his health had taken a turn for the worse, and instead of sleeping in his room as I usually did, I was asked to sleep in another room. My master's closest assistant and master of ceremonies, Lama Chokden, had been with my master longer than anyone. He was a silent, serious, ascetic man with piercing eyes and sunken cheeks, and a dignified and elegant but humble manner. Chokden was known for his fundamental integrity, his deep, human decency, his courtesy of heart, and his extraordinary memory: He seemed to remember every word my master said, and every story, and he knew the smallest details of all the most intricate rituals and their significance. He was also an exemplary practitioner and a teacher in his own right. We watched, then, as Lama Chokden continued to carry my master's meals into his room, but the expression on his face was somber. We kept asking how Khyentse was, and Chokden would only say: "He is just the same." In certain traditions, after a master has died, and during the time he remains in meditation after death, it is important to maintain secrecy. It was only three days later, as I have said, that we finally heard that he had died.

The Government of India then sent a telegram to Peking. From there the message went out to my master's own monastery, Dzongsar, in Tibet, where many of the monks were already in tears, because somehow they knew he was dying. Just before we had left, Khyentse had made a mysterious pledge that he would return once before he died. And he did. On New Year's Day that year, about six months before he actually passed away, when a ritual dance was being performed, many of the older monks had a vision of him, just as he used to be, appearing in the sky. At the monastery my master had founded a study college, famous for producing some of the most excellent scholars of recent times. In the main temple stood a huge statue of the future Buddha, Maitreya. Early one morning, soon after the New Years' Day when the vision had appeared in the sky, the caretaker of the temple opened the door: Khyentse was sitting in the Buddha Maitreya's lap.

My master passed away in "the sleeping lion's posture." All the signs were there to show that he was still in a state of meditation, and no one touched the body for three whole days. The moment when he then came out of his meditation will stay with me all my life: His nose suddenly deflated, the color in his face drained away, and then his head fell slightly to one side. Until that moment there had been a certain poise and strength and life about his body.

It was evening when we washed the body, dressed it, and took it from his bedroom up into the main temple of the palace. Crowds of people were there, filing around the temple to show their respect.

Then something extraordinary happened. An incandescent, milky light, looking like a thin and luminous fog, began to appear and gradually spread everywhere. The palace temple had four large electric lamps outside; normally at that time of the evening they shone brightly, as it was already dark by seven o'clock. Yet they were dimmed by this mysterious light. Apa Pant, who was then Political Officer to Sikkim, was the first to ring and inquire what on earth it could be. Then many others started to call; this strange, unearthly light was seen by hundreds of people. One of the other masters then told us that such manifestations of light are said in the Tantras to be a sign of someone attaining Buddhahood.

It was originally planned that Jamyang Khyentse's body was to be kept in the palace temple for one week, but very soon we started receiving telegrams from his disciples. It was 1959; many of them, including Dilgo Khyentse Rinpoche, had just arrived in exile, having made the long and dangerous escape from Tibet. They all begged that the body be kept so that they could have a chance to see it. So we kept it for two more weeks. Each day there were four different prayer sessions with hundreds of monks, headed by Lamas of all the different schools, and often with the lineage holders presiding, and thousands upon thousands of butter-lamps were offered. The body did not smell or start to decay, so we kept it for another week. India is fiercely hot in the summer, but even though week after week went by, the body showed no signs of decay. We ended up keeping Jamyang Khyentse's body for six months; a whole environment of teaching and practice evolved in its holy presence: teachings that Jamyang Khyentse had been giving, which were incomplete when he died, were finished by his oldest disciples, and many, many monks were ordained.

Finally we took the body to the place he had chosen for the cremation. Tashiding is one of the most sacred sites in Sikkim, and stands on top of a hill. All the disciples went there, and we constructed the *stupa* for his relics by ourselves, although in India all grueling manual work is usually done by hired laborers. Everybody, young and old, from even a master like Dilgo Khyentse Rinpoche to the most ordinary person, carried stones up the hill and built the whole thing with their own bare hands. It was the greatest possible testimony to the devotion he inspired.

No words would ever be able to convey the loss of Jamyang Khyentse's death. In leaving Tibet I and my family lost all

our lands and possessions, but I was too young to have
formed any attachment to them. But losing Jamyang
Khyentse was a loss so enormous that I still mourn it, so
many years later. My entire childhood had been lived in the
sunlight of his presence. I had slept in a small bed at the foot
of his bed, and woke for many years to the sound of him
whispering his morning prayers and clicking his mala, his
Buddhist rosary. His words, his teachings, the great peaceful
radiance of his presence, his smile, all of these are indelible
memories for me. He is the inspiration of my life, and it is his
presence as well as Padmasambhava's that I always invoke
when I am in difficulties or when I teach. His death was an
incalculable loss for the world and an incalculable loss for
Tibet. I used to think of him, as I thought also of Dilgo
Khyentse Rinpoche, that if Buddhism was destroyed and only
he remained, nevertheless Buddhism would still be alive, for
he was the complete embodiment of what Buddhism means.
With Jamyang Khyentse's passing, a whole epoch, sometimes
it seems a whole dimension of spiritual power and knowledge, passed with him.

He died when he was only sixty-seven, and I often
wonder how the entire future of Tibetan Buddhism would
have been different if Jamyang Khyentse had lived to inspire
its growth in exile and in the West with the same authority
and infinite respect for all traditions and lineages that had
made him so beloved in Tibet. Because he was the master
of masters, and since the lineage-holders of all the traditions had received initiations and teachings from him and so
revered him as their root-teacher, he was able naturally to
draw them together, in a spirit of devoted harmony and
cooperation.

And yet, a great master never dies. Jamyang Khyentse is
here inspiring me as I write this; he is the force behind this
book and whatever I teach; he is the foundation and basis of
the spirit behind everything I do; it is he who goes on giving
me my inner direction. His blessing and the confidence it
gives me have been with me, guiding me through all the
difficulties of trying to represent, in whatever way I can, the
tradition of which he was so sublime a representative. His
noble face is more alive to me now than any of the faces of
the living, and in his eyes I always see that light of transcendent wisdom and transcendent compassion that no power in
heaven or earth can put out.

May all of you who read this book come to know him a little as I know him, may all of you be as inspired as I have been by the dedication of his life and the splendor of his dying, may all of you draw from his example of total dedication to the welfare of all sentient beings the courage and wisdom you will need to work for the truth in this time!

SEVENTEEN

Intrinsic Radiance

AS THE GROUND LUMINOSITY DAWNS AT DEATH, an experienced practitioner will maintain full awareness and merge with it, thereby attaining liberation. But if we fail to recognize the Ground Luminosity, then we encounter the next bardo, the luminous bardo of dharmata.

The teaching on the bardo of dharmata is a very special instruction, one specific to Dzogchen practice and treasured at the heart of the Dzogchen teachings over the centuries. Initially I felt some hesitation about publicly presenting this most sacred of teachings, and in fact if there had not been any precedent I might not have done so at all. However, the *Tibetan Book of the Dead* and a number of other books that refer to the bardo of dharmata have already been published, and have led to some naive conclusions. I feel it is extremely important, and timely, to make available a straightforward clarification of this bardo, putting it into its authentic context. I should stress that I have not gone into any detail about the advanced practices involved; none of these practices could, under any circumstances, ever be done effectively except with the instructions and guidance of a qualified master, and when the commitment and connection with that master is kept completely pure.

I have gathered insights from many different sources in order to make this chapter, which I feel is one of the most important in this book, as lucid as possible. I hope that through it some of you will make a connection with this extraordinary teaching, and be inspired to investigate further and to begin to practice yourselves.

THE FOUR PHASES OF DHARMATA

The Sanskrit word *dharmata*, *chö nyi* in Tibetan, means the intrinsic nature of everything, the essence of things as they are. Dharmata is the naked, unconditioned truth, the nature of reality, or the true nature of phenomenal existence. What we are discussing here is something fundamental to the whole understanding of the nature of mind and the nature of everything.

The end of the dissolution process and dawning of the Ground Luminosity has opened up an entirely new dimension, which now begins to unfold. One helpful way I have found to explain it is to compare it with the way night turns into day. The final phase of the dissolution process of dying is the black experience of the stage of "full attainment." It is described as "like a sky shrouded in darkness." The arising of the Ground Luminosity is like the clarity in the empty sky just before dawn. Now gradually the sun of dharmata begins to rise in all its splendor, illuminating the contours of the land in all directions. The natural radiance of Rigpa manifests spontaneously and blazes out as energy and light.

Just as the sun rises in that clear and empty sky, the luminous appearances of the bardo of dharmata will all arise from the all-pervading space of the Ground Luminosity. The name we give to this display of sound, light, and color is "spontaneous presence," for it is always and inherently present within the expanse of "primordial purity," which is its ground.

What is actually taking place here is a process of unfoldment, in which mind and its fundamental nature are gradually becoming more and more manifest. The bardo of dharmata is one stage in that process. For it is through this dimension of light and energy that mind unfolds from its purest state, the Ground Luminosity, toward its manifestation as form in the next bardo, the bardo of becoming.

I find it extremely suggestive that modern physics has shown that when matter is investigated, it is revealed as an ocean of energy and light. "Matter, as it were, is condensed or frozen light . . . all matter is a condensation of light into patterns moving back and forth at average speeds which are less than the speed of light," remarks David Bohm. Modern physics also understands light in a many-sided way: "It's energy and it's also information—content, form and structure. It's the potential for everything."[1]

The bardo of dharmata has four phases, each one of which presents another opportunity for liberation. If the opportunity is not taken, then the next phase will unfold. The explanation I am giving here of this bardo originates in the Dzogchen

Tantras, where it is taught that only through the special advanced practice of luminosity, Tögal, can the true significance of the bardo of dharmata be in any real sense understood. The bardo of dharmata, then, figures with far less prominence in other cycles of teachings on death in the Tibetan tradition. Even in the *Tibetan Book of the Dead,* which also belongs to the Dzogchen teachings, the sequence of these four phases is only implicit, as if slightly hidden, and does not appear there in such a clear and ordered structure.

I must stress, however, that all words could possibly do is give some conceptual picture of what might happen in the bardo of dharmata. The appearances of this bardo will remain just conceptual images until the practitioner has perfected the Tögal practice, when each detail of the description I am about to give becomes an undeniable personal experience. What I am trying to give you here is some sense that such a marvelous and amazing dimension could exist, and to complete my description of the whole of the bardos. I also profoundly hope that this complete description could act perhaps as some kind of reminder when you go through the process of death.

1. Luminosity—the Landscape of Light

In the bardo of dharmata, you take on a body of light. The first phase of this bardo is when "space dissolves into luminosity":

Suddenly you become aware of a flowing vibrant world of sound, light, and color. All the ordinary features of our familiar environment have melted into an all-pervasive landscape of light. This is brilliantly clear and radiant, transparent and multicolored, unlimited by any kind of dimension or direction, shimmering and constantly in motion. The *Tibetan Book of the Dead* calls it "like a mirage on a plain in the heat of summer." Its colors are the natural expression of the intrinsic elemental qualities of the mind: space is perceived as blue light, water as white, earth as yellow, fire as red, and wind as green.

How stable these dazzling appearances of light are in the bardo of dharmata depends entirely upon what stability you have managed to attain in Tögal practice. Only a real mastery of this practice will enable you to stabilize the experience and so use it to gain liberation. Otherwise the bardo of dharmata will simply flash by like a bolt of lightning; you will not even know that it has occurred. Let me stress again that only a practitioner of Tögal will be able to make the all-important recognition: that these radiant manifestations of light have no separate existence from the nature of mind.

2. Union—the Deities

If you are unable to recognize this as the spontaneous display of Rigpa, the simple rays and colors then begin to integrate and coalesce into points or balls of light of different sizes, called tiklé. Within them the "mandalas of the peaceful and wrathful deities" appear, as enormous spherical concentrations of light seeming to occupy the whole of space.

This is the second phase, known as "luminosity dissolving into union," where the luminosity manifests in the form of buddhas or deities of various size, color, and form, holding different attributes. The brilliant light they emanate is blinding and dazzling, the sound is tremendous, like the roaring of a thousand thunderclaps, and the rays and beams of light are like lasers, piercing everything.

These are the "forty-two peaceful and fifty-eight wrathful deities" depicted in the *Tibetan Book of the Dead*. They unfold over a certain period of "days," taking on their own characteristic mandala pattern of five-fold clusters. This is a vision that fills the whole of your perception with such intensity that if you are unable to recognize it for what it is, it appears terrifying and threatening. Sheer fear and blind panic can consume you, and you faint.

From yourself and from the deities, very fine shafts of light stream out, joining your heart with theirs. Countless luminous spheres appear in their rays, which increase and then "roll up," as the deities all dissolve into you.

3. Wisdom

If again you fail to recognize and gain stability, the next phase unfolds, called "union dissolving into wisdom."

Another fine shaft of light springs out from your heart and an enormous vision unfolds from it; however, every detail remains distinct and precise. This is the display of the various aspects of wisdom, which appear together in a show of unfurled carpets of light and resplendent spherical luminous tiklés:

First, on a carpet of deep blue light appear shimmering tiklés of sapphire blue, in patterns of five. Above that, on a carpet of white light, appear radiant tiklés, white like crystal. Above, on a carpet of yellow light, appear golden tiklés, and upon that a carpet of red light supports ruby red tiklés. They are crowned by a radiant sphere like an outspread canopy made of peacock feathers.

This brilliant display of light is the manifestation of the five wisdoms: wisdom of all-encompassing space, mirror-like wisdom, equalizing wisdom, wisdom of discernment, and all-accomplishing wisdom. But since the all-accomplishing wisdom is *only* perfected at the time of enlightenment, it does not appear yet. Therefore there is no green carpet of light and tiklés, yet it is inherent within all the other colors. What is being manifested here is our potential of enlightenment, and the all-accomplishing wisdom will only appear when we become a buddha.

If you do not attain liberation here through resting undistracted in the nature of mind, the carpets of light and their tiklés, along with your Rigpa, all dissolve into the radiant sphere of light, which is like the canopy of peacock feathers.

4. *Spontaneous Presence*

This heralds the final phase of the bardo of dharmata, "wisdom dissolving into spontaneous presence." Now the whole of reality presents itself in one tremendous display. First the state of primordial purity dawns like an open, cloudless sky. Then the peaceful and wrathful deities appear, followed by the pure realms of the buddhas, and below them the six realms of samsaric existence.

The limitlessness of this vision is utterly beyond our ordinary imagination. Every possibility is presented: from wisdom and liberation, to confusion and rebirth. At this point you will find yourself endowed with powers of clairvoyant perception and recollection. For example, with total clairvoyance and your senses unobstructed, you will know your past and future lives, see into others' minds, and have knowledge of all six realms of existence. In an instant you will vividly recall whatever teachings you have heard, and even teachings you have never heard will awaken in your mind.

The entire vision then dissolves back into its original essence, like a tent collapsing once its ropes are cut.

If you have the stability to recognize these manifestations as the "self-radiance" of your own Rigpa, you will be liberated. But without the experience of Tögal practice, you will be unable to look at the visions of the deities, which are "as bright as the sun." Instead, as a result of the habitual tendencies of your previous lives, your gaze will be drawn downward to the six realms. It is *those* that you will recognize and which will lure you again into delusion.

In the *Tibetan Book of the Dead,* periods of days are allotted to the experiences of the bardo of dharmata. These are not solar days of twenty-four hours, because in the sphere of dharmata we have gone completely beyond all limits such as time and space. These days are "meditation days," and refer to the length of time we have been able to rest undistracted in the nature of mind, or in one single state of mind. With no stability in meditation practice, these days could be minutely short, and the appearance of the peaceful and wrathful deities so fleeting that we cannot even register they have arisen.

UNDERSTANDING DHARMATA

Now when the bardo of dharmata dawns upon me,
I will abandon all fear and terror,
I will recognize whatever appears as the display of my own Rigpa,
And know it to be the natural appearance of this bardo;
Now that I have reached this crucial point,
I will not fear the peaceful and wrathful deities, that arise from the
    nature of my very own mind.

The key to understanding this bardo is that all the experiences that take place in it are the natural radiance of the nature of our mind. What is happening is that different aspects of its enlightened energy are being released. Just as the dancing rainbows of light scattered by a crystal are its natural display, so too the dazzling appearances of dharmata cannot be separated from the nature of mind. *They are its spontaneous expression.* So however terrifying the appearances may be, says the *Tibetan Book of the Dead,* they have no more claim on your fear than a stuffed lion.

Strictly speaking, however, it would be wrong to call these appearances "visions" or even "experiences," because vision and experience depend upon a dualistic relationship between a perceiver and something perceived. If we can recognize the appearances of the bardo of dharmata as the wisdom energy of our very own mind, there is no difference between perceiver and perceived, and this is an experience of non-duality. To enter into that experience completely is to attain liberation. For, as Kalu Rinpoche says, "Liberation arises at that moment

in the after-death state when consciousness can realize its
experiences to be nothing other than mind itself."[2]

However, now that we are no longer grounded or shielded
by a physical body or world, the energies of the nature of
mind released in the bardo state can look overwhelmingly
real, and appear to take on an objective existence. They seem
to inhabit the world outside of us. And without the stability
of practice, we have no knowledge of anything that is non-dual,
that is not dependent on our own perception. Once we mistake the appearances as separate from us, as "external visions,"
we respond with fear or hope, which leads us into delusion.

Just as in the dawning of the Ground Luminosity recognition was the key to liberation, so here in the bardo of dharmata it is also. Only here it is the recognition of *the self-
radiance of Rigpa,* the manifesting energy of the nature of
mind, that makes the difference between liberation or continuing in an uncontrolled cycle of rebirth. Take, for example,
the appearances of the hundred peaceful and wrathful deities,
which occur in the second phase of this bardo. These consist
of the buddhas of the five buddha families, their female counterparts, male and female bodhisattvas, the buddhas of the six
realms, and a number of wrathful and protective deities. All
emerge amidst the brilliant light of the five wisdoms.

How are we to understand these buddhas or deities? "Each
one of these pure forms expresses an enlightened perspective
of a part of our impure experience."[3] The five masculine buddhas are the pure aspect of the five aggregates of ego. Their five
wisdoms are the pure aspect of the five negative emotions. The
five female buddhas are the pure elemental qualities of mind,
which we experience as the impure elements of our physical
body and environment. The eight bodhisattvas are the pure
aspect of the different types of consciousness, and their
female counterparts are the objects of these consciousnesses.

Whether the pure vision of the buddha families and their wisdoms manifests, or the impure vision of the aggregates and
negative emotions arises, they are intrinsically the same in
their fundamental nature. The difference lies in *how we recognize them,* and whether we recognize that they emerge from
the ground of the nature of mind as its enlightened energy.

Take, for example, what manifests in our ordinary mind as
a thought of *desire;* if its true nature is recognized, it arises,
free of grasping, as the "wisdom of discernment." Hatred and
anger, when truly recognized, arise as diamond-like clarity, free
of grasping; this is the "mirror-like wisdom." When *ignorance*

is recognized, it arises as vast and natural clarity without concepts: the "wisdom of all-encompassing space." *Pride,* when
recognized, is realized as non-duality and equality: the "equalizing wisdom." *Jealousy,* when recognized, is freed from par-
tiality and grasping, and arises as the "all-accomplishing
wisdom." So the five negative emotions arise as the direct
result of our not recognizing their true nature. When truly
recognized, they are purified and liberated, and arise themselves as none other than the display of the five wisdoms.

In the bardo of dharmata, when you fail to recognize the
brilliant lights of these wisdoms, then self-grasping enters
your "perception," just as, one master says, a person who
is seriously ill with a high fever will begin to hallucinate and
see all kinds of delusions. So, for example, if you fail to recognize the red, ruby light of the wisdom of discernment,
it arises as fire, for it is the pure essence of the fire element;
if you fail to recognize the true nature of the golden radiance
of the equalizing wisdom, then it arises as the element
earth, because it is the pure essence of the earth element;
and so on.

This is how, when self-grasping enters into the "perception" of the appearances of the bardo of dharmata, they are
transformed, you could almost say solidified, through that
into the various bases of delusion of samsara.

One Dzogchen master uses the example of ice and water to
show how this lack of recognition and self-grasping unfold:
Water is usually liquid, an element with wonderful qualities,
that purifies and quenches thirst. But when it freezes, it solidifies into ice. In a similar way, whenever self-grasping arises
it solidifies both our inner experience and the way we perceive the world around us. Yet just as in the heat of the sun
ice will melt into water, so in the light of recognition, our
unbound wisdom nature is revealed.

Now we can see exactly how, after the dawning of the
Ground Luminosity and the bardo of dharmata, samsara
actually arises as a result of two successive failures to recognize the essential nature of mind. In the first the Ground
Luminosity, the ground of the nature of mind, is not recognized; if it had been, liberation would have been attained.
In the second the energy nature of the nature of mind manifests, and a second chance for liberation presents itself; if that
is not recognized, arising negative emotions start to solidify
into different false perceptions, which together go on to create
the illusory realms we call samsara, and which imprison us in

the cycle of birth and death. The whole of spiritual practice, then, is dedicated to directly reversing what I would call this progress of ignorance, and so of de-creating, de-solidifying those interlinked and interdependent false perceptions that have led to our entrapment in the illusory reality of our own invention.

Just as when the Ground Luminosity dawned at the moment of death, here too in the bardo of dharmata, liberation cannot be taken for granted. For when the brilliant light of wisdom shines out, it is accompanied by a display of simple, comforting, cozy sounds and lights, less challenging and overwhelming than the light of wisdom. These dim lights·-- smoky, yellow, green, blue, red, and white—are our habitual, unconscious tendencies accumulated by anger, greed, ignorance, desire, jealousy, and pride. These are the emotions that create the six realms of samsara: hell, hungry ghost, animal, human, demigod, and god realms respectively.

If we have not recognized and stabilized the dharmata nature of mind in life, we are instinctively drawn toward the dim lights of the six realms, as the basic tendency toward grasping, which we have built up during life, begins to stir and awaken. Threatened by the dynamic brilliance of wisdom, the mind retreats. The cozy lights, the invitation of our habitual tendencies, lure us toward a rebirth, determined by the particular negative emotion that dominates our karma and our mindstream.

Let us take an example of the appearance of one of the peaceful buddhas from the *Tibetan Book of the Dead,* which will illustrate this whole process. The master or spiritual friend addresses the consciousness of the dead person:

> *O son/daughter of an enlightened family, listen without distraction!*
>
> *On the third day, a yellow light will arise which is the pure essence of the element earth. Simultaneously, from the yellow southern buddhafield known as "The Glorious," the Buddha Ratnasambhava will appear before you, his body yellow in color, and holding a wishfulfilling jewel in his hand. He presides upon a throne borne up by horses and is embraced by the supreme female consort, Mamaki. Around him are the two male bodhisattvas, Akashagarbha and Samantabhadra,[4] and the two female bodhisattvas, Mala and Dhupa, so that six buddha bodies appear from within the expanse of rainbow light.*

The inherent purity of the skandha of feeling—which is the "equalizing wisdom"—a yellow light, dazzling and adorned with tiklés of light, large and small, radiant and clear, and unbearable to the eyes, will stream toward you from the heart of Ratnasambhava and his consort, and pierce your heart so that your eyes cannot stand to gaze at it.

At exactly the same time, together with the light of wisdom, a dull blue light representing the human realm will come toward you and pierce your heart. Then, driven by pride, you will flee in terror from the intensity of the yellow light, but delight in the dim blue light of the human realm, and so become attached to it.

At this moment do not be afraid of the piercing yellow light, in all its dazzling radiance, but recognize it as wisdom. Let your Rigpa rest in it, relaxed, at ease, in a state free of any activity. And have confidence in it; have devotion and longing towards it. If you recognize it as the natural radiance of your own Rigpa, even though you do not have devotion and have not said the necessary prayer of inspiration, all the buddha bodies and rays of light will merge inseparably with you, and you will attain buddhahood.

If you do not recognize it as the natural radiance of your own Rigpa, then pray to it with devotion, thinking, "This is the light of the compassionate energy of Buddha Ratnasambhava. I take refuge in it." Since it is in fact the Buddha Ratnasambhava coming to guide you amid the terrors of the bardo, and it is the light-ray hook of his compassionate energy, so fill your heart with devotion to it.

Do not delight in the dim blue light of the human realm. This is the seductive path of habitual tendencies which you have accumulated through intense pride. If you are attached to it you will fall into the human realm, where you will experience the suffering of birth, old age, sickness, and death, and you will miss the chance to emerge from the swamp of samsara. This (dull blue light) is an obstacle blocking the path to liberation, so do not look at it, but abandon pride! Abandon its habitual tendencies! Do not be attached (to the dull blue light)! Do not yearn for it! Feel devotion and longing for the dazzling, radiant yellow light, focus with total attention on the Buddha Ratnasmabhava, and say this prayer:

Alas!
When through intense pride I wander in samsara,
May the Buddha Ratnasambhava lead the way
On the radiant path of light which is the "equalizing wisdom,"
May the supreme female consort Mamaki walk behind me;
Ma they help me through the dangerous pathway of the bardo,
And bring me to the perfect buddha state.

By saying this prayer of inspiration with deep devotion, you will dissolve into rainbow light in the heart of the Buddha Ratnasambhava and his consort and become a Sambhogakaya Buddha[5] in the southern buddha-field known as "The Glorious."

This description of the appearance of the Buddha Ratnasambhava concludes by explaining that through this "showing" by the master or spiritual friend, liberation is certain, however weak the dead person's capacities may be. Yet, even after being "shown" many times, the *Tibetan Book of the Dead* says, there are those who, because of negative karma, will not recognize and gain liberation. Disturbed by desire and obscurations, and terrified by the different sounds and lights, they will flee. So, on the following "day," the next buddha, Amitabha, the Buddha of Limitless Light, with his mandala of deities, will appear in all the splendor of his dazzling red light, manifesting together with the dim, seductive, yellow light-path of the hungry ghosts, which is created out of desire and meanness. And so the *Tibetan Book of the Dead* introduces the appearance of each of the peaceful and wrathful deities in turn in a similar way.

I am often asked: "Will the deities appear to a Western person? And if so, will it be in familiar, Western forms?"

The manifestations of the bardo of dharmata are called "spontaneously present." This means that they are inherent and unconditioned, and exist in us all. Their arising is not dependent on any spiritual realization we may have; only the recognition of them is. They are not unique to Tibetans; they are a universal and fundamental experience, but the way they are perceived depends on our conditioning. Since they are by nature limitless, they have the freedom then to manifest in any form.

Therefore the deities can take on forms we are most familiar with in our lives. For example, for Christian practitioners, the deities might take the form of Christ or the Virgin Mary. Generally, the whole purpose of the enlightened manifestation of the buddhas is to help us, so they may take on whatever form is most appropriate and beneficial for us. But in whatever form the deities appear, it is important to recognize that there is definitely no difference whatsoever in their fundamental nature.

RECOGNITION

In Dzogchen it is explained that just as a person will not recognize the Ground Luminosity without a true realization of the nature of mind and a stable experience of Trekchö practice, so without the stability of Tögal hardly anyone can recognize the bardo of dharmata. An accomplished Tögal practitioner who has perfected and stabilized the luminosity of the nature of mind has already come to a direct knowledge in his or her life of the very same manifestations that will emerge in the bardo of dharmata. This energy and light, then, lie within us, although at the moment they are hidden. Yet when the body and grosser levels of mind die, they are naturally freed, and the sound, color, and light of our true nature blaze out.

However, it is not only through Tögal that this bardo can be used as an opportunity for liberation. Practitioners of Tantra in Buddhism will relate the appearances of the bardo of dharmata to their own practice. In Tantra the principle of deities is a way of communicating. It is difficult to relate to the presence of enlightened energies if they have no form or ground for personal communication. The deities are understood as metaphors, which personalize and capture the infinite energies and qualities of the wisdom mind of the buddhas. Personifying them in the form of deities enables the practitioner to recognize them and relate to them. Through training in creating and reabsorbing the deities in the practice of visualization, he or she realizes that the mind that perceives the deity and the deity itself are not separate.

In Tibetan Buddhism practitioners will have a *yidam,* that is, a practice of a particular buddha or deity with which they have a strong karmic connection, which for them is an embodiment of the truth, and which they invoke as the heart of their practice. Instead of perceiving the appearances of the dharmata as external phenomena, the Tantric practitioners will relate them to their yidam practice, and unite and merge with the appearances. Since in their practice they have recognized the yidam as the natural radiance of the enlightened mind, they are able to view the appearances with this recognition, and let them arise as the deity. With this pure perception, a practitioner recognizes whatever appears in the bardo as none other than the display of the yidam. Then, through the power of his practice and the blessing of the deity, he or she will gain liberation in the bardo of dharmata.

This is why in the Tibetan tradition the advice given to lay people and ordinary practitioners unfamiliar with the yidam practice is that whatever appearances arise, they should consider them, and recognize them immediately and essentially as Avalokiteshvara, the Buddha of Compassion, or Padmasambhava, or Amitabha—whichever they have been most familiar with. To put it briefly, whichever way you have practiced in life will be the very same way by which you try to recognize the appearances of the bardo of dharmata.

Another revealing way of looking at the bardo of dharmata is to see it as duality being expressed in its ultimately purest form. We are presented with the means to liberation, yet we are simultaneously seduced by the call of our habits and instincts. We experience the pure energy of mind, and its confusion at one and the same time. It is almost as if we were being prompted to make up our mind—to choose between one or the other. It goes without saying, however, that whether we even have this choice at all is determined by the degree and perfection of our spiritual practice in life.

EIGHTEEN

The Bardo of Becoming

THE EXPERIENCE OF DEATH, for most people, will simply mean passing into a state of oblivion at the end of the process of dying. The three stages of the inner dissolution can be as quick, it is sometimes said, as three snaps of a finger. The white and red essences of father and mother meet at the heart, and the black experience called "full attainment" arises. The Ground Luminosity dawns, but we fail to recognize it and we faint into unconsciousness.

As I have said, this is the first failure to recognize, or stage of ignorance, called *Ma Rigpa* in Tibetan, the opposite of Rigpa. This marks the beginning in us of another cycle of samsara, which was interrupted for an instant at the moment of death. The bardo of dharmata then occurs, and it simply flashes past, unrecognized. This is the second failure of recognition, a second stage of ignorance, Ma Rigpa.

The first thing that we are aware of is "as if the sky and earth were separating again": We suddenly awaken into the intermediate state that lies between death and a new rebirth. This is called the bardo of becoming, the *sipa bardo,* and is the third bardo of death.

With our failure to recognize the Ground Luminosity and our failure to recognize the bardo of dharmata, the seeds of all our habitual tendencies are activated and reawakened. The bardo of becoming spans the time between their reawakening and our entering the womb of the next life.

The word *sipa* in sipa bardo, which is translated as "becoming," also means "possibility" and "existence." In the sipa bardo, as the mind is no longer limited and obstructed by the physical body of this world, the "possibilities" are infinite for "becoming" reborn in different realms. And this bardo has the outer "existence" of the mental body and the inner "existence" of the mind.

The outstanding feature of the bardo of becoming is that *mind* takes on the predominant role, whereas the bardo of dharmata unfolded within the realm of Rigpa. So, in the bardo of dharmata we have a body of light, and in the bardo of becoming we have a mental body.

In the bardo of becoming the mind is endowed with immense clarity and unlimited mobility, yet the direction in which it moves is determined solely by the habitual tendencies of our past karma. So it is called the "karmic" bardo of becoming, because as Kalu Rinpoche says: "It is an entirely automatic or blind result of our previous actions or karma, and nothing that occurs here is a conscious decision on the part of the being; we are simply buffeted around by the force of karma."[1]

At this point the mind has arrived at the next stage in its process of gradual unfolding: out of its purest state—the Ground Luminosity—through its light and energy—the appearances of the bardo of dharmata—and so into the yet grosser manifestation of a mental form in the bardo of becoming. What takes place now at this stage is a reverse process of dissolution: the winds reappear, and along with them come the thought states connected with ignorance, desire, and anger. Then, because the memory of our past karmic body is still fresh in our mind, we take on a "mental body."

THE MENTAL BODY

Our mental body in the bardo of becoming has a number of special characteristics. It possesses all its senses. It is extremely light, lucid, and mobile, and its awareness is said to be seven times clearer than in life. It is also endowed with a rudimentary kind of clairvoyance, which is not under conscious control, but gives the mental body the ability to read others' minds.

At first this mental body will have a form similar to the body of the life just lived, yet it is without any defects and in the prime of life. Even if you were handicapped or sick in this life, you will have a perfect mental body in the bardo of becoming.

One of the ancient teachings of Dzogchen tells us that the mental body is about the size of a child of eight to ten years old.

Because of the force of conceptual thinking, also known as "the karmic wind," the mental body is unable to remain still, even for an instant. It is ceaselessly on the move. It can go wherever it wishes unobstructedly, just by thinking. Because the mental body has no physical basis, it can pass through solid barriers such as walls or mountains.[2]

The mental body can see through three-dimensional objects. Yet since we lack the father and mother essences of the physical body, we no longer have the light of sun or moon, but only a dim glow illuminating the space immediately in front of us. We can see other bardo beings, but we cannot be seen by living beings, except those who have the kind of clairvoyance developed through deep experience of meditation.[3] So we can meet and converse for fleeting moments with many other travelers in the bardo world, those who have died before us.

Because of the presence of the five elements in its makeup, the mental body seems to us to be solid, and we still feel pangs of hunger. The bardo teachings say that the mental body lives off odors and derives nourishment from burnt offerings, but it can only benefit from offerings dedicated specially in its name.

In this state mental activity is very rapid: thoughts come in quick succession, and we can do many things at once. The mind continues to perpetuate set patterns and habits, especially its clinging to experiences, and its belief that they are ultimately real.

THE EXPERIENCES OF THE BARDO

During the first weeks of the bardo, we have the impression that we are a man or woman, just as in our previous life. We do not realize that we are dead. We return home to meet our family and loved ones. We try to talk to them, to touch them on the shoulder. But they do not reply, or even show they are aware we are there. As hard as we try, nothing can make them notice us. We watch, powerless, as they weep or sit stunned and heartbroken over our death. Fruitlessly we try to make use of our belongings. Our place is no longer laid at table, and arrangements are being made to dispose of our possessions. We feel angry, hurt, and frustrated, "like a fish," says the *Tibetan Book of the Dead,* "writhing in hot sand."

If we are very attached to our body, we may even try, in vain, to reenter or hover around it. In extreme cases the mental body can linger near its possessions or body for weeks or even years. And still it may not dawn on us we are dead. It is only when we see that we cast no shadow, make no reflection in the mirror, no footprints on the ground, that finally we realize. And the sheer shock of recognizing we have died can be enough to make us faint away.

In the bardo of becoming we relive all the experiences of our past life, reviewing minute details long lost to memory, and revisiting places, the masters say, "where we did no more than spit on the ground." Every seven days we are compelled to go through the experience of death once again, with all its suffering. If our death was peaceful, that peaceful state of mind is repeated; if it was tormented, however, that torment is repeated too. And remember that this is with a consciousness seven times more intense than that of life, and that in the fleeting period of the bardo of becoming, all the negative karma of previous lives is returning, in a fiercely concentrated and deranging way.

Our restless, solitary wandering through the bardo world is as frantic as a nightmare, and just as in a dream, we believe we have a physical body and that we really exist. Yet all the experiences of this bardo arise only from our mind, created by our karma and habits returning.

The winds of the elements return, and as Tulku Urgyen Rinpoche says, "One hears loud sounds caused by the four elements of earth, water, fire, and wind. There is the sound of an avalanche continuously falling behind one, the sound of a great rushing river, the sound of a huge blazing mass of fire like a volcano, and the sound of a great storm."[4] Trying to escape them in the terrifying darkness, it is said that three different abysses, white, red, and black, "deep and dreadful," open up in front of us. These, the *Tibetan Book of the Dead* tells us, are our own anger, desire, and ignorance. We are assailed by freezing downpours, hailstorms of pus and blood; haunted by the sound of disembodied, menacing cries; hounded by flesh-eating demons and carnivorous beasts.

We are swept along relentlessly by the wind of karma, unable to hold onto any ground. The *Tibetan Book of the Dead* says: "At this time, the great tornado of karma, terrifying, unbearable, whirling fiercely, will drive you from behind." Consumed by fear, blown to and fro like dandelion seeds in the wind, we roam, helpless, through the gloom of the bardo. Tormented by hunger and thirst, we seek refuge here and there. Our mind's perceptions change every moment, projecting us, "like out of a catapult," says the *Tibetan Book of the Dead,* into alternate states of sorrow or joy. Into our minds comes the longing for a physical body, and yet we fail to find one, which plunges us into further suffering.

The whole landscape and environment is molded by our karma, just as the bardo world can be peopled by the nightmarish images of our own delusions. If our habitual conduct in life was positive, our perception and experience in the bardo will be mixed with bliss and happiness; and if our lives were harmful or hurtful to others, our experiences in the bardo will be ones of pain, grief, and fear. So, it was said in Tibet, fishermen, butchers, and hunters are attacked by monstrous versions of their former victims.

Some who have studied the near-death experience in detail, and especially the "life-review" that is one of its common features, have asked themselves: How could we possibly imagine the horror of the bardo experiences of a drug baron, a dictator, or a Nazi torturer? The "life-review" seems to suggest that, after death, we can experience *all* the suffering for which we were both directly and indirectly responsible.

THE DURATION OF THE BARDO OF BECOMING

The whole of the bardo of becoming has an average duration of forty-nine days, and a minimum length of one week. But it varies, just as now some people live to be a hundred years old, and others die in their youth. Some can even get stuck in the bardo, to become spirits or ghosts. Dudjom Rinpoche used to explain that during the first twenty-one days of the bardo, you still have a strong impression of your previous life, and this is therefore the most important period for the living to be able to help a dead person. After that, your future life slowly takes shape and becomes the dominant influence.

We have to wait in the bardo until we can make a karmic connection with our future parents. I sometimes think of the bardo as something like a transit lounge, in which you can wait for up to forty-nine days before transferring to the next life. But there are two special cases who don't have to wait in the intermediate state, because the intensity of the power of their karma sweeps them immediately on to their next rebirth. The first are those who have lived extremely beneficial and positive lives, and so trained their minds in spiritual practice that the force of their realization carries them directly into a good rebirth. The second case are those whose lives have been negative and harmful; they travel swiftly down to their next birth, wherever that might be.

JUDGMENT

Some accounts of the bardo describe a judgment scene, a kind of life-review similar to the post-mortem judgment found in many of the world's cultures. Your good conscience, a white guardian angel, acts as your defense counsel, recounting the beneficial things you have done, while your bad conscience, a black demon, submits the case for the prosecution. Good and bad are totalled up as white and black pebbles. The "Lord of Death," who presides, then consults the mirror of karma and makes his judgment.[5]

I feel that in this judgment scene there are some interesting parallels with the life-review of the near-death experience. *Ultimately all judgment takes place within our own mind. We are the judge and the judged.* "It is interesting to note," said Raymond Moody, "that the judgment in the cases I studied came not from the being of light, who seemed to love and accept these people anyway, but rather from within the individual being judged."[6]

A woman who went through a near-death experience told Kenneth Ring: "You are shown your life—and you do the judging. . . . You are judging yourself. You have been forgiven all your sins, but are you able to forgive yourself for not doing the things you should have done, and some little cheating things that maybe you've done in life? Can you forgive yourself? This is the judgment."[7]

The judgment scene also shows that what really counts, in the final analysis, is the motivation behind our every action, and that there is no escaping the effects of our past actions, words, and thoughts, and the imprints and habits they have stamped us with. It means that we are entirely responsible, not only for this life, but for our future lives as well.

THE POWER OF THE MIND

As our mind is so light, mobile, and vulnerable in the bardo, whatever thoughts arise, good or bad, have tremendous power and influence. Without a physical body to ground us, thoughts actually become reality. Imagine the sharp grief and anger we might feel on seeing a funeral service performed carelessly on our behalf, or greedy relatives squabbling over our possessions, or friends we loved deeply, and thought had loved us, talking about us in a sneering or hurtful or simply condescending way. Such a situation could be very dangerous, because our reaction, in its violence, could drive us directly toward an unfortunate rebirth.

The overwhelming power of thought, then, is *the* key issue in the bardo of becoming. This crucial moment finds us completely exposed to whatever habits and tendencies we have allowed to grow and dominate our lives. If you don't check those habits and tendencies now in life, and prevent them from seizing hold of your mind, then in the bardo of becoming you will be their helpless victim, buffeted to and fro by their power. The slightest irritation, for example, in the bardo of becoming can have a devastating effect, and that is why traditionally the person reading the *Tibetan Book of the Dead* had to be someone with whom you had a good connection; if not, the very sound of his or her voice could infuriate you, with the most disastrous consequences.

The teachings give us many descriptions of the rawness of the mind in the bardo of becoming; the most striking of these says that our mind in this bardo is like a flaming red-hot iron bar that can be bent in whichever way you want until it cools, when whatever form it finds itself in rapidly solidifies. In just the same way, it is said, a single positive thought in this bardo can lead directly to enlightenment, and a single negative reaction can plunge you into the most prolonged and extreme suffering. The *Tibetan Book of the Dead* could not warn us more strongly:

> *Now is the time which is the border line between going up and going down; now is the time when by slipping into laziness even for a moment you will endure constant suffering; now is the time when by concentrating for an instant you will enjoy constant happiness. Focus your mind single-mindedly; strive to prolong the results of good karma!*

The *Tibetan Book of the Dead* tries to awaken any connection with spiritual practice the dead person may have had, and it encourages us: to give up attachment to people and possessions, to abandon yearning for a body, not to give in to desire or anger, to cultivate kindness rather than hostility, and not even to contemplate negative actions. It reminds the dead person there is no need to fear: On the one hand, it tells them that the terrifying bardo figures are nothing more than their own deluded projections and by nature empty; and on the other hand, that they themselves have only "a mental body of habitual tendencies," and are therefore empty too. "So emptiness cannot harm emptiness."

The shifting and precarious nature of the bardo of becoming can also be the source of many opportunities for liberation, and the susceptibility of mind in this bardo can be turned to our advantage. All we have to do is remember one instruction; all it needs is for one positive thought to spring into our mind. If we can recall any teaching that has inspired us to the nature of mind, if we have even one good inclination toward practice, or a deep connection with a spiritual practice, then that alone can free us.

In the bardo of becoming, the buddha realms do not appear spontaneously as they do in the bardo of dharmata. Just by remembering them, however, you can transfer yourself there directly by the power of your mind, and proceed toward enlightenment. It is said that if you can invoke a buddha, he will immediately appear before you. But remember, even though the possibilities are limitless, we must have at least some, if not total, control over our mind in this bardo; and this is extremely difficult, because the mind here is so vulnerable, fragmented, and restless.

So in this bardo, whenever you can suddenly retrieve your awareness, even for a moment, immediately recall your connection with spiritual practice, remember your master or buddha, and invoke them with all your strength. If in life you have developed the natural reflex of praying whenever things become difficult or critical, or slip beyond your control, then instantly you will be able to invoke or call to mind an enlightened being, such as Buddha or Padmasambhava, Tara or Avalokiteshvara, Christ or the Virgin Mary. If you are able to invoke them fervently with one-pointed devotion, and with all your heart, then through the power of their blessing, your mind will be liberated into the space of their wisdom mind. Prayer in this life may seem sometimes to bring little result, but its effects in the bardo are unprecedentedly powerful.

Yet the description that I have given you of the bardo shows the sheer difficulty of focusing the mind at this juncture, if we have had no previous training. Think how almost impossible it is to remember something like a prayer in a dream or nightmare, how impotent and powerless we feel in them; in the bardo of becoming it is just as hard, if not harder, to collect our thoughts at all. This is why the watchword of the *Tibetan Book of the Dead*, repeated over and over again, is: "Do not be distracted." As it points out:

*This is the dividing line where buddhas and sentient beings are
    separated . . .*
*"In an instant they are separated, in an instant complete
    enlightenment."*

REBIRTH

As, in the bardo of becoming, the time for rebirth gets
closer, you crave more and more for the support of a material
body, and you search for any one that might be available in
which to be reborn. Different signs will begin to appear,
warning you of the realm in which you are likely to take
rebirth. Lights of various colors shine from the six realms of
existence, and you will feel drawn toward one or another,
depending on the negative emotion that is predominant in
your mind. Once you have been drawn into one of these
lights, it is very difficult to turn back.

Then images and visions will arise, linked to the different
realms. As you become more familiar with the teachings, you
will become more alert to what they really mean. The signs
vary slightly according to different teachings. Some say that if
you are to be reborn as a god, you will have a vision of entering a heavenly palace with many stories. If you are to be
reborn as a demigod, you will feel you are amidst spinning
circular weapons of fire, or going onto a battlefield. If you are
to be reborn as an animal, you find yourself in a cave, a hole
in the ground, or a nest made of straw. If you have a vision of
a tree stump, a deep forest, or a woven cloth, you are to be
reborn as a hungry ghost. And if you are to be reborn in hell,
you will feel you are being led, powerless, into a black pit,
down a black road, into a somber land with black or red
houses, or toward a city of iron.

There are many other signs, such as the way in which
your gaze or movement is aligned, which indicate the realm
for which you are heading. If you are to be reborn in a god or
human realm, your gaze will be directed upward; if in an animal realm, you will look straight ahead, as do birds; and if in
a hungry ghost or hell realm, you will look downward, as
though you were diving.

If any of these signs appear, you should be on guard not to
fall into any of these unfortunate rebirths.

At the same time, you will have an intense desire and longing for certain realms, and you are drawn toward them all too
instinctively. The teachings warn us that at this point there is
a great danger that out of your avid eagerness to be reborn,

you will rush to any place at all that seems to offer some security. If your desire is frustrated, the anger that arises will of itself bring the bardo abruptly to an end, as you are swept into your next rebirth by the current of that negative emotion. And so, as you can see, your future rebirth is directly determined by desire, anger, and ignorance.

Imagine that you run toward a place of refuge, simply to escape the onslaught of the bardo experiences. Then, terrified to leave, you might become attached and take on a new birth, no matter where, just in order to have one. You might even, the *Tibetan Book of the Dead* explains, become confused and mistake a good birthplace for a bad one, or a bad one for a good one. Or hear the voices of your loved ones calling you, or seductive singing, and follow these, only to find yourself being lured down into the lower realms.

You must take great care not to enter blindly into one of these undesirable realms. Yet what is wonderful is that the instant you become aware of what is happening to you, you can actually begin to influence and change your destiny.

Swept along by the wind of karma, you will then arrive at a place where your future parents are making love. Seeing them, you become emotionally drawn in; and because of past karmic connections, you begin spontaneously to feel strong attachment or aversion. Attraction and desire for the mother and aversion or jealousy for the father will result in your being born as a male child, and the reverse a female.[8] But if you succumb to such strong passions, not only will you be reborn, but that very emotion may draw you into birth in a lower realm.

Is there anything now that we can do to avoid being reborn or to direct our next rebirth? The bardo teachings give two specific kinds of instructions: methods for preventing a rebirth, or failing that, for choosing a good birth. First are the guidelines for *closing the entrance to another birth:*

The best method is to abandon the emotions such as desire, anger, or jealousy, and recognize that none of these bardo experiences have any ultimate reality. If you can realize this and then rest the mind in its true, empty nature, this in itself will prevent rebirth. The *Tibetan Book of the Dead* here warns us:

Alas! the father and mother, the great storm, the whirlwind, the thunder, the terrifying projections and all these apparent phenomena are illusory in their real nature. However they appear, they are not real. All substances are false and untrue. They are like a mirage, they are not permanent, they are not changeless. What is the use of desire? What is the use of fear? It is regarding the nonexistent as existent . . .

The *Tibetan Book of the Dead* goes on to advise us:

"All substances are my own mind, and this mind is emptiness, unarisen and unobstructed." *Thinking this, keep your mind natural and undiluted, self-contained in its own nature like water poured into water, just as it is, loose, open and relaxed. By letting it rest naturally and loosely, you can be sure that the womb-entrance to all the different kinds of birth will certainly be closed.*[9]

The next best method to prevent rebirth is to see your potential parents as the buddha, or your master, or yidam deity. And at the very least, you should try to generate a feeling of renunciation against being drawn into feelings of desire, and to think of the pure realms of the buddhas. This will prevent rebirth and may cause you to be reborn in one of the buddha realms.

If you are unable to stabilize the mind enough to do even this kind of practice, then there remain the methods for *choosing a rebirth,* which are linked to the landmarks and signs of the different realms. If you must take rebirth, or you intentionally wish to be reborn in order to pursue your spiritual path and be of benefit to others, you should not enter any but the human realm. It is only there that conditions are favorable for spiritual progress. If you are going to be born in a fortunate situation in the human realm, the teachings tell us, you will feel you are arriving at a sumptuous and beautiful house, or in a city, or among a crowd of people, or you will have a vision of couples making love.

Otherwise, generally we have no choice. We are drawn toward our birthplace "as inexorably as a bird lured into a cage, dry grass catching fire, or an animal sinking into a marsh." The *Tibetan Book of the Dead* says: "O son/daughter of an enlightened family, even though you do not want to go, you have no power of your own; you are helpless and compelled to go."

Yet, as the teachings are always so inspiringly reminding us, there is always hope; *now* is the time for prayer. By wishing and concentrating intensely, even at this moment, you can still be reborn in one of the buddha realms, or else you can generate a deep aspiration to be reborn in a human family where you may be able to meet the spiritual path and continue toward liberation. If you have a strong karma that impels you toward a particular realm, you may have no choice; however, your past aspiration and prayers can help you to reshape your destiny, so you may be reborn into a life that will lead one day to liberation.

Even as you enter the womb, you can go on praying for this to happen. Even now, you can visualize yourself as any enlightened being, traditionally the masters say as Vajra-sattva,[10] bless the womb you are entering as a sacred environment, "a palace of the gods," and continue to practice.

> Now when the bardo of becoming dawns upon me,
> I will concentrate my mind one-pointedly,
> And strive to prolong the results of good karma,
> Close the entrance to rebirth, and try to keep from being reborn.
> This is the time when perseverance and pure perception are needed;
> Abandon negative emotions, and meditate on the master.

Ultimately it is the mind's urge to inhabit a particular realm that impels us toward reincarnation, and its tendency to solidify and to grasp that finds its ultimate expression in physical rebirth. This is the next stage in the process of manifestation that we have seen taking place throughout the bardos.

If you succeed in directing the mind toward a human birth, you have come full circle. You are poised to be born again into the natural bardo of this life. When you see your father and mother in intercourse, your mind is ineluctably drawn in, and enters the womb. This signals the end of the bardo of becoming, as your mind rapidly reexperiences yet again the signs of the phases of dissolution and the dawning of the Ground Luminosity. Then the black experience of full attainment arises again, and at the same moment the connection to the new womb is made.

So life begins, as it ends, with the Ground Luminosity.

NINETEEN

Helping after Death

SO OFTEN IN THE MODERN WORLD when someone dies, one of the deepest sources of anguish for those left behind to mourn is their conviction that there is nothing they can now do to help their loved one who has gone, a conviction that only aggravates and darkens the loneliness of their grief. But this is not true. There are many, many ways we can help the dead, and so help ourselves to survive their absence. One of the unique features of Buddhism, and one of the ways in which the omniscient skill and compassion of the buddhas is most profoundly demonstrated, is in the many special practices that are available to help a dead person, and so also comfort the bereaved. The Tibetan Buddhist vision of life and death is an all-encompassing one, and it shows us clearly that there are ways of helping people in every conceivable situation, since there are no barriers whatever between what we call "life" and what we call "death." The radiant power and warmth of the compassionate heart can reach out to help in all states and all realms.

WHEN WE CAN HELP

The bardo of becoming, as it has already been described, may seem a very disturbed and disturbing time. Yet there is great hope in it. The qualities of the mental body during the bardo of becoming that make it so vulnerable—its clarity, mobility, sensitivity, and clairvoyance—*also make it particularly receptive to help from the living.* The fact that it has no physical form or basis makes it very easy to guide. The *Tibetan Book of the Dead* compares the mental body to a horse, which can be readily controlled by a bridle, or to a huge tree trunk, which may be almost immovable on land, yet once floated in water can be effortlessly directed wherever you wish.

The most powerful time to do spiritual practice for someone who has died is during the forty-nine days of the bardo
of becoming, placing special emphasis on the first twenty-one
days. It is during these first three weeks that the dead have a
stronger link with *this* life, which makes them more accessible
to our help. So it is then that spiritual practice has a far greater
possibility of influencing their future, and of affecting their
chances for liberation, or at least a better rebirth. We should
employ every means possible to help them then, as after the
physical form of their next existence begins gradually to be
determined—and this is said to happen between the twenty-
first and forty-ninth day after death—the chance for real
change is very much more limited.

Help for the dead, however, is not confined to the forty-
nine days after death. *It is never too late to help someone who has
died, no matter how long ago it was.* The person you want to help
may have been dead a hundred years, but it will still be of
benefit to practice for them. Dudjom Rinpoche used to say
that even if someone has gained enlightenment and become a
buddha, they will still need all the assistance they can possibly get in their work of helping others.

HOW WE CAN HELP

The best and easiest way to help a dead person is to do the
essential practice of phowa I have taught in chapter 13, Spiritual Help for the Dying, as soon as we hear that someone
has died.

In Tibet we say that just as it is the nature of fire to burn
and of water to quench thirst, the nature of the buddhas is to
be present as soon as anyone invokes them, so infinite is their
compassionate desire to help all sentient beings. Don't for one
moment imagine that it would be less effective for *you* to
invoke the truth to help your dead friend than if a "holy
man" prays for them. Because you are close to the person
who has died, the intensity of your love and the depth of
your connection will give your invocation an added power.
The masters have assured us: Call out to them, and the
buddhas *will* answer you.

Khandro Tsering Chödrön, the spiritual wife of Jamyang
Khyentse, often says that if you really have a good heart, and
really mean well, and then pray for someone, that prayer
will be very effective. So be confident that if someone you
love very much has died, and you pray for them with true
love and sincerity, your prayer *will* be exceptionally powerful.

The best and most effective time to do the phowa is before the body is touched or moved in any way. If this is not possible, then try to do the phowa in the place where the person died, or at least picture that place very strongly in your mind. There is a powerful connection between the dead person, the place of death, and also the time of death, especially in the case of a person who died in a traumatic way.

In the bardo of becoming, as I have said, the dead person's consciousness goes through the experience of death every week, on exactly the same day. So you should perform the phowa, or whatever other spiritual practice you have chosen to do, on any day of the forty-nine day period, but *especially* on the same day of the week that the person died.

Whenever your dead relative or friend comes into your mind, whenever you hear his or her name being mentioned, send the person your love, and then focus on doing the phowa, and do it for as long and as often as you wish.

Another thing you can do, whenever you think of someone who has died, is to say immediately a mantra such as OM MANI PADME HUM (pronounced by Tibetans: Om Mani Pémé Hung), the mantra of the Buddha of Compassion, which purifies each of the negative emotions that are the cause of rebirth[1]; or OM AMI DEWA HRIH, the mantra of Buddha Amitabha, the Buddha of Limitless Light. You can then follow that again with the practice of phowa.

But whether you do any of these practices or not to help your loved one who has died, don't ever forget that the consciousness in the bardo is acutely clairvoyant; simply directing good thoughts toward them will be most beneficial.

When you pray for someone who was close to you, you can, if you wish, extend the embrace of your compassion to include other dead people in your prayers: the victims of atrocities, wars, disasters, and famines, or those who died and are now dying in concentration camps, such as those in China and Tibet. You can even pray for people who died years ago, like your grandparents, long-dead members of your family, or victims of wars, such as those in the World Wars. Imagine your prayers going especially to those who lost their lives in extreme anguish, passion, or anger.

Those who have suffered *violent or sudden death* have a particularly urgent need for help. Victims of murder, suicide, accident, or war can easily be trapped by their suffering, anguish, and fear, or may be imprisoned in the actual experience of death and so be unable to move on through the process of rebirth. When you practice the phowa for them, do it more strongly and with more fervor than you have ever done it before:

Imagine tremendous rays of light emanating from the buddhas or divine beings, pouring down all their compassion and blessing. Imagine this light streaming down onto the dead person, purifying them totally and freeing them from the confusion and pain of their death, granting them profound, lasting peace. Imagine then, with all your heart and mind, that the dead person dissolves into light and his or her consciousness, healed now and free of all suffering, soars up to merge indissolubly, and forever, with the wisdom mind of the buddhas.

Some Western people who recently visited Tibet told me about the following incident they had witnessed. One day a Tibetan walking by the side of the road was knocked over and killed instantly by a Chinese truck. A monk, who happened to be passing, quickly went over and sat next to the dead man lying on the ground. They saw the monk lean over him and recite some practice or other close to his ear; suddenly, to their astonishment, the dead man revived. The monk then performed a practice they recognized as the transference of consciousness, and guided him back calmly into death. What had happened? Clearly the monk had recognized that the violent shock of the man's death had left him terribly disturbed, and so the monk had acted swiftly: first to free the dead man's mind from its distress, and then, by means of the phowa, to transfer it to a buddha realm or toward a good rebirth. To the Westerners who were watching, this monk seemed to be just an ordinary person, but this remarkable story shows that he was in fact a practitioner of considerable power.

Meditation practices and prayers are not the only kind of help that we can give to the dead. We can offer charity in their name to help the sick and needy. We can give their possessions to the poor. We can contribute, on their behalf, to humanitarian or spiritual ventures such as hospitals, aid projects, hospices, or monasteries.

We could also sponsor retreats by good spiritual practitioners, or prayer meetings led by great masters in sacred places, like Bodhgaya. We could offer lights for the dead person, or sponsor works of art related to spiritual practice. Another method of helping the dead, especially favored in Tibet and the Himalayas, is to save the lives of animals due to be slaughtered, and release them again into freedom.

It is important to dedicate all the merit and well-being that springs from any such acts of kindness and generosity to the dead person, and in fact to all those who have died, so that everyone who has died may obtain a better rebirth and favorable circumstances in their next life.

THE CLAIRVOYANCE OF THE DEAD PERSON

Remember, the clairvoyant consciousness of the person in the bardo of becoming is seven times clearer than in life. This can bring them *either great suffering or great benefit*.

So it is essential that after someone you love has died, you are as aware as possible in all your behavior, so as not to disturb them or hurt them. For when the dead person returns to those left behind, or those invited to practice on their behalf, they are able, in their new state of being, not only to see what is going on but to read minds directly. If relatives are only scheming and quarreling about how to divide up their possessions, only talking and thinking of attachment and aversion, with no real love for the dead person, this can cause them intense anger and hurt or disillusion, and they will then be drawn by these turbulent emotions into an unfortunate rebirth.

For example, imagine if a dead person saw spiritual practitioners supposedly practicing for him but with no sincere thought in their minds for his benefit, and with their minds preoccupied with trivial distractions; the dead person could lose any faith he might ever have had. Imagine too if a dead person had to watch her loved ones distraught and helpless with grief; it could plunge her into deep grief also. And if a dead person were to discover, for example, that relatives only made a show of loving her because of her money, she could become so painfully disillusioned that she returned as a ghost to haunt the inheritor of her wealth. You can see now that what you do and how you think and how you behave after people have died can be of crucial importance, and have a far greater impact on their future than you can possibly imagine.[2]

You will see now why it is absolutely essential for the peace of mind of the dead person that those who are left behind should be harmonious. This is why, in Tibet, when

all the friends and relatives of the dead person assembled,
they were encouraged to practice together and to say, as much
as possible, a mantra such as: OM MANI PADME HUM.
This is something that everyone in Tibet could do and knew
would definitely help the dead person, and which inspired
them all to an act of fervent communal prayer.

The clairvoyance of the dead person in the bardo of becoming is also what makes the practice done by a master or experienced spiritual practitioner on his or her behalf of such
exceptional benefit.

What a master does is to rest in the primordial state of
Rigpa, the nature of mind, and invoke the mental body
of the dead person roaming in the bardo of becoming. When
the mental body comes into the master's presence, through
the power of meditation, he or she can point out the essential
nature of Rigpa. Through the power of its clairvoyance, the
bardo being then can see directly into the master's wisdom
mind, and so there and then be introduced to the nature of mind
and be liberated.

Whatever practice an ordinary practitioner can do as well
for a close friend who has died can, for the same reason, be of
enormous help. You might do the practice, for example, of the
Hundred Peaceful and Wrathful Deities associated with the
Tibetan Book of the Dead, or you might simply rest in a steady
state of compassion; especially if you then invoke the dead
person and invite him or her into the heart-core of your practice, it can be of immense benefit.

Whenever Buddhist practitioners die we inform their master, all their spiritual teachers, and their spiritual friends, so
they can immediately start practicing for them. Usually I collect the names of people who have died, and send them to great
masters I know in India and the Himalayas. Every few weeks
they will include them in a purification practice, and once a
year in a ten-day intensive group practice in the monasteries.[3]

TIBETAN BUDDHIST PRACTICES FOR THE DEAD

1. The Tibetan Book of the Dead

In Tibet, once the phowa practice has been done for the
dying person, the *Tibetan Book of the Dead* is read repeatedly
and the practices associated with it are done. In eastern Tibet

we used to have a tradition of reading the *Tibetan Book of the Dead* for the whole forty-nine days after death. Through the reading, the dead are shown what stage of the process of death they are in, and given whatever inspiration and guidance they need.

Westerners often ask me: How can a person who is dead *hear* the *Tibetan Book of the Dead*?

The simple reply is that the consciousness of the dead person, when it is invoked by the power of prayer, is able to read our minds and can feel exactly whatever we may be thinking or meditating on. That is why there is no obstacle to the dead person's understanding the *Tibetan Book of the Dead* or practices done on their behalf, even though they may be recited in Tibetan. For the dead person, language is no barrier at all, for the essential *meaning* of the text can be understood fully and directly by his or her mind.

This makes it all the more vital that the practitioner should be as focused and attentive as possible when doing the practice, and not merely performing it by rote. Also, as the dead person is living the actual experiences, he or she may have a greater capacity to understand the truth of the *Tibetan Book of the Dead* than we do!

I am sometimes asked: "But what happens if the consciousness has already fainted into an oblivious state at the moment of death?" Since we do not know how long the dead person will remain in that state of unconsciousness, and at what point he or she will enter the bardo of becoming, the *Tibetan Book of the Dead* is read and practiced repeatedly, to cover any eventuality.

But what about people who are not familiar with the teachings or the *Tibetan Book of the Dead*: Should we read it to them? The Dalai Lama has given us this clear guidance:

> *Whether you believe in religion or not it is very important to have a peaceful mind at the time of death. . . . From a Buddhist point of view, whether the person who dies believes in rebirth or not, their rebirth exists, and so a peaceful mind, even if it is neutral, is important at the time of death. If the person is a non-believer, reading the* Tibetan Book of the Dead *could agitate their mind. . . . it could arouse aversion and so even harm them instead of helping them. In the case of a person who is open to it, however, the mantras or the names of the buddhas might help them to generate some kind of connection, and so it could be helpful. It is important to take into account, above all, the attitude of the dying person.*"[4]

2. Né Dren and Chang Chok

Hand in hand with the reading of the *Tibetan Book of the Dead* goes the practice of *Né Dren,* the ritual for guiding the dead, or *Chang Chok,* the ritual purification, in which a master will guide the consciousness of the dead person to a better rebirth.

Ideally the Né Dren or Chang Chok should be done immediately after death, or at least within forty-nine days. If the corpse is not present, the consciousness of the deceased is summoned into an effigy or card bearing their likeness and name, or even a photograph, called a *tsenjang.* The Né Dren or Chang Chok derive their power from the fact that during the period immediately after death, the dead person will have a strong feeling of possessing the body of its recent life.

Through the power of the master's meditation, the consciousness of the dead person, roaming aimlessly in the bardo, is called into the tsenjang, which represents the dead person's identity. The consciousness is then purified; the karmic seeds of the six realms are cleansed; a teaching is given just as in life; and the dead person is introduced to the nature of the mind. Finally the phowa is effected, and the dead person's consciousness is directed toward one of the Buddha realms. Then the tsenjang, representing the individual's old—now discarded—identity, is burned, and their karma is purified.

3. The Purification of the Six Realms

My master Dilgo Khyentse Rinpoche often used to say that the practice known as "the Purification of the Six Realms" was the best possible purification practice for a practitioner who has died.

The Purification of the Six Realms is a practice used in life that employs visualization and meditation to purify the body of each of the six main negative emotions, along with the realms of existence they create. It can also be used very effectively for the dead, and is particularly powerful because it purifies the root of their karma, and so of their connection with samsara. This is essential; if these negative emotions are not purified, they will dictate which realm of samsara the dead person will be reborn in.

According to the Dzogchen Tantras, the negative emotions accumulate in the psycho-physical system of subtle channels, inner air, and energy, and gather at particular energy centers in the body. So the seed of the hell realm and its cause, anger, are located at the soles of the feet; the hungry ghost

realm and its cause, avarice, rest at the base of the trunk; the
animal realm and its cause, ignorance, rest at the navel; the
human realm and its cause, doubt, rest at the heart; the
demigod realm and its cause, jealousy, rest at the throat;
and the god realm and its cause, pride, rest at the crown of
the head.

In this practice of the Purification of the Six Realms, when
each realm and its negative emotion is purified, the practitioner imagines that all the karma created by that particular
emotion is now exhausted, and that specific part of his body
associated with the karma of a particular emotion dissolves
entirely into light. So when you do this practice for a dead
person, imagine with all your heart and mind that, at the end
of the practice, all their karma is purified, and their body and
entire being dissolve into radiant light.[5]

4. The Practice of the Hundred Peaceful and Wrathful Deities

Another means to help the dead is the practice of the Hundred Peaceful and Wrathful Deities. (These deities are
described in chapter 17, "Intrinsic Radiance.") The practitioner
considers his or her entire body as the mandala of the Hundred Peaceful and Wrathful Deities; the peaceful deities are
visualized in the energy center in the heart, and the wrathful
dieties in the brain. The practitioner then imagines that the
deities send out thousands of rays of light, which stream out
to the dead and purify all their negative karma.

The mantra of purification the practitioner recites is the
mantra of Vajrasattva, the presiding deity of all the Tantric
mandalas, and the central deity of the mandala of the Hundred Peaceful and Wrathful Deities, whose power is invoked
especially for purification and for healing. This is the "Hundred Syllable Mantra," which includes "seed syllables" of each
of the Hundred Peaceful and Wrathful Deities.[6]

You can use a short, six-syllable form of the Vajrasattva
mantra: OM VAJRA SATTVA HUM (pronounced by Tibetans: Om Benza Satto Hung). The essential meaning of this
mantra is, "O Vajrasattva! Through your power may you
bring about purification, healing, and transformation." I
strongly recommend this mantra for healing and purification.

Another important mantra, which appears in the Dzogchen Tantras and the practices associated with the *Tibetan Book
of the Dead*, is 'A A HA SHA SA MA. The six syllables of this
mantra have the power to "close the gates" to the six realms
of samsara.

5. Cremation

Generally in many Eastern traditions, *cremation* is the way of disposing of the corpse. In Tibetan Buddhism, there are also specific practices for cremation. The crematorium or funeral pyre is visualized as the mandala of Vajrasattva, or the Hundred Peaceful and Wrathful Deities, and the deities are strongly visualized and their presence is invoked. The dead person's corpse is seen as actually representing all his or her negative karma and obscurations. As the corpse burns, these are consumed by the deities as a great feast and transmuted and transformed by them into their wisdom nature. Rays of light are imagined streaming out from the deities; the corpse is visualized dissolving completely into light, as all the impurities of the dead person are purified in the blazing flames of wisdom. As you visualize this, you can recite the hundred-syllable or six-syllable mantra of Vajrasattva. This simple practice for a cremation was transmitted and inspired by Dudjom Rinpoche and Dilgo Khyentse Rinpoche.

The ashes of the body, and the tsenjang, can then be mixed with clay to make little images called *tsatsa*. These are blessed and dedicated on behalf of the dead person, so creating auspicious conditions for a future good rebirth.

6. The Weekly Practices

In a Tibetan environment practices and rituals happen regularly every seventh day after death, or if the family can afford it, for each of the forty-nine days. Monks are invited to do practice, especially the lamas who are close to the family and had a link with the dead person. Lights are offered and prayers said continuously, especially until the time the body is taken out of the house. Offerings are made to masters and to shrines, and alms are given to the poor in the name of the dead person.

These "weekly" practices on behalf of the dead person are considered essential, since the mental body in the bardo of becoming undergoes every week, on the same day, the experience of death. If the dead person has enough merit as a result of positive actions in the past, then the benefit of these practices can give them the impetus to transfer to a pure realm. Strictly speaking, if a person passed away on a Wednesday before noon, the first week's practice day would fall on the following Tuesday. If the person died after noon, it would fall on the following Wednesday.

Tibetans regard the fourth week after death as specially significant, because some say that most ordinary beings do not stay in the bardo longer than four weeks. The seventh week is also considered a critical juncture, as forty-nine days is taught to be generally the longest stay in the bardo. So on these occasions, masters and practitioners will be invited to the house, and the practices, offerings, and donations to the needy are performed on a grander scale.

Another offering ceremony and feast is held one year after the death, to mark the dead person's rebirth. Most Tibetan families would have annual ceremonies on the anniversaries of their teachers, parents, husbands, wives, brothers, and sisters, and on these days they will also give donations to the poor.

HELPING THE BEREAVED

Among Tibetans, whenever someone dies it's natural for their relatives and friends to gather round, and everyone always finds some way or another to give a helping hand. The whole community provides strong spiritual, emotional, and practical support, and the dead person's family is never left feeling helpless or at a loss or wondering what they can do. Everyone in Tibetan society knows that as much as possible is being done for the dead person, and that knowledge empowers those who are left behind to endure, accept, and survive the death of their loved ones.

How different it is now in modern society, where such community support has been almost entirely lost! I often think how such support could save the grief of bereavement from being prolonged and needlessly difficult, as it so often is.

My students who work as bereavement counselors in hospices have told me that one of the severest sources of anguish for a bereaved person is the belief that neither they nor anyone else can do anything for their loved one who has died. But there is, as I have been showing, a great deal that anyone can do to help the dead.

One way of comforting the bereaved is to encourage them to do something for their loved ones who have died: by living even more intensely on their behalf after they have gone, by practicing for them, and so giving their death a deeper meaning. In Tibet relatives may even go on a pilgrimage for the dead person, and at special moments and at holy places they will think of their dead loved ones and practice for them. The Tibetans never forget the dead: They will make offerings at shrines on their behalf; at great prayer meetings they will sponsor prayers in their name; they will keep making donations, for them, to spiritual projects; and whenever they meet masters they will request special prayers for them. The greatest consolation for a Tibetan would be to know that a master was doing practice for their dead relative.

Don't let us half die with our loved ones, then; let us try to live, after they have gone, with greater fervor. Let us try, at least, to fulfill the dead person's wishes or aspirations in some way, for instance by giving some of his belongings to charity, or sponsoring in her name a project she held particularly dear.

Tibetans often write letters of condolence to friends who are bereaved that might say something like this:

> All things are impermanent, and all things die. You know this. It was only natural that your mother died when she did; the older generation is expected to die first. She was elderly and unwell, and will not resent having had to leave her body. And because you can help her now by sponsoring practices and doing good actions in her name, she will be happy and relieved. So please do not be sad.

If our friend has lost a child or someone close to them who seemed too young to die so soon, we tell them:

> Now your little boy has died, and it seems as if your whole world has been shattered. It seems, I know, so cruel and illogical. I cannot explain your son's death, but I do know that it must be the natural result of his karma, and I believe and know that his death must have purified some karmic debt that you and I cannot know about. Your grief is my grief. But take heart because now you and I can help him, through our practice and our good actions and our love; we can take his hand and walk by his side, even now, even when he's dead, and help him to find a new birth and a longer life next time.

In other cases we might write:

> I know your grief is vast, but when you are tempted to despair, just think how fortunate your friend is to have the masters practicing for her. Just think too, that at other times and in other places there has been no such spiritual help at all for those who died. Think, when you remember your loved one dying, how many people are dying in the world today, alone, forgotten, abandoned, and unsupported by any spiritual vision. Think of the people who died in the terrible, inhuman years of the Cultural Revolution in Tibet, where spiritual practice of any kind was forbidden.

Remember too when despair menaces you that giving in to it will only disturb the one who has died. Your sorrow may even drag her back from the path she may be taking toward a good rebirth. And if you are consumed by grief, you will cripple yourself from being able to help her. The steadier you are, the more positive your state of mind, the more comfort you will give her, and the more you will enable her to free herself.

When you are sad, have the courage to say to yourself: "Whatever feelings I am experiencing, they will all pass: even if they return, they cannot last." Just as long as you do not try to prolong them, all your feelings of loss and grief will naturally begin to dissolve and fall away.

In our world, however, where we do not know that it is even possible to help the dead, and where we have not faced the fact of death at all, such a serene and wise reflection cannot be easy. A person who is going through bereavement for the first time may simply be shattered by the array of disturbing feelings, of intense sadness, anger, denial, withdrawal, and guilt that they suddenly find are playing havoc inside them. Helping those who have just gone through the loss of someone close to them will call for all your patience and sensitivity. You will need to spend time with them and to let them talk, to listen silently without judgment as they recall their most private memories, or go over again and again the details of the death. Above all, you will need simply to be there with them as they experience what is probably the fiercest sadness and pain of their entire lives. Make sure you make yourself available to them at all times, even when they don't seem to need it. Carol, a widow, was interviewed for a video series on death one year after her husband had died. "When you look back on the last year," she was asked, "who would you say had helped you the most?" She said: "The people who kept calling and coming by, even though I said 'no.'"

People who are grieving go through a kind of death. Just like a person who is actually dying, they need to know that the disturbing emotions they are feeling are natural. They need to know too that the process of mourning is a long and often tortuous one, where grief returns again and again in cycles. Their shock and numbness and disbelief will fade, and will be replaced by a deep and at times desperate awareness of the immensity of their loss, which itself will settle eventually into a state of recovery and balance. Tell them that this is a pattern that will repeat itself over and over again, month after month, and that all their unbearable feelings and fears, of being unable to function as a human being any more, are normal. Tell them that although it may take one year or two, their grief will definitely reach an end and be transformed into acceptance.

As Judy Tatelbaum says:

> Grief is a wound that needs attention in order to heal. To work through and complete grief means to face our feelings openly and honestly, to express and release our feelings fully and to tolerate and accept our feelings for however long it takes for the wound to heal. We fear that once acknowledged grief will bowl us over. The truth is that grief experienced does dissolve. Grief unexpressed is grief that lasts indefinitely.[7]

But so often, tragically, friends and family of the bereaved person expect them to be "back to normal" after a few months. This only intensifies their bewilderment and isolation as their grief continues, and sometimes even deepens.

In Tibet, as I've said, the whole community, friends and relatives, would take part during the forty-nine days after the death, and everyone was fully occupied in the activity of the spiritual help being given to the dead person, with all the hundred things there were to do. The bereaved would grieve, and they would cry a little, as is only natural, and then when everyone had left, the house would look empty. Yet in so many subtle, heartwarming ways, the bustle and support of those forty-nine days had helped them through a great part of their mourning.

Facing loss alone in our society is very different. And all the usual feelings of grief are magnified intensely in the case of a sudden death, or a suicide. It reinforces the sense that the bereaved is powerless in any way to help their loved one who is gone. It is very important for survivors of sudden death to go and see the body, otherwise it can be difficult to realize that death has actually happened. If possible, people should sit quietly by the body, to say what they need to, express their love, and start to say goodbye.

If this is not possible, bring out a photo of the person who has just died and begin the process of saying goodbye, completing the relationship, and letting go. Encourage those who have suffered the sudden death of a loved one to do this, and it will help them to accept the new, searing reality of death.

Tell them too of these ways I've been describing of helping a dead person, simple ways they too can use, instead of sitting hopelessly going over again and again the moment of death in silent frustration and self-recrimination.

In the case of a sudden death, the survivors may often experience wild and unfamiliar feelings of *anger* at what they see as the cause of the death. Help them express that anger, because if it is held inside, sooner or later it will plunge them into a chronic depression. Help them to let go of the anger and uncover the depths of pain that hide behind it. Then they can begin the painful but ultimately healing task of letting go.

It happens often too that someone is left after the death of a loved one feeling intense *guilt,* obsessively reviewing mistakes in the past relationship, or torturing themselves about what they might have done to prevent the death. Help them to talk about their feelings of guilt, however irrational and crazy they may seem. Slowly these feelings will diminish, and they will come to forgive themselves and go on with their lives.

A HEART PRACTICE

I would now like to give you a practice that can truly help you when you are suffering from deep sorrow and grief. It is a practice my master Jamyang Khyentse always used to give to people who were going through emotional torment or mental anguish and breakdown, and I know from my own experience it can bring enormous relief and solace. The life of someone teaching in a world like ours is not an easy one. When I was younger there were many moments of crisis and difficulty, and then I would always invoke Padmasambhava, as I still always do, thinking of him as the same as all my masters. And so I discovered for myself how transforming this practice is, and why all my masters used to say that the practice of Padmasambhava is the most useful when you go through turmoil, because it has the power you need to take on and survive the chaotic confusion of this age.

So whenever you are desperate, anguished, or depressed, whenever you feel you cannot go on, or you feel your heart is breaking, I advise you to do this practice. The only conditions to the effectiveness of this practice are that you need to do it with all your might, and that you need to ask, really to ask, for help.

Even if you practice meditation you will have emotional pain and suffering, and a lot of things from your past lives or this one may emerge that will be difficult to face. You may find you do not have the wisdom or the stability in your meditation to deal with them, and that your meditation on its own is not enough. What you need then is what I call "a heart practice." I always feel sad that people don't have a practice like this to help them in times of desperation, because if you do, you will find you have something immeasurably precious, which will also become a source of transformation and continuing strength.

1. Invocation

Invoke in the sky in front of you the presence of whichever enlightened being inspires you the most, and consider that this being is the embodiment of all the buddhas, bodhisattvas, and masters. For me, as I have said, this embodiment is Padmasambhava. Even if you cannot imagine in your mind's eye any one form, just feel the presence strongly and invoke his or her infinite power, compassion, and blessing.

2. Calling Out

Open your heart and invoke him or her with all the pain and suffering you feel. If you feel like crying, don't hold back: let your tears flow, and really ask for help. Know that there *is* someone who is absolutely there for you, someone who listens to you, who understands you with love and compassion, without ever judging you: an ultimate friend. Call to him or her from the depths of your pain, using the mantra OM AH HUM VAJRA GURU PADMA SIDDHI HUM, the mantra that has been used for centuries by hundreds of thousands of beings as a healing spring of purification and protection.

3. Filling the Heart with Bliss

Imagine and know now that the buddha you are crying out to responds, with all his or her love, compassion, wisdom, and power. Tremendous rays of light stream out toward you from him or her. Imagine that light as nectar, filling your heart up completely, and transforming all your suffering into bliss.

One way in which Padmasambhava appears is simply sitting in meditation posture, wrapped in his gown and robes, exuding an enchanting feeling of warm and cozy comfort, and with a loving smile on his face. In this emanation he is called "Great Bliss." His hands lie relaxed in his lap, cradling a cup made from the top of a skull. It is full of the nectar of Great Bliss, swirling and sparkling, the source of all healing. He sits serenely on a lotus blossom, ringed by a shimmering sphere of light.

Think of him as infinitely warm and loving, a sun of bliss, comfort, peace, and healing. Open your heart, let out all your suffering; cry out for help. And say his mantra: OM AH HUM VAJRA GURU PADMA SIDDHI HUM.

Imagine now thousands of rays of light streaming out of his body or from his heart: Imagine that the nectar of Great Bliss in the skull cup in his hands overflows with joy and pours down over you in a continuous stream of soothing, golden liquid light. It flows into your heart, filling it and transforming your suffering into bliss.

This nectar flow from the Padmasambhava of Great Bliss is the wonderful practice that my master used to teach: it has never failed to give me great inspiration and help in times of real need.

4. Helping the Dead

As you do this practice again and again, saying the mantra and filling your heart with bliss, slowly your suffering will dissolve in the confident peace of the nature of your mind. You will realize, with joy and delight, that the buddhas are not outside of you but always with you, inseparable from the nature of your mind. And what they have done through their blessing is to empower and nourish you with the confidence of the buddha within you.

Now, with all the power and confidence this practice has given you, imagine you are sending this blessing, the light of healing compassion of the enlightened beings, to your loved one who has died. This is especially vital in the case of someone who has suffered a traumatic death, as it transforms their suffering and brings them peace and bliss. In the past, you may have felt helpless in your grief and impotent to help your dear friend, but now through this practice you can feel consoled, encouraged, and empowered to help the dead person.

KEEPING THE HEART OPEN

Don't expect immediate results, or a miracle. It may only be after a while, or even much later, when you least expect it, that your suffering will shift. Do not have any expectation that it is going to "work," and end your grief once and for all. Be open to your grief, as open as you are to the enlightened beings and buddhas in the practice.

You may even come to feel mysteriously grateful toward your suffering, because it gives you such an opportunity of working through it and transforming it. Without it you would never have been able to discover that hidden in the nature and depths of suffering is a treasure of bliss. The times when you are suffering can be those when you are most open, and where you are extremely vulnerable can be where your greatest strength really lies.

Say to yourself then: "I am not going to run away from this suffering. I want to use it in the best and richest way I can, so that I can become more compassionate and more helpful to others." Suffering, after all, can teach us about compassion. If you suffer you will know how it is when others suffer. And if you are in a position to help others, it is through your suffering that you will find the understanding and compassion to do so.

So whatever you do, don't shut off your pain; accept your pain and remain vulnerable. However desperate you become, accept your pain as it is, because it is in fact trying to hand you a priceless gift: the chance of discovering, through spiritual practice, what lies behind sorrow. "Grief," Rumi wrote, "can be the garden of compassion." If you keep your heart open through everything, your pain can become your greatest ally in your life's search for love and wisdom.

And don't we know, only too well, that protection from pain doesn't work, and that when we try to defend ourselves from suffering, we only suffer more and don't learn what we can from the experience? As Rilke wrote, the protected heart that is "never exposed to loss, innocent and secure, cannot know tenderness; only the won-back heart can ever be satisfied: free, through all it has given up, to rejoice in its mastery."[8]

ENDING GRIEF AND LEARNING THROUGH GRIEF

When you are overwhelmed by your suffering, try to inspire yourself in one of those many ways I mentioned when I spoke of meditation practice in chapter 5, "Bringing the Mind Home." One of the most powerful methods I have found to soothe and dissolve sorrow is to go into nature, and especially to stand and contemplate by a waterfall, and let your tears and grief pour out of you and purify you, like the water

flowing down. Or you could read a moving text on impermanence or sorrow, and let its wisdom bring you solace.

To accept and end grief *is* possible. One way that many
people have used and found helpful is a variation on the
method I explained for completing unfinished business. No
matter how long ago your loved one died, you will find this
most effective.

Visualize that all the buddhas and enlightened beings are in
the sky above and around you, shining down their rays of
compassionate light and giving you their support and blessing. In their presence grieve and say what you have to say,
what is really in your heart and mind, to your loved one who
has died.

Visualize that the person who is dead is looking at you
with a greater love and understanding than he or she ever had
while alive. Know that the dead person wants you to understand that he or she loves you and forgives you for whatever
you may have done, and wants to ask for and receive *your*
forgiveness.

Allow your heart to open and put into words any anger,
any feelings of hurt, you may have been harbouring, and let
go of them completely. With your whole heart and mind,
let your forgiveness go out toward the dead person. Tell him
or her of your forgiveness; tell him or her of the regrets you
feel for all the pain you may have caused.

Now feel with your whole being his or her forgiveness and
love streaming toward you. Know in the depths of yourself
that you are lovable and deserve to be forgiven, and feel your
grief dissolve.

At the end of the practice, ask yourself if you can now
truly say farewell and really let go of the person. Imagine the
person turning and leaving, and then conclude by doing the
phowa, or another practice for helping the dead.

This practice will give you the chance of showing your
love once more, doing something to help the person who has
died, and completing and healing the relationship in your
heart.

You can learn so much, if you let yourself, from the grief
and loss of bereavement. Bereavement can force you to look
at your life directly, compelling you to find a purpose in it
where there may not have been one before. When suddenly
you find yourself alone after the death of someone you love,

it can feel as if you are being given a new life and are being asked "What will you do with this life? And why do you wish to continue living?"

Loss and bereavement can also remind you sharply what can happen when in life you do not show your love and appreciation, or ask for forgiveness, and so can make you far more sensitive to your loved ones who are alive. Elisabeth Kübler-Ross said, "What I try to teach people is to live in such a way that you say those things while the other person can still hear it."[9] And Raymond Moody, after his life's work in near-death research, wrote: "I have begun to realise how near to death we all are in our daily lives. More than ever now I am very careful to let each person I love know how I feel."[10]

So my heartfelt advice to those in the depths of grief and despair after losing someone they dearly loved is to pray for help and strength and grace. Pray you will survive and discover the richest possible meaning to the new life you now find yourself in. Be vulnerable and receptive, be courageous, and be patient. Above all, look into your life to find ways of sharing your love more deeply with others now.

TWENTY

The Near-Death Experience: A Staircase to Heaven?

WE HAVE BECOME very familiar now in the West with the near-death experience, the name given to the range of experiences reported by people who have survived an incident of near or clinical death. The near-death experience has been reported throughout history, in all mystical and shamanic traditions, and by writers and philosophers as varied as Plato, Pope Gregory the Great, some of the great Sufi masters, Tolstoy, and Jung. My favorite example from history is the story told by the great English historian, the monk Bede, in the eighth century.

About this time, a noteworthy miracle, like those of olden days, occurred in Britain. For, in order to arouse the living from spiritual death, a man already dead returned to bodily life and related many notable things that he had seen, some of which I have thought it valuable to mention here in brief. There was a head of a family living in a place in the country of the Northumbrians known as Cunningham, who led a devout life with all his household. He fell ill and grew steadily worse until the crisis came, and in the early hours of one night he died. But at daybreak he returned to life and suddenly sat up to the great consternation of those weeping around the body, who ran away; only his wife, who loved him more dearly, remained with him, though trembling and fearful. The man reassured her and said: "Do not be frightened; for I have truly risen from the grasp of death, and I am allowed to live among men again. But henceforth I must not live as I used to, and must adopt a very different way of life" . . . Not long afterward, he abandoned all worldly responsibilities and entered the monastery of Melrose . . .

Bede goes on:

This was the account he used to give of his experience: "A handsome man in a shining robe was my guide, and we walked in silence in what appeared to be a northeasterly direction. As we traveled onward, we came to a very broad and deep valley of infinite length . . . He soon brought me out of darkness into an atmosphere of clear light, and as he led me forward in bright light, I saw before us a tremendous wall which seemed to be of infinite length and height in all directions. As I could see no gate, window, or entrance in it, I began to wonder why we went up to the wall. But when we reached it, all at once—I know not by what means—we were on top of it. Within lay a very broad and pleasant meadow . . . Such was the light flooding all this place that it seemed greater than the brightness of daylight or of the sun's rays at noon . . .

"(The guide said) 'You must now return to your body and live among men once more; but, if you will weigh your actions with greater care and study to keep your words and ways virtuous and simple, then when you die, you too will win a home among these happy spirits that you see. For, when I left you for a while, I did so in order to discover what your future would be.' When he told me this I was most reluctant to return to my body; for I was entranced by the pleasantness and beauty of the place I could see and the company I saw there. But I did not dare to question my guide, and meanwhile, I know not how, I suddenly found myself alive among men once more."

Bede ends his account with these words:

This man of God would not discuss these and other things he had seen with any apathetic or careless-living people, but only with those who were . . . willing to take his words to heart and grow in holiness.[1]

The skill of modern medical technology has added a new and exciting dimension to the extent of the near-death experience; many people have now been revived from "death," for example, after accidents, heart attack, or serious illness, or in operations or combat. The near-death experience has been the subject of a great deal of scientific research and philosophical speculation. According to an authoritative 1982 Gallup poll, an extraordinary number of Americans—up to 8 million, or one in twenty in the population—have had at least one near-death experience.[2]

Although no two people have exactly the same experience, just as no two people could have identical experiences of the bardos, a common pattern of different phases in the near-death experience, a "core experience," appears:

1. They experience an altered state of feeling, of peace and well-being, without pain, bodily sensations, or fear.

2. They may be aware of a buzzing or rushing sound, and find themselves separated from their body. This is the so-called "out-of-the-body experience": They can view the body, often from a point somewhere above it; their sense of sight and hearing is heightened; their consciousness is clear and vividly alert, and they can even move through walls.

3. They are aware of another reality, of entering a darkness, floating in a dimensionless space, and then moving rapidly through a tunnel.

4. They see a light, at first a point in the distance, and are magnetically drawn toward it and then enveloped in light and love. This light is described as a blinding light of great beauty, but the eyes are unhurt by it. Some people report meeting "a being of light," a luminous, seemingly omniscient presence that a few call God or Christ, who is compassionate and loving. Sometimes in this presence they may witness a life-review, seeing everything they have done in their life, good and bad. They communicate telepathically with the presence, and find themselves in a timeless and usually blissful dimension in which all ordinary concepts like time and space are meaningless. Even if the experience lasts only one or two minutes in normal time, it can be of a vast elaboration and richness.

5. Some see an inner world of preternatural beauty, paradisal landscapes and buildings, with heavenly music, and they have a feeling of oneness. A very few, it seems, report terrifying visions of hellish realms.

6. They may reach a boundary beyond which they cannot go; some meet dead relatives and friends and talk to them. They decide (often reluctantly) or are told to return to the body and this life, sometimes with a sense of mission and service, sometimes to protect and care for their family, sometimes simply to fulfill the purpose of their life, which has not been accomplished.

The most important aspect of the near-death experience, as reported again and again in the literature about it, is the complete transformation it often makes in the lives, attitudes, careers, and relationships of the people who have this experience. They may not lose their fear of pain and dying, but they lose their fear of death itself; they become more tolerant and loving; and they become interested in spiritual values, the "path of wisdom," and usually in a universal spirituality rather than the dogma of any one religion.

How, then, should the near-death experience be interpreted? Some Western writers, who have read the *Tibetan Book of the Dead,* equate these experiences with the experiences of the bardos taught in the Tibetan tradition. At first glance there do seem to be tantalizing parallels between the two, but how exactly do the details of the near-death experience relate to the teachings on the bardos? I feel that this would require a special study beyond the scope of this book, but there are a number of similarities and differences that we can see.

THE DARKNESS AND THE TUNNEL

The final phase of the dissolution process of the bardo of dying, you will remember, is when the black experience of "full attainment" dawns "like an empty sky shrouded in utter darkness." At this point, the teachings speak of a moment of bliss and joy. One of the main features of the near-death experience is the impression of moving "at a terrific speed" and "feeling weightless" through a black space, "a total, peaceful, wonderful blackness," and down a "long, dark, tunnel."

One woman told Kenneth Ring: "It's just like a void, a nothing and it's such a peaceful—it's so pleasant that you can keep going. It's a complete blackness, there is no sensation at all, there was no feeling . . . sort of like a dark tunnel. Just a floating. It's like being in mid-air."[3]

And another woman told him:

The first thing I remember was a tremendous rushing sound, a tremendous . . . It's hard to find the right words to describe. The closest thing that I could possibly associate it with is, possibly, the sound of a tornado—a tremendous gushing wind, but almost pulling me. And I was being pulled into a narrow point from a wide area.[4]

A woman told Margot Grey:

I was in what felt like outer space. It was absolutely black out there and I felt like I was being drawn towards an opening like at the end of a tunnel. I knew this because I could see a light at the end; that's how I knew it was there. I was vertical and I was being drawn towards the opening. I know it wasn't a dream, dreams don't happen that way. I never once imagined it was a dream.[5]

THE LIGHT

At the moment of death, the Ground Luminosity or Clear Light dawns in all its splendor. The *Tibetan Book of the Dead* says: "O son/daughter of an enlightened family . . . your Rigpa is inseparable luminosity and emptiness and dwells as a great expanse of light; beyond birth or death, it is, in fact, the Buddha of Unchanging Light."

Melvin Morse, who has specialized in the research of near-death experiences in children, remarks: "Nearly every near-death experience of children (and about one fourth of those of adults) has in it an element of light. They all report that the light appears at the final stages of the near-death experience, after they have had an out-of-body experience or have travelled up the tunnel."[6]

One of the best descriptions of the approach to the light was reported by Margot Grey:

> Then gradually you realize that way, far off in the distance, an unmeasurable distance, you may be reaching the end of the tunnel, as you can see a white light, but it's so far away I can only compare it to looking up into the sky and in the distance seeing a single star, but visually you must remember that you are looking through a tunnel, and this light would fill the end of the tunnel. You concentrate on this speck of light because as you are propelled forward you anticipate reaching this light.
>
> Gradually, as you travel towards it at an extreme speed it gets larger and larger. The whole process on reflection only seems to take about one minute. As you gradually draw nearer to this extremely brilliant light there is no sensation of an abrupt end of the tunnel, but rather more of a merging into the light. By now, the tunnel is behind you and before you is this magnificent, beautiful blue-white light. The brilliance is so bright, brighter than a light that would immediately blind you, but absolutely does not hurt your eyes at all.[7]

Many near-death experiencers describe the light itself:

> My description of the light was—well, it was not a light, but the absence of darkness, total and complete . . . Well, you think of light as a big light shining on things making shadows and so forth. This light was really the absence of darkness. We're not used to that concept because we always get a shadow from the light unless the light is all around us. But this light was so total and complete that you didn't look at the light, you were in the light.[8]

One person told Kenneth Ring, "It was not bright. It was like a shaded lamp or something. But it wasn't that kind of light that you get from a lamp. You know what it was? Like someone had put a shade over the sun. It made me feel very, very peaceful. I was no longer afraid. Everything was going to be all right."[9]

A woman told Margot Grey: "The light is brighter than anything you could possibly imagine. There are no words to describe it. I was so happy, it's impossible to explain. It was such a feeling of serenity, it was a marvelous feeling. The light is so bright that it would normally blind you, but it doesn't hurt one's eyes a bit."

Others recount how they not only see the light, but enter directly into the light, and they speak of the feelings they have: "I had no sense of separate identity. I was the light and one with it."[10]

A woman who had undergone two major operations in two days told Margot Grey: "Only my essence was felt. Time no longer mattered and space was filled with bliss. I was bathed in radiant light and immersed in the aura of the rainbow. All was fusion. Sounds were of a new order, harmonious, nameless (now I call it music)."[11]

Another man who reached this point of entering the light describes it in this way:

> The following series of events appear to happen simultaneously, but in describing them I will have to take them one at a time. The sensation is of a being of some kind, more a kind of energy, not a character in the sense of another person, but an intelligence with whom it is possible to communicate. Also, in size it just covers the entire vista before you. It totally engulfs everything, you feel enveloped.
>
> The light immediately communicates to you, in an instant telekinesis your thought waves are read, regardless of language. A doubtful statement would be impossible to receive. The first message I received was "Relax, everything is beautiful, everything is OK, you have nothing to fear." I was immediately put at absolute ease. In the past if someone like a doctor had said "It's OK you have nothing to fear, this won't hurt," it usually did—you couldn't trust them.
>
> But this was the most beautiful feeling I have ever known, it's absolute pure love. Every feeling, every emotion is just perfect. You feel warm, but it has nothing to do with temperature. Everything there is absolutely vivid and clear. What the light communicates to you is a feeling of true, pure love. You experience this for the first time ever. You can't compare it to the love of your wife, or the love of your children or sexual love. Even if all those things were combined, you cannot compare it to the feeling you get from this light.[12]

A man who had almost drowned at the age of fourteen recalled:

As I reached the source of the Light, I could see in. I cannot begin to describe in human terms the feelings I had over what I saw. It was a giant infinite world of calm, and love, and energy, and beauty. It was as though human life was unimportant compared to this. And yet it urged the importance of life at the same time as it solicited death as a means to a different and better life. It was all being, all beauty, all meaning for all existence. It was all the energy of the universe forever in one place.[13]

Melvin Morse has written movingly of the near-death experiences of children, and tells how they describe the light in their simple eloquence: "I have a wonderful secret to tell you. I have been climbing a staircase to heaven." "I just wanted to get to that Light. Forget my body, forget everything. I just wanted to get to that Light." "There was a beautiful Light that had everything good in it. For about a week, I could see sparks of that Light in everything." "When I came out of the coma in the hospital, I opened my eyes and saw pieces of the Light everywhere. I could see how everything in the world fits together."[14]

SIMILARITIES WITH THE BARDO OF BECOMING

In the near-death experience, the mind is momentarily released from the body, and goes through a number of experiences akin to those of the mental body in the bardo of becoming.

1. Out-of-Body Experience

The near-death experience very often begins with an out-of-body experience: people can see their own body, as well as the environment around them. This coincides with what has already been said about the *Tibetan Book of the Dead*:

"I remember coming round from the anesthetic and then drifting off and finding myself out of my body, over the bed looking down at my carcass. I was aware only of being a brain and eyes, I do not remember having a body."[15]

A man who had suffered a heart attack told Kenneth Ring: "It seemed like I was up there in space and just my mind was active. No body feeling, just like my brain was up in space. I had nothing but my mind. Weightless, I had nothing."[16]

2. Helplessly Watching Relatives

I have described how, in the bardo of becoming, the dead are able to see and hear their living relatives, but are unable, sometimes frustratingly, to communicate with them. A woman from Florida told Michael Sabom how she looked down on her mother from a point near the ceiling: "The biggest thing I remember was that I felt so sad that I couldn't somehow let her know that I was all right. Somehow I knew that I was all right, but I didn't know how to tell her . . ."[17]

"I remember seeing them down the hall . . . my wife, my oldest son and my oldest daughter and the doctor . . . I didn't know why they were crying."[18]

And a woman told Michael Sabom: "I was sitting way up there looking at myself convulsing and my mother and my maid screaming and yelling because they thought I was dead. I felt so sorry for them, . . . Just deep, deep sadness. But I felt I was free up there and there was no reason for suffering."[19]

3. Perfect Form, Mobility, and Clairvoyance

The mental body in the bardo of becoming is described in the *Tibetan Book of the Dead* as being "like a body of the golden age," and as having almost supernatural mobility and clairvoyance. The near-death experiencers also find that the form they have is complete and in the prime of life.

"I was floating and I was a much younger man . . . The impression I got was that I was able to see myself some way through a reflection or something where I was twenty years younger than what I actually was."[20]

They find also that they can travel instantaneously, simply by the power of thought. A Vietnam veteran told Michael Sabom:

"I felt like I could have thought myself anywhere I wanted to be instantly . . . I just felt exhilarated with a sense of power. I could do what I wanted to . . . It's realer than here, really."[21]

"I remember all of a sudden going right back to the battlefield where I had been lost . . . It was almost like you materialize there and all of a sudden the next instant you were over here. It was just like you blinked your eyes."[22]

Many near-death experiencers also report a clairvoyant sense of total knowledge "from the beginning of time to the end of time."[23] A woman told Raymond Moody: "All of a sudden, all knowledge of all that had started from the very beginning, that would go on without end—for a second I knew all the secrets of the ages, all the meaning of the universe, the stars, the moon—of everything."[24]

"There was a moment in this thing—well, there isn't any way to describe it—but it was like I knew all things . . . For a moment, there, it was like communication wasn't necessary. I thought whatever I wanted to know could be known."[25]

"While I was there I felt at the center of things. I felt enlightened and cleansed. I felt I could see the point of everything. Everything fitted in, it all made sense, even the dark times. It almost seemed, too, as if the pieces of jigsaw all fitted together."[26]

4. Meeting Others

In the Tibetan teachings the mental body in the bardo of becoming is described as meeting other beings in the bardo. Similarly the near-death experiencer is often able to converse with others who have died. Michael Sabom's Vietnam veteran said that as he lay unconscious on the battlefield, viewing his own body:

The thirteen guys that had been killed the day before that I had put in plastic bags were right there with me. And more than that, during the course of that month of May, my particular company lost forty-two dead. All forty-two of those guys were there. They were not in the form we perceive the human body . . . But I know they were there. I felt their presence. We communicated without talking with our voices.[27]

A woman whose heart stopped under anesthetic during a dental extraction said:

Then I found myself, I was in a beautiful landscape, the grass is greener than anything seen on earth, it has a special light or glow. The colors are beyond description, the colors here are so drab by comparison . . . In this place I saw people that I knew had died. There were no words spoken, but it was as if I knew what they were thinking, and at the same time I knew that they knew what I was thinking.[28]

5. Different Realms

In the bardo of becoming, as well as many other kinds of visions, the mental body will see visions and signs of different realms. A small percentage of those who have survived a near-death experience report visions of inner worlds, of paradises, cities of light, with transcendental music.

One woman told Raymond Moody:

Off in the distance . . . I could see a city. There were buildings—separate buildings. They were gleaming, bright. People were happy in there. There was sparkling water, fountains . . . a city of light I guess would be the way to say it . . . It was wonderful. There was beautiful music. Everything was just glowing, wonderful . . . But if I had entered into this, I think I would never have returned . . . I was told that if I went there I couldn't go back . . . that the decision was mine.[29]

Another person told Margot Grey:

I seemed to find myself in what appeared to be some type of structure or building, but there were no walls that I can remember. There was only this all-pervading beautiful golden light . . . I noticed about me many people that seemed to be walking or milling about; they didn't even appear to walk, but seemed somehow to glide. I didn't feel apart from them at all; one of the feelings I remember most about them was the feeling of unity, of being totally a part of everything around me and about me.[30]

6. Hellish Visions

Not all descriptions in the near-death experience, however, are positive, as you would expect from what we have spoken of in the Tibetan teachings. Some people report terrifying experiences of fear, panic, loneliness, desolation, and gloom, vividly reminiscent of the descriptions of the bardo of becoming. One person reported by Margot Grey spoke of being sucked into "a vast black vortex like a whirlpool," and those who have negative experiences tend to feel, rather like those about to be reborn in lower realms in the bardo of becoming, that they are traveling downward instead of upward:

I was moving along as part of a river of sound—a constant babble of human noise . . . I felt myself sinking into and becoming part of the stream and slowly being submerged by it. A great fear possessed me as if I knew that once overcome by this ever growing mass of noise that I would be lost.[31]

I was looking down into a large pit, which was full of swirling gray mist and there were all these hands and arms reaching up and trying to grab hold of me and drag me in there. There was a terrible wailing noise, full of desperation.[32]

Other people have even experienced what can only be called hellish visions, of intense cold or unbearable heat, and heard the sounds of tormented wailing or a noise like that of wild beasts. A woman reported by Margot Grey said:

I found myself in a place surrounded by mist. I felt I was in hell. There was a big pit with vapor coming out and there were arms and hands coming out trying to grab mine . . . I was terrified that these hands were going to claw hold of me and pull me into the pit with them . . . an enormous lion bounded towards me from the other side and I let out a scream. I was not afraid of the lion, but I felt somehow he would unsettle me and push me into that dreadful pit . . . It was very hot down there and the vapor or steam was very hot.[33]

A man who suffered a cardiac arrest reported: "I was going down, down deep into the earth. There was anger and I felt this horrible fear. Everything was gray. The noise was fearsome, with snarling and crashing like maddened wild animals, gnashing their teeth."[34]

Raymond Moody writes that several people claimed to have seen beings who seemed trapped by their inability to surrender their attachments to the physical world: possessions, people, or habits. One woman spoke of these "bewildered people":

What you would think of as their head was bent downward; they had sad depressed looks; they seemed to shuffle, as someone would on a chain gang . . . they looked washed out, dull, gray. And they seemed to be forever shuffling and moving around, not knowing where they were going, not knowing who to follow, or what to look for.

As I went by they didn't even raise their heads to see what was happening. They seemed to be thinking, "Well, it's all over with. What am I doing? What's it all about?" Just this absolute, crushed, hopeless demeanor—not knowing what to do or where to go or who they were or anything else.

They seemed to be forever moving, rather than just sitting, but in no special direction. They would start straight, then veer to the left and take a few steps and veer back to the right. And absolutely nothing to do. Searching, but for what they were searching I don't know.[35]

In the accounts we have of the near-death experience, a border or limit is occasionally perceived; a point of no return is reached. At this border the person then chooses (or is instructed) to return to life, sometimes by the presence of light. Of course in the Tibetan bardo teachings there is no parallel to this, because they describe what happens to a person who actually dies. However, in Tibet there was a group of people, called *déloks*, who had something like a near-death experience, and what they report is fascinatingly similar.

THE DÉLOK: A TIBETAN NEAR-DEATH EXPERIENCE

A curious phenomenon, little known in the West, but familiar to Tibetans, is the délok. In Tibetan *dé lok* means "returned from death," and traditionally déloks are people who seemingly "die" as a result of an illness, and find themselves traveling in the bardo. They visit the hell realms, where they witness the judgment of the dead and the sufferings of hell, and sometimes they go to paradises and buddha realms. They can be accompanied by a deity, who protects them and explains what is happening. After a week the délok is sent back to the body with a message from the Lord of Death for the living, urging them to spiritual practice and a beneficial way of life. Often the déloks have great difficulty making people believe their story, and they spend the rest of their lives recounting their experiences to others in order to draw them toward the path of wisdom. The biographies of some of the more famous déloks were written down, and are sung all over Tibet by traveling minstrels.

A number of aspects of the délok correspond not only with, as you would expect, the bardo teachings such as the *Tibetan Book of the Dead,* but also with the near-death experience.

Lingza Chökyi was a famous délok who came from my part of Tibet and lived in the sixteenth century. In her biography she tells how she failed to realize she was dead, how she found herself out of her body, and saw a pig's corpse lying on her bed, wearing her clothes. Frantically she tried in vain to communicate with her family, as they set about the business of the practices for her death. She grew furious with them when they took no notice of her and did not give her her plate of food. When her children wept, she felt a "hail of pus and blood" fall, which caused her intense pain. She tells us she felt joy each time the practices were done, and immeasurable happiness when finally she came before the master who was practicing for her and who was resting in the nature of mind, and her mind and his became one.

After a while she heard someone whom she thought was her father calling to her, and she followed him. She arrived in the bardo realm, which appeared to her like a country. From there, she tells us, there was a bridge that led to the hell realms, and to where the Lord of Death was counting the good or evil actions of the dead. In this realm she met various people who recounted their stories, and she saw a great yogin who had come into the hell realms in order to liberate beings.

Finally Lingza Chökyi was sent back to the world, as there had been an error concerning her name and family, and it was not yet her time to die. With the message from the Lord of Death to the living, she returned to her body and recovered, and spent the rest of her life telling of what she had learned.

The phenomenon of the délok was not simply a historical one; it continued up until very recently in Tibet. Sometimes a délok would leave the body for about a week, and meet people who had died, sometimes quite unknown to the délok, who would give messages for their living relatives and ask these relatives to do certain kinds of practices on their behalf. The délok would then return to his or her body and deliver their messages. In Tibet this was an accepted occurrence, and elaborate methods were devised for detecting whether déloks were fraudulent or not. Dilgo Khyentse Rinpoche's daughter told Françoise Pommaret, author of a book on the déloks, that in Tibet, while the délok was undergoing his or her experience, the orifices of the body were stopped with butter, and a paste made from barley flour put over the face.[36] If the butter did not run, and the mask did not crack, the délok was recognized as authentic.

The tradition of déloks continues in the Tibetan Himalayan regions today. These déloks are quite ordinary people, often women, who are very devoted and have great faith. They "die" on special days in the Buddhist calendar, for a number of hours, and their major function is to act as messengers between the living and the dead.

THE MESSAGE OF THE NEAR-DEATH EXPERIENCE

As we have seen, there are significant similarities between the near-death experience and the bardo teachings; there are also significant differences. The greatest difference, of course, is the fact that the near-death experiencers do *not* die, whereas the teachings describe what happens to people as they die, after actual physical death, and as they take rebirth. The fact that the near-death experiencers do not go further on the journey into death—some of them are only "dead" for one minute—must go some way to explaining at least the possibility for disparities between the two accounts.

Some writers have suggested the near-death experience expresses the stages of the dissolution process in the bardo of dying. It is premature, I feel, to try to link the near-death experience too precisely with the bardo descriptions, because the person who has survived the near-death experience has only been—literally—"near death." I explained to my master Dilgo Khyentse Rinpoche the nature of the near-death experience, and he called it a phenomenon that belongs to the natural bardo of *this* life, because the consciousness merely leaves the body of the person who has "died," and wanders temporarily in various realms.

Dilgo Khyentse Rinpoche implied that the near-death experiencers are experiencing their clinical death within the natural bardo of this life. Perhaps they are standing on the threshold of the bardos, but they have not actually entered into them and returned. Whatever they experience, they are still in the natural bardo of this life. Is their experience of the light similar to the dawning of the Ground Luminosity? Could it be that just before its vast sun rises, they catch a strong glimpse of the first rays of dawn?

Whatever the ultimate meaning of the details of the near-death experience, I remain extremely moved by the many accounts I have heard or read, and struck especially by some of the attitudes that flow from these experiences, attitudes that mirror so richly the Buddhist view of life. Two I have already spoken of: the profound transformation and spiritual awakening that takes place in those who have been through this experience; and the implications for our lives of the life-review. The life-review happens again and again in the near-death experience, and demonstrates so clearly the inescapability of karma and the far-reaching and powerful effects of all our actions, words, and thoughts. The central message that the near-death experiencers bring back from their encounter with death, or the presence or "being of light," is exactly the same as that of Buddha and of the bardo teachings: that the essential and most important qualities in life are love and knowledge, compassion and wisdom.

They are surely beginning to see what the bardo teachings tell us: that life and death are in the mind itself. And the confidence that many of them seem to have after this experience reflects this deeper understanding of mind.

There are also certain, fascinating similarities between the near-death experience and its results, and mystical states and altered states of consciousness. For example, a number of paranormal phenomena have been reported by the near-death experiencers. Some have precognitive or prophetic planetary visions, or "life previews" that turn out to be uncannily accurate; after the near-death experience, some report experiences of what appears to be the energy of *kundalini*[37]; others find they have real and amazing powers of clairvoyance, or psychic or physical healing.

Many of those who have come near death speak in a personal, undeniably eloquent way of the beauty, love, peace and bliss and wisdom of what they have experienced. To me this sounds like they have had certain glimpses of the radiance of the nature of mind, and it is hardly surprising that such glimpses should have resulted in true spiritual transformation, again and again. Yet as Margot Grey points out, "We do not need nearly to die in order to experience a higher spiritual reality."[38] That higher spiritual reality is here and now, in life, if only we can discover and enter it.

I would like to make one essential caution: Don't let these accounts of the near-death experience, which are so inspiring, lull you into believing that all you have to do in order to dwell in such states of peace and bliss is to die. It is not, and could not be, that simple.

Sometimes when people are going through suffering and pain, they feel they cannot bear it anymore; and hearing the near-death stories might, it is conceivable, tempt them to put an end to it all by taking their lives. This might seem like a simple solution, but it overlooks the fact that whatever we go through is part of life. It's impossible to run away. If you run away, you will only come to face your suffering in an even deeper way later on.

Besides, while it is true that the majority of near-death experiences that have been collected have been good ones, there is still some speculation as to whether this reflects the actual rarity of negative, terrifying experiences, or merely the difficulty in recollecting them. People may not want or consciously be able to remember the darker or more frightening experiences. Also the near-death experiencers themselves stress that what they have learned is the importance of transforming our lives *now*, while we are still alive, for we have, they say "a more important mission while we're here."[39]

This transformation of our lives now is the urgent and essential point. Wouldn't it be tragic if this central message of the near-death experience—that life is inherently sacred and must be lived with sacred intensity and purpose—was obscured and lost in a facile romanticizing of death? Wouldn't it be even more tragic if such a facile optimism further deepened that disregard for our actual responsibilities to ourselves and our world that is menacing the survival of the planet?

THE MEANING OF
THE NEAR-DEATH EXPERIENCE

Inevitably some have tried to show that the events of the near-death experience constitute something other than a spiritual experience, and reductionist scientists have tried to explain it away in terms of physiological, neurological, chemical, or psychological effects. The near-death experience researchers, however, doctors and scientists themselves, have countered these objections lucidly one by one, and insist that they cannot explain the whole of the near-death experience. As Melvin Morse writes at the end of his magnificent book, *Closer to the Light: Learning from Children's Near-Death Experiences:*

> But near-death experiences appear to be a cluster of events so that one cannot understand the total by looking at its various pieces. One cannot understand music by studying the various frequencies of sound that generate each note, nor does one need to have a deep understanding of acoustical physics to enjoy Mozart. The near-death experience remains a mystery.[40]

Melvin Morse also says:

> I feel that just understanding near-death experiences will be our first step at healing the great division between science and religion that started with Isaac Newton almost three hundred years ago. Educating physicians, nurses, and ourselves about what people experience in those final hours will shatter our prejudices about the ways we think about medicine and life.[41]

In other words the very advance in medical technology is simultaneously providing the means to revolutionize itself. Melvin Morse says:

> I find it ironic that it is our medical technology that has led to this plethora of near-death experiences. . . . There have been near-death experiences throughout the centuries, but it has only been in the last twenty years that we have had the technology to resuscitate patients. Now they are telling us about their experiences, so let's listen to them. This to me is a challenge for our society. . . . Near-death experiences, to my mind, are a natural, psychological process associated with dying. I'm going to boldly predict if we can reintegrate this knowledge into our society, not only will it help with dying patients, but it will

help society as a whole. I see medicine today as being devoid of spirit. . . . There is no reason why technology and the spirit cannot exist side by side.[42]

One of the reasons I have written this book is to show I believe what Melvin Morse says is possible: Technology and the spirit can and must exist side by side, if our fullest human potential is to be developed. Wouldn't a complete, and completely useful, human science have the courage to embrace and explore the facts of the mystical, the facts of death and dying as revealed in the near-death experience and in this book?

Bruce Greyson, one of the leading figures in near-death research, says:

Science must try to explain the near-death experience because therein lies the key to its own growth. . . . History tells us that only in trying to explain phenomena which are currently beyond our reach will science develop new methods. I believe the near-death experience is one of the puzzles that just might force scientists to develop a new scientific method, one that will incorporate all sources of knowledge, not only logical deduction of the intellect, and empirical observation of the physical, but direct experience of the mystical as well.[43]

Bruce Greyson has also said he believes near-death experiences occur for a reason: "Based on my watching near-death experiences for a number of years, I think that we have these experiences in order to learn how to help others."

Kenneth Ring sees yet another extraordinary possibility and meaning to the near-death experiences. He asks why so many people are now having such experiences and going through spiritual transformation at *this* time. For many years one of the bravest pioneers in the field of near-death research, he has come to see the near-death experiencers as being "messengers of hope," speaking of a higher and more noble spiritual reality, and calling us to change urgently every facet of how we live now; to end all war, all divisions between religions and peoples, and to protect and save the environment:

I believe . . . that humanity as a whole is collectively struggling to awaken to a newer and higher mode of consciousness, . . . and that the near-death Experience can be viewed as an evolutionary device to bring about this transformation, over a period of years, in millions of persons.[44]

It may be that whether this is true or not depends on all of us: on whether we really have the courage to face the implications of the near-death experience and the bardo teachings, and by transforming ourselves transform the world around us, and so by stages the whole future of humanity.

PART FOUR

Conclusion

TWENTY-ONE

The Universal Process

FORTY YEARS AFTER the Chinese occupation of Tibet, the world is still ignorant of what has happened, ignorant of the extent of the terror, destruction, and systematic genocide that the Tibetan people have endured and are still enduring. Over 1 million people out of a population of 6 million have died at the hands of the Chinese; Tibet's vast forests, as indispensable as those of the Amazon to the ecology of the world, have been cut down; its wildlife has been almost totally massacred; its plateaus and rivers have been polluted with nuclear waste; the vast majority of its six-and-a-half thousand monasteries lie gutted or destroyed; the Tibetan people face extinction, and the glory of their own culture in their homeland has been almost entirely obliterated.

From the very beginning of the Chinese occupation of Tibet in the 1950s, many terrible atrocities were committed. Spiritual masters, monks, and nuns were the first targets, because the Chinese Communists wanted above all to break the spirit of the people by wiping out all traces of religious life. Many, many stories have reached me over the years of extraordinary and moving deaths, in the worst possible circumstances, that witnessed and paid final tribute to the splendor of the truth the Chinese were desperate to destroy.

In the part of Tibet I come from, the province of Kham, there was an old *khenpo,* or abbot, who had spent many years in retreat in the mountains. The Chinese announced that they were going to "punish" him, which everyone knew meant torture and death, and sent a detachment of soldiers to his hermitage to arrest him. The khenpo was elderly and unable to walk, and the Chinese found him an old and mangy horse for his last journey. They sat him on the horse, tied him to it, and led the horse down the path from his hermitage to the army camp. The khenpo began to sing. The Chinese could not understand the words, but the monks who were taken with him said later that he was singing "songs of experience," beautiful songs that sprang spontaneously from the depth and the joy of his realization. Slowly the party wound its way down the mountain, the soldiers in a stony silence and many of the monks sobbing; the khenpo, however, sang all the way.

Not long before the party arrived at the army camp, he stopped singing and closed his eyes, and the group then moved on in silence. As they crossed through the gate into the camp, they found the khenpo had passed away. He had quietly left his body.

What did he know that made him so serene, even in the face of death? What gave him even in those final moments the joy and fearlessness to sing? Perhaps he was singing something like these verses from "The Immaculate Radiance," the last testament of the fourteenth-century Dzogchen master Longchenpa:

In a cloudless night sky, the full moon,
"The Lord of Stars," is about to rise . . .
The face of my compassionate lord, Padmasambhava,
Draws me on, radiating its tender welcome.

My delight in death is far, far greater than
The delight of traders at making vast fortunes at sea,
Or the lords of the gods who vaunt their victory in battle;
Or of those sages who have entered the rapture of perfect absorption.
So just as a traveler who sets out on the road when the time has come
*   to go,*
I will not remain in this world any longer,
But will go to dwell in the stronghold of the great bliss of deathlessness.

This, my life, is finished, my karma is exhausted, what benefit
*   prayers could bring has worn out,*
All worldly things are done with, this life's show is over.
In one instant, I will recognize the very essence of the manifestation of
*   my being*
In the pure, vast realms of the bardo states;
I am close now to taking up my seat in the ground of primordial
*   perfection.*

The riches found in myself have made the minds of others happy,
I have used the blessing of this life to realize all the benefits of the
island of liberation;
Having been with you, my noble disciples, through all this time,
The joy of sharing the truth has filled me and satisfied me.

Now all the connections in this life between us are ending,
I am an aimless beggar who is going to die as he likes,
Do not feel sad for me, but go on praying always.
These words are my heart talking, talking to help you;
Think of them as a cloud of lotus-blossoms, and you in your devotion
as bees plunging into them to suck from them their transcendent joy.

Through the great good of these words
May the beings of all the realms of samsara,
In the ground of primordial perfection, attain Nirvana.

These are unmistakably the words of someone who has achieved the highest realization with all that it can bring: that joy and fearlessness and freedom and understanding that are the goal of the teachings and of human life. I think of masters like Longchenpa, and my own masters Jamyang Khyentse, Dudjom Rinpoche, Dilgo Khyentse Rinpoche, and I imagine beings who have their depth of realization as magnificent mountain eagles, who soar above both life and death and see them for what they are, in all their mysterious, intricate interrelation.

To see through the eyes of the mountain eagle, the view of realization, is to look down on a landscape in which the boundaries that we imagined existed between life and death shade into each other and dissolve. The physicist David Bohm has described reality as being "unbroken wholeness in flowing movement." What is seen by the masters, then, seen directly and with total understanding, is that flowing movement and that unbroken wholeness. What we, in our ignorance, call "life," and what we, in our ignorance, call "death," are merely different aspects of that wholeness and that movement. This is the vast and transforming vision opened up to us by the bardo teachings, and embodied in the lives of the supreme masters.

THE REVELATION OF THE BARDOS

To see death, then, through realized eyes, is to see death in the context of this wholeness, and as part, and only part, of this beginningless and endless movement. The uniqueness and power of the bardo teachings is that they reveal to us, by showing with total clarity the actual process of death, the actual process of life as well.

Let us look now again at what happens to a person who dies, at each of the three crucial stages of death:

1. At the culmination of the process of dying, after the dissolution of elements, senses, and thought-states, the ultimate nature of mind, the Ground Luminosity, is for a moment laid bare.

2. Then, fleetingly, the radiance of that nature of mind is displayed and shines out in appearances of sound, colors, and light.

3. Next the dead person's consciousness awakens and enters into the bardo of becoming; his or her ordinary mind returns, and takes on a manifestation—the form of the mental body—subject to the dictates of past karma and habits. These drive the ordinary mind to cling onto the illusory bardo experiences as something real and solid.

So what do the bardo teachings show us that death is? Nothing less than three phases of a process of gradual manifestation of mind: from out of its very purest state of the essential nature of mind, through light and energy (the radiance of the nature of mind), and into increasing crystallization into a mental form. What unravels with such clarity in the bardo of dying, the bardo of dharmata, and the bardo of becoming, the teachings show us, is a threefold process: first, enfoldment leading to laying bare; second, spontaneous radiance; and third, crystallization and manifestation.

The teachings draw us to go further. What they in fact show us—and I think this is a truly revolutionary insight, one which, when it is understood, changes our view of everything—is that this threefold pattern does not only unfold in the process of dying and death: It is unfolding now, *at this moment, at every moment,* within our mind, in our thoughts and emotions, and at every single level of our conscious experience.

Another way the teachings offer us of understanding this process is by looking at *what is revealed* at each phase of dying and death. The teachings speak of three levels of being, to which the Sanskrit name kaya is given. This word *kaya* literally means "body," but signifies here dimension, field, or basis.

So let us look now at the threefold process from this perspective:

1. The absolute nature, uncovered at the moment of death in the Ground Luminosity, is called the Dharmakaya, the dimension of "empty," unconditioned truth, into which illusion and ignorance, and any kind of concept, have never entered.

2. The intrinsic radiance of energy and light that is spontaneously displayed in the bardo of dharmata is called Sambhogakaya, the dimension of complete enjoyment, the field of total plenitude, of full richness, beyond all dualistic limitations, beyond space or time.

3. The sphere of crystallization into form revealed in the bardo of becoming is called Nirmanakaya, the dimension of ceaseless manifestation.

Remember now that when we looked at the nature of mind, we saw that it had these three same aspects: its empty, sky-like *essence,* its radiant luminous *nature,* and its unobstructed, all-pervasive, compassionate *energy,* which are all simultaneously present and interpenetrating as one within the Rigpa. Padmasambhava describes this in the following way:

> *Within this Rigpa, the three kayas are inseparable and fully present as one:*
> *Since it is empty and not created anywhere whatsoever, it is the Dharmakaya,*
> *Since its luminous clarity represents the inherent transparent radiance of emptiness, it is the Sambhogakaya.*
> *Since its arising is nowhere obstructed or interrupted, it is the Nirmanakaya.*
> *These three being complete and fully present as one, are its very essence.*[1]

The three kayas, then, refer to these three intrinsic aspects of our enlightened mind; they also, of course, refer to different capacities of our perception. The vast majority of us are limited in our vision, and only perceive the Nirmanakaya dimension of form and manifestation. This is the reason that for most of us the moment of death is a blank and a state of oblivion, for we have neither encountered nor evolved any way of recognizing the Dharmakaya reality when it arises as the Ground Luminosity. Nor do we have any hope of recognizing the Sambhogakaya fields as they appear in the bardo of dharmata. Because our entire life has been lived out within the realm of the impure perceptions of the Nirmanakaya manifestation, so at the moment of death we are transported directly back into that dimension; we awaken, frantic and distracted, in the bardo of becoming in the mental body, taking illusory experiences for solid and real just as we have in lives before, and stumbling helplessly, propelled by past karma, toward rebirth.

Highly realized beings, however, have awakened in themselves a perception completely different from our own, one that is purified, evolved, and refined to such an extent that, while they still dwell in a human body, they actually perceive reality in a totally purified form, transparent to them in all its limitless dimension. And for them, as we have seen, the experience of death holds no fear or surprises; it is embraced, in fact, as an opportunity for final liberation.

THE PROCESS IN SLEEP

The three phases of the process we see unfolding in the bardo states in death can be perceived in other levels of consciousness in life also. Consider them in the light of what occurs in sleep and dream:

1. When we fall asleep, the senses and grosser layers of consciousness dissolve, and gradually the absolute nature of mind, we could say the Ground Luminosity, is briefly laid bare.

2. Next there is a dimension of consciousness, comparable to the bardo of dharmata, which is so subtle that we are normally completely unaware of its very existence. How many of us, after all, are aware of the moment of sleep before dreams begin?

3. For most of us, all that we are aware of is the next stage, when the mind becomes yet again active, and we find ourselves in a dream-world similar to the bardo of becoming. Here we take on a dream-body and go through different dream-experiences to a great extent influenced and shaped by the habits and activities of our waking state, all of which we believe to be solid and real, without ever realizing that we are dreaming.

THE PROCESS IN THOUGHTS AND EMOTIONS

Exactly the same process can be recognized in the workings of thoughts and emotions, and the manner in which
they arise:

1. The Ground Luminosity, the absolute nature of mind,
is the primordial state of Rigpa that exists before any thought
or emotion.
2. Within its unconditioned space, a fundamental energy
stirs, the spontaneous radiance of Rigpa, which begins to arise
as the basis, the potential, and the fuel for raw emotion.
3. This energy can then take on the forms of emotions
and thoughts, which eventually propel us into action and
cause us to accumulate karma.

It is when we become intimately familiar with meditation
practice that we can see this process with unmistakable
clarity:

1. As thoughts and emotions gradually fall silent, and die
away and dissolve into the nature of mind, we may momentarily glimpse the nature of mind, the Rigpa itself: the primordial state.
2. Then we become aware that out of the stillness and
calm of the nature of mind unfolds a movement and raw
energy, its very self-radiance.
3. If any grasping enters into the rising of that energy, the
energy inevitably crystallizes into thought-forms, which in
turn will carry us back into conceptual and mental activity.

THE PROCESS IN EVERYDAY LIFE

Now that we have looked at the way this process repro-
duces itself in sleep and dream, and the very formation of
thought and emotion, let us see it at work in our day-to-day
experience of our everyday life.

This is best done by looking closely at one movement of
joy or anger. Examine that movement and you will see that
there exists always a space or gap before any emotion begins
to arise. That pregnant moment before the energy of emotion
has a chance to arise is a moment of pure, pristine awareness,
in which we could, if we let ourselves, have a glimpse of the
true nature of mind. For an instant the spell of ignorance is
broken; we are totally freed from any need or possibility of
grasping, and even the notion of "clinging" is made ridiculous

and redundant. However, instead of embracing the "emptiness" of that gap, in which we could find the bliss of being
free from and unburdened by any idea, reference, or concept,
we grasp at the dubious security of the familiar, comforting
drama of our emotions, driven by our deep habitual tendencies. And this is how an inherently unconditioned energy arising from the nature of mind is crystallized into the form of an
emotion, and how its fundamental purity is then colored and
distorted by our samsaric vision to provide a continuous
source of everyday distractions and delusions.

If we really examine every aspect of our life, as I have
shown, we will discover how we go through, again and
again, in sleep and dream, in thoughts and emotions, that
same process of the bardos. And the teachings reveal to us
that it is precisely this fact—that we go through the process of
the bardos again and again, in both life and death, and at all
the different levels of consciousness—that gives us innumerable opportunities, now and also in death, for liberation. The
teachings show us that it is the character, form, and uniqueness of the process that offer us either the chance for liberation or the potential for continuing in confusion. For every
aspect of the whole process hands us at the same time the
chance for liberation, or the chance for confusion.

The bardo teachings are opening a door to us, showing us
how we can step out of the uncontrolled cycle of death and
rebirth, the repetitive treadmill of ignorance, life after life.
They are telling us that throughout this process of the bardos
of life and death, whenever we can recognize and maintain a
stable awareness of the nature of mind, Rigpa, or even when
we can gain some measure of control over our mind, we can
walk through that door toward liberation. Depending on the
phase of the bardos it is applied in, depending on your
familiarity with the View of the nature of mind itself, and
depending on the depth of your understanding of your mind,
its thoughts and emotions, this recognition will be different.

What the bardo teachings are also telling us, however, is
that what happens in our mind now in life is *exactly* what
will occur in the bardo states at death, since essentially there
is no difference; life and death are one in "unbroken wholeness" and "flowing movement." This is why one of the
most accomplished Tibetan masters of the seventeenth
century, Tsele Natsok Rangdrol, explains the heart practices

THE UNIVERSAL PROCESS   347

for each of the bardos—this life, dying, dharmata, and becoming—in terms of the state of our present understanding of the nature of thoughts and emotions, and of mind and its perceptions:

> Recognize this infinite variety of appearances as a dream,
> As nothing but the projections of your mind, illusory and unreal.
> Without grasping at anything, rest in the wisdom of your Rigpa, that
>   transcends all concepts:
> This is the heart of the practice for the bardo of this life.
>
> You are bound to die soon, and nothing then will be of any real help.
> What you experience in death is only your own conceptual thinking.
> Without fabricating any thoughts, let them all die into the vast
>   expanse of your Rigpa's self-awareness:
> This is the heart of the practice for the bardo of dying.
>
>
> Whatever grasps at appearance or disappearance, as being good or
>   bad, is your mind.
> And this mind itself is the self-radiance of the Dharmakaya, just
>   whatever arises.
> Not to cling to the risings, make concepts out of them, accept or reject
>   them:
> This is the heart of the practice for the bardo of dharmata.
>
>
> Samsara is your mind, and nirvana is also your mind,
> All pleasure and pain, and all delusions exist nowhere apart from
>   your mind.
> To attain control over your own mind;
> This is the heart of the practice for the bardo of becoming.

We are now ready to look at one particular bardo, to see how our meditation practice, our understanding of emotions and thoughts, and our experiences in that bardo are all inextricably interlinked, and how our experiences in that bardo reflect back into our ordinary life. Perhaps the most helpful bardo to study is the bardo of dharmata, which is where the pure energy that will become emotion begins to emerge spontaneously as the intrinsic radiance of the nature of mind; and emotions, I know, are a main, almost obsessive preoccupation of people in the modern world. Truly to understand the nature of emotion is to advance very far on the path to liberation.

The deepest aim of meditation is to be able to rest, undistracted, in the state of Rigpa, and with that View to realize that whatever arises in the mind is never anything but the display of your own Rigpa, just as the sun and its million rays are one and indivisible. As Tsele Natsok Rangdrol says in his verse for the bardo of dharmata: "Whatever grasps at appearance or disappearance, as being good or bad, is your mind. And this mind itself is the self-radiance of the Dharmakaya . . ."

So when you are in the state of Rigpa, and when thoughts and emotions arise, you recognize exactly what they are and where they are springing from: then whatever arises becomes the self-radiance of that wisdom. If you lose the presence of that pristine, pure awareness of Rigpa, however, and you fail to recognize whatever arises, then it will become separate from you. It goes on to form what we call "thought," or an emotion, and this is the creation of duality. To avoid this and its consequences is why Tsele Natsok Rangdrol says: "Not to cling to the risings, make concepts out of them, accept or reject them: this is the heart of the practice for the bardo of dharmata."

That separateness, between you and the risings in your mind, and the duality it engenders, become spectacularly magnified after death. This explains how, without that essence of recognition of the true nature of the arisings within the mind, in the bardo of dharmata the sounds, lights, and rays that manifest can take on the objective reality of shocking, external phenomena that are happening to *you*. So what could you possibly do in such a situation but flee from the brilliant radiance of the peaceful and wrathful deities, and run to the dim, seductive, habitual lights of the six realms? The crucial recognition, then, in the bardo of dharmata is that it is the wisdom energy of your mind that is dawning: The buddhas and the lights of wisdom are in no sense separate from you, but your own wisdom energy. To realize that is an experience of non-duality, and to enter into it is liberation.

What is occurring in the bardo of dharmata at death, and whenever an emotion begins to arise in our minds in life, is the same natural process. What is at question is whether or not we recognize the true nature of the arising. If we can recognize the arising of an emotion for what it really is, the spontaneous energy of the nature of our own mind, then we are empowered to free ourselves from the negative effects or possible dangers of that emotion, and let it dissolve back into the primordial purity of the vast expanse of Rigpa.

This recognition, and the freedom it brings, can only be the fruit of many, many years of the most disciplined practice of meditation, for it requires a long familiarity with and stabilization of Rigpa, the nature of mind. Nothing less will bring us that calm and blissful freedom from our own habitual tendencies and conflicting emotions that we all long for. The teachings may tell us that this freedom is hard to win, but the fact that this possibility really exists is a tremendous source of hope and inspiration. There *is* a way to understand thought and emotion, mind and its nature, life and death completely, and that is to achieve realization. For the enlightened ones, as I have said, see life and death as if in the palm of their hand, because they know, as Tsele Natsok Rangdrol wrote: "Samsara is your mind, and nirvana is also your mind; all pleasure and pain, and all delusions exist nowhere apart from your mind." And this clear knowledge, stabilized through long practice and integrated with every movement, every thought, every emotion of their relative reality, has made them free. Dudjom Rinpoche said: "Having purified the great delusion, the heart's darkness, the radiant light of the unobscured sun continuously rises."

THE ENERGY OF DELIGHT

I often think of what Dudjom Rinpoche wrote: "The nature of mind is the nature of everything." I wonder if this threefold process the bardos reveal is true not only, as we discovered, of all the different levels of consciousness and of all the different experiences of consciousness, both in life and death, but also perhaps of the actual nature of the universe itself.

The more I reflect about the three kayas and the threefold process of the bardos, the more fertile and intriguing parallels I find with the innermost vision of other spiritual traditions, and many seemingly very different fields of human endeavor. I think of the Christian vision of the nature and activity of God as represented by the Trinity, of Christ the incarnation being manifested in form out of the ground of the Father through the subtle medium of the Holy Spirit. Could it not be at least illuminating to envision Christ as similar to the Nirmanakaya, the Holy Spirit as akin to the Sambhogakaya, and the absolute ground of both as like the Dharmakaya? In Tibetan Buddhism the word *tulku*, incarnation, actually means Nirmanakaya, the constantly reappearing embodiment and activity of compassionate, enlightened energy. Isn't this understanding very like the Christian notion of incarnation?

I think also of the Hindus' threefold vision of the essence of God, called in Sanskrit *satcitananda* (sat-cit-ananda), which roughly translated means "manifestation, consciousness, and bliss." For Hindus God is the simultaneous, ecstatic explosion of all these forces and powers at once. Again, fascinating parallels with the vision of the three kayas could be made: the Sambhogakaya could perhaps be compared to *ananda*—the bliss energy of the nature of God—Nirmanakaya to *sat,* and Dharmakaya to *cit.* Anyone who has seen the great sculpture of Shiva in the caves of Elephanta in India, with its three faces representing the three faces of the absolute, will have some idea of the grandeur and majesty of this vision of the divine.

Both of these mystical visions of the essence, nature, and action of the divine dimension show a distinct yet suggestively similar understanding to the Buddhist one of the different and interpenetrating levels of being. Isn't it at least thought-provoking that a threefold process is seen at the heart of each of these different mystical traditions, even though they do view reality from their own unique standpoint?

Thinking about what the nature of manifestation might be, and the different but linked approaches to understanding it, leads me naturally to think about the nature of human creativity, the manifestation in form of the inner world of humanity. I have often wondered over the years how the unfolding of the three kayas and bardos could throw light on the whole process of artistic expression, and hint at its true nature and hidden goal. Each individual act and manifestation of creativity, whether it is in music, art, or poetry, or indeed in the moments and unfoldings of scientific discovery, as many scientists have described, arises from a mysterious ground of inspiration and is mediated into form by a translating and communicating energy. Are we looking here at yet another enactment of the interrelated threefold process we have seen at work in the bardos? Is this why certain works of music and poetry, and certain discoveries in science, seem to have an almost infinite meaning and significance? And would this explain their power to guide us into a state of contemplation and joy, where some essential secret of our nature and the nature of reality is revealed? From where did Blake's lines come?

To see a World in a Grain of Sand
And a Heaven in a Wild Flower
Hold Infinity in the palm of your hand
And Eternity in an hour.[2]

In Tibetan Buddhism the Nirmanakaya is envisioned as the manifestation of enlightenment, in an infinite variety of forms and ways, in the physical world. It is traditionally defined in three ways. One is the manifestation of a completely realized Buddha, such as Gautama Siddhartha, who is born into the world and teaches in it; another is a seemingly ordinary being who is blessed with a special capacity to benefit others: a tulku; and the third is actually a being through whom some degree of enlightenment works to benefit and inspire others through various arts, crafts, and sciences. In their case this enlightened impulse is, as Kalu Rinpoche says, "a spontaneous expression, just as light radiates spontaneously from the sun without the sun issuing directives or giving any conscious thought to the matter. The sun is, and it radiates."[3] So couldn't one explanation of the power and nature of artistic genius be that it derives its ultimate inspiration from the dimension of Truth?

This does not mean that great artists can in any way be said to be enlightened; it is clear from their lives that they are not. Nevertheless it's also clear that they can be, in certain crucial periods and in certain exceptional conditions, instruments and channels of enlightened energy. Who, really listening to the greatest masterpieces of Beethoven or Mozart, could deny that another dimension at times seems to be manifesting through their work? And who, looking at the great cathedrals of medieval Europe like Chartres, or the mosques of Isfahan, or the sculptures of Angkor, or the beauty and richness of the Hindu temples of Ellora, could fail to see that the artists who created them were directly inspired by an energy that springs from the ground and source of all things?

I think of a great work of art as like a moon shining in the night sky; it illuminates the world, yet its light is not its own but borrowed from the hidden sun of the absolute. Art has helped many toward glimpsing the nature of spirituality. Is one of the reasons for the limitations of much of modern art, however, the loss of this knowledge of art's unseen sacred origin and its sacred purpose: to give people a vision of their true nature and their place in the universe, and to restore to them, endlessly afresh, the value and meaning of life, and its infinite possibilities? Is the real meaning of inspired artistic expression, then, that it is akin to the field of the Sambhogakaya, that dimension of ceaseless, luminous, blissful energy, which Rilke calls "the wingèd energy of delight," that radiance which transmits, translates, and communicates the purity and infinite meaning of the absolute to the finite and the relative, from the Dharmakaya, in other words, to the Nirmanakaya?

AN UNFOLDING VISION OF WHOLENESS

One of the many ways in which the example of His Holiness the Dalai Lama has inspired me has been in his unfailing curiosity about, and openness to, all the various facets and discoveries of modern science.[4] Buddhism, after all, is often called "a science of the mind," and as I contemplate the bardo teachings, it is their precision and vast, sober clarity that move me again and again to awe and gratitude. If Buddhism is a science of the mind, then for me Dzogchen and the bardo teachings represent the heart essence of that science, the innermost visionary and practical seed, out of which a vast tree of interconnected realizations have flowered and will go on to flower in ways that cannot now be imagined, as humanity continues to evolve.

Over the years and over many meetings with scientists of all kinds, I have become increasingly struck by the richness of the parallels between the teachings of Buddha and the discoveries of modern physics. Fortunately many of the major philosophical and scientific pioneers of the West have also become aware of these parallels and are exploring them with tact and verve and a sense that from the dialogue between mysticism, the science of mind and consciousness, and the various sciences of matter, a new vision of the universe and our responsibility to it could very well emerge. I have been more and more convinced that the bardo teachings themselves, with their threefold process of unfoldment, have a unique contribution to make to this dialogue.

From all the possible alternatives, I would like to focus here on one particular scientific vision, one which has especially absorbed me—that of the physicist David Bohm. Bohm has imagined a new approach to reality that, while being controversial, has inspired a great sympathetic response from researchers in all sorts of different disciplines: physics itself, medicine, biology, mathematics, neuroscience, psychiatry, and among artists and philosophers. David Bohm has conceived a new scientific approach to reality based, as the bardo teachings are, on an understanding of the totality and oneness of existence as an unbroken and seamless whole.

The multidimensional, dynamic order he sees at work in the universe has essentially three aspects. The most obvious one is our three-dimensional world of objects, space, and time, which he calls the *explicate* or *unfolded* order. What does he believe this order is unfolded from? A universal, unbroken field, "a ground beyond time," the *implicate* or *enfolded* order, as he terms it, which is the all-encompassing background to our entire experience. He sees the relationship between these two orders as a continuous process where what is unfolded in the explicate order is then re-enfolded into the implicate order. As the source that organizes this process into various structures, he "proposes" (a word he likes to use since his whole philosophy is that ideas should be created out of the free flow of dialogue, and be always vulnerable) the *super-implicate order*, a yet subtler and potentially infinite dimension.

Could not a vivid parallel be drawn between these three orders and the three kayas and the process of the bardos? As David Bohm says: "The whole notion of the implicate order is, to begin with, a way of discussing the origin of form from out of the formless, via the process of explication or unfolding."[5]

I am also inspired by David Bohm's imaginative extension of this way of understanding matter that arose out of quantum physics to consciousness itself, a leap which I think will come to be seen as more and more necessary as science opens and evolves. "The mind," he says, "may have a structure similar to the universe and in the underlying movement we call empty space there is actually a tremendous energy, a movement. The particular forms which appear in the mind may be analogous to the particles, and getting to the ground of the mind might be felt as light."[6]

Hand in hand with his notion of implicate and explicate order, David Bohm has imagined a way of looking at the relationship between the mental and the physical, between mind and matter, called *soma-significance*. As he writes: "The notion of soma-significance implies that soma (or the physical) and its significance (which is mental) are not in any sense separately existent, but rather that they are two aspects of one over-all reality."[7]

For David Bohm, the universe manifests three mutually enfolding aspects: matter, energy, and meaning.

From the point of view of the implicate order, energy and matter are imbued with a certain kind of significance which gives form to their over-all activity and to the matter which arises in that activity. The energy of mind and of the material substance of the brain are also imbued with a kind of significance which gives form to their over-all activity. So quite generally, energy enfolds matter and meaning, while matter enfolds energy and meaning . . . But also meaning enfolds both matter and energy . . . So each of these basic notions enfolds the other two. [8]

Simplifying an exceptionally subtle and refined vision, you could say that for David Bohm meaning has a special and wide-ranging importance. He says: "This implies, in contrast to the usual view, that meaning is an inherent and essential part of our overall reality, and is not merely a purely abstract and ethereal quality having its existence only in the mind. Or to put it differently, in human life, quite generally, meaning *is* being . . ." In the very act of interpreting the universe, we are creating the universe: "In a way, we could say that we are the totality of our meanings." [9]

Could it not be helpful to begin to imagine parallels between these three aspects of David Bohm's notion of the universe and the three kayas? A deeper exploration of David Bohm's ideas might perhaps show that meaning, energy, and matter stand in a similar relationship to each other as do the three kayas. Could this possibly suggest that the role of *meaning,* as he explains it, is somehow analogous to the Dharma-kaya, that endlessly fertile, unconditioned totality from which all things rise? The work of *energy,* through which meaning and matter act upon one another, has a certain affinity to the Sambhogakaya, the spontaneous, constant springing forth of energy out of the ground of emptiness, and the creation of *matter,* in David Bohm's vision, has resemblances to the Nir-manakaya, the continuous crystallization of that energy into form and manifestation.

Thinking about David Bohm and his remarkable explana-tion of reality, I am tempted to wonder what a great scientist who was also a really accomplished spiritual practitioner trained by a great master could discover. What would a scien-tist and sage, a Longchenpa and an Einstein in one, have to tell us about the nature of reality? Will one of the future flowerings of the great tree of the bardo teachings be a scientific mystical dialogue, one that we can still only barely imagine, but which we seem to be on the threshold of? And what would that mean for humanity?

The deepest parallel of all between David Bohm's ideas and the bardo teachings is that they both spring from a vision of wholeness. This vision, if it was able to invigorate individuals to transform their consciousness and so influence society, would restore to our world a desperately needed sense of living interconnection and meaning.

What I am proposing here is that man's general way of thinking of the totality, i.e. his general world view, is crucial for overall order of the human mind itself. If he thinks of the totality as constituted of independent fragments, then that is how his mind will tend to operate, but if he can include everything coherently and harmoniously in an overall whole that is undivided, unbroken, and without a border (for every border is a division or break) then his mind will tend to move in a similar way, and from this will flow an orderly action within the whole.[10]

All the great masters would be in perfect agreement with David Bohm when he writes:

A change of meaning is necessary to change this world politically, economically and socially. But that change must begin with the individual; it must change for him . . . if meaning is a key part of reality, then, once society, the individual and relationships are seen to mean something different a fundamental change has taken place.[11]

Ultimately the vision of the bardo teachings and the deepest understanding of both art and science all converge on one fact, our responsibility to and for ourselves; and the necessity of using that responsibility in the most urgent and far-reaching way: to transform ourselves, the meaning of our lives, and so the world around us.

As the Buddha said: "I have shown you the way to liberation, now you must take it for yourself."

TWENTY-TWO

Servants of Peace

ONE OF MY OLDEST STUDENTS, who has watched this book develop over the years, asked me not so long ago: "What in your heart of hearts do you really want to happen through this book when it is published?" The image immediately came into my mind of Lama Tseten, whom as a boy I had seen dying, and of his calm and gentle dignity in death. I found myself saying: "I want every human being not to be afraid of death, or of life; I want every human being to die at peace, and surrounded by the wisest, clearest, and most tender care, and to find the ultimate happiness that can only come from an understanding of the nature of mind and of reality."

Thomas Merton wrote: "What can we gain by sailing to the moon if we are not able to cross the abyss that separates us from ourselves? This is the most important of all voyages of discovery, and without it, all the rest are not only useless, but disastrous."[1] We spend millions of dollars every minute on training people to kill and destroy, and on bombs and planes and missiles. But we spend hardly anything, in comparison, on teaching human beings the nature of life and death, and helping them, when they come to die, to face and understand what is happening to them. What a terrifying, sad situation this is, and how revealing it is of our ignorance and our lack of true love for ourselves and for each other! More than anything, I pray that the book I have written could contribute in some small way to changing this situation in the world, could help awaken as many people as possible to the urgency of the need for spiritual transformation, and the urgency of the need to be responsible for ourselves and others. We are all potential buddhas, and we all desire to live in peace and die in peace. When will humanity really understand that, and truly create a society that reflects in all of its areas and activities that simple, sacred understanding? Without it, what is life worth? And without it, how can we die well?

It is crucial now that an enlightened vision of death and dying should be introduced throughout the world at all levels of education. Children should not be "protected" from death, but introduced, while young, to the true nature of death and what they can learn from it. Why not introduce this vision, in its simplest forms, to all age groups? Knowledge about death, about how to help the dying, and about the spiritual nature of death and dying should be made available to all levels of society; it should be taught, in depth and with real imagination, in schools and colleges and universities of all kinds; and especially and most important, it should be available in teaching hospitals to nurses and doctors who will look after the dying and who have so much responsibility toward them.

How can you be a truly effective doctor when you do not have at least some understanding of the truth about death, or how really to care spiritually for your dying patient? How can you be a truly effective nurse if you have not begun to face your own fear of dying and have nothing to say to those who are dying when they ask you for guidance and wisdom? I know many well-meaning doctors and nurses, people of the most sincere openness to new ideas and new approaches. I pray that this book will give them the courage and the strength they will need to help their institutions absorb the lessons of the teachings and adapt to them. Isn't it time now that the medical profession should understand that the search for the truth about life and death and the practice of healing are inseparable? What I hope from this book is that it will help inspire everywhere a debate about what exactly can be done for the dying, and the best conditions for doing it. A spiritual and practical revolution in the training of doctors and nurses, in the vision of hospital care, and in the actual treatment of the dying, is urgently needed, and I hope this book will make a humble contribution to it.

I have expressed again and again my admiration for the pioneering work that is being done in the hospice movement. In it at last we see the dying being treated with the dignity they deserve. I would like here to make a deep plea to all the governments of the world that they should encourage the creation of hospices and fund them as generously as possible.

It is my intention to make this book the foundation of several different kinds of training programs. These would be for people of all kinds of backgrounds and professions, and specifically for all those implicated in the care of the dying: families, doctors, nurses, clergy of all denominations, counselors, psychiatrists, and psychologists.

There is a whole, rich, as yet far too little-known, body of medical revelations in Tibetan Buddhism, as well as prophecies by Padmasambhava, concerning in detail the diseases of this age. I would like to make a strong plea here for funding to be poured into serious research of these astonishing teachings. Who can say what healing discoveries might not be made, and how the anguish of diseases such as cancer and AIDS, and even those which have not yet manifested, might not be alleviated?

So what is it I hope for from this book? To inspire a quiet revolution in the whole way we look at death and care for the dying, and so the whole way we look at life and care for the living.

While this book was being written, my great master Dilgo Khyentse Rinpoche left his body on Friday, September 27, 1991, in Thimphu, Bhutan. He was eighty-two years old, and had spent his entire life in the service of all beings. Who of any of those who saw him will ever forget him? He was a huge, glowing mountain of a man, and his majesty would have been overwhelming had there not always emanated from him the most profound calm and gentleness and rich, natural humor, and that peace and bliss that are the signs of ultimate realization. For me and for many others he was a master of the accomplishment and importance and grandeur of Milarepa, of Longchenpa, of Padmasambhava, even of the Buddha himself. When he died it was as if the sun had gone out of the sky, leaving the world dark, and a whole glorious age of Tibetan spirituality had come to its close. Whatever the future holds for us, I am certain none of us will ever see anyone like him again. Just to have seen him once, even for a moment, I believe, is to have had sown in you a seed of liberation that nothing will ever destroy, and which will one day flower completely.

There were many astonishing signs before and after Dilgo Khyentse Rinpoche's death that witnessed his greatness, but the one that shook and moved me most happened more than four thousand miles away, in southern France, in a place called Lerab Ling, near Montpellier, which is going to be dedicated to the creation of a retreat center under his blessing. Let one of my students who lives and works at the center tell you what happened:

> That morning the sky stayed dark longer than usual, and the first sign of dawn was a deep red line on the distant horizon. We were going to town; and as we approached the top of our road, the tent that houses the shrine, pitched on the site of our future temple, came into view on the crest of the hill on our right. Suddenly a beam of sharp sunlight pierced the half-light and fell directly onto the white shrine tent, making it glow intensely in the early morning. We carried on, and as we came to the turning in the road to take us into town, some sudden impulse made us glance back toward the tent. By now the sky was light. We were astounded. A brilliant rainbow stretched across the entire valley, its colors so bright and alive, it felt as though we could reach out and touch it. Rising up from the horizon on our left, it arched across the sky. What was mysterious was that there was not a hint of rain—just the rainbow itself, vivid and radiant against the vast, empty sky. It was not until the following evening that we heard that this was the very day that Dilgo Khyentse Rinpoche had passed away in Bhutan. We all felt certain that the rainbow was a sign of his blessing, descending on us all, and on Lerab Ling.

When Buddha lay dying in a forest grove in Kushinagara, surrounded by five hundred of his disciples, he said to them, with his last breath: "It is in the nature of all things that take form to dissolve again. Strive with your whole being to attain perfection." Those words have come to me often since the passing of Dilgo Khyentse Rinpoche. Is there any more poignant teaching on impermanence than the passing of a supreme master, one who had seemed the very axis of the world? It made all of us who knew him and were his disciples feel alone, thrown back upon ourselves. Now it is up to all of us to carry forward and try to embody as far as we can that tradition he so nobly represented. It is up to us to do what the Buddha's disciples did, when left alone in the world without his radiance: to "strive with our whole being to attain perfection."

That rainbow that arched over the morning sky of France and over the valley by Lerab Ling is a sign, I feel, that Dilgo Khyentse Rinpoche is blessing, and will continue to bless, the whole world. Freed of his body he lives now in the unconditioned, timeless splendor of the Dharmakaya, with the power all those who attain enlightenment have of being able to help across all limitations of time or space. Believe in the level of his attainment and call upon him with your whole heart, and you will find that he will be with you instantly. How could he, who loved all beings with such a perfect love, ever abandon us? And where would he go to, who had become one with everything?

How fortunate we were that a master such as he, who embodied all that the Tibetan tradition was, should be with us for thirty years after the fall of Tibet, and teach in the Himalayas, in India, in Europe, in Asia, in the United States. How fortunate we are to have hundreds of hours of tapes of his voice and his teachings, many videos that convey something of the majesty of his presence, translations into English and other languages of some of the rich outpourings of his wisdom mind. I think in particular of the teachings he gave in the south of France near Grenoble in the last year of his life, when, gazing out toward the valley and the mountains, in a setting of almost Tibetan grandeur, he granted the transmission of the most important Dzogchen teachings to 1,500 students, many of them, which gave me particular joy, students of mine from all over the world. A number of the masters present felt that through this act in the last year of his life, Dilgo Khyentse Rinpoche was placing his seal definitively on the coming of these teachings to the West, and blessing their reception with the accumulated power of lifetimes of meditation. For my part, I felt, with amazed gratitude, that he was giving his blessing also to all that I had been trying to do for the teachings in the West over the years.

To think of Dilgo Khyentse Rinpoche and of what he has done for humanity is to find gathered and displayed in one person the greatness of the gift Tibet is giving to the world.

It has always seemed to me far more than a coincidence that Tibet fell finally in 1959, just at the moment when the West was about to open its heart and mind to the traditions of Eastern wisdom. So just at the moment when the West was receptive, some of the deepest teachings of that tradition, which had been preserved in the pure solitude of the mountain land of Tibet, could be given to humanity. It is vital now, at all costs, to preserve this living tradition of wisdom, which the Tibetan people have suffered immeasurably to make available to us. Let us remember them always in our hearts, and let us all, also, work to see that their land and its traditions are returned to them. These great teachings I have shared with you cannot be practiced openly by the very people who guarded them so long. May the day come soon when the monasteries and nunneries of Tibet rise again from their rubble, and the vast spaces of Tibet again are dedicated to peace and the pursuit of enlightenment.

A large part of the future of humanity may depend on the reestablishment of a free Tibet, a Tibet that would act as a sanctuary for seekers of all kinds and of all faiths, and as the wisdom heart of an evolving world, the laboratory in which highest insights and sacred technologies could be tested, refined, and enacted again, as they were for so many centuries, to serve now as an inspiration and help to the whole human race in its hour of danger. It is hard to find the perfect environment to practice this wisdom in a world like ours; a Tibet restored, purified by tragedy and with a determination renewed by all that it has suffered, would be that environment, and so of crucial importance for the evolution of humanity.

I would like to dedicate this book to the hundreds of thousands who died in the terror in Tibet, witnessing at the end their faith and the wonderful vision of the Buddha's teachings, and to those who have died in this century in similarly appalling conditions: to the Jews, to the Cambodians, to the Russians, to the victims of two world wars, to all those who died abandoned and unremembered, and to all those who go on and on being deprived of the opportunity to practice their spiritual path.

Many masters believe that the Tibetan teachings are now entering into a new age; there are a number of prophecies by Padmasambhava and other visionary masters that foretell of their coming to the West. Now that this time has come, I know that the teachings will take on a new life. This new life will necessitate changes, but I believe that any adaptations must spring from a very deep understanding, in order to avoid betraying the purity of the tradition or its power, or the timelessness of its truth. If a depth of understanding of the tradition is fused with a real awareness of the problems and challenges of modern life, adaptations will arise that will only strengthen, enlarge, and enrich the tradition, revealing ever deeper layers of the teachings themselves, and making them even more effective in dealing with the difficulties of our time.

Many of the great Tibetan masters who have visited the West in the last thirty years have now passed away, and I am certain that they died praying that the teachings would benefit not only Tibetans, not only Buddhists, but the whole world. I think they knew exactly how valuable and how revelatory the teachings would be when the modern world grew ready to receive them. I think of Dudjom Rinpoche and Karmapa, who chose to die in the West itself, as if to bless it with the power of their enlightenment. May their prayers for the transformation of the world and for the illumination of the hearts and minds of humanity be fulfilled! And may we who received their teachings be responsible to them, and strive to embody them!

The greatest challenge that spiritual teachings such as Buddhism face in this transition from their ancient settings to the West is how, in a turbulent, fast-paced, and restless world, students of these teachings can find ways to practice them with the calm and steady consistency that they require for the realization of their truth to be possible. Spiritual training, after all, is the highest and in some ways the most demanding form of education, and it must be followed with the same dedicated and systematic application as any other kind of serious training. How can we accept that to train to be a doctor requires years of study and practice, but all we require for our spiritual path through life are chance blessings, initiations, and occasional encounters with different masters? In the past, people stayed in one place and followed a master all their lives. Think of Milarepa, serving Marpa for years before he was spiritually mature enough to leave him and practice on his own. Spiritual training requires a continuous transmission, working with the master and learning, following him or her with ardor and subtle skill. The main question for the future of the teaching in the modern world is how those who are following the teachings can be helped and inspired to find the right inner and outer environment in which fully to practice them, follow them through, and come to realize and embody their heart essence.

The teachings of all the mystical paths of the world make it clear that there is within us an enormous reservoir of power, the power of wisdom and compassion, the power of what Christ called the Kingdom of Heaven. If we learn how to use it—and this is the goal of the search for enlightenment —it can transform not only ourselves but the world around us. Has there ever been a time when the clear use of this sacred power was more essential or more urgent? Has there ever been a time when it was more vital to understand the nature of this pure power and how to channel it and how to use it for the sake of the world? I pray that all of you who read this book may come to know and believe in the power of enlightenment, and come to recognize the nature of your mind, for to recognize the nature of your mind is to engender in the ground of your being an understanding that will change your entire world view, and help you discover and develop, naturally and spontaneously, a compassionate desire to serve all beings, as well as a direct knowledge of how best you can do so, with whatever skill or ability you have, in whatever circumstances you find yourself. I pray then that you will come to know in the very core of your being the living truth of these words by Nyoshul Khenpo:

> *An effortless compassion can arise for all beings who have not realized their true nature. So limitless is it that if tears could express it, you would cry without end. Not only compassion, but tremendous skillful means can be born when you realize the nature of mind. Also you are naturally liberated from all suffering and fear, such as the fear of birth, death, and the intermediate state. Then if you were to speak of the joy and bliss that arise from this realization, it is said by the buddhas that if you were to gather all the glory, enjoyment, pleasure, and happiness of the world and put it all together, it would not approach one tiny fraction of the bliss that you experience upon realizing the nature of mind.*

To serve the world out of this dynamic union of wisdom and compassion would be to participate most effectively in the preservation of the planet. Masters of all the religious traditions on earth now understand that spiritual training is *essential* not solely for monks and nuns, but for all people, whatever their faith or way of life. What I have tried to show in this book is the intensely practical, active, and effective nature of spiritual development. As a famous Tibetan teaching says: "When the world is filled with evil, all mishaps should be transformed into the path of enlightenment." The danger we are all in together makes it essential now that we no longer think of spiritual development as a luxury, but as a necessity for survival.

Let us dare to imagine now what it would be like to live in a world where a significant number of people took the opportunity offered by the teachings, to devote part of their lives to serious spiritual practice, to recognize the nature of their mind, and so to use the opportunity of their deaths to move closer to buddhahood, and to be reborn with one aim, that of serving and benefiting others.

This book is giving you a sacred technology, by which you can transform not only your present life and not only your dying and your death, but also your future lives, and so the future of humanity. What my masters and I are hoping to inspire here is a major leap forward toward the conscious evolution of humanity. To learn how to die is to learn how to live; to learn how to live is to learn how to act not only in this life, but in the lives to come. To transform yourself truly and learn how to be reborn as a transformed being to help others is really to help the world in the most powerful way of all.

The most compassionate insight of my tradition and its noblest contribution to the spiritual wisdom of humanity has been its understanding and repeated enactment of the ideal of the bodhisattva, the being who takes on the suffering of all sentient beings, who undertakes the journey to liberation not for his or her own good alone but to help all others, and who eventually, after attaining liberation, does not dissolve into the absolute or flee the agony of samsara, but chooses to return again and again to devote his or her wisdom and compassion to the service of the whole world. What the world needs more than anything is active servants of peace such as these, "clothed," as Longchenpa said, "in the armor of perseverance," dedicated to their bodhisattva vision and to the spreading of wisdom into all reaches of our experience. We need bodhisattva lawyers, bodhisattva artists and politicians, bodhisattva doctors and economists, bodhisattva teachers and scientists, bodhisattva technicians and engineers, bodhisattvas everywhere, working consciously as channels of compassion and wisdom at every level and in every situation of society, working to transform their minds and actions and those of others, working tirelessly in the certain knowledge of the support of the buddhas and enlightened beings, for the preservation of our world, and for a more merciful future. As Teilhard de Chardin said: "Some day, after we have mastered the winds, the waves, the tides and gravity, . . . we shall harness . . . the energies of love. Then, for the second time in the history of the world, man will have discovered fire." In the wonderful prayer of Rumi:

O love, O pure deep love, be here, be now
Be all; worlds dissolve into your stainless endless radiance,
Frail living leaves burn with you brighter than cold stars:
Make me your servant, your breath, your core.

One of my deepest hopes for this book is that it could be an unfailing, loyal companion to anyone who makes the choice to become a bodhisattva, a source of guidance and inspiration to those who really face the challenge of this time, and undertake the journey to enlightenment out of compassion for all other beings. May they never grow weary or disappointed or disillusioned; may they never give up hope whatever the terrors and difficulties and obstacles that rise up against them. May those obstacles only inspire them to even deeper determination. May they have faith in the undying love and power of all those enlightened beings that have blessed and still bless the earth with their presence; may they take heart, as I have constantly taken heart, from the living examples of the great masters, men and women like us, who have with infinite courage heeded the Buddha's deathbed words to strive with their whole being to attain perfection. May the vision that so many mystic masters of all traditions have had, of a future world free of cruelty and horror, where humanity can live in the ultimate happiness of the nature of mind, come, through all our efforts, to be realized. Let us all pray together for that better world, first with Shantideva and then with St. Francis:

For as long as space exists
And sentient beings endure,
May I too remain,
To dispel the misery of the world.

Lord make me an instrument
Of thy peace, where there is hatred,
Let me sow love;
Where there is injury, pardon;
Where there is doubt, faith;
Where there is despair, hope;
Where there is darkness, light;
And where there is sadness, joy.
O Divine Master, grant that
I may not so much seek
To be consoled as to console;
To be understood as to understand;
To be loved as to love;
For it is in giving that we receive,
It is in pardoning that we
Are pardoned, and it is in dying
That we are born to eternal life.

Let this book be dedicated to all my masters: for those who have passed away, may their aspirations be fulfilled, and for those who are living, may their lives be long, may their great and sacred work meet with ever more shining success, and may their teachings inspire, encourage, and hearten all beings. I pray with all my heart for the swift rebirth of Dilgo Khyentse Rinpoche in as powerful and fully enlightened an incarnation as possible, to help us through the dangers of this age!

Let this book be dedicated also to all those whom you have read about in it who have died: Lama Tseten, Lama Chokden, Samten, Ani Pelu, Ani Rilu, and A-pé Dorje. Remember them in your prayers, and remember too those of my students who have died, and those who are dying now, whose devotion and courage have so inspired me.

Let this book be dedicated to all beings, living, dying, or dead. For all those who are at this moment going through the process of dying, may their deaths be peaceful and free of pain or fear. May all those who at this moment are being born, and those who are struggling in this life, be nourished by the blessings of the buddhas, and may they meet the teachings, and follow the path of wisdom. May their lives be happy and fruitful, and free from all sorrow. May whoever reads this book derive rich and unending benefit from it, and may these teachings transform their hearts and minds. This is my prayer.

May every single being, of all the six realms, attain, all together, the ground of primordial perfection!

My Teachers

Jamyang Khyentse Chökyi Lodrö (1896–1959) was the most outstanding Tibetan master of this century. Authority on all traditions and holder of all lineages, he was the heart of the "non-partisan" movement in Tibet.

Dudjom Rinpoche (1904–1987), one of Tibet's foremost yogins, scholars, and meditation masters. Considered to be the living representative of Padmasambhava, he was a prolific author and revealer of the "treasures" concealed by Padmasambhava. Photo by Arnaud Desjardins.

Dilgo Khyentse Rinpoche (1910–1991)) was acknowledged as a peerless master of the Dzogchen teachings, and discoverer of the spiritual treasures of Padmasambhava. He was the greatest disciple of Jamyang Khyentse Chökyi Lodrö, and master of many important lamas, including H. H. the Dalai Lama. Photo by Julian Engelsman.

Khandro Tsering Chödrön was the spiritual wife of Jamyang Khyentse Chökyi Lodrö and is regarded as the foremost woman master in Tibetan Buddhism. Photo by Mark B. Tracy.

Questions about Death

THE SKILL OF MEDICAL SCIENCE and advances in medical technology have been responsible for saving countless lives and alleviating untold suffering. Yet at the same time they pose many ethical and moral dilemmas for the dying, their families, and their doctors, which are complex and sometimes anguishingly difficult to resolve. Should we, for example, allow our dying relative or friend to be connected to a life-support system, or removed from one? To avoid prolonging the agony of a dying person, should doctors have the power to terminate a life? And should those who feel they are condemned to a long and painful death be encouraged, or even assisted, in killing themselves? People often ask me questions such as these about death and dying, and I would like to review some of them here.

STAYING ALIVE

Even forty years ago most people died at home, but now the majority of us die in hospitals and nursing homes. The prospect of being kept alive by a machine is a real and frightening one. People are asking themselves more and more what they can do to ensure a humane and dignified death, without their lives being unnecessarily prolonged. This has become a very complicated issue. How do we decide whether to begin life-support for a person, for instance, after a serious accident? And what if the person is comatose, cannot speak, or has been rendered mentally incapable because of a degenerative illness? What if it is an infant who is severely deformed and brain-damaged?

There are no easy answers to questions such as these, but there are some basic principles that might guide us. According to the teaching of Buddha, all life is sacred; all beings have buddha nature, and life offers them, as we have seen, the possibility of enlightenment. To avoid destroying life is taken as one of the first principles of human conduct. Yet Buddha also advised very strongly against dogmatism, and I believe we cannot take a fixed view, or an "official" position, or make rules about issues such as these. We can only act with whatever wisdom we have, according to each situation.

And, as always, everything depends on our motivation and on the compassion behind it.

Is there any point in keeping people alive artificially when they otherwise would die? The Dalai Lama has indicated one essential factor—the state of mind of the dying person: "From the Buddhist point of view if a dying person has any chance of having positive, virtuous thoughts, it is important—and there is a purpose—for them to live for even just a few minutes longer." He highlights the stress on the family in such a situation: "If there is no such chance for positive thoughts, and in addition a lot of money is being spent by relatives simply in order to keep someone alive, then there seems to be no point. But each case must be dealt with individually; it is very difficult to generalize."[1]

Life-support measures or resuscitation can be a cause of disturbance, annoyance, and distraction at the critical moment of death. We have seen from both the Buddhist teachings and the evidence of the near-death experience that even when people are in a coma they can have total awareness of everything that is going on around them. What happens just before death, at death, and until the final separation of body and consciousness are moments of immense importance for anyone, and especially for a spiritual practitioner seeking to practice or rest in the nature of the mind.

In general there is a danger that life-sustaining treatment that merely prolongs the dying process may only kindle unnecessary grasping, anger, and frustration in a dying person, especially if this was not his or her original wish. Relatives who are faced with difficult decisions, and overwhelmed with the responsibility of letting their loved one die, should reflect that if there is no real hope of recovery, the quality of the final days or hours of their loved one's life may be more important than simply keeping the person alive. Besides, as we never really know whether the consciousness is still in the body, we may even be condemning them to imprisonment in a useless body.

Dilgo Khyentse Rinpoche said:

> To use life-support mechanisms when a person has no chance of recovery is pointless. It is far better to let them die naturally in a peaceful atmosphere and perform positive actions on their behalf. When the life-support machinery is in place, but there is no hope, it is not a crime to stop it, since there is no way in which the person can survive, and you are only holding onto their life artificially.

Attempts at resuscitation can also sometimes be needless and an unnecessary disturbance to a dying person. One doctor writes:

> The hospital erupts into a spasm of frenzied activity. Dozens of people rush to the bedside in a last-ditch effort to resuscitate the patient. The essentially dead patient is pumped full of drugs, stabbed with dozens of needles, and jolted with electric shocks. Our dying moments are closely documented by heart rate,

levels of oxygen in the blood, brain wave readings, and so forth. Finally, when the last doctor has had enough, this technohysteria comes to an end.[2]

You may not wish to have life-support mechanisms or be resuscitated, and you may want to be left undisturbed for some time after clinical death. How can you ensure that your wishes for the kind of peaceful environment recommended by the masters for dying will be respected?

Even if you state your wishes about wanting or refusing certain kinds of treatment in the hospital, your requests may not be respected. If your next of kin does not agree with your wishes, he or she may ask for particular procedures to be started even while you are still conscious and able to talk. Unfortunately, it is not uncommon for doctors to comply with family's wishes rather than those of the dying person. Of course the best way to have some control over your medical care when you are dying is to die at home.

In some parts of the world, documents known as Living Wills exist, through which you can state your desires for treatment in case the time comes when you can no longer make decisions for your own future. These are a sensible precaution, and help doctors if they are faced with a dilemma. However, they are not legally binding, and cannot anticipate the complexities of your illness. In the United States you can draw up what is called a "Durable Power of Attorney for Health Care" with a lawyer. This is the most effective way to state your choices and ensures, as far as possible, that they will be respected. In it you name an agent, a legal spokesperson who understands your attitudes and wishes, who can respond to the special circumstances of your illness, and who can make crucial decisions on your behalf.

My advice (as I indicated in chapter 11, "Heart Advice on Helping the Dying") is to find out whether or not your doctor is comfortable honoring your wishes, especially if you want to have life-support measures withdrawn when you are dying, and you do not wish to be resuscitated if your heart stops. Make sure that your doctor informs the hospital staff and has your wishes written onto your chart. Discuss the issue of your dying with your relatives. Ask your family or friends to request the staff to disconnect any monitors and IV lines once the process of dying has begun, and to move you from an intensive care unit into a private room if feasible. Explore ways in which the atmosphere around you can be made as quiet, peaceful, and as free from panic as possible.

ALLOWING DEATH TO HAPPEN

In 1986 the American Medical Association ruled it was ethical for doctors to remove life-support, including food and water, from terminally ill patients about to die and from those who could linger in a coma. Four years later a Gallup poll showed that 84 percent of

Americans would prefer to have treatment withheld if they were on life-support and had no hope of recovering.[3]

The decision to limit or withhold life-sustaining treatments is often called "passive euthanasia." Death is allowed to happen naturally, by refraining from medical intervention or heroic measures that can only lengthen a person's life by days or hours, and where their condition is not amenable to treatment. It would include terminating aggressive treatments or therapies aimed at curing the dying person, refusing or discontinuing life-support machinery and intravenous feeding, and dispensing with cardiac resuscitation. This passive form of euthanasia also takes place when the family and doctor choose not to treat a secondary condition that will result in death. For example, a person dying in the final stages of bone cancer may develop pneumonia, which if not treated may lead to a death that is more peaceful, and less painful and prolonged.

What about people who are terminally ill and decide to take themselves off life-support? By ending their lives, are they committing a negative action? Kalu Rinpoche has answered this question very precisely:

> The person who decides that they have had enough suffering and wish to be allowed to die is in a situation that we cannot call virtuous or non-virtuous. We certainly cannot blame someone for making that decision. It is not a karmically negative act. It is simply the wish to avoid suffering, which is the fundamental wish of all living beings. On the other hand, it is not a particularly virtuous act, either. . . . Rather than being a wish to end one's life, it's a wish to end suffering. Therefore it is a karmically neutral act.

What if we are caring for a dying person who asks us to remove life-support? Kalu Rinpoche said:

> We may not be able to save the patient's life. We may not be able to relieve the person's suffering. But we are trying our best, motivated in the purest way possible. Whatever we do, even if it is not ultimately successful, can never be thought of as karmically damaging or karmically negative.
>
> When a healer is instructed by a patient to remove life-support systems, that puts the healer in a difficult position, because the instincts of the healer may be telling them, "If this person stayed on the life-support system they would remain alive. If I take them off, they will die." The karmic consequences depend upon the healer's intent because the healer will be depriving someone of the means to stay alive, regardless of the fact that it was that person that told us to do it. If the basic motivation of the healer has always been to help and benefit that person and relieve their suffering, then from that state of mind it seems as though nothing karmically negative can develop.[4]

CHOOSING TO DIE

The same 1990 Gallup poll cited earlier showed that 66 percent of people in the United States believed that a person in great pain, with "no hope of improvement," had a moral right to take his or her own life. In a country like Holland, ten thousand people are said to choose euthanasia each year. The doctors who help them to die must prove that the patient consents, that he or she discussed the alternatives with them fully, and that the doctor consulted a colleague for a second opinion. In the United States matters have come to such a head that a book clearly describing methods of suicide for people faced with a terminal illness has become a runaway bestseller, and movements have been begun to legalize "active euthanasia" or "aid in dying."

But what would happen if euthanasia were legal? Many people are afraid that patients labeled as terminal, especially those in great pain, might choose to die even though their pain might be manageable, and their lives might be longer. Others fear that the elderly might simply feel it is their duty to die, or choose suicide simply to spare their families' lives and money.

Many of those who work with the dying feel that higher standards of terminal care are the answer to requests for euthanasia. When she was asked about the pending legislation on euthanasia, Elisabeth Kübler-Ross replied: "I find it sad that we have to have laws about matters like this. I think that we should use our human judgment, and come to grips with our own fear of death. Then we could respect patients' needs and listen to them, and would not have a problem such as this."[5]

People are afraid that dying will be unbearable, that they will be overtaken by immobilizing, even dementing illness, and intolerable and meaningless pain. The Buddhist teachings offer us a different attitude to suffering, one that gives it a purpose. The Dalai Lama points out that

> Your suffering is due to your own karma, and you have to bear the fruit of that karma anyway in this life or another, unless you can find some way of purifying it. In that case, it is considered to be better to experience the karma in this life of a human where you have more abilities to bear it in a better way, than, for example, an animal who is helpless and can suffer even more because of that.

According to the Buddhist teachings we should do everything we can to help the dying cope with their deterioration, pain, and fear, and offer them the loving support that will give the end of their lives meaning. Dame Cicely Saunders, founder of St. Christopher's Hospice in London, said: "If one of our patients requests euthanasia, it means we are not doing our job." She argues against the legalization of euthanasia, and says,

> We are not so poor a society that we cannot afford time and trouble and money to help people live until they die. We owe it to all those for whom we can kill the pain which traps them in fear and bitterness. To do this we do not

have to kill them. . . . To make voluntary [active] euthanasia lawful would be an irresponsible act, hindering help, pressuring the vulnerable, abrogating our true respect and responsibility to the frail and the old, the disabled and dying.[6]

SOME OTHER QUESTIONS

What happens to the consciousness of a baby that is aborted, or dies very young? What can the parents do to help the baby?

Dilgo Khyentse Rinpoche explained:

The consciousness of those who die before birth, at birth, or in infancy will travel once again through the bardo states, and take on another existence. The same meritorious practices and actions can be done for them as are usually performed for the dead: the purification practice and mantra recitation of Vajrasattva, offering of lights, purification of the ashes, and so on.

In the case of an abortion, in addition to these usual practices, if the parents feel remorse they can help by acknowledging it, asking for forgiveness, and performing ardently the purification practice of Vajrasattva. They can also offer lights, and save lives, or help others, or sponsor some humanitarian or spiritual project, dedicating it to the well-being and future enlightenment of the baby's consciousness.

What happens to the consciousness of a person who commits suicide?

Dilgo Khyentse Rinpoche said:

When a person commits suicide, the consciousness has no choice but to follow its negative karma, and it may well happen that a harmful spirit will seize and possess its life force. In the case of suicide, a powerful master must perform special kinds of practices, such as fire ceremonies and other rituals, in order to free the dead person's consciousness.

Should we donate our organs when we die? What if they have to be removed while the blood is still circulating or before the process of dying is complete? Doesn't this disturb or harm the consciousness at the moment before death?

Masters whom I have asked this question agree that organ donation is an extremely positive action, since it stems from a genuinely compassionate wish to benefit others. So, as long as it is truly the wish of the dying person, it will not harm in any way the consciousness that is leaving the body. On the contrary, this final act of generosity accumulates good karma. Another master said that any suffering and pain that a person goes through in the process of giving his or her organs, and every moment of distraction, turns into a good karma.

Dilgo Khyentse Rinpoche explained: "If the person is definitely going to die within a few moments, and has expressed the wish to give his organs, and his mind is filled with compassion, it is alright for them to be removed even before the heart stops beating."

What about cryonics, where a person's body, or just their head, is frozen to await the time when medical science has advanced to the point where they can be resuscitated?

Dilgo Khyentse Rinpoche called this utterly meaningless. One's consciousness cannot enter one's body again after one is actually dead. The belief that one's corpse is being kept for future revival can obviously trap the person's consciousness in a tragically increased attachment to the body, and so aggravate its suffering immensely and block the process of rebirth. One master compares cryonics to going directly to a cold hell, without even passing through the bardo state.

What can we do for an aging parent, a father, for example, who has become senile or demented?

At that point it may be of no use to try to explain the teachings, but practicing quietly or saying mantras or the names of the buddhas in his presence will definitely help. Kalu Rinpoche explains:

You will be planting seeds. Your own aspirations and altruistic concern for him in this situation are very important. In offering this service to your father in his unhappy circumstances, you must go about it with the best of intentions, out of a true concern for his welfare and happiness. That is a very important factor in your relationship to him in these times . . . The karmic connection between parents and children is very strong. Much benefit can be worked on subtle levels because of that bond, if our approach to our parents is marked by compassion and concern and our involvement in spiritual practice is not only for our sake, but for the benefit of other beings as well, particularly, in this case, our parents.[7]

APPENDIX THREE

Two Stories

MY STUDENTS AND FRIENDS in the West have told me many inspiring accounts of people they knew who were helped, as they died, by the teachings of Buddha. Let me tell you here the stories of two of my students, and of the way they have faced death.

DOROTHY

Dorothy was a student of mine who died from cancer at St. Christopher's Hospice in London in England. She had been a talented artist and embroiderer, art historian, and tour guide, as well as a color therapist and healer. Her father was a well-known healer, and she had a great respect for all religions and spiritual traditions. It was late in her life when she discovered Buddhism, and became, as she said "hooked"; she said she found its teachings gave her the most compelling and complete view of the nature of reality. Let some of her spiritual friends, who cared for her while she died, tell you in their own words how Dorothy let the teachings help her when she came to die:

Dorothy's death was an inspiration to us all. She died with such grace and dignity, and everyone who came in contact with her felt her strength—doctors, nurses, auxiliary helpers, other patients, and not least her spiritual friends, who were fortunate enough to be around her during the last weeks of her life.

When we visited Dorothy at home before she went into the hospice, it was clear that the cancer was in a very aggressive phase, and her organs were beginning to fail. She had been on morphine for over a year and now she could hardly eat or drink; yet she never complained, and you would never have known that she was in fact in considerable pain. She had grown terribly thin, and there were moments when she was obviously exhausted. But whenever people came to visit her, she would greet them and entertain them, radiating a remarkable energy and joy, unfailingly serene and considerate. One of her favorite things was to lie on her couch, and listen to tapes of Sogyal Rinpoche's teachings, and she was delighted when he sent her some tapes from Paris, which he said would have a special meaning for her.

Dorothy prepared and planned for her death right down to the last detail. She wanted there to be no unfinished business for others to sort out, and spent months working on all the practical arrangements. She didn't seem to have any fear of dying, but wanted to feel that there was nothing left undone, and that she could then approach death without distraction. She derived a lot of comfort from the knowledge that she had done no real harm to others in her life, and that she had received and followed the teachings; as she said "I've done my homework."

When the time came for Dorothy to go into the hospice, and leave her flat for the last time—a flat once full of beautiful treasures collected over the years—she left with just a small holdall and without even a backward glance. She had already given most of her personal possessions away, but she took a small picture of Rinpoche that she always kept with her, and his small book on meditation. She had essentialized her life into that one small bag: "traveling light," she called it. She was very matter-of-fact about leaving, almost as though she were only going as far as the shops; she simply said "Bye bye, flat," waved her hand and walked out of the door.

Her room in the hospice became a very special place. There was always a candle lit on her bedside table in front of Rinpoche's picture, and once, when someone asked if she would like to talk to him, she smiled, looked at the photograph, and said: "No, there's no need, he's always here!" She often referred to Rinpoche's advice on creating the "right environment," and had a beautiful painting of a rainbow put on the wall directly in front of her; there were flowers everywhere, brought by her visitors.

Dorothy remained in command of the situation, right up to the end, and her trust in the teachings seemed never to waver, even for a second. It felt as though she was helping us, rather than the other way round! She was consistently cheerful, confident, and humorous, and had a dignity about her, which we saw sprung from her courage and self-reliance. The joy with which she always welcomed us secretly helped us to understand that death is by no means somber or terrifying. This was her gift to us, and it made us feel honored and privileged to be with her.

We had almost come to depend on Dorothy's strength, so it was humbling for us when we realized that she needed our strength and support. She was going through some final details about her funeral, when suddenly we saw that, after having been so concerned about others, what she needed now was to let go of all these details and turn her attention toward herself. And she needed us to give her our permission to do so.

It was a difficult, painful death and Dorothy was like a warrior. She tried to do as much as possible for herself, so as not to make work for the nurses, until the moment when her body would no longer support her. On one occasion, when she was still able to get out of bed, a nurse asked her very discreetly if she would like to sit on the commode. Dorothy struggled up, then laughed and said, "Just look at this body!" as she showed us her body, reduced almost to a skeleton. Yet because her body was falling apart, her spirit seemed to radiate and soar. It was as though she were acknowledging that her body had done its job: It was no longer really "her" but something she had inhabited and was now ready to let go of.

For all the light and joy that surrounded Dorothy, it was clear that dying was by no means easy; in fact it was very hard work. There were bleak and harrowing moments, but she went through them with tremendous grace and fortitude. After one particularly painful night when she had fallen over, she became afraid that she might die at any moment, all alone, and so she asked for one of us to stay with her all the time. It was then that we began the 24-hour rotation.

Dorothy practiced every day, and the purification practice of Vajrasattva was her favorite practice. Rinpoche recommended teachings on death for her to read, which included an essential practice of phowa. Sometimes we would sit together reading passages out loud to her; sometimes we would chant Padmasambhava's mantra; sometimes we would simply rest in silence for a while. So we developed a gentle, relaxed rhythm of practice and rest. There were times when she would doze, and wake up to say: "Oh, isn't this lovely!" When she appeared more energetic and alive, and if she felt like it, we would read passages from the bardo teachings, so that she could identify the stages she would go through. We were all astonished at how bright and alert she was, but she wanted to keep her practice very simple—just the essence. When we arrived to change "shifts" we would always be struck by the peaceful atmosphere in the room, Dorothy lying there, her eyes wide open, gazing into space, even while she was sleeping, and her attendant sitting or quietly reciting mantras.

Rinpoche would often telephone to find out how she was getting on, and they talked freely about how near she was to death. Dorothy would speak in a down-to-earth way, and say things like, "Just a few more days to go, Rinpoche." One day the nurses wheeled in the telephone trolley saying, "Telephone call from Amsterdam." Dorothy brightened up immediately, and glowed with pleasure as she took the call from Rinpoche. After she hung up she beamed at us and said he had told her that she should no longer concentrate on reading texts, and that now was the time simply to "rest in the nature of mind; rest in the luminosity." When she was very close to death, and Rinpoche called her for the last time, she told us he had said, "Don't forget us; look us up some time!"

Once when the doctor came round to check on how she was and adjust her medication, Dorothy explained, in a disarmingly simple and straightforward way, "You see, I am a student of Buddhism, and we believe that when you die you see lots of light. I think I'm beginning to see a few flashes of light, but I don't think I've really quite seen it yet." The doctors were astounded by her clarity and her liveliness, particularly, they told us, in her advanced stage of illness, when they would normally have expected her to have been unconscious.

As death came closer, the distinction between day and night seemed to blur, and Dorothy went deeper and deeper into herself. The color in her face changed and her moments of consciousness became fewer. We thought we could detect the signs of the elements dissolving. Dorothy was ready to die, but her body was not ready to let go, because her heart was strong. So each night turned into an ordeal for her, and she would be surprised in the morning that she had made it through to another day. She never complained, but we could see how she was suffering; we did everything we could to make her more comfortable, and when she could no longer take fluids, we would moisten her lips. Right up until the last thirty-six hours, she politely refused any drugs which would interfere with her awareness.

Not long before Dorothy died, the nurses moved her. She lay curled up in a fetal position, and even though her body had now wasted away to almost nothing, and she could neither move nor speak, her eyes were still open and alive, looking directly ahead, through the window in front of her, out into the sky. In the moment just before she died, she moved, almost imperceptibly, looked Debbie straight in the eye, and communicated something strongly; it was a look of recognition, as if to say, "This is it," with a hint of a smile. Then she gazed back out at the sky, breathed once or twice, and passed away. Debbie gently let go of Dorothy's hand, so that she could continue, undisturbed, through the inner dissolution.

The staff at the hospice said that they had never seen anyone so well prepared for death as Dorothy, and her presence and inspiration were still remembered by many people at the hospice even a year after her death.

RICK

Rick lived in Oregon and had AIDS. He had worked as a computer operator, and was forty five when, a few years ago, he came to the annual summer retreat I lead in the United States, and spoke to us about what death, and life, and his illness meant to him. I was amazed by how Rick, who had only studied the Buddhist teachings with me for two years, had taken them to heart. In this brief period he had, in his own way, captured the essence of the teachings: devotion, compassion, and the View of the nature of mind, and made them a part of his life. Rick sat in his chair and faced us all and told us how he felt about dying. I hope that these excerpts will give you some flavor of this moving occasion:

When I thought I was dying, two years ago, I did what was natural: I cried out, and I was answered. And it took me through several weeks of horrible fevers, where I thought I was going to go in the middle of the night . . . This devotion, this crying out . . . When this is all you can do, we have that promise from Padmasambhava that he is there. And he doesn't lie: he has proved himself to me many times.

If it were not for Padmasambhava, whom Rinpoche teaches us is the nature of our own mind, our own buddha nature, if it were not for that glorious shining presence, I couldn't go through what I'm going through. I just know I couldn't.

The first thing I realized was that you must take personal responsibility for yourself. The reason I am dying is that I have AIDS. That is my responsibility; no one else is to blame. In fact there is no one to blame, not even myself. But I take responsibility for that.

I made a vow to myself and to whatever gods there may be, before I came into Buddhism, that I just wanted to be happy. When . . . I made that decision, I stuck to it. And this is very important in doing any kind of training of the mind. You must make the decision that you really want to change. If you don't want to change, no one is going to do the work for you.

Our part . . . is to work with the daily aspects of our situation. First is to be *grateful* that you are in this body, and on this planet. That was the beginning for me—realizing gratitude for the earth, for living beings. Now that I feel things slowly slipping out, I am becoming so much more grateful for everyone and everything. So my practice now centers on this gratitude, simply a constant offering of praise to life, to Padmasambhava, who is living all of these multitudinous forms.

Don't make the mistake I did for so many years, that "practice" means sitting straight and saying mantras, thinking, "I'll be glad when this is over!" Practice is much bigger than that. Practice is every person you meet; practice is every unkind word you hear or that may even be directed at you.

When you stand up from your practice seat, that's when practice really begins. We have to be very artful and creative in how we apply the practice to life. There is always something in our environment we can connect with, to do the practice. So if I'm too dizzy to visualize Vajrasattva above my head, I stand up, and I go and wash my morning dishes, and the plate I'm holding in my hand is the world and all its suffering beings. Then I say the mantra . . . OM VAJRA SATTVA HUM . . . and I'm washing away the suffering of beings. When I take a shower, it's not a shower; that's Vajrasattva above my head. When I go out in the sunshine, it is the light, like hundred thousand suns, shining from Vajrasattva's body and entering me, and I just take it in. When I see a beautiful person walking down the street, I might in the beginning think, "What a nice-looking person," but the next instant I am offering that up to Padmasambhava with my full heart, and letting it go. You have to take real life situations and make them your practice. Otherwise you will have only an empty belief that gives you no solace, no strength, when hard times start. It's just a belief: "Oh, some day, I'll go to heaven. Some day I'll be a Buddha." Well, some day you won't be a Buddha. You are a Buddha, now. And when you practice, you are practicing at being who you are. . . .

It's very important to take situations that are occurring in your life and use them. As Rinpoche keeps saying, if you have practiced calling out and asking for help, then in the bardos it will be natural to do the same . . . I made a mantra out of this line by Dudjom Rinpoche: "Lama of unrepayable kindness, I only remember you." Some days, it is all I can manage to think; it is the only practice I can get out. But it works great.

So . . . happiness, self-responsibility, gratitude . . . don't confuse a dead, ritualistic practice for a living, ongoing, changing, fluid, opening, glorious practice. Because, and it's my experience right now—and I know it sounds like words perhaps, but I know in my heart it's not—I see Padmasambhava everywhere. That's just my practice. Every person, especially the difficult ones, that are making life difficult for others around them, to me that is the blessing of the master. To me this illness is the blessing of the master. It is grace. So much grace I could chew on it.

But this has happened because I have trained my mind . . . When I started, I used to judge things constantly in my mind. I would judge this person; I would judge that one. I would judge the way he looked; I would judge the way she sat; I would judge, "I don't like today, it's too rainy, too gray. Oh, poor me . . . Oh love me . . . Oh help!" So I started with that. It was just a constant commentary in my mind. But I made a start. I would write myself little notes and stick them on my refrigerator. "Don't judge!"

When you live in your mind—that is choosing between this and that, "This is good . . . this is bad, I don't want it," between hope and fear, between hate and love, between joy and sorrow, when you are actually grasping for one of those extremes—the essential peace of your mind is disturbed. A Zen patriarch says: "The Great Way is not difficult for those who have no preferences." Because your buddha nature is there. Happiness is everywhere.

So I began to work with my conceptual mind. At first it seemed like an impossible thing to do. But the more I practiced at it . . . I found out: If you leave the risings in their own place, they are perfectly fine, where they are. Just be with them, and be happy, because you know you have the buddha nature.

You don't have to *feel* like you have the buddha nature. That's not the point. The point is trust, which is faith. The point is devotion, which is surrender. That, for me, is the essence. If you can trust what the master is saying, and study and try to bring the teaching back to yourself in difficult times, and train your mind not to fall into its habitual patterns, if you can just be with what is happening, with bare attention, after a while you notice that nothing stays around very long. Not even negative thoughts. Especially not our bodies. Everything changes. If you leave it in its place, it will liberate itself.

In a situation like mine, when fear becomes so obvious to you, and so predominant, and you feel like you are being swallowed by the fear, you must take your mind in hand. I have realized that fear is not going to kill me. This is just something that is passing through my mind. This is a thought and I know that thoughts will liberate themselves if I just keep my hands off. I also realize that's what happens in the bardos, when and if you see a vision coming at you that might be frightening; it's not coming anywhere other than from you! All those energies we have kept damped down into our bodies are being released.

I also discovered, early on, when I was training my mind, there is a certain point, a certain line you must draw, and beyond that point you cannot let your mind go. If you do, you risk mental problems, you risk moroseness, you risk being a real downer for everybody around you: that would be the least. But you could flip out. People do flip out, get unbalanced by believing what their minds are telling them about reality. We all do it, but there is a certain line beyond which you cannot go . . . I used to have panic attacks. I thought there was a big black hole in the ground in front of me. Since I have allowed myself the privilege, and the grace of being happy, all the time, I don't see black holes any more.

Some of you have been dearer to me than my family. Because you allow Padmasambhava to come to me in just another way, through your care and your concern and your love. You don't seem to care that I have AIDS. No one has ever asked me: "Well, how did you get it?" No one has ever intimated that this might be a curse on me; except one old friend of mine who called me a week or so ago and said, "Aren't you afraid that this is God's curse on you?" After I stopped laughing, I said, "You believe that God has cursed the earth and the human body is impure. I, on the other hand, believe that blessing is the original starting point, not a curse." From beginningless time, everything has already been accomplished, pure and perfect.

So what I do now is just rest in the radiance. It's everywhere. You can't get away from it. It is so intoxicating that sometimes I feel like I am just floating in the radiance. I am letting Padmasambhava, as he flies through the sky of the mind, just let me tag along.

Now if I were sitting out there listening to this, I would say, "OK then, why aren't you healed?" People have asked me that. It's not that I haven't tried: I bought a whole suitcase full of pills. But I stopped that question quite a while ago. I guess the reason I did was because it seemed it would be manipulating and interfering with the process that has started. This process is very cleansing for me. I know there is a lot of karma being burned up. It's cleansing perhaps for my mother, because I offer this for her. She suffers quite a bit. Then there are spiritual friends in this group whom I love like brothers and sisters; they suffer too. I have made this covenant with Padmasambhava: If I have to stay around and suffer so that some of it could help cleanse and purify you as well as me, what a blessing that would be! This is my prayer. And I'm not a person who likes to suffer, I can guarantee you that! But I feel that grace, that blessing, pushing me gently into that suffering.

And at this point, from studying what I have studied of Rinpoche's teachings on the bardos, death is not an enemy. Just like our thoughts are not to be seen as enemies. . . . And life is not an enemy. Life is something glorious, because in this life we can awaken to who we truly are.

So I beg you—from the bottom of my heart—not to waste the opportunity you have, while you are still relatively healthy, to work with what Rinpoche is offering you . . . He knows how to get to the point in speaking and teaching about what Dzogchen is, and he knows how to take you there in the heart. That is so important: and especially when you are getting ready to die.

So I'm here to say goodbye. At least for this time around . . . I want to say goodbye to all those of you who have become my brothers and sisters, those of you whom I know but have not had the privilege of getting to know better, those of you I have not even met . . . I have a feeling that within the next six months I may die. It could be within the next three months. So I hold you all in my heart, and I see you all bright and shining. There is no darkness. It is just light from Padmasambhava's heart, pervading all of us. Thanks to the master's blessing.

APPENDIX FOUR

Two Mantras

The two most famous mantras in Tibet are the mantra of Padmasambhava, called the Vajra Guru Mantra, OM AH HUM VAJRA
GURU PADMA SIDDHI HUM, and the mantra of Avalokiteshvara,
the Buddha of Compassion, OM MANI PADME HUM. Like most
mantras they are in Sanskrit, the ancient sacred language of India.

THE VAJRA GURU MANTRA

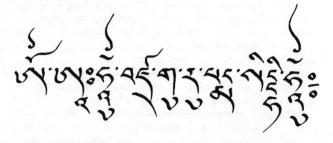

The Vajra Guru mantra, OM AH HUM VAJRA GURU PADMA
SIDDHI HUM, is pronounced by Tibetans: Om Ah Hung Benza
Guru Péma Siddhi Hung. This exploration of its meaning is based
on explanations by Dudjom Rinpoche and Dilgo Khyentse Rinpoche.

OM AH HUM

The syllables OM AH HUM have outer, inner, and "secret" meanings. At each of these levels, however, OM stands for the body, AH for
the speech, and HUM for the mind. They represent the transformative
blessings of the body, speech, and mind of all the buddhas.

Externally OM purifies all the negative actions committed through
your body, AH through your speech, and HUM through your mind.[1]
By purifying your body, speech, and mind, OM AH HUM grants the
blessing of the body, speech, and mind of the buddhas.

OM is also the essence of form, AH the essence of sound, and HUM the essence of mind. So by reciting this mantra, you are also purifying the environment, as well as yourself and all other beings within it. OM purifies all perceptions, AH all sounds, and HUM the mind, its thoughts and emotions.

Internally OM purifies the subtle channels, AH the wind, inner air or flow of energy, and HUM the creative essence.[2]

On a deeper level, OM AH HUM represent the three kayas of the Lotus family of buddhas: OM is the Dharmakaya: the Buddha Amitabha, Buddha of Limitless Light; AH is the Sambhogakaya: Avalokiteshvara, the Buddha of Compassion; and HUM is the Nirmanakaya: Padmasambhava. This signifies, in the case of this mantra, that all three kayas are embodied in the person of Padmasambhava.

At the innermost level, OM AH HUM bring the realization of the three aspects of the nature of mind: OM brings the realization of its unceasing Energy and Compassion, AH brings the realization of its radiant Nature, and HUM brings the realization of its sky-like Essence.

VAJRA GURU PADMA

VAJRA is compared to the diamond, the strongest and most precious of stones. Just as a diamond can cut through anything but is itself completely indestructible, so the unchanging, non-dual wisdom of the buddhas can never be harmed or destroyed by ignorance, and can cut through all delusion and obscurations. The qualities and activities of the body, speech, and wisdom mind of the buddhas are able to benefit beings with the piercing, unhindered power of the diamond. And like a diamond, the Vajra is free of defects; its brilliant strength comes from the realization of the Dharmakaya nature of reality, the nature of the Buddha Amitabha.

GURU means "weighty"; someone replete with every wonderful quality, who embodies wisdom, knowledge, compassion, and skillful means. Just as gold is the weightiest and most precious of metals, so the inconceivable, flawless qualities of the Guru—the master—make him unsurpassable, and above all things in excellence. GURU corresponds to the Sambhogakaya, and to Avalokiteshvara, the Buddha of Compassion. Also, since Padmasambhava teaches the path of Tantra, which is symbolized by the Vajra, and through the practice of Tantra he attained supreme realization, so he is known as "the VAJRA GURU."

PADMA means lotus, and signifies the Lotus family of the buddhas, and specifically their aspect of enlightened speech. The Lotus family is the buddha family to which human beings belong. As Padmasambhava is the direct emanation, the Nirmanakaya, of Buddha Amitabha, who is the primordial buddha of the Lotus family, he is known as "PADMA." His name Padmasambhava, the

"Lotus-born," in fact refers to the story of his birth on a blossoming lotus flower.

When the syllables VAJRA GURU PADMA are taken together, they also signify the essence and the blessing of the View, Meditation, and Action. VAJRA means the unchanging, diamantine, indestructible Essence of the truth, which we pray to realize in our View. GURU represents the luminosity Nature and noble qualities of enlightenment, which we pray to perfect in our Meditation. PADMA stands for Compassion, which we pray to accomplish in our Action.

Through reciting the mantra, then, we receive the blessing of the wisdom mind, the noble qualities and the compassion of Padmasambhava and all the buddhas.

SIDDHI HUM

SIDDHI means "real accomplishment," "attainment," "blessing," and "realization." There are two kinds of siddhis: ordinary and supreme. Through receiving the blessing of ordinary siddhis, all obstacles in our lives, such as ill-health, are removed, all our good aspirations are fulfilled, benefits like wealth and prosperity and long life accrue to us, and all of life's various circumstances become auspicious and conducive to spiritual practice, and the realization of enlightenment.

The blessing of the supreme siddhi brings about enlightenment itself, the state of complete realization of Padmasambhava, that benefits both ourselves and all other sentient beings. So by remembering and praying to the body, speech, mind, qualities, and activity of Padmasambhava, we will come to attain both ordinary and supreme siddhis.

SIDDHI HUM is said to draw in all the siddhis like a magnet that attracts iron filings.

HUM represents the wisdom mind of the buddhas, and is the sacred catalyst of the mantra. It is like proclaiming its power and truth: "So be it!"

The essential meaning of the mantra is: "I invoke you, the Vajra Guru, Padmasambhava, by your blessing may you grant us ordinary and supreme siddhis."

Dilgo Khyentse Rinpoche explains:

It is said that the twelve syllables OM AH HUM VAJRA GURU PADMA SIDDHI HUM carry the entire blessing of the twelve types of teaching taught by Buddha, which are the essence of his eighty four thousand Dharmas. Therefore to recite the Vajra Guru mantra once is equivalent to the blessing of reciting . . . or practicing the whole teaching of the Buddha. These twelve branches of the teachings are the antidotes to free us from the "Twelve Links of Interdependent Origination," which keep us bound to samsara: ignorance, karmic formations, discursive consciousness, name and form, senses, contact, sensation, craving, grasping, existence, birth, old age, and death.

These twelve links are the mechanism of samsara, by which samsara is kept alive. Through reciting the twelve syllables of the Vajra Guru mantra, these twelve links are purified, and you are able to remove and purify completely the layer of karmic emotional defilements, and so be liberated from samsara.

Although we are not able to see Padmasambhava in person, his wisdom mind has manifested in the form of mantra; these twelve syllables are actually the emanation of his wisdom mind, and they are endowed with his entire blessing. The Vajra Guru Mantra is Padmasambhava in the form of sound. So when you invoke him with the recitation of the twelve syllables, the blessing and merit you obtain is tremendous. In these difficult times, just as there is no buddha or refuge we can call upon who is more powerful than Padmasambhava, so there is no mantra that is more fitting than the Vajra Guru mantra.

THE MANTRA OF COMPASSION

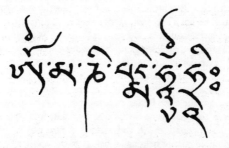

The Mantra of Compassion, OM MANI PADME HUM, is pronounced by Tibetans: Om Mani Pémé Hung. It embodies the compassion and blessing of all the buddhas and bodhisattvas, and invokes especially the blessing of Avalokiteshvara, the Buddha of Compassion. Avalokiteshvara is a manifestation of the Buddha in the Sambhogakaya, and his mantra is considered the essence of the Buddha's compassion for all beings. Just as Padmasambhava is the most important *master* for the Tibetan people, Avalokiteshvara is their most important *buddha*, and the karmic deity of Tibet. There is a famous saying that the Buddha of Compassion became so embedded in the Tibetan consciousness that any child who could say the word "mother" could also recite the mantra OM MANI PADME HUM.

Countless ages ago, it is said, a thousand princes vowed to become buddhas. One resolved to become the Buddha we know as Gautama Siddhartha; Avalokiteshvara, however, vowed not to attain enlightenment until all the other thousand princes had themselves become buddhas. In his infinite compassion, he vowed too to liberate all sentient beings from the sufferings of the different realms of samsara. Before the buddhas of the ten directions, he prayed: "May I help all beings, and if ever I tire in this great work, may my body be shattered into a thousand pieces." First, it is said, he descended into the hell realms, ascending gradually through the world of hungry ghosts, up to the realm of the gods. From there he happened to look down and saw, aghast, that though he had saved innumerable beings from hell, countless more were pouring in. This plunged him into the profoundest grief; for a moment he almost lost faith in that noble vow he had taken, and his body exploded into a thousand pieces. In his desperation, he called out to all the buddhas for help, who came to his aid from all directions of the universe, as one text said, like a soft blizzard of snowflakes. With their great power the buddhas made him whole again, and from then on Avalokiteshvara had eleven heads, and a thousand arms, and on each palm of each hand was an eye, signifying that union of wisdom and skillful means that is the mark of true compassion. In this form he was even more resplendent and empowered than before to help all beings, and his compassion grew even more intense as again and again he repeated this vow before the buddhas: "May I not attain final buddhahood before all sentient beings attain enlightenment."

It is said that in his sorrow at the pain of samsara, two tears fell from his eyes: through the blessings of the buddhas, they were transformed into the two Taras. One is Tara in her green form, who is the active force of compassion, and the other is Tara in her white form, who is compassion's motherly aspect. The name Tara means "she who liberates": she who ferries us across the ocean of samsara.

It is written in the Mahayana Sutras that Avalokiteshvara gave his mantra to the Buddha himself, and Buddha in turn granted him the special and noble task of helping all beings in the universe toward buddhahood. At this moment all the gods rained flowers on them, the earth shook, and the air rang with the sound OM MANI PADME HUM HRIH.

In the words of the poem:

Avalokiteshvara is like the moon
Whose cool light puts out the burning fires of samsara
In its rays the night-flowering lotus of compassion
Opens wide its petals.

The teachings explain that each of the six syllables of the mantra—OM MA NI PAD MÉ HUM—has a specific and potent effect in bringing about transformation at different levels of our being. The six syllables purify completely the six poisonous negative emotions, which are the manifestation of ignorance, and which cause us to act negatively with our body, speech, and mind, so creating samsara and our suffering in it. Pride, jealousy, desire, ignorance, greed, and anger are transformed, through the mantra, into their true nature, the wisdoms of the six buddha families that become manifest in the enlightened mind.[3]

So when we recite OM MANI PADME HUM, the six negative emotions, which are the cause of the six realms of samsara, are purified. This is how reciting the six syllables prevents rebirth in each of the six realms, and also dispels the suffering inherent in each realm. At the same time reciting OM MANI PADME HUM completely purifies the aggregates of ego, the skandhas, and perfects the six kinds of transcendental action of the heart of the enlightened mind, the *paramitas* of: generosity, harmonious conduct, endurance, enthusiasm, concentration, and insight. It is also said that OM MANI PADME HUM grants strong protection from all kinds of negative influences, and various different forms of illness.

Often HRIH, the "seed-syllable" of Avalokiteshvara, is added to the mantra to make OM MANI PADME HUM HRIH. The essence of the compassion of all the Buddhas, HRIH, is the catalyst that activates the compassion of the Buddhas to transform our negative emotions into their wisdom nature.

Kalu Rinpoche writes:

Another way of interpreting the mantra is that the syllable OM is the essence of enlightened form; MANI PADME, the four syllables in the middle, represent the speech of enlightenment; and the last syllable, HUM, represents the mind of enlightenment. The body, speech, and mind of all the buddhas and bodhisattvas are inherent in the sound of this mantra. It purifies the obscurations of body, speech and mind, and brings all beings to the state of realization. When it is joined with our own faith and efforts in meditation and recitation, the transformative power of the mantra arises and develops. It is truly possible to purify ourselves in this way.[4]

For those who are familiar with the mantra and have recited it with fervor and faith all their lives, the *Tibetan Book of the Dead* prays that in the bardo: "When the sound of dharmata roars like a thousand thunders, may it all become the sound of the six-syllables." Similarly we read in the Surangama Sutra:

How sweetly mysterious is the transcendental sound of Avalokiteshvara. It is the primordial sound of the universe . . . It is the subdued murmur of the sea-tide setting inward. Its mysterious sound brings liberation and peace to all sentient beings who in their pain are calling out for help, and it brings a sense of serene stability to all those who are seeking Nirvana's boundless peace.

Notes

PREFACE

1. *Rinpoche,* a term of respect meaning "Precious One," is given to highly revered teachers in Tibet. It was widely used in the central part of the country; but in eastern Tibet the title was held in such esteem that it tended to be applied only to the greatest masters.

2. A bodhisattva is a being whose sole wish is to benefit all sentient beings, and who therefore dedicates his or her entire life, work and spiritual practice to the attainment of enlightenment, in order to be of the greatest possible help to other beings.

3. Jamyang Khyentse was also a leader, one who inspired movements of spiritual change; in everything he did, he promoted harmony and unity. He supported monasteries when they fell on hard times; he discovered unknown practitioners of great spiritual attainment; and he encouraged masters of little known lineages, giving them his backing so they were recognized in the community. He had great magnetism and was like a living spiritual center in himself. Whenever there was a project that needed accomplishing, he attracted the best experts and craftsmen to work on it. From kings and princes down to the simplest person, he gave everyone his unstinting personal attention. There was no one who met him who did not have their own story to tell about him.

1. IN THE MIRROR OF DEATH

1. The name Lakar was given to the family by the great Tibetan saint Tsongkhapa in the fourteenth century, when he stopped at their home on his way to central Tibet from the northeastern province of Amdo.

2. Chagdud Tulku Rinpoche, *Life in Relation to Death* (Cottage Grove, OR: Padma Publishing, 1987), 7.

3. Jose Antonio Lutzenberger quoted in the London *Sunday Times,* March 1991.

4. Robert A. F. Thurman in *"MindScience" An East-West Dialogue* (Boston: Wisdom, 1991), 55.

5. Samsara is the uncontrolled cycle of birth and death in which sentient beings, driven by unskilful actions and destructive emotions, repeatedly perpetuate their own suffering. Nirvana is a state beyond suffering, the realization of the ultimate truth, or Buddhahood. Dilgo Khyentse Rinpoche says: "When the nature of mind is recognized, it is called nirvana. When it is obscured by delusion, it is called samsara."

2. IMPERMANENCE

1. Michel de Montaigne, *The Essays of Michel de Montaigne,* translated and edited by M. A. Screech (London: Allen Lane, 1991), 95.

2. Milarepa, *The Hundred Thousand Songs of Milarepa,* vol. 2, translated by Garma C. C. Chang (Boston: Shambhala, 1984), 634.

3. *Songs of Spiritual Change: Selected Works of the Seventh Dalai Lama,* translated by Glenn H. Mullin (Ithaca, NY: Snow Lion, 1982), 61.

4. Kenneth Ring, *Heading Towards Omega: In Search of the Meaning of the Near-Death Experience* (New York: Quill, 1985), 69.

5. Raymond Moody, Jr., M.D., *Life After Life* (New York: Bantam, 1976), 65–67.

6. Ring, *Heading Towards Omega,* 67.

7. In the Mahaparinirvana Sutra.

8. Gary Zukav, *The Dancing Wu Li Masters* (New York: Bantam, 1980), 197.

3. REFLECTION AND CHANGE

1. Kenneth Ring, *Heading Towards Omega: In Search of the Meaning of the Near-Death Experience* (New York: Quill, 1985), 99.

2. Margot Grey, *Return from Death: An Exploration of the Near-Death Experience.* (London: Arkana, 1985), 97.

3. Dr. R. G. Owens and Freda Naylor, G.P., *Living While Dying* (Wellingborough, England: Thorsons, 1987), 59.

4. Tibet has its own traditional system of natural medicine, and its own particular understanding of disease. Tibetan doctors recognize certain disorders that are difficult for medicine alone to cure, so they recommend spiritual practices along with medical treatment. Patients who follow this practice are in many cases healed completely; at the very least they will become more receptive to the treatment they are being given.

5. Nyoshul Khen Rinpoche, *Rest in Natural Great Peace: Songs of Experience* (London: Rigpa, 1987), 27.

6. Portia Nelson, quoted in Charles L. Whitfield, M.D., *Healing the Child Within* (Orlando, FL: Health Communications, 1989).

7. "Eternity" in *Blake: Complete Writings,* edited by Geoffrey Keynes (Oxford and New York: OUP, 1972), 179.

8. Alexandra David-Neel and Lama Yongden, *The Superhuman Life of Gesar of Ling* (Boston: Shambhala, 1987), Introduction.

9. In the Samadhirajasutra, quoted in *Ancient Futures: Learning from Ladakh,* Helena Norbert-Hodge (London: Rider, 1991), 72.

10. Chagdud Tulku Rinpoche, *Life in Relation to Death* (Cottage Grove, OR: Padma Publishing, 1987), 28.

11. His Holiness the Dalai Lama, *A Policy of Kindness: An Anthology of Writings by and about the Dalai Lama* (Ithaca, NY: Snow Lion, 1990), 113–14.

12. In *Letters to a Young Poet,* Rainer Maria Rilke, translated by Stephen Mitchell (New York: Vintage Books, 1986), 92.

13. A famous verse by Milarepa, quoted by Patrul Rinpoche in his *Kunzang Lamé Shyalung.*

4. THE NATURE OF MIND

1. Dudjom Rinpoche, *Calling the Lama from Afar* (London: Rigpa, 1980).

2. Chögyam Trungpa, *The Heart of the Buddha* (Boston: Shambhala, 1991), 23.

3. In this book, the ordinary mind, *Sem,* is referred to as "mind," and the essential innermost pure awareness, *Rigpa,* is referred to as the "nature of mind."

4. Nyoshul Khen Rinpoche (Nyoshul Khenpo), *Rest in Natural Great Peace: Songs of Experience* (London: Rigpa, 1989), 4.

5. John Myrdhin Reynolds, *Self-Liberation through Seeing the Naked Awareness* (New York: Station Hill, 1989), 10.

5. BRINGING THE MIND HOME

1. Thich Nhat Hanh, *Old Path, White Clouds* (Berkeley, CA: Parallax Press, 1991), 121.

2. The ferocious wild animals that were a threat in ancient times have today been replaced by other dangers: our wild and uncontrolled emotions.

3. Marion L. Matics, *Entering the Path of Enlightenment: The Bodhicarya-vatara of the Buddhist Poet Shantideva* (London: George, Allen and Unwin, 1971), 162.

4. Calm Abiding and Clear Seeing are the two central practices of Buddhist meditation, called in Sanskrit *Shamatha* and *Vipashyana,* and in Tibetan *Shyiné* and *Lhaktong.* Their deepening and development forms the link between basic meditation practice and the more advanced meditation practices of Mahamudra and Dzogchen (See chapter 10, "The Innermost Essence"). I hope in a future book to be able to explore in greater depth the precise way in which the path of meditation develops through Shamatha and Vipashyana to Dzogchen.

5. The future Buddha, Maitreya, is in fact portrayed sitting on a chair.

6. You may not be following this practice now, but keeping the eyes open creates an auspicious condition for your practicing it in the future. See chapter 10, "The Innermost Essence."

7. See Appendix 4 for an explanation of this mantra.

8. Although I have given here a full instruction on the practice, it should be borne in mind that meditation cannot truly be learned from a book, but only with the guidance of a qualified teacher.

9. Rainer Maria Rilke in *Duino Elegies.*

10. Lewis Thompson, *Mirror to the Light* (Coventure).

6. EVOLUTION, KARMA, AND REBIRTH

1. Adapted from the "Middle Length Sayings," quoted in H. W. Schumann, *The Historical Buddha* (London: Arkana, 1989), 54–55.

2. Quoted in Hans TenDam, *Exploring Reincarnation* (London: Arkana, 1990), 377. Other figures in the West in modern history who have apparently believed in rebirth have included: Goethe, Schiller, Sweden-borg, Tolstoy, Gauguin, Mahler, Arthur Conan Doyle, David Lloyd George, Kipling, Sibelius, and General Patton.

3. Some Buddhist scholars prefer the word rebirth to "re-incarnation," which they feel implies the notion of a "soul" that incarnates, and it is therefore not appropriate to Buddhism. The American statistics for belief

in reincarnation appear in: George Gallup Jr., with William Proctor, *Adventures in Immortality: A Look Beyond the Threshold of Death* (London: Souvenir, 1983). A poll in the London *Sunday Telegraph*, April 15, 1979, indicated that 28 percent of British people believed in reincarnation.

4. Joan Forman, *The Golden Shore* (London: Futura, 1989), 159–63.

5. Ian Stevenson, *Twenty Cases Suggestive of Reincarnation* (Charlottesville: Univ. Press of Virginia, 1974); *Cases of the Reincarnation Type*, vols. 1–4 (Charlottesville: Univ. Press of Virginia, 1975–1983); *Children Who Remember Previous Lives* (Charlottesville: University of Virginia Press, 1987).

6. Kalsang Yeshi, "Kamaljit Kour: Remembering a Past Life," in *Dreloma*, no. 12 (New Delhi, June 1984): 25–31.

7. Raymond A. Moody, Jr., *Life After Life* (New York: Bantam, 1986), 94.

8. Margot Grey, *Return from Death: An Exploration of the Near-Death Experience* (Boston and London: Arkana, 1985), 105.

9. Kenneth Ring, *Heading Towards Omega: In Search of the Meaning of the Near-Death Experience* (New York: Quill, 1985), 156.

10. Interestingly Mozart, in a letter to his father, referred to death as "the true and best friend of humanity . . . the key which unlocks the door to our true state of happiness." "At night," he wrote," I never lie down in my bed without thinking that perhaps (young as I am) I shall not live to see the next day and yet not one among my acquaintances could say that in my intercourse with them I am stubborn or morose—and for this source of happiness I thank my Creator every day and wish with all my heart the same for my fellow-creatures." *Mozart's Letters*, an illustrated edition, translated by Emily Anderson (London: Barrie and Jenkins, 1990).

11. *Plato's Republic*, translated by F. M. Cornford (Oxford: Oxford University Press, 1966), 350.

12. An explanation given by His Holiness the Dalai Lama during a public teaching in New York, October 1991.

13. His Holiness the Dalai Lama, in a dialogue with David Bohm, in *Dialogues with Scientists and Sages: The Search for Unity*, edited by Renée Weber (London: Routledge and Kegan Paul, 1986), 237.

14. H. W. Schumann, *The Historical Buddha* (London: Arkana, 1989), 139.

15. Schumann, *The Historical Buddha*, 55.

16. Shantideva, *A Guide to the Bodhisattva's Way of Life (Bodhicaryavatara)*, translated by Stephen Batchelor (Dharamsala: Library of Tibetan Works and Archives, 1979), 120.

17. His Holiness the Dalai Lama, *A Policy of Kindness: An Anthology of Writings by and about the Dalai Lama:* (Ithaca, NY: Snow Lion, 1990), 58.

18. Saddharmapundarika Sutra, quoted in Tulku Thondup, *Buddha Mind* (Ithaca, NY: Snow Lion, 1989), 215.

19. David Lorimer treats this topic in depth in his *Whole in One: The Near-Death Experience and the Ethic of Interconnectedness* (London: Arkana, 1990).

20. Raymond A. Moody, Jr., *Reflections on Life After Life* (London: Corgi, 1978), 35.

21. Ring, *Heading Towards Omega*, 71.

22. Raymond A. Moody, Jr., *The Light Beyond* (London: Pan, 1989), 38.

23. P. M. H. Atwater, *Coming Back to Life* (New York: Dodd, Bead, 1988), 36.

24. From Albert Einstein, *Ideas and Opinions,* translated by Sonja Bargmann (New York: Crown Publishers, 1954), quoted in Weber, ed., *Dialogues with Scientists and Sages,* 203.

25. His Holiness the Dalai Lama, *My Land and My People: The Autobiography of the Dalai Lama* (London: Panther, 1964), 24.

7. BARDOS AND OTHER REALITIES

1. *Egyptian Book of the Dead* is itself an artificial title coined by its translator, E. A. Wallis Budge, after the Arab *Book of the Deceased,* and having as little to do with the original title: "Coming Forth into the Day."

2. See chapter 10, "The Innermost Essence," on Dzogchen. The Dzogchen Tantras are the original teachings of Dzogchen compiled by the first human Dzogchen master, Garab Dorje.

3. In Tibet masters did not make a show of their realization. They may have had immense psychic powers, but nearly always they kept them to themselves. This is what our tradition recommends. True masters never, on any occasion, use their powers for self-aggrandizement. They use them only when they know they will be of real benefit to others; or in special circumstances and a special environment, they may allow a few of their closest students to witness them.

8. THIS LIFE: THE NATURAL BARDO

1. Tulku Thondup, *Buddha Mind* (Ithaca, NY: Snow Lion, 1989), 211.

2. Kalu Rinpoche, *Essence of the Dharma* (Delhi, India: Tibet House), 206.

3. From "The Marriage of Heaven and Hell," *Blake: Complete Writings* (Oxford and New York: OUP, 1972), 154.

4. The three kayas are the three aspects of the true nature of mind described in chapter 4: its empty essence, radiant nature, and all-pervasive energy; see also chapter 21, "The Universal Process."

5. Shunryu Suzuki, *Zen Mind, Beginner's Mind* (New York: Weatherhill, 1973), 21.

9. THE SPIRITUAL PATH

1. The Tantras are the teachings and writings that set out the practices of Vajrayana Buddhism, the stream of Buddhism prevalent in Tibet. The Tantric teachings are based on the principle of the transformation of impure vision into pure vision, through working with the body, energy, and mind. Tantric texts usually describe the mandala and meditation practices associated with a particular enlightened being or deity. Although they are called Tantras, the Dzogchen Tantras are a

specific category of the Dzogchen teachings, which are not based on transformation but on self-liberation (see chapter 10, The Innermost Essence).

2. Dilgo Khyentse, *The Wish-Fulfilling Jewel: The Practice of Guru Yoga According to the Longchen Nyingthig Tradition* (London and Boston: Shambhala, 1988), 51.

3. A dakini is a female embodiment of enlightened energy.

4. A stupa is a three-dimensional construction symbolizing the mind of the buddhas. It often contains the relics of great masters.

5. Dilgo Khyentse, *The Wish-Fulfilling Jewel*, 11. This quotation contains many traditional elements, and a similar praise of the master is found in the writings of Patrul Rinpoche.

6. Matthew 7:7.

7. Dilgo Khyentse, *The Wish-Fulfilling Jewel*, 3.

8. From the Guru Yoga in Jikmé Lingpa's famous preliminary practice to his cycle of Dzogchen teachings: *Longchen Nyingtik*.

9. Dilgo Khyentse, *The Wish-Fulfilling Jewel*, 83.

10. THE INNERMOST ESSENCE

1. The Ngöndro is divided traditionally into two parts. The Outer Preliminaries, beginning with the Invocation of the Lama, consist of contemplation on the uniqueness of human life, impermanence, karma, and the suffering of samsara. The Inner Preliminaries are Taking Refuge, Generating Bodhicitta (the Heart of the Enlightened Mind), Vajrasattva purification, Mandala Offering, and then finally, Guru Yoga, followed by the Phowa (the Transference of Consciousness) and the dedication.

2. This is not the place to explore in detail these preliminary practices. I hope in future to be able to publish a full explanation of them for those who are interested in following them.

3. Dzogchen Monastery was a monastic university founded in the seventeenth century in Kham, eastern Tibet, which was one of the largest and most influential centers of the tradition of Padmasambhava and the Dzogchen teachings until its destruction by the Chinese in 1959. It had a renowned study college, and produced scholars and teachers of the very highest caliber, such as Patrul Rinpoche (1808–87) and Mipham (1846–1912). With the blessing of the Dalai Lama, the monastery has been rebuilt in exile by the Seventh Dzogchen Rinpoche in Mysore in the south of India.

4. Quoted in Tulku Thondup Rinpoche, *Buddha Mind*, 128.

5. A mandala usually means the sacred environment and dwelling of a buddha, bodhisattva, or deity, which is visualized by the practitioner in Tantric practice.

6. One sure way I have found of discerning whether you are in the state of Rigpa is by the presence of its sky-like Essence, its radiant Nature, and its unimpeded Energy of compassion, as well as the five wisdoms, with their qualities of openness, precision, all-embracing equality, discernment, and spontaneous accomplishment, as described on page 153.

7. Through the practice of Tögal, an accomplished practitioner can realize the three kayas in one lifetime (see chapter 21, "The Universal Process"). This is the Fruition of Dzogchen.

8. From a teaching given in Helsinki, Finland, in 1988.

11. HEART ADVICE ON HELPING THE DYING

1. Elisabeth Kübler-Ross, *On Death and Dying* (New York: Collier, 1970), 50.

2. Dame Cicely Saunders, "I Was Sick and You Visited Me," *Christian Nurse International,* 3, no. 4 (1987).

3. Dame Cicely Saunders, "Spiritual Pain," a paper presented at St. Christopher's Hospice Fourth International Conference, London 1987, published in *Hospital Chaplain* (March 1988).

4. Kübler-Ross, *On Death and Dying,* 36.

5. I strongly recommend her forthcoming detailed book on how to care for the dying, *Facing Death and Finding Hope.*

12. COMPASSION: THE WISH-FULFILLING JEWEL

1. Often people have asked me: "Does this mean that it is somehow wrong to look after ourselves, and care for our own needs?" It cannot be said too often that the self-cherishing which is destroyed by compassion is *the grasping and cherishing of a false self,* as we saw in chapter 8. To say that self-cherishing is the root of all harm should never be misunderstood as meaning either that it is selfish, or wrong, to be kind to ourselves or that by simply thinking of others our problems will dissolve of their own accord. As I have explained in chapter 5, being generous to ourselves, making friends with ourselves, and uncovering our own kindness and confidence, are central to, and implicit in, the teachings. We uncover our own Good Heart, our fundamental goodness, and that is the aspect of ourselves that we identify with and encourage. We shall see later in this chapter, in the "Tonglen" practice, how important it is to begin by working on ourselves, strengthening our love and compassion, before going on to help others. Otherwise our "help" could ultimately be motivated by a subtle selfishness; it could become just a burden to others; it could even make them dependent on us, so robbing them of the opportunity to take responsibility for themselves, and obstructing their development.

Psychotherapists say too that one of the core tasks for their clients is to develop self-respect and "positive self-regard," to heal their feelings of lack and inner impoverishment, and to allow them the experience of well being that is an essential part of our development as human beings.

2. Shantideva, *A Guide to the Bodhisattva's Way of Life (Bodhicaryavatara),* translated by Stephen Batchelor (Dharamsala: Library of Tibetan Works and Archives, 1979), 120–21.

3. The Dalai Lama, *A Policy of Kindness: An Anthology of Writings by and about the Dalai Lama* (Ithaca, NY: Snow Lion, 1990), 53.

4. Quoted in *Acquainted with the Night: A Year on the Frontiers of Death,* Allegra Taylor (London: Fontana, 1989), 145.

5. Shantideva, *A Guide to the Bodhisattva's Way of Life*, 34.

6. In chapter 13, "Spiritual Help for the Dying," I shall explain how the dying person can practice Tonglen.

7. Shantideva, *A Guide to the Bodhisattva's Way of Life*, 119.

13. SPIRITUAL HELP FOR THE DYING

1. Dame Cicely Saunders, "Spiritual Pain," a paper presented at St. Christopher's Hospice Fourth International Conference, London 1987, published in *Hospital Chaplain* (March 1988).

2. Stephen Levine, interviewed by Peggy Roggenbuck, *New Age Magazine*, September 1979, 50.

3. Jamyang Khyentse Chökyi Lodrö wrote this in his *Heart Advice* for my great aunt Ani Pelu (London: Rigpa Publications, 1981).

4. An audio cassette of readings from the *Tibetan Book of Living and Dying* will be available soon to help people who are dying.

5. "Son/daughter of an enlightened family": All sentient beings are at one stage or another of purifying and revealing their inherent buddha nature and are therefore collectively known as "the enlightened family."

6. The Sanskrit word *Dharma* has many meanings. Here it means the Buddhist teaching as a whole. As Dilgo Khyentse Rinpoche says: "The expression of the Buddha's wisdom for the sake of all sentient beings." Dharma can mean Truth or ultimate reality; dharma also signifies any phenomenon or mental object.

7. Lama Norlha in Kalu Rinpoche, *The Dharma* (Albany: State Univ. of New York Press, 1986), 155.

8. Marion L. Matics, *Entering the Path of Enlightenment: The Bodhicarya-vatara of the Buddhist Poet Shantideva* (London: George, Allen and Unwin, 1971), 154; Shantideva, *A Guide to the Bodhisattva's Way of Life (Bodhicaryavatara)*, translated by Stephen Batchelor (Dharamsala: Library of Tibetan Works and Archives, 1979), 30–32.

14. THE PRACTICES FOR DYING

1. Lati Rinbochay and Jeffrey Hopkins, *Death, Intermediate State and Rebirth in Tibetan Buddhism* (Ithaca, NY: Snow Lion, 1985), 9.

2. A collection of photographs of the people and places mentioned in this book will be published in the near future.

3. From Francesca Fremantle and Chögyam Trungpa, *Tibetan Book of the Dead* (Boston: Shambhala, 1975), 68.

4. See appendix 4 for an explanation of this mantra.

5. See chapter 15, "The Process of Dying."

6. One text explains: "The route through which the consciousness escapes determines the future rebirth. If it escapes through the anus, rebirth will be in the hell realm; if through the genital organ, the animal realm; if through the mouth, the hungry ghost realm; if through the nose, the human and spirit realms; if through the navel, the realm of 'desire gods'; if through the ears, the demigods; if through the eyes, the 'form god' realm; and if through the top of the head (four finger-widths back from the hairline), the 'formless god' realm. If the consciousness

escapes through the crown of the head, the being will be reborn in Dewachen, the western paradise of Amitabha." In Lama Lodö, *Bardo Teachings* (Ithaca, NY: Snow Lion, 1987), 11.

7. The research was reported in "Psychophysiological Changes Due to the Performance of the Phowa Ritual," *Research for Religion and Parapsychology,* Journal No. 17 (December 1987), published by the International Association for Religion and Parapsychology, Tokyo, Japan.

8. Dilgo Khyentse Rinpoche told me of a number of such cases. When the famous Dzogchen master Khenpo Ngakchung was still a young boy, he once saw the corpse of a calf that had died of starvation at the end of winter. He was filled with compassion and prayed strongly for the animal, visualizing its consciousness traveling to the paradise of Buddha Amitabha. At that moment a hole appeared in the top of the calf's skull, from which blood and fluid flowed.

9. There are also certain buddhas who pledged that whoever hears their name at the moment of death will be helped. Simply reciting their names into the ear of the dying person can be of benefit. This is also done for animals when they die.

10. Literally the "prana-mind": one master explains that "prana" expresses mind's aspect of mobility, and "mind" its aspect of awareness, but they are essentially one and the same thing.

11. Padmasambhava's explanation is quoted by Tsele Natsok Rangdrol in his well-known explanation of the cycle of four bardos, published in English as the *Mirror of Mindfulness* (Boston: Shambhala, 1989).

15. THE PROCESS OF DYING

1. These are methods of observing your shadow in the sky at certain times and on particular days of the month.

2. *Ambrosia Heart Tantra,* annotated and translated by Dr. Yeshi Dhondhen and Jhampa Kelsang (Dharamsala: Library of Tibetan Works and Archives, 1977), 33.

3. In Kalu Rinpoche, *The Dharma* (Albany: State Univ. of New York Press, 1986), 59.

4. Dilgo Khyentse Rinpoche explains that the pure wisdom winds are present together with the impure karmic winds, but as long as the karmic winds are predominant, the wisdom winds are obstructed. When the karmic winds are brought into the central channel through yoga practice, they vanish, and only the wisdom winds circulate through the channels.

5. C. Trungpa Rinpoche, *Glimpses of Abhidharma* (Boulder: Prajna, 1975), 3.

6. In *Inquiring Mind,* 6, no. 2, Winter/Spring 1990, from a teaching by Kalu Rinpoche in 1982.

7. The order of appearance of Increase and Appearance varies. It can depend, Dilgo Khyentse Rinpoche says, on which emotion is stronger in the individual: desire or anger.

8. There are various accounts of this process of inner dissolution; here I have chosen one of the simpler descriptions, written by Patrul Rinpoche. Often the black experience is called "Attainment," and the

arising of the Ground Luminosity, which is recognized by a trained practitioner, "Full Attainment."

9. His Holiness the Dalai Lama, *The Dalai Lama at Harvard* (Ithaca, NY: Snow Lion, 1988), 45.

10. See chapter 21, "The Universal Process," and also C. Trungpa Rinpoche's commentary in *The Tibetan Book of the Dead*, Francesca Fremantle and Chögyam Trungpa (London: Shambhala, 1975), 1–29.

16. THE GROUND

1. "His Holiness in Zion, Illinois," in *Vajradhatu Sun*, vol. 4, no. 2 (Boulder, CO, Dec. 1981–Jan. 1982): 3. (It is now called *Shambhala Sun*.)

2. Bokar Tulku Rinpoche, in "An Open Letter to Disciples and Friends of Kalu Rinpoche," May 15, 1989.

3. The Sutras are the scriptures that are the original teachings of the Buddha; they often take the form of a dialogue between the Buddha and his disciples, explaining a particular theme.

17. INTRINSIC RADIANCE

1. In *Dialogues with Scientists and Sages: The Search for Unity*, edited by Renée Weber (London: Routledge and Kegan Paul, 1986), 45–46.

2. Kalu Rinpoche, *The Dharma* (Albany: State Univ. of New York Press, 1986), 61.

3. Kalu Rinpoche, *The Dharma*, 62.

4. This is the bodhisattva Samantabhadra and not the Primordial Buddha.

5. See chapter 21. In this passage, I am most grateful for the kind suggestions of Dr. Gyurme Dorje, whose translation of *The Tibetan Book of the Dead*, edited by himself and Graham Coleman, is scheduled to be published by Penguin in 1993.

18. THE BARDO OF BECOMING

1. Kalu Rinpoche, *The Dharma* (Albany: State Univ. of New York Press, 1986), 18.

2. It is said that there are only two places the mental body cannot go: the womb of its future mother and Vajrasana, the place where all the buddhas become enlightened. These two places represent the entrance to samsara and nirvana. In other words, to be reborn or gain enlightenment would bring an end to its life in this bardo.

3. There exist accounts of masters who were able to perceive bardo beings, or even travel to the bardo realm.

4. Chökyi Nyima Rinpoche, *The Bardo Guidebook* (Kathmandu: Rangjung Yeshe, 1991), 14.

5. This scene occurs in Tibetan folk dramas and operas, and is also reported by the "déloks" (see chapter 20, "The Near-Death Experience: A Staircase to Heaven?").

6. Raymond A. Moody, Jr., *Reflections on Life After Life* (New York: Bantam, 1977), 32.

7. Kenneth Ring, *Heading Towards Omega: In Search of the Meaning of the Near-Death Experience* (New York: Quill, 1985), 70.

8. It is said that whenever a couple make love, crowds of bardo beings gather, hoping to have the karmic connection to be reborn. One succeeds and the others die of despair; this can occur as the weekly experience of death in the bardo.

9. Fremantle and Trungpa, *Tibetan Book of the Dead,* 86.

10. Vajrasattva is the central deity of the Hundred Peaceful and Wrathful Deities. See chapter 19, "Helping after Death."

19. HELPING AFTER DEATH

1. See Appendix 4 for an explanation of this mantra.

2. Yet, in the case of a spiritual practitioner who has died, and who sees friends and relatives grasping and insincere after his death, it is possible that instead of being hurt and angry, he might be able to realize that all their behavior is simply the nature of samsara. From this he might generate a deep sense of renunciation and compassion, which could be of great benefit to him in the bardo of becoming.

3. When we ask a master to practice and pray for a dead person, it is a custom to send a donation of money, however small it might be. The donation establishes a tangible connection between the dead person and the master, who will always use this money exclusively to pay for the rituals for the dead, or make offerings at holy shrines, or dedicate it in their name to his or her work.

4. An answer given by His Holiness the Dalai Lama to a number of questions on death and dying. See Appendix 2, note 1.

5. Traditional practices such as this require training and cannot be followed simply from this book. Certain practices also require transmission and empowerment from a qualified master. I look forward to organizing training programs in the future on the Buddhist approach to death and caring for the dying, which will include some of these methods. A simple ceremony and guidance for the dead will then be available, based on the advice of Dilgo Khyentse Rinpoche.

6. The Hundred Syllable Mantra is: OM VAJRA SATTVA SAMAYA MANUPALAYA VAJRA SATTVA TENOPA TISHTHA DRI DHO ME BHAWA SUTO KHAYO ME BHAWA SUPO KHAYO ME BHAWA ANURAKTO ME BHAWA SARWA SIDDHI ME PRAYATSA SARWA KARMA SUTSA ME TSITTAM SHRIYAM KURU HUM HA HA HA HA HO BHAGAWAN SARWA TATHAGATA VAJRA MAME MUNTSA VAJRI BHAWA MAHA SAMAYA SATTVA AH.

7. Judy Tatelbaum, *The Courage to Grieve: Creative Living, Recovery and Growth through Grief* (New York: Harper & Row, 1980).

8. From "Dove that Ventured Outside" in *The Selected Poetry of Rainer Maria Rilke,* edited and translated by Stephen Mitchell (New York: Vintage Books, 1984), 293.

9. Elisabeth Kübler-Ross in "The Child Will Always Be There. Real Love Doesn't Die," by Daniel Goleman, *Psychology Today* (September 1976), 52.

10. Raymond A. Moody, Jr., *Reflections on Life After Life* (New York: Bantam, 1977), 112.

20. THE NEAR-DEATH EXPERIENCE: A STAIRCASE TO HEAVEN?

1. Bede, *A History of the English Church and People,* translated by Leo Sherley-Price (Harmondsworth, England: Penguin Books 1968), 420–21.

2. In George Gallup Jr., with William Proctor, *Adventures in Immortality: A Look Beyond the Threshold of Death* (London: Souvenir, 1983).

3. Kenneth Ring, *Life at Death: A Scientific Investigation of the Near-Death Experience* (New York: Quill, 1982), 55.

4. Ring, *Life at Death,* 63.

5. Margot Grey, *Return from Death: An Exploration of the Near-Death Experience* (Boston and London: Arkana, 1985), 42.

6. Melvin Morse, *Closer to the Light: Learning from Children's Near-Death Experiences* (New York: Villard, 1990), 115.

7. Grey, *Return from Death,* 47.

8. Michael Sabom, *Recollections of Death: A Medical Investigation of the Near-Death Experience* (London: Corgi, 1982), 66.

9. Ring, *Life at Death,* 59.

10. Grey, *Return from Death,* 46.

11. Grey, *Return from Death,* 33.

12. Grey, *Return from Death,* 53.

13. Morse, *Closer to the Light,* 120.

14. Morse, *Closer to the Light,* 181.

15. Grey, *Return from Death,* 35.

16. Ring, *Life at Death,* 45.

17. Sabom, *Recollections of Death,* 37.

18. Sabom, *Recollections of Death,* 155.

19. Sabom, *Recollections of Death,* 37.

20. Sabom, *Recollections of Death,* 40.

21. Sabom, *Recollections of Death,* 56.

22. Sabom, *Recollections of Death,* 54–55.

23. Kenneth Ring, *Heading Towards Omega: In Search of the Meaning of the Near-Death Experience* (New York: Quill, 1985), 199.

24. Raymond A. Moody, Jr., *Reflections on Life After Life* (London: Corgi, 1978), 10.

25. Moody, *Reflections,* 14.

26. Grey, *Return from Death,* 52.

27. Sabom, *Recollections of Death,* 71.

28. Grey, *Return from Death,* 50.

29. Moody, *Reflections,* 17.

30. Grey, *Return from Death,* 51.

31. Grey, *Return from Death,* 59.

32. Grey, *Return from Death,* 65.

33. Grey, *Return from Death,* 63.

34. Grey, *Return from Death,* 70.

35. Moody, *Reflections,* 19.

36. Françoise Pommaret, *Les Revenants de l'Au-Delà dans le Monde Tibétain* (Paris: Editions du CNRS, 1989).

37. In the Hindu tradition, kundalini refers to the awakening of the

subtle energy that can bring about a psycho-physiological transformation and union with the divine.

38. Grey, *Return from Death*, 194.

39. Ring, *Life at Death*, 145.

40. Morse, *Closer to the Light*, 193.

41. Morse, *Closer to the Light*, 93.

42. From *The NDE: As Experienced in Children*, a lecture for IANDS.

43. From *The NDE: Can It Be Explained in Science?*, a lecture for IANDS.

44. Ring, *Heading Towards Omega*, 7.

21. THE UNIVERSAL PROCESS

1. J. M. Reynolds, *Self-Liberation through Seeing with Naked Awareness* (New York: Station Hill, 1989), 13.

2. In "Auguries of Innocence," Blake: Complete Writings (Oxford and New York: Oxford Univ. Press, 1972), 431.

3. Kalu Rinpoche, *The Dharma*, 38.

4. See, for example, the Dalai Lama, *et al.*, *MindScience: An East-West Dialogue* (Boston: Wisdom, 1991).

5. Renée Weber, ed., *Dialogues with Scientists and Sages: The Search for Unity* (London: Routledge and Kegan Paul, 1986), 93–94.

6. Weber, *Scientists and Sages*, 48.

7. David Bohm, *Unfolding Meaning: A Weekend of Dialogue with David Bohm* (London: Ark, 1987), 73.

8. David Bohm, *Unfolding Meaning*, 90–91.

9. Paavo Pylkkänen, ed., *The Search for Meaning* (Wellingborough: Crucible, 1989), 51; Bohm, *Unfolding Meaning*, 93.

10. David Bohm, *Wholeness and the Implicate Order* (London: Ark 1988), xi.

11. Bohm, *Unfolding Meaning*, 107, 96.

22. SERVANTS OF PEACE

1. Thomas Merton, *The Wisdom of the Desert* (New York: New Directions, 1960), 11.

APPENDIX 2: QUESTIONS ABOUT DEATH

1. I have asked His Holiness the Dalai Lama, Dilgo Khyentse Rinpoche, and other masters a number of questions about death and dying, including issues such as life support and euthanasia, and throughout this chapter I shall quote some of their replies. I hope to publish their answers in detail in the future.

2. Melvin Morse, *Closer to the Light* (New York: Villard Books, 1990), 72.

3. Gallup poll cited in *Newsweek*, August 26, 1991, p. 41.

4. Kalu Rinpoche, *The Gem Ornament* (Ithaca, NY: Snow Lion, 1986), 194.

5. In Elisabeth Kübler-Ross, *Questions on Death and Dying* (New York: Macmillan, 1974), 84.

6. Dame Cicely Saunders in "A Commitment to Care," *Raft, The Journal of the Buddhist Hospice Trust,* 2, Winter 1989/90, London, p. 10.

7. Kalu Rinpoche, *The Gem Ornament,* 194.

APPENDIX 4: TWO MANTRAS

1. There are three negative activities of the body: taking life, stealing, and sexual misconduct; four of the speech: lies, harsh words, slander, and gossip; and three of the mind: avarice, malice, and wrong views.

2. *Nadi, prana,* and *bindu* in Sanskrit; *tsa, lung,* and *tiklé* in Tibetan. See chapter 15, "The Process of Dying."

3. Five buddha families and five wisdoms usually appear in the teachings; the sixth buddha family here embraces all the other five together.

4. Kalu Rinpoche, *The Dharma* (Albany: State Univ. of New York Press, 1986), 53.

Selected Bibliography

TRADITIONAL TIBETAN TEACHINGS ON DEATH AND DYING

Chagdud Tulku Rinpoche. *Life in Relation to Death.* Cottage Grove, OR: Padma Publishing, 1987.

Chökyi Nyima Rinpoche. *The Bardo Guidebook.* Kathmandu: Rangjung Yeshe, 1991.

Fremantle, Francesca and Chögyam Trungpa. *The Tibetan Book of the Dead.* Boston: Shambhala, 1975.

Lama Lodö. *Bardo Teachings.* Ithaca, NY: Snow Lion, 1987.

Lati Rinbochay and Jeffrey Hopkins. *Death, Intermediate State and Rebirth.* Ithaca, NY: Snow Lion, 1985.

Mullin, Glenn H. *Death and Dying: The Tibetan Tradition.* London: Arkana, 1986.

Tsele Natsok Rangdrol. *The Mirror of Mindfulness.* Boston: Shambhala, 1989.

CARING FOR THE DYING

Beckman, Robert. *I Don't Know What to Say: How to Help and Support Someone Who Is Dying.* London: Macmillan, 1988.

Duda, Deborah. *Coming Home: A Guide to Dying at Home with Dignity.* New York: Aurora Press, 1987.

Kübler-Ross, Elisabeth. *On Death and Dying.* New York: Collier, 1970.

———. *Questions and Answers on Death and Dying.* New York: Collier, 1974.

———. *To Live Until We Say Goodbye.* Englewood Cliffs, NJ: Prentice Hall, 1978.

Levine, Stephen. *Who Dies? An Investigation of Conscious Living and Conscious Dying.* Garden City, NY: Doubleday, 1982.

Saunders, Cicely and Mary Baines. *Living with Dying: The Management of Terminal Disease.* Oxford and New York: Oxford University Press, 1989.

Stoddard, Sandol. *The Hospice Movement: A Better Way to Care for the Dying.*
New York: Vintage Books/Random House, 1991.

Taylor, Allegra. *Acquainted with the Night: A Year on the Frontiers of Death.*
London: Fontana, 1989.

HELPING THE BEREAVED

Crenshaw, David. *Bereavement: Counselling the Grieving through the Life Cycle.*
New York: Continuum, 1990.

Gaffney, Donna. *The Seasons of Grief: Helping Children Grow through Loss.*
New York: Plume/Penguin, 1988.

Schiff, Harriet Sarnoff. *The Bereaved Parent.* Crown Publishing, 1977.

Staudacher, Carol. *Beyond Grief: A Guide for Recovering from the Death of a
Loved One.* Oakland: New Harbinger Publications, 1987.

Tatelbaum, Judy. *The Courage to Grieve: Creative Living, Recovery and Growth
through Grief.* New York: Harper & Row, 1980.

THE NEAR-DEATH EXPERIENCE

Grey, Margot. *Return from Death: An Exploration of the Near-Death Experience.*
Boston and London: Arkana, 1985.

Lorimer, David. *Whole in One: The Near-Death Experience and the Ethic of
Interconnectedness.* London: Arkana, 1990.

Moody, Jr., M.D., Raymond A. *Life After Life.* Atlanta: Mockingbird
Books, 1975; New York: Bantam, 1986.

———. *Reflections on Life After Life.* Atlanta: Mockingbird Books, 1977;
London: Corgi, 1978.

Morse, Melvin. *Closer to the Light: Learning from Children's Near-Death Experiences.* New York: Villard Books, 1990.

Ring, Kenneth. *Heading Towards Omega: In Search of the Meaning of the Near-
Death Experience.* New York: Quill, 1985.

———. *Life at Death: A Scientific Investigation of the Near-Death Experience.*
New York: Quill, 1982.

Sabom, Michael B. *Recollections of Death: A Medical Investigation of the Near-
Death Experience.* New York: Harper & Row, 1981; London: Corgi,
1982.

SCIENTIFIC PARALLELS

Bohm, David. *Unfolding Meaning: A Weekend of Dialogue with David Bohm.*
London: Ark, 1987.

Dalai Lama, et al. *MindScience, An East-West Dialogue.* Boston: Wisdom
1991.

Pylkkänen, Paavo, ed. *The Search for Meaning.* Wellingborough, England:
Crucible, 1989.

Weber, Renée. *Dialogues with Scientists and Sages: The Search for Unity.* London: Routledge and Kegan Paul, 1986.

BOOKS BY THE DALAI LAMA

A Policy of Kindness: An Anthology of Writings by and about the Dalai Lama. Ithaca, NY: Snow Lion, 1990.

The Dalai Lama at Harvard. Ithaca, NY: Snow Lion, 1988.

Freedom in Exile: An Autobiography of the Dalai Lama of Tibet. San Francisco: Harper San Francisco; London: Hodder and Stoughton, 1990.

The Fourteenth Dalai Lama. *Kindness, Clarity and Insight.* Ithaca, NY: Snow Lion, 1984.

THE BUDDHA AND HIS TEACHING

Dilgo Khyentse. *The Wish-Fulfilling Jewel: The Practice of Guru Yoga According to the Longchen Nyingthig Tradition.* Boston and London: Shambhala, 1988.

Goldstein, Joseph and Jack Kornfield. *Seeking the Heart of Wisdom: The Path of Insight Meditation.* Boston and London: Shambhala, 1987.

Kalu Rinpoche. *The Dharma.* Albany: State Univ. of New York Press, 1986.

Shantideva. *A Guide to the Bodhisattva's Way of Life (Bodhicaryavatara).* Translated by Stephen Batchelor. Dharamsala: Library of Tibetan Works and Archives, 1979.

Suzuki, Shunryu. *Zen Mind, Beginner's Mind.* New York: Weatherhill, 1973.

The Twelfth Tai Situpa. *Relative World, Ultimate Mind.* Boston and London: Shambhala, 1992.

Thich Nhat Hanh. *Being Peace.* Berkeley: Parallax Press, 1987.

———. *The Miracle of Mindfulness.* Boston: Beacon Press, 1976.

———. *Old Path, White Clouds.* Berkeley: Parallax Press, 1991.

OTHER BOOKS ON DEATH AND HEALING

Borysenko, Joan. *Minding the Body, Mending the Mind.* New York: Bantam, 1988.

Grof, Stanislav and Joan Halifax. *The Human Encounter with Death.* New York: E. P. Dutton, 1978.

Kushner, Harold. *When Bad Things Happen to Good People.* New York: Schoken Books, 1981.

Siegel, Bernie. *Peace, Love and Healing.* New York: HarperCollins, 1989.

Wennberg, Robert. *Terminal Choices: Euthanasia, Suicide, and the Right to Die.* Grand Rapids, MI: Eerdmans, 1989.

Acknowledgments

IN THE TASK OF PRESENTING the teachings contained in
this book authentically, and yet in a way that reaches out to
modern minds, I have been continually inspired by the example of His Holiness the Dalai Lama, and by how he embodies
all the authenticity and purity of the tradition while display-
ing an all-embracing openness to the modern world. There
are no words to express the depth of my gratitude to him; he
is a constant source of courage and inspiration not only to the
Tibetan people, but also to countless individuals all over the
world whose hearts have been moved and whose lives have
been transformed by his message. I have been told that the
connection I have with him stretches back over many lives,
and in the strength and closeness of the affinity I feel for him,
I somewhere know this to be true.

For their inspiration and their teachings, the essence of
which are this book, I thank every one of my masters, and I
offer it to them all. Jamyang Khyentse Chökyi Lodrö, who
recognized me and brought me up, gave me the ground and
the meaning of life; he gave me in fact the two most precious
things I have: devotion and understanding. His spiritual wife,
Khandro Tsering Chödrön, the foremost yogini in Tibetan
Buddhism, has, in her love and care, been truly like a master
to me as well; for me she is completely inseparable from
Jamyang Khyentse, and I only have to think of her to see his
majestic presence reflected in her. She is like a spiritual mother
to me: I feel always protected on account of her prayers and
her love, and I pray that she lives for many, many more years.
It was Dudjom Rinpoche who made flower those seeds of
understanding Jamyang Khyentse had sowed in me, through
his personal kindness and his teaching. The affection he
showed me was almost, I sometimes think, as though I had
been his own son. And then Dilgo Khyentse Rinpoche was

there to deepen whatever understanding I have and to give it eloquence. As the years went by, he took on more and more the role of teacher for me, with the personal attention and advice he gave me so freely, and with his gentle, unending kindness. Increasingly, when I have thought of "the master," my mind has turned to Dilgo Khyentse Rinpoche, and he became for me the embodiment of the entire teaching, a real living Buddha.

These great masters continue to move me and guide me always, and not a day goes by that I do not remember them and their unrepayable kindness, and talk about them to my students and friends. I pray that something of their wisdom, compassion, and power, and their vision for humanity, may live through the pages of this book they have so inspired.

Nor shall I ever forget my uncle Gyalwang Karmapa, who showed me such special affection from my childhood on, and the very thought of whom moves me to tears. I often think too of the great Kalu Rinpoche, the Milarepa of our times, who gave me enormous encouragement through his belief in me, and in the warmth and respect with which he treated me.

I would like to acknowledge here as well the debt of inspiration I owe to other great teachers, such as His Holiness Sakya Trizin, a close friend from my childhood, who has been my teacher and yet also like a brother, encouraging me at every turn. I give my deep thanks to Dodrupchen Rinpoche, who is a constant guide, especially on this book, and a source of refuge to me and to all of my students. Some of the most precious moments over recent years have been spent with Nyoshul Khen Rinpoche, with whom I have had the great good fortune to clarify the teachings in the light of his seemingly limitless learning and wisdom. Two other outstanding and eminent masters who are special springs of inspiration to me are Tulku Urgyen Rinpoche and Trulshik Rinpoche, and I must thank also the very learned Khenpo Appey and Khenpo Lodrö Zangpo, who played such an important part in my studies and education. Nor will I ever forget Gyaltön Rinpoche, who showed me such kindness after my master Jamyang Khyentse had passed away.

I wish to pay special tribute to the encouragement and marvellous vision of Penor Rinpoche, an outstanding master who works tirelessly to maintain the unbroken transmission of the rich tradition of teachings that come directly from Padmasambhava.

I am deeply grateful to Dudjom Rinpoche's family: his wife, Sangyum Kusho Rikzin Wangmo, for her kindness and understanding, and his son and daughters, Shenphen Rinpoche, Chime Wangmo, and Tsering Penzom, for their constant support. For their warm and generous help, I would like to thank too both Chökyi Nyima Rinpoche, whose work has inspired parts of this book and, Tulku Pema Wangyal Rinpoche, who has been so instrumental in bringing the teachings and the greatest teachers to the West.

Among the younger generation of masters, I must single out Dzongsar Jamyang Khyentse Rinpoche, the "activity emanation" of my master Jamyang Kyentse Chökyi Lodrö. The brilliance and freshness of his teaching continue to fascinate me and fill me with great hope for the future. Likewise I should like to thank, for his wonderful and spontaneous help, Shechen Rabjam Rinpoche, who is the heir to Dilgo Khyentse Rinpoche, and who received teachings from him continuously from the age of five.

I am always moved and encouraged too by a master who is very close to my heart, whose work and mine are one: Dzogchen Rinpoche. Having now reconstructed the famous Dzogchen Monastery with immense vitality in southern India, he has already taken on, in his learning and the dazzling purity and natural simplicity of his presence, the bearing of the great master he will be in the future.

A number of masters have answered in detail certain specific questions about the teachings presented in this book: His Holiness the Dalai Lama, Dilgo Khyentse Rinpoche, Nyoshul Khen Rinpoche, Trulshik Rinpoche, Dzongsar Khyentse Rinpoche, Lati Rinpoche, and Alak Dzengkar Rinpoche. To them I am deeply grateful. I would like to express my gratitude as well to Ringu Tulku Rinpoche, for his friendship over the years, his kind and constant help to both my students and myself, and his wonderful translation work, which includes the translation of this book into Tibetan.

I wish to thank and salute the pioneers of the Buddhist teachings, those masters of different traditions whose work has for decades brought help to so many people in the West. I think especially of Suzuki Roshi, Chögyam Trungpa, Tarthang Tulku, and Thich Nhat Hanh.

I would like also to thank my mother and my father for their support, and all the help they have given me to accomplish what I have done so far: my father, Tsewang Paljor, who was Jamyang Khyentse's secretary and personal

assistant from the age of eighteen, is himself a great
practitioner and yogin; and my mother, Tsering Wangmo,
who has always urged me onward and encouraged me in my
work. My gratitude goes too to my brother Thigyal and my
sister Dechen, for all their help and loyalty.

Let me express here my gratitude to the country of
Sikkim and its people, the late King, the Queen Mother, the
late Crown Prince Tenzin Namgyal, the present King
Wangchuk, and all the royal family, as well as Professor
Nirmal C. Sinha, former Director of the Sikkim Research
Institute.

Someone who was always a great source of inspiration and
encouragement to me, and especially in this book, was David
Bohm, to whom I would like to express my gratitude. I also
wish to thank a number of other scientists and scholars,
especially Dr. Kenneth Ring, an old friend of mine; Dr. Basil
Hiley; and Geshe Thubten Jinpa, His Holiness the Dalai
Lama's translator, who very kindly read through parts of this
book, and offered their advice. I would like to thank Tenzin
Geyche Tethong, H.H. the Dalai Lama's secretary; Lodi Gyari
Rinpoche, Special Envoy of H.H. the Dalai Lama and President
of the International Campaign for Tibet; and Konchog Tenzin,
Dilgo Khyentse Rinpoche's secretary and attendant, for their
help.

My thanks also go to my friend Andrew Harvey, a well-
known and very gifted writer, for the dedicated, impassioned,
and selfless way in which he has shaped this book and helped
the majesty of the teachings to shine through the words with
radiant simplicity and brilliance. He offers his work to his own
masters: to Thuksey Rinpoche, whom I remember well as
someone who positively radiated with love, and who looked
on me with so much affection that I have always longed to
repay his kindness; and to Mother Meera and her work of
harmony between all religions in the world.

I thank Patrick Gaffney for his unfailing patience, his
devoted perseverance, his ardor, and the sacrifices he has
made to see this book through its many transformations over
many years. He is one of my oldest and closest students; and
if anyone were to understand my mind or my work, it is him.
This book is as much his book as mine, for without him I
cannot imagine that it would have been possible. I would like
to dedicate his work to his own spiritual development, and to
the happiness of all beings.

I am grateful to Christine Longaker for all the invaluable
insights she has shared with me from her long experience of

helping the dying, and teaching on death and dying. I must salute also Harold Talbott, one of my first western friends and students, as well as Michael Baldwin, for their dedication in helping establish the teaching of Buddha in the West, and for the encouragement they have always given me. At HarperSan Francisco, I should like to thank Amy Hertz, Michael Toms, and all the staff for their priceless and enthusiastic assistance with this book.

I would like to take this opportunity as well to thank Philip Philippou, Dominique Side, Mary Ellen Rouiller, Sandra Pawula, Doris Wolter, Ian Maxwell, Giles Oliver, Lisa Brewer, Mauro de March, Dominique Cowell, Sabah Cheraiet, Tom Bottoms and Ross Mackay for their continuous help and dedication, and John Cleese, Alex Leith, Alan Madsen, Bokara Legendre, Lavinia Currier, Peter and Harriet Cornish, Robin Relph, Patrick Naylor and John Van Praag for their vision and support.

I thank all my students and friends who in a way have been like teachers to me, who have shared this book at every stage of its making, and who have put up with me with their deep devotion. They are a constant source of inspiration to me. My gratitude goes to those too who have truly worked with these teachings and put them into practice, especially those who are caring for the dying and bereaved, and who have contributed many useful insights to this book. I am moved by the efforts of all my students in trying to understand and apply the teachings, and I pray that they will be successful.

I have done my best here to convey the heart of the teachings, and for whatever is missing, whatever imprecision or errors there may be, I ask the reader's indulgence, and pray that my masters and the protectors of the teachings forgive me!

Index

Mockingbird Books, Inc., for excerpts from *Reflections on Life after Life*, by Raymond A. Moody. Reprinted by permission of Mockingbird Books, Inc.

Rider, Random Century Group for excerpts from *Ancient Futures: Learning from Ladakh*, by Helena Norberg-Hodge. Reprinted by permission of Rider Books.

Carol Publishing Group for excerpts from *The Hundred Thousand Songs of Milarepa*, edited and translated by Garma C. C. Chang. Copyright © 1977 by Garma C. C. Chang. Published by arrangement with Carol Publishing Group.

Routledge for excerpts from *Wholeness and the Implicate Order*, by David Bohm; excerpts from *Unfolding Meaning*, by David Bohm.

Souvenir Press for excerpts from *Closer to the Light*, by Melvin Morse and Paul Perry. Reprinted by permission of Souvenir Press.

About the Author

SOGYAL RINPOCHE was born in Tibet, and brought up by one of the most accomplished spiritual masters of this century, Jamyang Khyentse Chökyi Lodrö. With the Chinese occupation of Tibet he went into exile with his master, who passed away in Sikkim, in the Himalayas, in 1959. Rinpoche then received a modern education, studying at university in Delhi and Cambridge. He began to teach in 1974, while continuing to study with his many other teachers, especially Dudjom Rinpoche and Dilgo Khyentse Rinpoche, who have been the main inspiration behind his work.

Few teachers have Rinpoche's gift for communication, and living in the west now for over twenty years has given him a profound insight into the western mind. The ease, humour, warmth and intimacy with which he teaches have made him one of the best loved and most sought after interpreters of Tibetan Buddhism to the modern world. Rinpoche travels extensively, teaching in Europe, North America, Australia and Asia. He is the founder and spiritual director of Rigpa, an international network of centres and groups around the world which practise the Buddhist path under his guidance.

Sogyal Rinpoche has become among the most important Buddhist masters teaching today, considered by many senior Tibetan masters as having a special role to play in the future of Buddhism, both in the West and in the East.

RIGPA

Sogyal Rinpoche has given the name Rigpa to the unique network of centers and groups around the world who follow the teachings of Buddha under his guidance. Their vision, and their aim, is to make the Buddhist teachings available to as many people as possible, across all possible barriers of race, color, and creed, and to create supportive and inspiring environments to encourage their study and practice.

In order to respond to the enormous wave of interest in Sogyal Rinpoche's work and in *The Tibetan Book of Living and Dying*, Rigpa publishes a regular newsletter, informing those who have read Rinpoche's book about related teachings, news and events. A range of trainings, based on this book, are being developed as part of a program offering spiritual care for both the living and the dying, and a network for caregivers has already been created, to exchange ideas and resources. This program will explore ways of developing spiritual care services, creating buddhist hospices, and envisaging new approaches to health and psycho-spiritual care.

In various countries around the world, Rigpa has city centers that offer regular courses on meditation, compassion, and every aspect of Buddhist wisdom for the modern world. Rigpa has played a major part in presenting the most eminent Buddhist masters of all traditions to the West, including His Holiness the Dalai Lama. In Rigpa's International Center in London, alongside the Buddhist teachings, different contemporary approaches are explored, from psychotherapy and healing, the arts and sciences, to the study of death and caring for the dying.

One of the great problems facing people in the modern world is the lack of a complete spiritual education, and the lack of a spiritual environment in which to experience fully the truth of the teachings and integrate them into daily life. Central to

Rigpa's program, therefore, is the intensive training conducted by Sogyal Rinpoche during retreats of up to three months in length. They take place every year in Europe, the United States and Australia. Rinpoche has founded retreat centers in the countryside in France and Ireland.

Rigpa also supports the work of many great masters in the East, and sponsors the Dzogchen Monastery and its reconstruction in Kollegal, Mysore, southern India.

Following on from *The Tibetan Book of Living and Dying*, Rinpoche's next book will draw on his considerable experience teaching in the west to explore how those wishing to follow the spiritual path can create a spiritual environment, in which they can find a personal meaning in the teachings, and truly integrate them into their everyday lives. It will be a practical guide on how to work with the mind and emotions, how actually to apply the practice of compassion, and how to meet the challenges of living a spiritual life in the world today.

For details of Sogyal Rinpoche's teaching program and courses at Rigpa, for information on anything referred to in this book, for audio cassettes of Sogyal Rinpoche's teachings, or for details on how to make an offering for the dead, please contact the following addresses:

Britain
London
RIGPA
330 Caledonian Road
London N1 1BB

Tel: (44 71) 700 0185
Fax: (44 71) 609 6068

Germany
Berlin
RIGPA
Skalitzer Str. 82
10967 Berlin
Tel: (49 30) 618 3833
Fax: (49 30) 618 3849

France
Paris
RIGPA
40 rue Blanche
75009 Paris
Tel: (33 1) 40 82 90 70
Fax: (33 1) 40 82 91 04

Switzerland
Zurich
RIGPA
P.O. Box 253
8059 Zurich
Tel: (41 1) 463 3353

Ireland
Dublin
3rd Floor, 12 Wicklow Street
Dublin 2
Tel: (353 1) 670 3358
Fax: (353 1) 670 3358

Australia
Sydney
PO Box K56
Haymarket, NSW 1204
Tel: (61 2) 9211 5304
Fax: (61 2) 9211 5289

USA

RIGPA USA
449 Powell Street
Suite 200,
San Francisco
CA 94102
Tel: 1.415 392 2055
Fax: 1.415 392 2056

Munich
RIGPA
Paul Gerhardt-Allee 34
81245 München
Tel: (49 89) 89 62 05 15
Fax: (49 89) 89 62 05 58

Montpellier
Lerab Ling Retreat Centre
L'Engayresque
34650 Roqueredonde
Tel: (33 467) 88 46 00
Fax: (33 467) 88 46 01

Netherlands
Amsterdam
Stichting RIGPA
Sint Agnietenstraat 22
1012 EG Amsterdam
Tel: (31 20) 623 8022

Dzogchen Beara
Garranes
Allihies
Tel: (353 27) 730 32
Fax: (353 27) 731 77

India
Rigpa House
RA46, Inderpuri
New Delhi, 110012
(91) 11 573 0660
(91) 11 576 7852

There are many other local groups in these countries; please ask for information from the national centers given above.

A Note from the Publisher

Sogyal Rinpoche's book *The Tibetan Book of Living and Dying*, Published in 1992, is widely regarded as one of the most complete and authoritative presentations of the Tibetan Buddhist teachings ever written. It has demonstrated how these teachings can be at one and the same time accessible to everyone, and yet totally authentic and faithful to the tradition. Acclaimed by people of all ages and backgrounds, as well as by Buddhist practitioners, Rinpoche's book has been adopted for use in courses, workshops and retreats by a variety of groups and disciplines, therapeutic and spiritual. Many readers have remarked on how it carries all the immediacy and force of an oral teaching, and how, with repeated study and reflection, deeper meanings are continually revealed. Since first publication over 875,000 copies of *The Tibetan Book of Living and Dying*, in 22 languages, have been sold in 36 countries worldwide.

MEDITATION

A Little Book of Wisdom

Sogyal Rinpoche

'The gift of learning to meditate is the greatest gift you can give yourself in this life. For it is only through meditation that you can undertake the journey to discover your true nature, and to find the stability and confidence you will need to live, and die, well.'

In this selection from his highly acclaimed **The Tibetan Book of Living and Dying**, Buddhist meditation master Sogyal Rinpoche offers a lucid and complete introduction to the practice of meditation.

Written to inspire all who read it to explore the path to enlightenment, this is a simple and beautiful guide to the profound art of bringing the mind home to its true nature.

GLIMPSE AFTER GLIMPSE

Daily Reflections on Living and Dying

Sogyal Rinpoche

Inspired by Sogyal Rinpoche's modern spiritual classic, the bestselling **The Tibetan Book of Living and Dying**, these thought-provoking reflections and teaching stories are a rich source of contemplation, serenity and joy throughout the day.

Elegantly illustrated with original calligraphy by Sogyal Rinpoche and rare photographs of great Tibetan masters, **Glimpse After Glimpse** addresses the trials and rewards of the spiritual path, acceptance of death, meditation, karma, compassion in action, and much more – all with Sogyal Rinpoche's eloquent and engaging warmth, wit and wisdom.

THE MIND AND THE WAY

Buddhist Reflections on Life

Ajahn Sumedho

This lively, highly readable book offers a radically simple approach to life that is attractively clear to our confused and anxious society. Ajahn Sumedho's advice to live simply, to contemplate the way things are and to let go of suffering brings alive the possibilities of inner peace, wholeness and happiness that is not dependent on external conditions.

A renowned Western meditation master, Ajahn Sumedho is the spiritual director of several monasteries in Britain, including the Amaravati Buddhist Centre, and others around the world. In his new book he draws on his own experience and a centuries-old Theravadan Buddhist tradition to provide practical advice to all those interested in freeing the mind and opening the heart – through formal meditation as well as in daily life.

Written with warmth, compassion and humour, **The Mind and the Way** is an invaluable resource for both the beginner seeking an introduction to Buddhist teaching and the experienced practitioner seeking renewed inspiration.

If you would like to order any of the following or to receive our catalogue please fill in the form below:

Meditation by sogyal Rinpoche
Glimpse After Glimpse by Sogyal Rinpoche
The Mind and the Way by Ajahn Sumedho
The Good Heart by the Dalai Lama
The Buddhist Handbook by John Snelling
Taming the Tiger by Akong Tulku Rinpoche
Enlightened Management by Akong Tulku Rinpoche with Dona Witten
Tibet : The Road Ahead by Dawa Norbu
The Miracle of Mindfulness by Thich Nhat Hanh
The Buddha in Daily Life by Richard Causton

HOW TO ORDER

BY POST: TBS Direct, TBS Ltd, Colchester Road, Frating Green, Essex CO7 7DW

Please send me _____ copies of _____ @ £ _____ each

☐ I enclose my cheque for £ _____ payable to Rider Books

☐ Please charge £ _____ to my American Express/Visa/Mastercard account*
  (*delete as applicable)

Card No ☐☐☐☐☐☐☐☐☐☐☐☐☐☐☐☐☐☐☐

Expiry Date: ☐☐☐☐ Signature _____

Name _____

Address _____

_____ Postcode _____

Delivery address if different _____

_____ Postcode _____

Or call our credit card hotline on
01206 255800. Please have your card details handy
Please quote reference TBLDB-1

Rider is an imprint of Random House UK Ltd
Please tick here if you do not wish to receive further information from Rider or associated companies ☐